WITHDRAWN
HARVARD LIBRARY
WITHDRAWN

# The Politics of Spirit

SUNY series, Issues in the Study of Religion
———————
Bryan Rennie, editor

# The Politics of Spirit

Phenomenology, Genealogy, Religion

TIM MURPHY

SUNY PRESS

Published by State University of New York Press, Albany

© 2010 State University of New York

All rights reserved

Printed in the United States of America

No part of this book may be used or reproduced in any manner whatsoever without written permission. No part of this book may be stored in a retrieval system or transmitted in any form or by any means including electronic, electrostatic, magnetic tape, mechanical, photocopying, recording, or otherwise without the prior permission in writing of the publisher.

For information, contact State University of New York Press, Albany, NY
www.sunypress.edu

Production by Eileen Meehan
Marketing by Michael Campochiaro

Library of Congress Cataloging-in-Publication Data

Murphy, Tim, 1956–
 The politics of spirit : phenomenology, genealogy, religion / Tim Murphy.
   p. cm. — (SUNY series, Issues in the study of religion)
 Includes bibliographical references (p. ) and index.
 ISBN 978-1-4384-3287-8 (hardcover : alk. paper)
 1. Religion—Philosophy—History.  2. Phenomenology—History.
I. Title.

BL51.M8764 2010
210—dc22                                                    2010004938

10 9 8 7 6 5 4 3 2 1

*In Memoriam:*
Gary Lease
Teacher, Colleague, Friend

# Contents

Acknowledgments     xi

## PART I
### Introduction, Background, Methodological Issues

**Chapter One**
The Phenomenology of Religion: Introduction and Background     3

    Traditional Historiography of the Phenomenology of Religion: Hegel versus Husserl     4

    *Geist* and the *Geisteswissenschaften* in Nineteenth-Century Continental Thought     10

    "Explanation versus Interpretation": Previous Critiques of the Phenomenology of Religion     15

    The Pedigree of Classical Phenomenology of Religion     23

    Terminology: "Phenomenology" and "History of Religions"     27

    Authorial Stance and Thesis     30

**Chapter Two**
Discourse, Text, Philosophemes: Elements of a Postcolonial-Genealogical Reading Strategy     35

    Overview: Method and *Rezeptionsgeschitche*     36

    Language (*Langue*) and Discourse     42

    Postcolonial Discourse Theory     55

    The Politics of *Geist*     63

## PART II
## Readings in the Discourse of the Phenomenology of Religion

### Chapter Three
### *Geist*, History, Religion: Hegel and the Structure of Phenomenology and *Religionswissenschaft* — 69

- The Nature of Historical Change: Hegel's Articulation of the Concept of *Entwicklung* ("Development") — 71
- *Geist* and the Unity and Stages of History — 72
- "In" History: Reason, Morality, and the State — 79
- *Geist* and the Stages of Religious Self-Consciousness — 82
- Spirit as Life and as Community — 96

### Chapter Four
### Religion in Essence and Development: C. P. Tiele, Early *Religionswissenschaft*, and the Phenomenology of Religion — 101

- The Concept of "*Entwicklung*" (Development) — 102
- Ontology, or the Essence of Religion — 108
- History of Religion/s — 114

### Chapter Five
### "Experience, Expression, Understanding": Wilhelm Dilthey on *Geist* and the Methodology of the *Geisteswissenschaft* — 133

- Experience (*Erlebnis*) — 133
- Expression (*Ausdruck*) — 144
- Understanding (*Verstehen*) — 148
- Dilthey and Hegel/*Geist und Natur* — 153

### Chapter Six
### *Geist*, Nature, and History: The Phenomenology of Rudolf Otto — 157

- *Geist* versus *Natur*: The Structure of the Religious A Priori — 159
- "The Deficient Rationalization and Moralization of Experience":"Primitive" Religion — 168
- The (Feminine) Passivity of the East versus the (Masculine) Vitality of the Gothic West — 169

The Stage of Monotheism: Judaism and Islam versus
    Christianity                                                    173
Conclusion                                                          177

Chapter Seven
Phenomenology as Empathetic Taxonomy: The
Phenomenological Approaches of Chantepie de la Saussaye
and W. B. Kristensen                                                179
    Chantepie: *Religionswissenschaft* as a Tripart Science          181
    Phenomenology as Taxonomic Operation                            182
    Ethnographic Part                                               186
    History of Religions                                            188
    W. Brede Kristensen                                             191
    The Representation of Religion                                  194
    The Tripart Science: Philosophy, History, and
        Phenomenology in *Religionswissenschaft*                     196
    Phenomenological Limit                                          199
    Classification of Religions                                     202

Chapter Eight
Experience, Expression, Empathy: Gerardus van der Leeuw's
Phenomenological Program                                            207
    Subject/Object; Experience/Expression;
        Inward/Outward                                              207
    Structure, Meaning, and Phenomenological
        Reconstruction                                              213
    Religion in History                                             217
    Limits of *Religionsphänomenologie*                              226

Chapter Nine
Overcoming the Foreign through Experience, Expression,
Understanding: The Method/ology of Joachim Wach                     229
    Experience                                                      230
    Expression                                                      236
    Understanding                                                   240
    History of Religions, Society, and Culture                      251

## Chapter Ten
### The Total Hermeneutics of the New Humanism: Mircea Eliade's Agenda for *Religionswissenschaft* — 259
- The Grounding of the Sacred as an "Irreducible Element" — 260
- Expression and Experience — 261
- Structure, History, Intelligibility — 263
- *Religionswissenschaft*, a Total Hermeneutic and the New Humanism — 268

## PART III
### Poststructuralist, Postcolonialist Analyses

## Chapter Eleven
### "The Center Does Not Hold": Decentering the "Centrisms" of the Discourse of the Phenomenology of Religion — 275
- Logocentrism — 276
- Eurocentrism — 286
- Christocentrism — 289
- Ethnocentrism — 292
- Phenomenology of Religion and/as Racism — 296

## Chapter Twelve
### The "End of Man" and the Phenomenology of Religion — 299
- "Man," Subject, Consciousness, *Geist* — 300
- The Sickness unto Death of "Man" — 306
- The Sicknesses of "Man" — 307
- Incipit: Post-"Man" — 315

Notes — 317

Bibliography — 379

Index — 387

# Acknowledgments

I would like to thank Bryan Rennie, editor of the *Issues in the Study of Religion* series, for giving me the opportunity to publish in this series. Bryan has been very supportive of my work through the years and that support is very much appreciated.

I would also like to thank the team at SUNY that made this book happen. An author produces a manuscript; the publisher produces a book. There's all the difference between the two. Nancy Ellgate deserves special mention for championing this book and for her patience with my tardiness in finishing it.

My thanks to the Research Activity Committee of The University of Alabama for their financial support for this project. Support for research in the Humanities is hard to come by and their consistent support of Alabama faculty is a great service to the academic community as a whole.

My thanks also to two colleagues who have been especially supportive over the years. Early in the development of this project Thomas Ryba gave critical but positive feedback on its basic conceptions. Jeppe Jensen has been extremely supportive as source of intellectual feedback and sage advice over the years. His concerns for my career and his friendship have made a very real difference.

I would also like to thank Hayden White, James Clifford, David Hoy, and Carlos Noreña, all of the University of California, Santa Cruz, for reading and commenting on a much earlier version of this project.

The support and engagement of my friends, Tiffany, Karl, and Jonlaura has been much appreciated.

I would like to thank my friend and colleague Lysa Rivera for her support for my work. Her collegiality and her role as interlocutor in an ongoing and wide-ranging conversation were invaluable to me.

Finally, my good friend Stephanie Brennan also deserves mention in that regard for her support and friendship throughout the years of work on this project. Anyone who can recite Ginsberg from memory and splice genes is good company, indeed. I thank her especially for the conversation we have been pursuing over many years. While it did not always bear directly on this work, it most definitely affected my sense of where this project belongs in the larger scheme of things.

# Part I

# Introduction, Background, Methodological Issues

# 1

# The Phenomenology of Religion

## Introduction and Background

> It is extremely interesting to trace philosophy's relationship to the rising history of religion [*Religionswissenschaft*] ... I shall only mention that throughout the nineteenth century and up to the present the so-called philosophy of religion, out of which the history of religion grew, took it upon itself to study the specific questions of the history of religion. Only very recently have empirical research and philosophical speculation been separated.
>
> —Joachim Wach, 1924[1]

In his article, "What Constitutes the Identity of a Religion?," Hubert Seiwert poses two questions: "What constitutes a historical reality?" and, "What is a religion?"[2] Using "Buddhism" as an example, he asks how it is that there can be an identity between specific acts, practices, beliefs, etc., in different times and in different places, all of which are identified as "Buddhist" and none of which have any direct contact with each other? In an analysis of the meaning of such an identity, he concludes:

> Obviously one cannot maintain that there is no difference whatsoever between Buddhism in China of the 8th century and Buddhism in Ceylon of the 20th century. This implies that we cannot speak of an identity between these two phenomena. We can generalize the issue: Every observable phenomenon, i.e., every empirical fact, has as one of its attributes a spatiotemporal specificity. No empirical phenomenon can, therefore, be identical with any other than itself. From this it follows that either there is no identity of Buddhism or that Buddhism is not an empirical phenomenon.[3]

Given that each empirical phenomenon is perfectly discreet, how is it that we form unities out of these multiplicities? How, in other words, how do we form categories such as "religion," "tradition," "faith," "Buddhism," "Christianity," etc.? The very idea of a systematic study of religion is predicated on some kind of answer to this question. The ongoing attempt to define "religion" is indicative of the field's continuing struggle with precisely this issue.

In the history of the study of religion there have been a variety of responses to this issue. One school, however, has had a profound impact on the development of Religious Studies[4] as an autonomous endeavor, namely, *the* phenomenology of religion, also known as classical phenomenology of religion.[5] Scholars such as Rudolf Otto, W. B. Kristensen, Gerardus van der Leeuw, Joachim Wach, and Mircea Eliade reformulated nineteenth-century *Religionswissenschaft* into a distinct enterprise, one which has had a constitutive influence on the development of Religious Studies in Europe, North America, and elsewhere in the world. What is characteristic of this research tradition is its answer to the question just posed. Although each figure mentioned above differed in many respects from the others, they all adamantly agreed that religion must be studied as a sui generis phenomenon of the human spirit. As shall be discussed at the end of this study, they did this by reformulating the Hegelian concept of *Geist*, or Spirit, into the less metaphysically aggressive concepts of "Man"[6] or "consciousness." They answer the question posed by Seiwert by arguing that underlying the multiplicity of historical and geographically dispersed religions was an ultimately metaphysical, transhistorical substratum, variously called *Geist*, "Man," "human nature," "mind," or "consciousness." This transhistorical substratum is an expressive agent with a uniform, essential nature. As such, by reading the data of the history of religions as "expressions," it is possible to understand them sympathetically by tapping into one's *own* human subjectivity. *Geist*—spirit, human spirit, human nature, and/or "Man"—then, is the basis for a philosophy of religion, a philosophy of history, and a hermeneutical theory.

## Traditional Historiography of the Phenomenology of Religion: Hegel versus Husserl

*Hegel versus Husserl*

Much of this is well known, of course. However, the historical origins of this approach and the issues that arise from it have been, in my view, seriously misunderstood. Most historians of the phenomenology of religion argue that the phenomenological approach of Edmund Husserl was the main methodological and philosophical source for that movement. Willard Oxtoby represents the standard view on this issue: "Understood strictly, the phenomenology of religion is supposed to be a precise application to religion of insights from the European philosophical movement known as phenomenology, launched by Edmund Husserl."[7] Walter Capps concurs that it was Husserlian phenomenology that influenced Religious Studies: "Merleau-Ponty has not received much attention among persons working religious studies. Husserl has been considerably more prominent."[8] Capps further notes that there is disagreement about the pedigree of the phenomenology of religion and that

> [t]he reason for this lack of agreement is there are at least two strands of thought—two intellectual points of departure—which can produce a phenomenology of religion. The most obvious one is the one that stems directly from post-Kantian and post-Hegelian continental philosophy. Regardless of whatever else it includes, the strand always lists Edmund Husserl (1859–1961) as its primary inspirer, founding father, and intellectual catalyst.[9]

Finally, Hans Penner notes that the phenomenology of religion is as an "approach to religion is often located in the phenomenological movement which began with Husserl."[10] Penner cites Douglas Allen as a particularly ardent advocate of this view: "He [Allen] places Otto, van der Leeuw and Eliade, 'the three most influential' scholars of religion, directly in the phenomenological movement and states that they 'have used a phenomenological method and have been influenced, at least partially, by [Husserlian] phenomenological philosophy.' "[11]

Clearly, *there is a tradition* of claiming Husserl as the founder or "intellectual catalyst," at least, of classical (if no other component) phenomenology of religion. Kristensen and van der Leeuw in particular are seen as having been influenced by Husserl's twin ideas of the *epoché* and the eidetic vision. In this tradition of origins these Husserlian ideas are not seen as mere icing but as fundamental concepts.

A closer reading of the texts of the phenomenologists of religion indicates that this emphasis on Husserl is simply not warranted. The argument of this study is that, rather than see Husserl as the *primary* source for classical phenomenology of religion, its primary inspiration is derived from Hegel. The main features of phenomenology's paradigm and its appropriation of Hegel are, in turn, drawn from the early history of *Religionswissenschaft*, especially from C. P. Tiele and P. D. Chantepie de la Saussaye. It is the appropriation and transformation of the concepts of this historical trajectory that make up the intellectual, discursive content of the phenomenology of religion.

Arguing for Hegel more than Husserl puts this study in agreement with several other historians of the phenomenology of religion. While all the supporting texts cannot be cited here, a few will suffice. In contrast to reductive, noninterpretive approaches: "The phenomenological approach thus originated as an attempt to construct a coherent methodology for the study of religion" and that

> [t]he philosophy of Hegel provided a basis on which to build. In his influential *The Phenomenology of Spirit* (1806), Hegel developed the thesis that essence (*Wesen*) is understood through the investigation appearances and [as] manifestations (*Erscheinung*). Hegel's intention was to show that this led to the understanding that all phenomena, in their diversity, were nevertheless grounded in an underlying essence or unity (*Geist* or Spirit). This play upon the relationship between essence and manifestation provided a basis for understanding how religion, in its diversity, could, in essence, be understood as a distinct entity.[12]

Erricker goes on to argue that "Hegel's influence is evident in the title of the first significant publication to outline a phenomenological approach to the study of religion in a coherent way, Gerardus van der Leeuw's *Phänomenologie der Religion* (1933)."[13]

Another scholar who sees Hegel's influence on the phenomenology of religion is Olof Pettersson who argues that, contrary to seeing van der Leeuw as the originator on the strength of the above named work of this approach:

> However, the phenomenological method applied to the study of religion has its roots in the 18th century. We may remember F. Hegel's *Phänomenologie des Geistes*, published in 1807, in which the author stated that essence can be approached through a study of appearances and manifestations. He wished to discern unity behind diversity, to reach an understanding of the one essence of religion behind its many manifestations.[14]

Pettersson goes on to note: "I do not hesitate to maintain that the comparative method used by the mentioned scholars [Tyler, Lang, Marrett], among others, was *de facto* the embryo of the method that was later named the phenomenology of religion."[15] As I, too, will argue, while evolutionary and phenomenological approaches are typically seen as polar opposites or enemy camps, it is clear that the latter appropriated the former via the Hegelian concepts Erricker cites above. The teleological schemes are turned into synchronic schemes, with much the same structures and valuations as the former—despite protestations to the contrary. Of Tiele he argues, as do others, that: "He may be regarded as the first conscious representative of the Dutch phenomenological school."[16]

Finally, Walter Capps, again, gives us an excellent summary of the history of the phenomenology of religion. As noted above, he argues that there are two strands in this history (and perhaps more; I only argue that the Hegelian strand is the "thickest"). While the Husserlian legacy is one such strand, when phenomenologists of religion "trace their intellectual roots, the genealogy they offer tends to reach back not to Husserl... but to such relatively obscure figures as Cornelius Petrus Tiele... and Pierre Daniel Chantepie de la Saussaye" both of whose work began in 1877.[17] He argues that, as with Hegel's agenda described above: "Both Tiele and Chantepie engaged in phenomenology of religion while maintaining methodological interest in questions regarding religion's essence and origin."[18] From the earliest forms of Continental *Religionswissenschaft* to the peak of its development in Eliade, the phenomenology of religion retained its Hegelian structure, viewing history as the field of manifestation through which *Geist/ Wesen* expresses itself; a hermeneutical/phenomenological method (even when called "history of religions") seeks to decipher these historical particulars *as manifestations* and relate them, diachronically or synchronically, to their essence. This is the way in which they answer those absolutely fundamental questions posed by Seiwert.

*Which Hegel?*

This immediately raises the question: "Which Hegel?" Hegel has been read in numerous and conflicting ways. The traditional Marxist historiography[19] reads nineteenth-century Hegelianism as having split early between the "Young" or "Left" Hegelians and the "Old" or "Right" Hegelians. The former group read Hegel as the "philosopher of contradiction," and saw his *Phenomenology of Spirit* (*Geist*) as the key work from which to interpret the master. The latter group read Hegel as the "philosopher of identity" and saw his more complete and systematic, yet more conservative *Enzyklopaedie der Wissenschaft* as the key work from which to interpret the master.[20] In the twentieth century, following Kojeve, the "French" reading of Hegel radicalized the Left Hegelian reading and returned Hegel to the "philosopher of contradiction," with a heavy emphasis on the "master/slave" dialectic and the problematic of "the Other." This reading influenced such major thinkers as Sartre, de Beauvoir, and Lacan. The Hegel who influenced classical phenomenology of religion is *clearly* the so-called "philosopher of identity," the more conservative Hegel who had been well established in the academy.[21]

Derrida tells us of Hegel that he "summed up the entire philosophy of the *logos*. He determined ontology as absolute logic; he assembled all the delimitations of philosophy as presence; he assigned to presence the eschatology of *parousia*, of the self-proximity of infinite subjectivity."[22] Logos, *ontos*, presence, subjectivity: the combination of these elements, played out differently in different scenes, form the skeletal structure of that specific concept-operation, or research paradigm, "*the* phenomenology of religion." It argues that the concrete is a manifestation of the essential, that individual moments of religious consciousness are rooted in consciousness, or Spirit/*Geist* and can only be properly understood as such. Using the symbol of the "Cosmic Tree" as an example, Mircea Eliade argues: "Suffice it to say that it is impossible to understand the meaning [or essence] of the Cosmic Tree by considering one or some of its variants [manifestations]. It is only by the analysis of a considerable number of its examples [the many] that the structure [the one] can be completely deciphered."[23] Or, as Joachim Wach will argue in his "search for universals in religion": "A comparative study of the *forms* of the expressions of religious experience, the world over, shows an amazing similarity in structure."[24] From the many, one. Essence, or unity trumps difference as a founding category.

I will argue that Hegel and these Hegelian motifs, more than Husserl, provided the philosophical foundations or research paradigm for the phenomenology of religion. The quote at the beginning of this chapter from Wach summarizes the main features of phenomenology's paradigm and its appropriation of Hegel: "the so-called philosophy of religion, out of which the history of religion grew," the nineteenth-century philosophy of religion out of which *Religionswissenschaft* grew, was *Hegelian* philosophy of religion (something quite different than what goes by that name in Anglophonic contexts). And it was from this philosophy, or conceptual structure, that the history of religion (or phenomenology; see below on terminology) "took it upon itself to study the specific questions of the *history* of religion." That is, the phenomenology of religion's theory of history was a Hegelian theory of history, to wit, history as the manifestation of objective Spirit.

These Hegelian motifs pass through, so to speak, the early history of *Religionswissenschaft*, especially from such figures as C. P. Tiele and P. D. Chantepie de la Saussaye, and are modified and appropriated by Otto, Wach, van der Leeuw, Kristensen, and Eliade. It is noteworthy that Chantepie de la Saussaye cites Hegel as the founder of *Religionswissenschaft*: "[W]e must see Hegel as its true founder, because he first carried out the vast idea of realizing, as a whole, the various modes for studying religion (metaphysical, psychological, and historical), and made us see the harmony between the idea and the realization of religion [*zwischem dem Begriff und der Erscheinung der Religion zur Anschauung zu bringen*]."[25]

*Hegel more than Husserl not rather than Husserl*

Clearly, both are important sources for the phenomenology of religion, as are Kant, Schleiermacher, and Dilthey among others. If we follow Derrida's reading of them, as is done here, both must be located in the larger discourse of Western metaphysics, or ontotheology.[26] Both participate in the "subjective turn" in Modern Philosophy with its central emphasis on the category of "consciousness." Clearly, they both have much in common as well: "Heidegger insists Hegelian philosophy and *its extension in Husserl's phenomenology* brings an 'end to philosophy.' "[27] While the latter claim is obviously contestable, there is good evidence all around that there are important continuities between the two arch-phenomenologists. From the reading offered here, discussed in chapter 2, a discursive/textual reading rather than a strictly philosophical/conceptual reading, their differences vis-à-vis ontotheology, significant as they are, are reduced rather than expanded.

Hegel more than Husserl for two reasons. First, historically, of course, Hegel precedes Husserl, and there is a significant, if heavily qualified, appeal to Hegel throughout the literature of early *Religionswissenschaft*, as well as in classical phenomenology of religion. Though none of these figures could be considered "Hegelians" in any strict sense, nevertheless, certain important Hegelian motifs recur in their works, and these at crucial junctures. These motifs show up in *Religionswissenschaft* well before Husserl's work. For instance, Tiele will classify religions according to a teleological conception of their degree of rationalization or spiritualization. Chantepie de la Saussaye will make use of the term *phenomenology* before Husserl, but he means something quite different by the term. Furthermore, as noted, Chantepie cites Hegel as the founder of the study of religion. Ergo, by the time Husserl's phenomenology is established, the idea of phenomenology is already well entrenched in *Religionswissenschaft*.

Second, at the level of paradigm structure, as the problematic laid out by Seiwert above indicates, the issue of identity in or through history is of basic concern, is perhaps even foundational, for the systematic study of religion. Here, not only does Hegel precede Husserl, the philosophy of history was central to his thinking, whereas Husserl is notorious for his lack of concern with precisely this issue.[28] Although the issue of identity in history is articulated by classical phenomenology of religion in direct opposition to Hegel's notion of *"Entwicklung"* or "development," it nevertheless consistently maintains the preeminently Hegelian view of history as the unified, expressive activity of the human spirit, or *Geist*. The paradigm for classical phenomenology of religion, then, is the same as Hegel's Science of Wisdom, namely, that of *"Wesen und Erscheinung"* or "essence and manifestation." Also, even when articulated in an explicitly synchronic framework, the structure of Hegel's metanarrative of *Geist* informs the structure of the synchronic taxonomy of classical phenomenology of religion.

## Geist and the Geisteswissenschaften in Nineteenth-Century Continental Thought

To understand the influence of Hegel more clearly, it is important to understand *how* it was that Hegel was appropriated within the academic world of Continental Europe. It is a paradoxical story. Hegel is, from the 1830s on, appropriated by way of the explicit *rejection* of Hegel. That is, in all the schools where Hegelian ideas appear, they are constantly attended by explicit statements of denunciation of the master. This is common among theologians and philosophers, among all members of the "Historical School," and, most famously, among the dialectical materialists.

This appropriation/rejection of Hegel must be understood within the context of the general position of the human sciences from the 1830s on. In order to maintain any sense of their individual identity, it was necessary on the one hand to resist their being subsumed into a system of Absolute Knowledge, or "speculation" as Wach describes it above, that is, subsumed into philosophy, while on the other hand, indicating why they offered a technical competency that was both like, yet different from, that of the natural sciences. As Herbert Schnädelbach notes:

> The need to maintain this double front, against philosophy and the natural sciences, which was especially characteristic of the historical consciousness in Germany, gave a considerable impetus to epistemological reflection among historians, and explains the strong, if also often indirect, influence of writers such as Droysen, Dilthey or Rickert on the way in which the human sciences understood themselves.[29]

What was *rejected* in Hegel was his notorious a priorism, along with his insistence that the essential element of science was not its facticity, but its systematicity.[30] This was a defensive maneuver against both the "subordination" of the specific sciences to the system of Absolute Knowledge, and, against the charges of unscientificness being leveled from the direction of the natural sciences.[31] This is what Wach was alluding to when he said, in the epigram to this chapter, that "only very recently have empirical research and philosophical speculation been separated." The "empirical research" was historical research, but historical research understood on an Hegelian, expressive model of history. It was this empirical element, that is, concrete historical materials, which made the *Geisteswissenschaften* scientific.

Consequently, to preserve this middle ground, what was *retained* from Hegel, even by his detractors, was the conception of history as *objective spirit*, and entailed by that, the idea of development as the unfolding of Spirit:

> the bitterness of the polemics between the parties [Hegelians and the Historical School] should not conceal how close to each other they nevertheless were.... For Hegel as for the Historical School, history is *spirit*, that is, a domain of reality *which is in essence not nature*, but depends on freedom, on action which is capable of becoming conscious and creative individuality, and hence is intelligible to the individual knower.[32]

The ambiguity of this position is reflected in Droysen's slogan, that the method of the historical sciences was that of "Understanding [*Verstehen*] observation."[33] Understanding is the a priori, conceptual element of research; observation, the empirical element.

The Hegelian idea of development was especially influential in the study of religion. As Frederick Gregory notes: "If the employment of Hegelian reason involved a movement toward the identity of the concept with its object, the same process was reflected in the development of religion in history. It is from the idea of development inspired by Hegel that his influence on Protestant theology was felt in the nineteenth century debate over the relation between religion and natural science."[34] As shall be discussed at some length, although van der Leeuw famously said, *"der Religionsphänomenologie wiess die 'Entwicklung' nichts"* ("the phenomenology of religion does not know 'development' "), and Eliade will frequently proclaim that "the sacred is a structure of consciousness, not a stage of history," all phenomenologists of religion nevertheless hold to the idea that individual religions are manifestations of the essence of religion. "Essence and manifestation," then, continues to be the paradigm for the study of religion, whether understood diachronically or synchronically. In a statement written in1924, Wach again summarizes the situation in a complete manner: "Hegelianism did not derive its categories and laws from the course of history but imposed them on it from above. It is nevertheless possible to inquire, quite apart from metaphysical speculation and construction, into the principles according to which religion as a manifestation of the objective spirit evolves historically."[35] Yes to objective spirit (because it is objective and subject to empirical research); no to a priori categories. Such is the way the phenomenologists of religion appropriated the master.

Underlying, as it were, this view of the atemporal nature of consciousness, is a philosophy of matter (or nature, or *Natur*). One of the central arguments of this book is that this philosophy of matter/nature underlies the entire project being discussed here, that is, both the diachronic metanarrative of *Geist* in Hegel and Tiele and the synchronic taxonomy of "consciousness" in van der Leeuw and Eliade. Hegel articulates this view more thoroughly and explicitly than any of the other authors in this tradition:

> It is a result of speculative Philosophy that Freedom is the sole truth of Spirit [*Geist*]. Matter possesses gravity in virtue of its tendency toward a central point. It is essentially composite: consisting of parts that exclude each other. It seeks its Unity out of itself. . . . Spirit, on the contrary, may be defined as that which has its center in itself. It has not a unity outside itself, but has already found it; it exists in

and with itself. Matter has its essence out of itself; Spirit is self-contained existence (*Bei-sich-selbst-seyn*).[36]

Rudolf Otto, for example (a figure who will be included in this study), agrees, arguing that "[t]he direct experience that spirit has of itself, of its individuality and freedom, of its incomparability with all that is beneath it, is far too constant and genuine to admit of its being put into a difficulty by a doctrine [materialism] which it has itself established."[37] *Natur/Matter* as such, cannot attain true selfhood or subjectivity, as the essence of subjectivity is to be "in-and-for-itself."[38] Matter's ontological determination is to have its being as "out-of-itself."

As shall be discussed below, one of the heinous outcomes of this construction of the structural relation between *Geist* and *Natur*, Spirit and Nature, becomes evident when it is applied to human beings, some of whom are classified as *Naturvölker*, while the correlation between *Kultur* and *objectiv Geist* is elevated to both a methodological and a metaphysical principle. The result is that "civilized" peoples are inherently free and *Naturvölker* are, as Nature/Matter itself is, inherently dependent, having their *telos* and purpose outside of themselves. This is, of course, a legitimation for the colonization and subordination of the latter by the former. This occurs both in practical terms, where Nature—including *Naturvölker*—is a repository of resources which exists *for* Spirit, and, in theoretical-scientific terms where, as objects of inquiry, "primitive" cultures are the Other by and through which Spirit comes to "*pure* self-recognition in absolute otherness."[39] Spirit is both subject and substance, the underlying reality that makes temporality "history," as opposed to mere flux or change. So, "higher civilizations" have a history, whereas "primitives" or *Naturvölker*, do not. The metaphysics of peoples, if you will, necessitates a colonial discourse reading of the phenomenology of religion, a reading that forms a major element of this study, as shall discussed in detail in chapter 2.

Besides being an ontology, the distinction between *Geist* and *Natur* becomes the basis for the structure of knowledge and for the explicit articulation of the methodology of the human sciences. As Charles Bambach notes: "In the work of different [post-Hegelian] philosophers ranging from Rickert and Windelband to Vaihinger, Simmel, Troeltsh, and Cassirer, one notices the same rigorous focus on developing a critical theory of knowledge divided by the dual spheres of subject and object, mind and nature, *Geist* and *Natur*."[40] In particular, the work of Wilhelm Windelband was formative for this paradigm:

Windelband argued that the traditional distinction between "*Natur* and *Geist* was a substantive dichotomy." (Windelband, "History and Natural Science," p. 173) In other words, its principle of classification was based on the object being investigated—its content rather than its form. *Naturwissenschaften*, according to this model of the disciplines, were simply those sciences dealing with the objects of nature: physics, biology, chemistry, geology, meteorology, and the like. *Geisteswissenschaften* were, by contrast, those sciences dealing with the objects of human life: history, moral philosophy, economy, politics, and society. In this scheme, the *Naturwissenschaften* were concerned with the external, corporeal world of nature, and the *Geisteswissenschaften*, with the internal, reflexive world.[41]

Far from being some obtuse intellectual exercise, this division becomes part of *the very structure of institutionalized knowledge*: "At all major German universities, the disciplines were distinguished either as *Naturwissenschaften* (natural sciences) or as *Geisteswissenschaften* (sciences of the mind)."[42]

The human sciences "save" themselves, so to speak, from being negated by the natural sciences by arguing that *Geist* is qualitatively distinct from *Natur* and must, as such, be studied by different methods. Dilthey's famous dictum expresses this point: "Nature is 'explained' [*Erklären*] but Spirit is 'understood' [*Verstehen*]."[43] He elaborates: "All science and scholarship is empirical, but all experience is originally connected, and given validity, by our *consciousness* (within which it occurs) indeed, by our whole nature."[44] While it may sound as if he is an empiricist, he is in fact denying that empiricism is adequate for understanding the inner workings of consciousness. It is, again, consciousness' apprehension of *itself*—free of external stimuli, i.e., *emperia*—by which understanding occurs. This is a commonly shared notion among the phenomenologists of religion and leads to many misunderstandings (discussed below) on the part of Anglophonic empiricists' readings. Given that this inner experience occurs in the pure interiority of consciousness, the method of *Verstehen*, then, is *explicitly* rooted in the metaphysics of Spirit. Furthermore, "*Verstehen*," understanding, is an act of subjectivity, an act of that infinite proximity of which Derrida spoke: I can understand the "expressions" of the ancients, for example, because, at some level they express the universal structure or nature of *Geist*, consciousness, or "Man": "Thus he [Dilthey] differs from Hegel ultimately on one thing only, that according to Hegel the homecoming of the spirit takes place in the philosophical concept whereas, for Dilthey, the philosophical concept is significant not as knowledge but as expression."[45]

*Dilthey's Importance*

Dilthey is a key figure in the transmission and translation of Hegelianism. This was accomplished by rendering the concept of "objective spirit" scientifically respectable. In so doing, he also laid out the basic structure of the *Geisteswissenschaft* as these would be understood by several generations of scholars. Like Hegel, Windelband, and others, held that the division between *Geist* and *Natur* was foundational. More than just a methodological divide or bureaucratic convenience, Dilthey felt that this was a fundamental metaphysical truth: "He even claimed that the actual division of the sciences according to nature and spirit was based on these metaphysical principles of first philosophy."[46]

Furthermore, Dilthey worked on formulating both a methodological foundation and an agenda for the *Geisteswissenschaften*.[47] As Bambach argues, it is from this context that the modern view of the sciences stems: "The term *Geisteswissenshaft(en)* is a crucial one for Dilthey and needs to be understood within the context of late-nineteenth-century German thought in general.... Hegel used the phrase *Wissenschaft des Geistes,* and it is the Hegelian notion of *Geist* (bound up with all the historical, cultural, and metaphysical implications of a 'philosophy of mind' or 'philosophy of spirit') which influenced Dilthey.... the term signified for Dilthey that group of studies dealing with the cultural spirit of humanity."[48]

Dilthey's appropriation of Hegel, then, becomes one of the major sources for what will later be known as "the History of Religion(s)," or "the phenomenology of religion." His formula of "experience-expression-understanding" may as well have been the motto for the phenomenology/history of religion. Traces of Dilthey's influence are evident in Otto and Eliade, but are quite explicit in Wach and van der Leeuw. Both of the latter could be, without serious violence, considered "Diltheians." For this reason, although he was not a phenomenologist of religion, I have devoted a chapter to his views of the nature and methodology of the *Geisteswissenschaften*.

## "Explanation versus Interpretation": Previous Critiques of the Phenomenology of Religion

The phenomenology of religion and its legacy in Religious Studies have come into direct conflict with another approach, namely those who understand the scientific study of religion to take the form of reductive or naturalistic explanations.[49] The conflict has left the field with a great deal of uncertainty about what may be called "meta-theoretical" issues. That is, we are at odds as to what the study of religion is supposed to accomplish: is it sympathetic *understanding* by way of a hermeneutical approach, or is it an objective, reductive *explanation*, modeled more or less on the natural sciences? A search for meaning or a search for causes? Contemporary philosophy of social science (and even natural science), however, has indicated that one of the keys to understanding scientific quandaries is to critically examine the *history* of a science, especially the history of its category formation. Contrary to earlier positivist views of science, contemporary theorists hold that categories, scientific discourses, and research paradigms structure the objects and possible objects of scientific research, and not the other way around. Historical examination of the hidden assumptions and histories embedded in research questions, then, can indicate ways in which data were selected and organized.[50] Critical historical analysis of this kind is able to uncover previously unrecognized metaphysical, epistemological, and ideological assumptions that turned out to be *constitutive* of the data being analyzed. It can also suggest alternative ways to select and organize data. The way out of unsatisfactory results is not to find new data, but to ask new questions.

The Anglophonic critics of phenomenology and Religious Studies, mostly in North America, have drawn upon a philosophy of science developed by thinkers such as Karl Popper and Imre Lakotas.[51] Such an analytical apparatus has a specific yield, as it were. I, however, want to analyze classical phenomenology of religion in light of a significantly different paradigm, namely, that of poststructuralist philosophy and postcolonial theory as informed by poststructuralism. This paradigm will show that what is taken to be the very strength of classical phenomenology's method, the empathetic/hermeneutic approach, is based upon not so much normative Christian theology, but upon ideological humanism, *Geist*, or a transcendent notion of subjectivity.[52] Ideological humanism, far from being a benign concern for "mankind," has been implicated by poststructuralism and postcolonial criticism in a variety of forms of Euro- and ethno-centrism, a point which shall be argued at length in chapter 11 of this study. Once classical phenomenology of religion's Hegelian heritage is delineated more fully, this critique will be much clearer. Such delineation requires a specific kind of reading of Hegel, however, a reading very different than that of traditional Anglo-American analytic philosophy. This reading of Hegel, and of phenomenology in general, has been one of the most important accomplishments of poststructuralism. This point will be discussed more thoroughly in chapter 2.

*Anglophonic-Empiricist Critiques of the Phenomenology of Religion*

At this point it will be helpful to the overall thesis of this study and to clarify the methodology it uses to review some of the main criticisms offered by the empirical-Anglophonic scholars and indicate some of the ways in which my own critique of the phenomenology of religion agrees with and differs from these empiricist-oriented critiques.

FIRST CRITIQUE: THE RELIGIOSITY OF THE PHENOMENOLOGY OF RELIGION

"Let us confront this situation bluntly and in all honesty. Theology is very much a part of what has become known as the history and phenomenology of religion"; "In brief, the phenomenology of religion and theology are two *sides* of the same coin."[53] Anglo-American critics of Religious Studies find this to be one of the great weaknesses of both the phenomenology of religion in general and Eliade in particular (and, by extension, Religious Studies). I will, at many points below, take criticisms of Eliade as stand-ins for more general criticisms of the phenomenology of religion. Donald Wiebe concurs with Penner, going even farther: "The scholarly study of religion is now and has always been an essentially religio-theological undertaking for the majority of those involved in the enterprise. It is and has always been predominantly informed, that is, by theological assumptions and religious commitments."[54] As I will argue below, one aspect of what this argument holds is that theological and religious commitments overstep their bounds, claiming to do work in an area for which they are not suited. Wiebe sometimes implies, at least on my reading, that this elision/confusion of boundaries is an act of dissimulation. The theologians and religionists are not totally open, or perhaps not completely intellectually honest about what they are doing.

Robert Segal makes a similar claim about the twofold strategy that religio-theological approaches take to the social scientific approach: "Religionists deploy two strategies to fend off the social sciences: neutralizing the social sciences and embracing them."[55] The phenomenology of religion accomplishes this by using, on the one hand an old-fashioned faculty psychology: man thinks, feels, and wills, or has intellect, emotion, volition.[56] These innate and universal faculties correspond to the various aspect of human life: science, art, and ethics. On the other hand, once this is done, phenomenologists tend to break down the work of the sciences into what they sometime call "regional ontologies," but more often simply list, in categorical fashion, the various disciplines and their appropriate objects/areas of investigation. This neutralizes the impact of, say Freud, by sharply, logically, and categorically isolating "psychology" from history or phenomenology.

Robert Baird believes that this leads to a normative, rather than a descriptive-analytical methodology for the study of religion. As Baird notes, essentialism is not simply an objective description of the abstract, logically determined specific difference of a class of things in the world. Rather: "The search for the 'essence' of religion is subtly normative rather than historical-descriptive."[57] This is a major component of what I will argue in this study: the ontotheological categories of the phenomenology of religion necessarily create an "economy of privilege" in which some things are given greater value, reality, and being than others. While I do not see this aspect as importing an extraneous criterion into the descriptive task as does Baird, it is also true that phenomenologists—as well as many other scholars of religion—do import such criteria. My argument, rather, is that *the very structure of the discourse* of the phenomenology of religion is latent with hierarchies that are "values" in a broad sense. Such acts of valuation, then, are a *necessary* component of this discourse. As such, it cannot be salvaged by merely "removing" the normative elements. The kind of elements I am describing cannot be removed as they are constitutive of the conceptual system of the phenomenology of religion as a whole.

I completely concur with the assessment of Religious Studies in general and phenomenological approach specifically as an intellectual structure saturated by metaphysical-religious concepts. The phenomenology of religion is "religious" in some broad sense. Its intellectual pedigree is thoroughly embedded within and saturated by religio-theological concepts. However, the kind of critique I offer does not simply see phenomenology's problem as primarily a matter of theology but of *ontotheology*. Following other poststructuralists, I see the metaphysical structures underlying phenomenology as being part of the larger Western metaphysical tradition with its distinct structures and functions. These have been detailed and critiqued by many great thinkers, Nietzsche and Heidegger readily come to mind, but I will elaborate on Derrida's specific version of the structural critique of this historical-structural reality embedded as it is, deep within the structures of the Western thought. This will be spelled out in the next chapter and in the last chapters of this study.

The shift from theology to ontotheology is quite drastic in that it allows a much broader range of critique. Naming phenomenology as theology—a name it does deserve, though "metaphysics" would be more felicitous—generates a critique about the provinces of knowledge and the truth or falsity of religion. Theology, if considered legitimate at all, is a discipline that has a distinct sphere of concern. Penner's (et al.) critique could be seen as saying that the problem is one of overstepping bounds, that is, theology's proper area of concern. Theology also raises the question of the truth of religion: by labeling the phenomenology of religion theology Penner (et al.) is accusing the phenomenology of *advocating* of the truth of religion in the guise of a bias-free descriptivism and taxonomy. Like most critics in this vein, Penner holds out for a notion of science that is value-free and objective. While each has a somewhat different way of defending and explaining it, each of these critiques believes that the problem with a theological-normative approach to the study of religion that advocates for religion is that it violates the value-free cannon of science.

The critique from ontotheology raises considerably different issues. It is a meta-critique of the "regimes of truth" that have been deployed throughout Western history. It sees the fundamental categorical structure of Western metaphysics—including such categories as being, consciousness, truth, God, meaning, the good, mind, reality (*ex mente*), objectivity, the subject, and reason—as not simply being false, but as being utterly interdependent. Any "philosophy" is a permutation of the many-yet-finite possibilities contained within the larger system of available concepts (the paradigm in structuralist terms). These permutations occur by the exclusion, even suppression, of some elements of the system and the favoring and foregrounding of others, often combining them in novel ways. This means that apparently opposite philosophical doctrines have more fundamental features in common than they have differences. For instance, rationalism and empirical realism both are predicated upon the Heliotrope, that is, the idea of knowledge as light, light of the mind versus the light of sight or seeing (empirical verification). The play of the Heliotrope, then, governs the possible permutations of these positions (and not the other way around). Deconstructing (versus rejecting or falsifying) these positions says, in effect, "a pox on both your houses." It does not take sides between rival positions but tries to lay bare these common, constitutive features of each position.

Another trajectory of critique that the perspective of ontotheology allows is the situating of the phenomenology vis-à-vis the issue of Euro-imperialism and/or colonialism. While this may seem to be yet another normative turn in theory—poststructuralism's norms this time—this is not the case. Tracing out the play of the constitutive concepts of ontotheology shows that the structures of the terms by which colonialists describe the colonized and the structure of terms by which "religion is put into discourse" in the phenomenology of religion are quite similar, showing many points of outright identity. Again, it is not a matter of moral condemnation, but of structural analysis of concepts that constitute the conceptual framework of the phenomenology of religion. Deconstructing these is not the same thing as imposing a grid of moral-normative concepts upon phenomenology. It is an analytical operation, not an axiological one—axiological categories are themselves part of ontotheology.

SECOND CRITIQUE: NON-EMPIRICAL AND AHISTORICAL

The flip side of this normative critique is the criticism in Penner's claim "that the academic study of religion has failed to carry out its original scientific agenda."[58] Dudley cites Eliade's approval of Levi-Strauss because: "he forces anthropologists to *think*, and to think hard. For the empirically minded Anglo-American anthropologist, this is a real calamity."[59] This shows that, *pace* the *Verstehen* tradition of the *Geisteswissenschaften*, Eliade has disdain for any unfiltered, non-categorical (in Kant's terms) access to external reality, namely, typical empirical notions predicated on the correspondence theory of truth. Most Anglo-American Religious Studies critics find this to be one of the great weaknesses of both the phenomenology of religion in general and Eliade in particular.[60]

While Eliade himself makes some claims to doing empirical work, especially as it concerns historical research, my guess is that this is more a matter of academic politics than actually methodological or metaphysical commitments. If we recall the difficult positioning of the *Geisteswissenschaften* discussed above, this makes perfect sense. As did Windelband et al., Eliade finds himself sandwiched between an "epistemological right" that insists that all academic research be strictly (even narrowly) empirical in method and an "epistemological left" that tends toward either philosophical idealism or existentialism, that is, an explicitly nonempirical philosophical approach. Eliade, as did his predecessors, wishes to defend the scientific nature of his work. To do so he must satisfy the empiricists while denying that his work is simply a philosophy of religion or a philosophy of *Existenz*. The appeal to history accomplishes both of these tasks—as it did in the nineteenth century; the redundancy of the debate is an interesting fact in its own right. It suggests that we are dealing with the antinomies of a paradigm, in this case a Cartesian theory of consciousness, and not the progressive-dialectic of a theoretical debate that is actually making advances by eliminating failed perspectives.

Segal asserts that any "preemptory dismissal of any effort by the social sciences to assess the truth of religion is unjustified,"[61] viz., dismissal or denunciation by phenomenologists of religion, or religionists in general: "Eliade's denunciation of the study of religion by other disciplines" including the disciplines of " 'physiology, psychology, sociology, economics, linguistics, art.' "[62] By rejecting even the potential usefulness of these, Segal argues that phenomenological religionists are being dogmatically and unscientifically nonempirical[63] in that they seek to avoid or elide the impact of the social sciences on their scholarly agenda. While I completely concur with the latter argument, my approach to this entails neither accusing phenomenologists of being dogmatic (they are no more nor less so than social scientists or poststructuralists all *can* be) or of employing the falsification technique to criticize their work (although, again, I think, not without some serious reservations, that is a fruitful approach). The "yield" of my critique will be quite different as it differs significantly in both methods and aims. However, I think the results, viz., that the phenomenology of religion is a dead enterprise, of both approaches are quite similar. We are all looking to get "beyond phenomenology," but in radically different ways[64] for radically different reasons.

While I agree that the phenomenology of religion is inadequately empirical in its research methods and especially in its underlying theory of history and consciousness, I believe that Segal and Wiebe have both misunderstood the arguments of the phenomenologists in some rather drastic ways. The main way this systemic misunderstanding comes about is by the *equivocal and nonhistorical usage* of the terms of empiricism as applied to the phenomenology of religion. The result is that they impose extraneous criteria on the agenda of the phenomenologists, criticizing them for failing to do things they never set out to do. As the historical discussion of the complex footing of the *Geisteswissenschaften* above shows, the idea of "the empirical" is quite different in that tradition than it is in the empiricist tradition used by Segal and Wiebe. This is, I am afraid to say, a "family failing" of empiricism: it fails to historicize things, using a static, Cartesian epistemological model instead (an abstracted, individualized subject in relation to an abstracted, individual object). Frankly, the phenomenologists are more sophisticated than the empiricists on this point, if on no other. Saying this does *not*, it should be noted, justify the phenomenologists' program. It just indicates that, insofar as Segal and Wiebe consistently misrepresent the position of the phenomenologists, their critiques are hampered rather than helped. The cure for their historical-exegetical failings is the work of Schändelbach and Bambich cited extensively above. My impression is that the empiricists do not *like* what the phenomenologists are up to, and so their agenda leads them to make fast and loose equivocations, equivocations that amount to normative ideas of what science *should* be.

Another critique of the phenomenology of religion is that it is ahistorical in nature. Given what has been said about its use of history, this may seem a paradoxical, even contradictory charge. However, there is a strong ahistorical tendency in the phenomenonological method as a taxonomic operation. Kristensen gathers examples from all religions (or "Christian" and "non-Christian" religions), arguing that phenomenology's goal is "to consider phenomena, not only in their historical context, but also in their ideal connection"; "it does not matter where we find them."[65] Eliade's procedure in *Patterns in Comparative Religion*, one of his most important works, is avowedly ahistorical, using a decontextualized, synchronic-taxonomic method, a kind of merger of Kant (a priori categories of the mind) and Plato (forms or essences that are common to all material instantiations).[66]

Clearly, it is true: much of the phenomenology of religion's work is ahistorical. One must be cautious here: this is exactly the claim of phenomenology; it is a structural, synchronic, taxonomic operation which seeks to see the *simile in multis*, the same, common, structural, universal elements of diverse religious phenomena. It seeks the meaning of "sacrifice itself," not this or that sacrifice.[67]

Perhaps the more damning critique is not that they are ahistorical but that in their search for universals, for the *simile in multis*, they are engaged in imposing the "tyranny of the Same" (Levinas) onto to their subjects, thus depriving them of their historical particularity—i.e., their cultural identity. These subjects are, rather, subsumed into a metaphysics of *hylé/morphè* (hylemorphism), or matter and form. As mere matter, they are once again, on the lower side of the *Geist* (immaterial, universal a priori categories) and *Natur* ("subject matter"; "it does not matter where we find them") dichotomy.[68] The logocentrism of this approach allows and/or entails the elision of the particular identities of the subjects under investigation. The treatment of these subjects will be reviewed in detail throughout this study, but a clue to its target is signaled by Kristensen's macro taxonomy of Christian/non-Christian religions. Wach makes similar distinctions throughout his work. This is the cost of dehistoricing: the Other is negated in their otherness in an imperialism of the Same. When Derrida talks about the "metaphysics of presence," an aspect of ontotheology, this is a perfect example of what he meant.

Hans Penner has argued that phenomenology has run into serious theoretical and philosophical difficulties, perhaps signaling its end:

> The difficulty is due to the critique that "post-structural" scholars have directed at phenomenology in general and Husserl in particular. This critique has dealt a devastating blow to Husserl's notion of a transcendental reduction and the apodictic value of his notion of the transcendental ego.[69] Foucault for example, describes his own project as a correction of "the search for origins, for formal *a prioris*, for founding acts . . . its aim is to free history from the grip of phenomenology."[70]

This is precisely what this study shall attempt to do. While the criticisms listed here bear much fruit, and I concur with much that has been said, it should be clear that a poststructuralist critique has a significantly different yield. The specific yield of this method will be taken up in the last chapters of this study.

## The Pedigree of Classical Phenomenology of Religion

"Although a wide variety of scholars employ the word *phenomenology* to describe their methodological intentions, they do not always agree on what the label means."[71] The pedigree of the phenomenology of religion reaches back to the earliest moments in the formation of *Religionswissenschaft* as an autonomous and distinct institutional entity.[72] Although F. Max Müller is widely credited as the "founder" of the science of religion, his influence was largely confined to England. In his institutional history of the field of Religious Studies, *Comparative Religion: A History*, Eric Sharpe notes that the Dutch scholar, C. P. Tiele, "was perhaps the continental equivalent of Friedrich Max Müller in England."[73] As such, the Dutch vein will be reviewed first. There are, however, two main veins of development in this research tradition: the Dutch and the German. We will review each in turn.

## The Dutch School

Tiele and Chantepie de la Saussaye, both of whom figure prominently as sources for classical phenomenology of religion, were the first two persons to hold chairs in Holland, and two of the first ever to hold chairs in the academic study of religion. As Sharpe notes, these chairs were set up as part of the Dutch Universities Act. This act legally separated the theological faculties of the universities from the Dutch Reformed Church, giving the former more independence from the latter. It also established the new chairs, specifically designated as chairs in the "History of Religions," at the four main universities: Amsterdam, Groningen, Leiden, and Utrecht. To this day, these chairs have been the most fertile source of scholars trained in phenomenology of religion in the entire field.

Tiele was given a chair at Leiden (in History of Religions [*Religionsgeschichte*] and Philosophy of Religion) in 1877 which he held until his retirement in 1900. In 1878, Chantepie took the new chair at Amsterdam and held it until 1899. He then went to Leiden and held a chair there in Theological Encyclopedia, Doctrine of God, and Ethics until his retirement in 1916.

Tiele's handpicked successor at Leiden was W. B. Kristensen, a Norwegian classicist who had studied with Tiele before receiving his PhD Kristensen assumed the chair in 1900 and held it until 1937. Shortly thereafter, a new chair was established in 1911 at Leiden for the explicit purpose of bringing the Swedish philosopher and historian of religion, Nathan Söderblom there. Both of these scholars became prominent figures in the initial phase of classical phenomenology of religion.[74]

Two of Kristensen's students attained notoriety in this field: Hendrick Kraemer succeeded him at Leiden, holding "a chair in the history and phenomenology of religions,"[75] from 1937 to 1947. More importantly, Kristensen influenced Gerardus van der Leeuw, an important figure in the history with which we are concerned. After receiving his ThD from Leiden, van der Leeuw held the chair at Groningen in History of Religions, Theological Encyclopedia, and, as did Kristensen, Egyptology.

## The German School

On the German side Rudolph Otto is the principal figure. He received a PhD from Tübingen and taught theology at Göttingen from 1914 to 1917. In 1917 he went to Marburg where he stayed until his retirement in 1929. A colleague of Otto's at Marburg was Friedrich Heiler, whom Sharpe describes as "a disciple of Söderblom and Otto,"[76] and who became a well-known figure in the phenomenological movement with works such as *Erscheinungsformen und Wesen der Religion* (1949, roughly "Forms of Manifestations and the Essence of Religion"). Otto's successor at Marburg was another well-known scholar, Heinrich Frick. Frick's principal contribution to the field was his work, *Vergleichende Religionswissenschaft* (1928, "Comparative Religion"). However, besides Otto himself, the most significant figure to come out of this group was Joachim Wach. Wach received his PhD at Leipzig in 1922 with a dissertation entitled "Basic Elements of a Phenomenology of Salvation." Sharpe tells us that "he was introduced to the comparative study of religion by Friedrich Heiler, and counted among his mentors Troeltsch, Harnack, Söderblom, Weber, and Otto."[77] Charles Long, a graduate of the University of Chicago, however, tells us that Otto was the main influence on Wach, a point borne out thoroughly by examining Wach's citations throughout his works.[78]

Wach emigrated from Germany to the United States in 1935 and taught History of Religions at Brown until 1945, at which time he went to the University of Chicago to do the same until his death in 1955. Wach's successor at Chicago was the Rumanian-born Mircea Eliade. Eliade received his PhD in philosophy from the University of Bucharest in 1940 with a dissertation on yoga. He taught at the Sorbonne from 1945 to 1957, when he took Wach's chair at Chicago which he held until his retirement in 1986.

Joseph Kitagawa joined the faculty at Chicago in 1951, holding a position in the History of Religions, specializing in Japanese religions. He was very active the International Association for the History of Religions and was an advisor to the *Encyclopedia Britannica* in the area of religion. He also edited the posthumous works of Wach. While not an original thinker per se, Kitagawa played a major role in the promotion and dissemination of the "history of religions," which is a kind of code word for the phenomenological of religion (i.e., the study of the concrete manifestations of religion as they appear in history).

Wach, Eliade, and Kitagawa, along with other faculty at Chicago, formed what has come to be known as the "Chicago School" in the study of religion. While some graduates of that program deny that such a thing exists, it has been *thought* to exist and *thought* to have a broad influence of the study of religion. Donald Wiebe describes this common perception, tying it to the kind of methodology he rejects:

> This humanistic or scholarly study of religion, which Kitagawa takes such pains to distinguish from religion and

theology.... is nevertheless a liberal form of Protestantism. And with its establishment in the Divinity School of the University of Chicago, it wielded immense influence in the development of the field of religious studies in colleges and universities throughout the United States.[79]

Wiebe cites Wach and Eliade as the major figures in the Chicago school, arguing that it was further established by "the work of Joachim Wach" but the "turning point in the growth of the Divinity School's national profile coincided with the arrival of Mircea Eliade in 1956."[80] Similarly, according to Bryan Rennie, Gregory Alles, an editor of some of Wach's work, argues that "[t]he critique from totality that results Alles considers to have a direct bearing upon the Chicago school's attempt (exemplified by Wach and Eliade) to articulate the totality of religion via hermeneutics."[81] Finally, Willard Oxtoby notes how, after 1959, Harvard's rise in the field threatened to "rival Chicago's formerly undisputed primacy in the field."[82] Again, it is clear that there is a broadly shared perception that such a school exists. As editor of Wach's works, Alles is in as good a position as anyone to know the facts of the case. Note that he also argues that Wach and Eliade are its main figures. Both will be treated in this study for that very reason.

The journal *The History of Religions* is the main mouthpiece of the Chicago school. As Wiebe notes, this school had at one time produced more professors of Religious Studies (as opposed to professors of Bible or Theology) in the United States than any other individual institution in the country. Its influence extends well beyond the number of its graduates and it has been the principal means by which phenomenology of religion has been disseminated in American cultural and intellectual life. As such, it forms the formal terminus of our pedigree of classical phenomenology of religion.

We would, however, be remiss if we did not at least mention some of the other principals and successors, and "branches" of the pedigree.[83] Chief among the principals would have to be C. J. Bleeker. He was one of van der Leeuw's successors in Holland, held a chair for many years at Amsterdam and has played an important role in the dissemination of the program of the phenomenology of religion by both his writings and his institutional and editorial work (most notably, with the International Association for the History of Religions and as editor for the journal *Numen*). Important successors include Jacques Waardenburg, who held a chair for many years at Utrecht and published the widely circulated three volume work, *Classical Approaches the Study of Religion*, the heart of which is a long section on precisely the tradition we are dealing with here. The Swede, Åke Hultkrantz has been a long-time advocate of phenomenology in approaches to Native American religion. Evan Zusse, an Africanist and graduate of Chicago, is likewise an advocate of phenomenological approaches to religion. These three, Waardenburg, Hultkrantz, and Zusse, constitute a "third wave" of the phenomenological movement in Religious Studies.[84] They advocate each in varying ways a "contextualist" approach to phenomenology as opposed to the essentialism of classical phenomenologists. As they come after the "classical" group of phenomenologists (Otto, Wach, Eliade, et al.) they will not be dealt with in this study. I leave it to others to investigate the question as to what in this study would or would not apply to these "third wave" phenomenologists, although I suspect one would find many, though not all, of the same problems.

Finally, one of the branches of phenomenology of religion that will *not* be dealt with directly here is the Scandinavian school.[85] This, for three reasons: (1) it has not had any real impact on either the program of Religious Studies in the United States (my main concern), or on the history of the study of religion in general (especially compared to the Dutch and German strands, though it has much in common with the Dutch approach; (2) it is a later, and more critical approach (i.e., rejecting theology and essentialism more thoroughly), and its problematics are therefore very different from the classical variety; (3) virtually none of Swedish works are available in the United States, in Swedish, English, or German versions.

## Terminology: "Phenomenology" and "History of Religions"

Before proceeding to the next chapter, a terminological note is necessary. There is much confusion around the meaning and intention behind the term *phenomenology of religion*. It is sometimes used as a substitute for the older term, *Religionswissenschaft*, and as such, to characterize the entire field of the study of religion as an independent enterprise.[86] As Dudley notes, "[H]istorians of religion have sought to anchor their identity in a new autonomous discipline, first known as *Religionswissenschaft* and more recently as the history of religions."[87] More often it is used to characterize a specific approach to the task of *Religionswissenschaft*, which is just one approach among others (*Religionsphänomenologie*, alongside *Religionspsychologie, Religionssoziologie*, etc.). In both cases, however, the term has always indicated approaching the study religion in a strictly nonreductive way. This nonreductive argument, I will argue, is a permutation of the distinction *Geist/Natur*.

In the United States (and elsewhere) the phenomenology of religion very often goes by the name of History of Religions. "History of Religions" carries the same ambiguity as does "phenomenology of religion" in that it has a more and a less general sense. By and large, however, "History of Religions" is also another name for a phenomenological, nonreductive approach to the study of religious history. It was Eliade's preferred term for the field.[88]

"History of Religions" is also the preferred translation in American English for *Religionswissenschaft*. This confusion is spelled out by Douglas Allen when he makes the following distinctions:

> By "history of religions" we mean the entire discipline of *Religionswissenschaft*, with which we may distinguish such "branches" as history, psychology, sociology, and phenomenology of religion (see Joachim Wach, *Sociology of Religion*). Within this context we take Eliade to be a historian of religions, and, more specifically, a phenomenologist of religion.[89]

This begs the question, of course, as to why "*Religionswissenschaft*" is translated as "history of religions," when it contains neither the word "history" (*Geschichte*) nor "religions" in the plural.[90] A direct translation would be "the science of religion," not "history of religions." The answer is, again, that there is a deeply Hegelian bias to both the idea of *Wissenschaft* and to history: it is the study of "objective Spirit," or the study of the manifestations in history of the transhistorical essence of religion.

Also, just to make matters more confusing, "Comparative Religion" has a dual meaning, sometimes being the name for a field, sometimes for an approach.[91] As a name for an approach, "comparative religion" is also ambiguous: early versions of comparative religion compared religions as whole units. Later versions compared "structural parallels," a concept closely associated with the taxonomic approach in the phenomenology of religion. As such, "comparative religion" is often used as yet another name for this approach. Guilford Dudley indicates how, even by the late 1950s:

> There was not only a lack of consensus on methodology there was not even a universally accepted title for the field. It was Mircea Eliade, Joseph Kitagawa, and Charles Long of

the University of Chicago who urged the name "history of religion." Wilfred C. Smith of Harvard called it "comparative religions." Erwin Goodenough of Yale referred to it as the "science of religions." W. Brede Kristensen of Leiden and Gerardus van der Leeuw of Gronigen produced studies in "phenomenology of religion," and Raffaele Pettazzoni of Rome and Joachim Wach of Chicago spoke of *"allgemeine* [universal] *Religionswissenschaft."*[92]

In the following sections, I will always use "the phenomenology of religion" to denote a specific research tradition.[93] When quoting authors I will, of course, have to follow their lead. But for the most part the term "History of Religion/s" as used by these authors will also refer to this specific research tradition. In other words, the term *the phenomenology of religion* is not a generic term. It refers the specific set of authors and a specific "school" of thought, one especially associated with Otto, van der Leeuw, Wach, and Eliade. As discussed above, there are many other scholars who could be included under this heading. However, they are not my concern. I am *only* concerned with what Waardenberg calls "classic phenomenologists of religion," that is, with the tradition that names Otto, Eliade, et al., as phenomenologists. This body of intertextual texts, mediated as it is by a heavily determined *Rezeptionsgeschichte* (discussed in chapter 2), is the object under analysis here.

Consequently, I will not take it as a criticism that I did not include so-and-so, such-and-such scholar or scholars. They are simply not my concern and I have no intention—and no need, I would argue—to include authors outside this group. It, I believe, would also be highly redundant to do so; the structures of the discourse(s) of the phenomenology of religion are, as we shall discuss in the next chapter and as will be demonstrated throughout this study, very repetitive and replicated, often with creative reformulation, over and over again in many, if not all, scholars that could be labeled "phenomenologists." Be that as it may, I only claim and am rigorously restricting my analyses to the set of texts and the research tradition within which they are embedded, which I will refer to as *"the* phenomenology of religion."[94]

The unity of this "school" was also at least *somewhat* self-conscious, as can be seen by a trail of citations. Dilthey credited Schleiermacher and was influenced by Hegel; Otto also edited Schleiermacher and was clearly influenced by him. In the opening lines of *The Sacred and the Profane*, Eliade credits Otto; in the beginning of *Patterns*, he cites van der Leeuw's *Phänomenologie der Religion*; van der Leeuw, cites Chantepie, "As regards Phenomenology itself, Chantepie's volume should be consulted."[95] Chantepie, in turn, cites Hegel, as well as Schleiermacher, but especially the former. This circle of references indicates that the phenomenology of religion was, indeed, an intertextual phenomenon.

## Authorial Stance and Thesis

For the sake of the greatest degree of clarity possible, I will state explicitly and what it is that this study attempts to accomplish. Unfortunately, many critiques of studies such as this are founded on faulty assumptions: they critique a study for something it never intended to do. To further advance the discussion of this very important school of thought, I will lay out my theses here in as bare a fashion as I can so that its critiques can be as pointed and as direct as possible. A good, solid, well-done critique of this study would be a most welcomed and valued accomplishment. Only such critiques can advance scholarship. If it turns out that my approach is a dead end, that will save many potential scholars from pursuing research in the manner, and so, by way of the *via negativa*, scholarship in this area gains something of value. The converse, of course, is also true: if this study withstands its critiques it will be of service for further research and other researchers laboring in this particular field. Either can *only* be accomplished by a clear, thorough, and accurate analysis of the major arguments and assertions of this study. As I tell my students: you can neither agree nor disagree with a position that you do not first understand.

The *form* of the argument advanced by this study is that of a hypothetical syllogism: "If this, then that." Insofar as the presuppositions of poststructuralism[96] prove to be valid, then my readings of these texts and the conclusions drawn from them should follow rather clearly. Conversely, should poststructuralism turn out to be a flawed theory then much, perhaps all, of this study would also be invalidated. Put another way, this study is written in the subjunctive mood: "Suppose..." This will not always be apparent in micro, or "tactical" instances, but it is my "authorial stance" at the macro, or strategic level. The subjunctive mood, obviously, is not the indicative mood (which will be used again, at the tactical level *in the service* of the subjunctive) and certainly not in the imperative mood (the mood of normative projects; the grammar of morality, the "mood" of prophetic denunciation). Insofar as I *appear* to use the latter, especially in summarizing the results of this study in the last chapters, it is embedded, surrounded, so to speak, within the larger subjunctive text. While some may be dubious of this last claim I have a completely clear conscience on the matter: I would abandon poststructuralism in a heartbeat if it proved to be false.[97]

The heuristic used in this study is poststructuralism informed by postcolonial theory (and vice versa). It will be immediately obvious, I would hope, that "proving" poststructuralism to be true is a problem far beyond the range of this type of study. I am not dogmatically asserting that poststructuralism is transparently true. I am assuming it, as all research must assume *some* set of principles, that is, a theory, as a working hypothesis that functions as a heuristic through which a particular body of data (here: the texts of the phenomenology of religion) is viewed. That is, while "the phenomenology of religion" is an extratextually determined phenomenon (relative to *this* text), the selection and organization of these texts is *always* a heuristic act. My heuristic: poststructuralism. A postcolonial discourse theory informed by poststructuralism will also form part of the matrix of concepts used to filter, select, and organize the texts of the phenomenology of religion.

My thesis has two components: a historical component and a structural component. Allow me to review each in turn.

As discussed above, my historical argument is that Hegel and Hegelian motifs provide the broader, structural discourse within which the phenomenology of religion is embedded in its most important, constitutive features. Those acquainted with classic phenomenology will immediately object, as did van der Leeuw cited above, that classic phenomenology rejects the idea of *Entwicklung*, or development (or cultural/*geistig* evolution) and that this is a fundamental difference between Hegelianism, so saturated with diachronic elements, and the synchronic approach of classic phenomenology of religion. Eliade's proclamation that "the sacred is a structure of consciousness, not a stage of history" is almost the motto of classic phenomenology of religion. However, as I will argue, the synchronic taxonomies of religion/s generated are often quite similar to the diachronic "stages." They retain much of the same perspective, terminology, and, I will argue, much of the same underlying conceptual structure—despite the repudiation of the concept of "stages." As we saw above in the history of the *Geisteswissenschaften*, the appropriation of Hegelian motifs was accomplished by means of their overt *rejection*. One must not be fooled by this rejection: it is a reformulation of those concepts (*Geist*, essence, higher and lower religions, etc.) for the sake of their preservation. This reformulation in classic phenomenology aimed only at keeping, preserving, and defending the *Grundbegriffen* of this conceptual structure. I will go to some pains to demonstrate this in the analyses of each author.

The basis of the similarity between Hegelianism and the phenomenology of religion is precisely their mutual appropriation of the metaphysical categories of consciousness, *Geist*, objective Spirit, subjectivity, and "Man." While they treat this in somewhat different ways, these terms circulate within this discourse and move in an often silent and unmarked way between all of the instantiations of this discourse. Hegelianism is the *langue* of classic phenomenology of religion and the latter is—to some degree; a significant degree, I shall argue—*parole* to the former.

The second thesis I put forward is indicated by the terms just used. Using insights from structuralism and poststructuralism, I will argue that the phenomenology of religion, taken as a whole (overdetermined as it is), can be studied as an intertextual discourse which "seeps" between each text, each set of texts, and each phase of the history of the phenomenology of religion. That is, this broader discourse, *langue* to each individual text, is treated as the paradigmatic and syntagmatic elements of this overall school of thought. It is by means of this method, described in detail in the next chapter, that the significance of the constant reappearance of such binary sets of terms, especially but not exclusively, the opposition noted above between *Geist* and *Natur*, can be elucidated. Analyzing these texts as an intertextual circulation of this discourse, constituted by these elemental binary pairs we can begin to see how the phenomenology of religion is "performed" in each text, how it is structured, and, how it structures the objects of its analysis. *Geist/Natur*, for instance, will immediately correlate to "nature religions" and "civilized" or "higher religions." Essence and manifestation will be used as (or in place of) an explanatory paradigm for how religion *happens*, so to speak, and, as a defense against materialist or other kinds of reductive approaches to understanding religion. It will also create a taxonomy of the identities of religion that bears a very strong similarity to that of Hegel. This can be seen in the way scholars treat such critical "weld points" in this area as they describe and classify Islam and Hinduism; the distinctions between nature religions and ethical religion; and most importantly, the way they deal with so-called primitive religions. While they do not treat each of these in an identical manner, by comparing them with each other we will see some a very similar *structuration* of the identities of these religious data. This reinforces the issue touched on above: the identities of these religions and peoples are elided rather than illuminated.

Once the structure and play of these binaries, or "philosophemes" as I will call them, is traced out, another aspect of this discursive structure appears, viz., the representation of non-European religions, and most often though not exclusively, the representation of non-European religions of people of color. Ergo, *Geist/Natur*, "slides" into European/non-European, and this has the latent (most often) implication of white/nonwhite. As such, we cannot ignore the relationship between the phenomenology of religion and the historical phenomenon of European colonialism and imperialism. The set of representations produced by the phenomenology of religion, despite all protests to the contrary, will turn out to have a very strong resemblance to the system of colonial representations as described by colonial/postcolonial discourse theory. It will be necessary therefore, to combine the structural/poststructuralist reading of the play of the philosophemes in the discourse of the phenomenology of religion with a postcolonial discourse reading. The outcome of this twin operation is that the phenomenology of religion, and the field of Religious Studies insofar as it is based upon this school, are complicit in the legitimation and reproduction of colonial representations of Europe's Other(s). The phenomenology of religion gives scholarly credence to that system of representations and so reinforces them as "real." A form of power/knowledge is at work: scholars laboring within this discursive structure produce "knowledge," an authorized, legitimated representation of reality, of the reality of the Other. As we will see, much of their sources are drawn from the letters and reports of colonizers. This "knowledge" then reinforces, authorizes, and implicitly legitimates the system of colonial representations. This circular movement creates (or reproduces) a discursive hegemony within which it becomes difficult to falsify claims and which systematically limits the ability to persuade to the contrary. The data for such refutation is prepackaged by the methods used to select it out of the plethora of possible choices of data.

The historical failure to recognize this situation and the failure to see the many ways it underlies the way we form departments, divide up scholarly labor, train scholars, teach students, and inform the public has allowed these colonial representations to circulate freely and with a yet greater degree of the authority to define the real. It is a cannon of intellectual endeavor that we seek for the truth, that the stronger argument should prevail over the weaker argument, and that we should be ready to abandon any position that proves to be untrue.

In this situation, that means that we must reverse these representations, contest them, deny them, and cease using them in our teaching and research. The result, then, of this study is that we must "speak truth to power" in the very specific sense of revoking the label "true" from the representations produced by the phenomenology of religion and all those representations heir to it. It is my stance, after years of studying this body of literature, that we can *only* contest it. It does not speak truth, its conceptual structures are irrevocably flawed, and its effects are negative both to scholarship and to society at large. I study the phenomenology of religion only to bury it.

In sum: the method used in this study is, relative to conventional methods, "unorthodox," and so perhaps more prone to generating misunderstandings. As such, it needs considerable explanation. This explanation will aim at two levels: method*ology*, the theoretical explanation of method, and method, the actual techniques used in the reading of texts. Such an explanation is doubly necessary because there is a growing consensus among theorists of literature that the reader of a text plays a significant role in constituting (or co-constituting) the meaning of a text. By extension, the methods of reading—and *all* readings have methods, whether implicit or explicit[98]—will largely determine the conclusions that can and will be drawn from that modality of reading. It is incumbent then, for critical reflection to be as explicit as possible about reading strategies and not *assume* the conventional modalities sedimented in traditional research. An overview will be given of that method as well as a more detailed description of it terms and concepts in chapter 2.

# 2

# Discourse, Text, Philosophemes
## Elements of a Postcolonial-Genealogical Reading Strategy

> To concern oneself with the founding concepts of the entire history of philosophy, to deconstitute them, is not to undertake the work of the philologist or of the classic historian of philosophy.
>
> —Jacques Derrida[1]

Whatever the world is *an sich*, it is only ever "received" by humans through some form of mediation. Previous theories about this mediating element focused on consciousness, sense perception, and structures of consciousness. More recent views, however, and the perspective taken in this study, is that the medium by which humans relate to the world *ex mente* is language, and specifically, language usage as institutionalized in both discreet macro units and many micro units. This institutionalized language usage is known as "discourse." As discussed in chapter 1, the method used in this study, as well as its aims, are not those of either tradition explication or of the history of ideas. It is predicated on a poststructuralist theory of discourse and a postcolonial discourse theory informed by poststructuralism. As this is an unconventional approach, and, more importantly, the results of this study will be correlated to its methodology, in order to avoid the misunderstandings that a polemical work such as this is likely to incite, it is necessary to spell out the terms and concepts of that methodology. These terms include: discourse and language, discourse and text, the philosophemes that constitute those texts (in the manner alluded to above by Derrida), how these philosophemes are situated in the historical construct "ontotheology," and the kind of postcolonial theory used here. This chapter will be entirely devoted to an examination of these concepts.

## Overview: Method and *Rezeptionsgeschitche*

This methodology and method differs from conventional methods such as the *explication de texte* (though it will take a very similar form), intellectual history, or history of ideas, in at least two main ways. First, this study does not attempt to explicate the entire systems of thought of Hegel, Tiele, Dilthey, Eliade, et al., *as such*. I do not attempt to explicate their "positions" as a whole. This study/analysis does not seek to explicate the chain of assertoric propositions which constitute the "argument" of a text.[2] The object of traditional explication is an "argument" or a "position," that is, the meaning of the text is rendered into logical form. We may ask, however, what *is* an "argument" or a "position"?[3] What is the *substancia*, the *esse*, the being, if you will, of a "position"? Is it not a set of concept-terms that exist within a larger system and/or history of concepts? This "system" (in a broad sense of the term) is a crucial aspect of what discourse *does*. Ergo, these conceptual-verbal structures are highly valuable targets for analysis. It is this point that I wish to emphasize as the main virtue of my method. As these structures form the *conditions for the possibility* (*langue*, not *parole*) of meaning, they are latent, quiet, and even silent in the way in which they function within and between texts. Consequently, they are difficult to render as the objects of traditional exegetical strategies.

To further explain this method, allow me to use an automotive metaphor: in examining a text, I do not look at the entire automobile, I do not even look at the entire frame of the automobile; I look at the *weld points* on the frame. I define these weld points as a set of critical terms that act as binding links between major clusters of concept-terms (usually very well known and easily recognized). William Connolly nicely refers to these weld points on the "frame" as places "where assumptions and insistences quietly hold discourse together."[4] Borrowing a term from Derrida, I refer to these weld points as "philosophemes," that is, an element within a system of elements. A philosopheme is an analogue of a "morpheme" in semantics or a "phoneme" in linguistics. It is a basic unit of the phenomenon being studied, here a set of texts that braid together philosophical, metaphysical, theological, and theoretical discourses drawn from many strands of Western history including those established by colonizers in the context of contact with non-European peoples. These units constitute the meaning of the text/discourse. They do not do so alone or in isolation, hence their designation as "elements." While not all sets of concepts everywhere come in the form of binary oppositions, it is an undeniable fact that in this particular body of texts/discourses the philosophemes that form the weld points on the structure of the discourse of the phenomenology of religion do. Examples of these binary paired philosophemes include: kernel/husk, universal religions/ethnic religions, unchanging essence/historical accretion, inner experience/outer expression, and, I shall argue, most importantly, *Geist/Natur*. This is why this is a *genealogy* of the phenomenology of religion and not an explication of "works" (in Barthes's terms) nor a history of "ideas"—inasmuch as it aims to trace out the *play* of these philosophemes within their given structures synchronically and trace the text-to-text appropriations of these philosophemes diachronically.

To illustrate my reading strategy it will help to look at how William Connolly, in his book *Political Theory and Modernity*, has undertaken a somewhat similar exercise. Given the vastness of the literature that falls under the heading of his topic, "modern political theory," he is forced to come up with a way of selecting some finite set of texts out of this vast milieu. He describes his method as follows:

> The positions which occupy privileged sites within modern discourse cannot be presented on a list. They might, though, be apprehended indirectly and imperfectly through a comparison of divergent texts... which, in their very diversity, help to reveal the field upon which they stand together. It may be, as I think it is, that a few classical texts exhibit beautifully the small set of alternative patterns into which modern conceptions of self, freedom and order can be woven.[5]

This is similar to the method used in this study. As the phenomenology of religion is rooted in classic Western metaphysics, its genealogy of could arguably go back to the Pre-Socratics. Or, in a synchronic fashion, one could look at the entire field of discourse within which it resides.[6] Such studies are impractical under "normal" academic conditions and more importantly, they would be largely redundant. It will not take *every* instance of this text/discourse formation to exhibit clearly and explicitly "the small set of alternative patterns [of] conceptions" at play within it. A few "classic" instances thoroughly analyzed will suffice. As Connolly noted about the body of texts he was examining, while these texts have a multiple-layered relation to each other—it is not one of pure identity, but it is not one of pure alterity, either—we may gain insight by "a comparison of divergent texts... which, in their very diversity, help to reveal the field upon which they stand together" and which "enable us to discern affinities and commonalities among these divergent theories."[7] In other words, approaching these all-too-well-known texts with this "unorthodox" method/ology, even with its limited number of sources, will likely throw into relief latent assumptions which move within and between them and which have not been the objects of previous research methods. *Something will be gained from this exercise,* even if it is partial, controversial, and only initial in its final result. The *instigation*, or furthering,[8] of controversy is itself a positive outcome of the deployment of a new method/ology.

At the beginning of this overview I said that my method/ology differs from conventional methods in at least two main ways. The first has been described above: it follows out a play of philosophemes, not a history of "ideas," nor the exposition of a text (taken as a self-contained object). The second difference between my method/ology and conventional methods is the crucial role that a very specific *Rezeptionsgeschichte* plays in it. This *Rezeptionsgeschichte* binds this body of texts/discourses together in two ways, at two different levels of abstraction. First: an institutional, discursive horizon of temporality: at the time Hegel wrote, at the time Tiele, Otto, van der Leeuw, wrote, even at the time Eliade wrote, "Religious Studies" (which is both the object and origin of this retroactive reading, this *Rezeptionsgeschichte*) was not a fixed entity and did not exist as we know it, as it exists here and now, in this time, in "our" present. Ergo, there is no way to write about these texts as episodes *within* a history of Religious Studies as no such entity existed during this span of time (ca.1825–1960), at least in the United States[9] As Willard Oxtoby writes in a historical overview of the field: "As late as 1959, the history-of-religions field in America seemed a sideline, even a dead end, peripheral to the main stream of scholarship in the study of religion. A scant eight years later, the field is prospering in American universities and colleges."[10] Guildford Dudley concurs with Oxtoby's statement, if for different reasons: "The scholar Willard G. Oxtoby is probably correct in stating that 1959 was a watershed in the development of discipline, for the decade following saw a resurgence of interest and expansion unprecedented for such a brief period."[11]

Even with Eliade, Religious Studies was only then taking shape. By the end of his life it had taken its current form. However, at the beginning of his career, at that crucial formative point at which he is the inheritor of a discursive formation whose structures and regularities were well in place—at that point of intersection between institutional history and Eliade's career development, Religious Studies as we now know it did not exist.

This way of looking at the formative role of the *Rezeptionsgeschichte* illustrates the difference between a *genealogy* and a *history*. To further understand genealogy, we may follow Alexander Nehamas when he says of Nietzsche, the arch-genealogist: "Nietzsche in effect claimed that nothing in the world has any intrinsic features of its own and that each thing is constituted solely through its interrelations with, and differences from, everything else."[12] "A thing," writes Nietzsche, "is the sum of its effects": "The properties of a thing are effects on other 'things': if one removes other 'things,' then a thing has no properties, i.e., there is no thing without other things, i.e., there is no 'thing-in-itself.' "[13] While the discourse of the phenomenology of religion is not "nothing," it is, nevertheless, not an obvious object in nature either. It comes to the fore or *ex*-sists (in this sense if in no other) by a specific dual reading of Religious Studies and a set of texts in relation to one another and to Religious Studies as an emergent institutional reality. It is an object, but "the object is generated by an interpretive hypothesis that links certain events to one another and distinguishes them from other groups. The object emerges through such events; it is in a serious sense their product and not their ground."[14] Put in terms of reading: the text is the sum of its readings. Ergo, "the phenomenology of religion" is the product of its *Rezeptionsgeschichte* in the post hoc formation, Religious Studies.

My genealogical reading strategy, then, is a hypothesis that calls into being a set of terms, texts, names, a history of transmission: all of which exist in their own right but are not naturally the effective object that they are individually outside of or independent of this genealogical hypothesis. Using these concept-operations, discourse, text, philosophemes, and reviewing this swath of Religious Studies we can with justice state that such an object, "the discourse of the phenomenology of religion," exists, and exists as the thing so characterized. A genealogical reading shows us both *that* it is and *what* it is.

This macro-level, the "disciplinary" level, the level of Religious Studies as a whole, is the first and higher level of abstraction (though no less real and effective for being abstract) of analysis of the *Rezeptionsgeschichte*, that historical process by which "phenomenology of religion" came into being. The second and more proximate level of the operation of this quite specific *Rezeptionsgeschichte* is the process of the grouping of these texts so named into a distinct entity, itself the effect of an interpretation and something that already imposes an interpretation upon these texts—a horizon of expectations under its specific title, viz., "the phenomenology of religion." This is a term that should be taken very carefully. It is easy to assume its meaning; it is fatal to do so, for it has multiple senses and multiple implications. First, the evocation of "phenomenology" is already a complex, overdetermined and internally as well as externally contested signifier. It evokes a definite, yet plural horizon of expectations once the appellation is applied to a given text or a group of texts. "Phenomenology" contains many elements, many of which are conflicting, and many of which are at complete odds with, or completely irrelevant to, the phenomenology of religion. Moreover, the term is both specific (e.g., Husserlian phenomenology) and generic (one can perform "*a* phenomenological analysis" of an object). Furthermore, it often blends into the different yet related term, "phenomenalism."

It is well known that "Religion" is a similarly overdetermined signifier. Rendering it in the singular (phenomenology of *religion*) embeds the term in a universalist viewpoint. Rendering it in the plural implicitly entails that there is a multiplicity of things that have a common nature, or, at least, a common set of characteristics. Further, rendering it as "the holy," or "the sacred" not only changes the meaning of "Religion," but is itself a theoretical postulate, namely, the end result of a very long string of enthymemes. All of these assertions have been hotly contested at least since Wilfred Cantwell Smith's *The Meaning and End of Religion* appeared in the mid-1960s. The syntagmatic linking of "phenomenology" with "religion" narrows and specifies the evocation entailed even further. It is at once recognizable, contradictory, historically specific yet also generic—one may say "*a* phenomenology of religion" intelligibly, as well as "*the* phenomenology of religion" intelligibly. However, both statements are of completely different orders whatever overlap they might share.

The main issue raised by such an exercise in *Rezeptionsgeschichte* of *the* phenomenology of religion is that it shows us that it is a *retroactive creation of a certain history*, of a certain interpretation, so to speak, of a body of texts, individual scholars, tropes of research methods (the *epoché*, empathetic understanding, understanding versus explanation, sui generis, etc.), and a set of well-known schools of method and training (the Dutch *Religionswissenschaft*, "Chicago School," "History of Religions," etc.). "*The* phenomenology of religion" is, I would argue, *our* idea, *our* invention.[15] Members of the Religious Studies guild (at least most of them, if not all) *know* what the term evokes: a set of concepts, *epoché*, eidetic vision, static taxonomic operations, nonreductive approaches, religious experience, empathetic understanding, and so forth. There is also a known concatenation of familiar names: Otto, Kristensen, van der Leeuw, Wach, and most of all, Eliade. There are also major texts associated with it, that is, read as a research tradition: *The Idea of the Holy*, *Religion in Essence and Manifestation*, and *The Sacred and the Profane*. It is a definite, recognizable element of the history of Religious Studies; these schools, terms, names, and texts spontaneously invoke the title, however loosely understood, "phenomenology of religion."

This is not to say that such a concatenation is historically or logically accurate; one could reasonably argue otherwise; there is a considerable amount of debate over which authors are actually phenomenologists. That this may be an erroneous configuration is not the point, or precisely the point I am *not* concerned to make.[16] What *is* important is that these texts, ideas, and names are, *in fact*, taken together, recognizable as such, *known* as such. My argument is that they have, rightly or wrongly, with or without exegetical justice, become an effective textual-discursive formation, a historically effective (Gadamer's *Wirkungsgeschichte*) body of discourse(s). This formation has had, and continues to have, a real historical effect on Religious Studies in the present, and, at the same time, determines to a large degree how we retroactively read these texts: its effect is circular in classic hermeneutical fashion. They have been *read* together (read as a group, but "read-together" as a verbal action, as in "glued together"). *That* they form this unity is data enough for me to offer the reading which is offered here. We have created "*the* phenomenology of religion" and it has created us.

Finally, what is the larger purpose of this reading? Why undertake such a project and undertake it in this manner? The ultimate target of this reading, one that exists extratextually and is also constitutive of these texts, is precisely the discursive formation that has emerged from the *Wirkungsgeschichte* of these texts having been "read-together." While the nature and scope of this textual effecticity may be and is disputed, I would argue, as have others, that its main effect goes by the name: "Religious Studies."[17] This discursive-institutional formation is the principal architectural means by which this unified discursive entity, "Religious Studies" was and has been formed, as well as it *apologia* for its existence.[18] Religious Studies retroactively created its own story, its own myth of origins. As this has been argued and documented elsewhere, I will not do so here. Suffice it to say that, *insofar as* (the subjunctive mood again) that discursive unity, "Religious Studies" has both formed and been formed by this other discursive unity, "*the* phenomenology of religion," the former is the real target of this reading. That is: the purpose of resorting to a genealogical reading rather than other conventional methods,[19] such as an institutional history, an intellectual history, a history of ideas, or the *explication de texte* of a diachronic series of texts grouped by genre, is to demonstrate that the underpinnings, that latent system of binary philosophemes, upon which Religious Studies has been founded, are faulty, misguided, and have led to and do lead to some rather dire consequences. These consequences are largely unintended and most often not recognized as such by many of its more cheerful advocates. In short: insofar as we *are* the heirs of "*the* phenomenology of religion," we have gone *wrong*, perhaps terribly, terribly wrong.[20] A genealogical reading such as this, then, is nothing short of a call to revolution.[21] If it is correct, a radical[22] revision of the entire basis of Religious Studies will be necessary: from the textbooks we use, the language by which our field is put into effect, the way in which we taxonomize our job categories, award positions, organize our departments, and the way in which—and most definitely *the institutions in which*—we train the professionals who assume those positions. It will not be possible to spell out, in detail, all of these implications in the same work that performs this genealogical reading. It suffices for now to state clearly where the ultimate trajectory of this genealogical reading is heading, viz., a revolution in our thinking in Religious Studies is necessary if it is going to be intellectually viable and if it is going to extricate itself from its role in re/producing colonialist representations. Without some kind of revolutionary, constitutive re-formation, Religious Studies does not have the intellectual right to continue to exist.

## Language *(Langue)* and Discourse

> There is no such thing as a prediscursive reality. Every reality is founded and defined by a discourse.
>
> —Jacques Lacan[23]

How then to study these texts? I have proposed the term *genealogy*, but this is a metonym for a complex operation. The elements of this operation include: a radicalized concept of discourse, a radicalized concept of the text, a radicalized concept of the relation between the subject and the text, a deconstructive understanding of the microelements of the text (the "weld points" I spoke of earlier), and finally locating all of these in a oppositional strategy of reading which I "borrow" from postcolonial theory. This and the following sections will unpack each of these operations.

## Discourse

We understand that discourse is a form of language usage, but what is the exact relationship between language and discourse? Foucault argues that "a language (*langue*) is still a system for possible statements, a finite body of rules that authorizes an infinite number of performances. The field of discursive events, on the other hand, is a grouping that is always finite and limited at any moment to the linguistic sequences that have been formulated."[24] Like language, discourse makes possible a body of statements (its archive, its "already said"); unlike language, discourse is circumscribed by numerous factors, some linguistic, some nonlinguistic.

Such is the description of discourse as a passive thing. Discourse, however, is a formative process which is often invisible but very active. Foucault calls this aspect of discourse a "discursive practice" and defines it as "a body of anonymous, historical rules, always determined in the time and space that have defined a given period, and for a given social, economic, geographical, or linguistic area, the conditions of operation of the enunciative function."[25]

As Sara Mills points out, Foucault's view of discourse is a more radical way of thinking about what discourse does. It must be understood

> not as a group of signs or a stretch of text, but as *"practices that systematically form the objects of which they speak."* In this sense, a discourse is something which produces something else (an utterance, a concept, an effect), rather than something which exists in and of itself and which can be analyzed in isolation. A discursive structure can be detected because of the systematicity of the ideas, opinions, concepts, ways of thinking and behaving which are formed within a particular context."[26]

Put another way, Foucault rejects the idea that discourses have a mimetic relationship to objects in the world. Rather, the study of discourse is: "To substitute for the enigmatic treasure of 'things' anterior to a discourse, the regular formation of objects that emerge only in discourse."[27] It is not the relation between a knowing subject, or a descriptive term, and its reference to an extralinguistic object that grounds or defines discourse. Rather, it is *the sheer systematicity* of discourse, its ability to replicate in speech (*parole*) certain forms of speech—not describe objects in a definitive manner.[28] When we can anticipate what a text is about to say, we are thinking within that text's discourse. We recognized familiar themes, phrases, and strings of concepts, and agreed upon enthymemes (whole "chunks" of silent yet accepted propositions) that make the "argument" possible.

For instance, in the phenomenology of religion the notion that consciousness is not reducible to matter is a given assumption for which there is necessary only an occasional *apologia*, not a foundational argument (something agreed upon/within the discourse to have "already been," "already written"). This agreement permeates the discourse of the phenomenology of religion. Its establishment is *alluded to only* (Descartes' cogito, Kant, Hegel, Husserl) but never truly substantiated—except by way of an antireductive, antimaterialist polemics. The agreed upon, then, constitutes the discourse; if it was not established and accepted, the threads of the discourse would unravel. Consciousness is the object of the "science of experience," or phenomenology, but it is an object constructed by the discourse within which it resides. This discourse is, as Foucault said, an anonymous set of rules, or discursive regularities.

*The Subject and Discourse*

The last point and the point above about the "systematicity of the ideas, opinions, concepts, ways of thinking and behaving," raises the question of the relationship between the subject, the individual, and the author, who has (or does not have) agency in regard to the production of discourse. As is well known, the poststructuralist method I am using in this study is notorious for its denial of the agency of the subject.

Against the idea of a controlling subject which produces discourse: Foucault on the "rarefaction of discourse," that is, "the surprising fact that although the utterances which could be produced by any one person are theoretically infinite, in fact, they are remarkably repetitive and remain within certain socially agreed-upon boundaries."[29] This is not a fact about an individual's production of discourse, but about the production of discourse across the "curriculum" of a discipline. It governs the way an entire field of researchers and teachers, each of whom is anonymous to the other, arrive at the same conclusions, use the same tropes, and "think the same," despite numerous differences of personal biography and training. As Diane Macdonell put it: "Discourse is considered as a kind of whole whose organization, at any given stage of history [or moment in its life], is 'irreducible either to the history of the careers, thought and intentions of individual agents (the authors of utterances) or to a supra-individual teleology of discovery and intellectual evolution (the truth of the utterances),' "[30] as such, "no person, no individual... could be called the creator of these changes of meaning."[31] Ergo, it is not the concatenation of names, of authors, that ultimately defines the phenomenology of religion, it is the *langue*, the underlying structures of discourse that are repeated within each author's text *without it being necessary to mention* these structural features. They are the anonymous conditions for the possibility of statements within that narrow field: "These principles of exclusion and choices, whose presence is manifold, whose effectiveness is embodied in practices and whose transformations are relatively autonomous, are not based on an agent of knowledge."[32] The subject, like the Author, like God, is dead.

## Discourse as Acting

We have seen what discourse is. We must now ask: What do discourses *do*? "Discourses structure both our sense of reality and our notion of our own identity."[33] Or as Victor Burgin argues: "[D]iscourse is itself a determinate and determining form of social practice; discourse does not *express* the meanings of a pre-existent social order, it *constructs* those meanings and that order."[34] More than simply trafficking in words, discourses *produce* "knowledge" and authorize it, claiming the right, however implicitly, to differentiate between knowledge and non-knowledge. Discourses produce truth, but truth "is something which societies have to work to produce, rather than something which appears in a transcendental way."[35]

Another way to make this point: "Discourses are, in point of fact, heavily policed cognitive systems which control and delimit both the mode and the means of *representation* in a given society."[36] The systematicity of discourse is usually, though not always, codified by some "regime of truth," that is, some implicit system of concept-formation and concept-contestation (rules for adjudicating conflicts between rival claims). These, then, govern "representation." As Paul Rabinow has argued, "[R]epresentations are social facts."[37] A history, an image, a map, a book, or a scholarly article is just such a re-presentation: it makes its content present to a community of text and image consumers other than that of the origin of that content (and simultaneously makes other content absent to its consumer). The governing of this re-presentation is precisely those anonymous rules shared by producer and consumer that say that "this is the correct," the "right" way, in all senses and connotations of the term, to *do that*. At the level of producer, it is that set of "professional standards" which are both explicitly and implicitly understood as shaping "true journalism," "true scholarship," etc. At the level of the consumer, the governing of representations is those set of semiconscious responses triggered when one knows one is reading (viewing, etc.) something "done right." It is the plausibility or believability of the fragment of discourse under consideration in the *way* it shapes its object, its content, totally irrespective of the content itself. These are, discourse theory holds, *purely formal properties* of the representation.

These claims raise the question of the authentication of knowledge, which since the "Subjective Turn" modern philosophy took in the seventeenth century, has been the province of epistemology.[38] However, as the paradigm of epistemology is historically structured by the relation between a subject and its object of apprehension, the critique of the subject above leads to the conclusion that Richard Rorty has claimed: epistemology is dead. It has been replaced by the idea that knowledge cannot be transcendental in nature but is never separate from specific sites/cites of the production of discourse. The silent work of discourse determines the true ("true" in the sense described above, i.e., "the social construction of the true" or of reality generally).

Foucault variously calls the site that "holds" these perceptions, concepts, and ways of thinking the archive or the episteme. "The new notion here, the 'episteme,' may be understood as the 'grounding of thought' on which at a particular time some statements—and not others—will count as knowledge. Foucault's studies argue that the very concepts knowledges produce are informed by definite rules: 'there is a regularity in their development, even though their practitioners are not conscious of these rules.' "[39] Therefore, no one individual is responsible for changes within discourse or the episteme. The discourse (*langue*) speaks *us* more than we speak it. Ruptures, invasions, and "marriages" happen in a chance fashion; they do not unfold according to a given teleological impetus with a predestined goal. We speak here of transformation, not "progress." At least in the human sciences, discourses simply layer human reality with yet one more network of concepts. The "history of ideas" is just this layering of conceptual grids or networks.

Just as Foucault said the difference between language and discourse lies in the fact that language can produce a theoretically infinite number of statements whereas discourse's finitude is created by its own structural principles, the episteme must be seen as historically specific and *not* a Kantian transcendental reality: "[T]he episteme is defined as the ensemble of 'relations that can be discovered, *for a given period*, between the sciences,' and the network of connections that can be found between knowledges, 'when one analyzes them at the level of discursive regularities.' "[40] As Gadamer might say, there is a temporal horizon to the episteme. It is not a collection of "ideas" thought by a universal subject (mind, self, reason); it is a network of relations which appear in the pure contingencies of time and place.

My argument in this book is that the discourse of phenomenology operates like an episteme, a discursive regularity, on the texts under consideration. The fact is that, despite their differences, these texts are "remarkably repetitive and remain within certain socially agreed-upon boundaries," or a shared set of concept/structures. I will argue later that one of the primary, structural features of the discourse of the phenomenology of religion is the radical, even apodictic, distinction between *Geist und Natur*. As I argued in chapter 1, this distinction underlies many, if not all, of the individual statements within each text and, in an intertextual manner, across a body of texts. At a metaphysical level, it is a distinction between consciousness or mind and the body or materiality generally. At the taxonomic level, it is the basis for the distinction between "nature religions" and "ethical religions," or "higher" and "lower" religions. At the level of geopolitics, it is the distinction between Europeans (*Geist*) and non-Europeans (*Natur*), most often as it turns out, non-Europeans of color.[41] While this initial distinction might at first glance seem simple enough, it is the engine that produces a whole series of discursive regularities.

*Nota bene*: the concatenation of distinctions which the *Geist/Natur* distinction sets off, so to speak, is not necessarily logical, correct, accurate, morally acceptable, or subject to empirical verification or falsification. As discussed in chapter 1, while most previous critics reject the phenomenology of religion precisely on account of these types of flaws, and flaws they are, discourse analysis is focused precisely on these fissures, these patches or weld points that *remain in discourse and are constantly reiterated in texts, despite the fact that they are conceptually and factually suspect*. This is what discursive regularity or systematicity does to "truth" or "knowledge": it traps itself in the (circular) circulation of its own established limitations. So, from Hegel to Otto and Otto to Eliade we will see these tropes iterated, reiterated, and reaffirmed as necessary truths. This regularity will manifest itself in a wide variety of ways even when texts and conceptual paradigms seem to disagree in some fundamental ways. So we find them in both the diachronic views of Hegel and Tiele and in the synchronic approaches of van der Leeuw and Eliade. Discourse operates at a para-logical level and *pre*-figures what will be objects for analysis. As such, falsification can only be done as an imminent action, that is, within a given discourse. The object as constituted by and in another discourse is powerless, for the most part, to change the object in its rival discourse. Hence, we get "schools" of continuous thought rather than a progressive narrowing of discourses that force other discourses to be discarded, or at least held at bay. Why is it that schools of thought that have ostensively been debunked yet continue to exist never, or very rarely admit that and close up shop? Discourse. "The phenomenology of religion," as previously described, is precisely such a phenomenon: a congealed network of discursive practices/elements which cannot, which will not, be easily disentangled because the circulation of its ideas is immanent within its field and so immune, at least to a great degree, to outside critique.

## Systematic Exclusion

"Some statements—and not others—will count," as Macdonell said above. Foucault puts the point as follows: "The question posed by language analysis of some discursive fact or other is always: according to what rules has a particular statement been made . . . how is it that one particular statement appeared *rather than* another."[42] One of the effects of discourse is that its finitude and its seen and unseen patterns allow for some statements and disallow others. Speaking of Foucault's examination of the "prodigious machinery designed to exclude," Mills notes that: "Exclusion is, in essence, paradoxically, one of the most important ways in which discourse is produced."[43] One need not posit conspiracy theories or the idea of agency in the "use" of power because, "there is a combined force of institutional and cultural pressure, together with the intrinsic structure of discourse, which always exceeds the plans and desires of the institution or of those in power."[44] As Foucault so famously said, power is both nonsubjective yet intentional. It is a complex latticework of the symbolic, of the coercive, of the productive, of those institutions, rules, and cultural norms that elide discourses other than its own, which elide the discourse of the Other. Exclusion is a fundamental feature of signification: it is an aspect of Saussure's notion of pure difference. A sign means not only because of what is there, relations *in presentia*; but even more so because of what is not there, relations *in absentia*.

There is in discourse, then, a *systematic set of exclusions*, a set of things that are always left out, or at least elided, passed over, there but not mentioned, there but not allowed to fully be. This other of institutionalized discourse comes in two forms, or at least can be analyzed in two forms: a formal system of binary terms which constitute discourse (the weld points on its frame) or, in geopolitical terms, those Others who are mentioned yet excluded—and certainly not voiced—in discourse. As we saw, the binary terms, *Geist/Natur* are (with all of its corollaries), I will argue, constitutive of the discourse of the phenomenology of religion. This binary immediately correlates to the geopolitical binary, Europe/not-Europe. The first type of analysis requires a deconstructive approach; the second requires a postcolonial discourse analysis. There is a union but not an identity between the two types of analysis, so each will be examined separately.

*Text and Discourse*

Where is the text in all of this? We do, after all, have *books*, concrete products of an individual's labor. It will be necessary to theorize, that is, explain formally, the nature of the text (or textuality) and its relationship to discourse and the subject.

There is a hierarchy of relations between language, discourse, and text, but only in terms of genus-species relations. Language is the most general term; discourse is subset of language, usually defined as units of language beyond the individual sentence; and text is a subset of discourse. If language is, as Saussure claimed, a system of differences, it follows then that discourse, as a type of language use, will also be constituted by or as a system of difference. So also then with the text. "Discourse is the umbrella term for either spoken or written communication beyond the level of the sentence. Text is the basic means of this communication, be it spoken or written. . . . Discourse is thus a more embracing term that calls attention to the situated uses of texts: it comprises both text and context."[45] Georgakopoulou and Goutsos rightly speak of "access to discourse through texts."[46] This point is key to my method. As Connolley argued above, we can access the field from which texts emerge (discourse or *langue*) by looking at a select few texts (understood as *parole*). The approach of analyzing the "weld points" will use only a limited number of texts from each author. Again, I am not claiming to give an exegesis of the entire corpus or the system of thought as a whole. My aims are more strategic, limited, and focused on particular elements of a text. But my access to these weld points is through this limited yet crucial set of texts.

Nicola Woods has described two different, yet related ways to analyze discourse: from the top down, or from the bottom up. In the former, "discourse analysts begin from an understanding or a conceptualization (their own) of the context in which the discourse is taking place."[47] One starts at the macro level, and works down to the level of individual units of language. The bottom-up approach begins with the "analysis of language... that are used in the discourse,"[48] or, from the units within the actual text, to the larger framework or discourse which it constitutes and by which it is constituted (as the condition for the possibility of its existence). Woods argues that the relationship between the two is: "an intricate (almost symbiotic) interplay between the approach that that interprets utterances from the starting point of the context in which the discourse takes place, and the approach that takes as its starting point the linguistic level at which the utterances are produced."[49] Both are used in this study. The macro approach is the framing of the texts of the phenomenology of religion within poststructuralism and postcolonialism, ontotheology, and the geopolitical condition of European colonization. The micro level is that described by Connelly, a reading of a few classic texts (as defined by the *Rezeptionsgeschichte*) and using this to "access discourse." The latter operation will appear in the *form* of an *explication de texte*, but its goal is quite different.[50]

Given that the text is the point of access to discourse it is necessary, therefore, to discuss the nature of the "text." The concept of the text "constitutes the founding assumptions of discourse studies. Text is a *primum datum*, a primary notion, for discourse analysis, in the same way that a phoneme is for phonology, or morpheme is for morphology."[51] The text cannot be seen as a self-contained system of signifiers/signifieds, for its system of meanings draws upon a series of preexistent meanings, formulae, tropes, clichés, conventions, genres, taxonomies, myths, characters, histories, ideologems, and other historico-cultural-linguistic items. A particular text comes into being as an ensemble of discourses, as "a multi-dimensional space in which a variety of writings, none of them original, blend and clash. The text is a tissue of quotations drawn from the innumerable centers of culture."[52] The specific text then, is *parole* to the *langue* of discourse. Foucault makes a similar claim:

> The frontiers of a book are never clear-cut: beyond the title, the first lines, and the last full stop, beyond its internal configurations and its autonomous form, it is caught up in a system of reference to other books, other texts, other sentences: *it is a node within a network*. And this network of reference is not the same in the case of a mathematical

treatise, a textual commentary, a historical account, and an episode in a novel cycle; the unity of the book, even in the sense of a group of relations, cannot be regarded as identical in each case. The book is not simply the object that one holds in one's hands ... its unity is variable and relative ... it indicates itself, constructs itself, only on the basis of a complex field of discourse.[53]

Roland Barthes makes a distinction between a "work" ("book" in Foucault's terms above) and a "text": "The difference is this: the work is a fragment of a substance, occupying a part of the space of books (in a library for example); the Text is a methodological field ... the work can be held in the hand, the text is held in language, only exists in the movement of a discourse."[54] As such, discourse and text are inseparable. While discourse is the broader reality, it is accessed by texts, but the being of the text is discourse. As discourse is finite yet overdetermined, the text is, in Barthes's words, "irreducibly plural." Its intertextual, composite nature diminishes the role of author even more: "The intertextual in which every text is held, itself being the text-between of another text, is not to be confused with some origin of the text."[55] This is precisely the case with the discourse of the phenomenology of religion. Each of its individual texts is a "text-between of another text," the other text being the larger discursive structures within which it resides which are themselves systematically structured, operate autonomously, and can neither be identified with any individual text nor with a mere aggregation of all the texts so named.

*Philosophemes as Binary Pairs*

As discourse is a subset of language, and the text a subset of discourse, so, at least in this genre of text, the philosopheme is the constitutive unit of the text. An individual text is a play of elements, a specific deployment, arrangement, and ordering of a finite set of terms, elements, or here, philosophemes. In artistic genres of literature, the novel, play, or poem, we talk of the use of metaphors or tropes, the interplay of which makes the work *mean*. In this genre of philosophical-theoretical literature, philosophemes function as the constitutive tropes.

As such, a philosopheme is an analogue of a "morpheme" in semantics or a "phoneme" in linguistics. It is a basic unit of the object of analysis, here a philosophical, metaphysical, theoretical set of texts and discourses. These units indicate *and* make the text/discourse intertextual, that is, a congealment of discourses that exist beyond the individual text. They do not do so alone or in isolation, hence their designation as "elements." They do so in the manner in which they are combined, arranged, prioritized, etc., within a text/discourse. In this particular body of texts/discourses philosophemes virtually always come in the form of binary oppositions, for example, kernel/husk, universal religions/ethnic religions, essence/inessential historical accretions, form/meaning, etc.[56] This study, then, is a genealogy of the phenomenology of religion inasmuch as it seeks to trace out the various scenes of the deployment and text-to-text appropriation of these philosophemes.

Drawing from but also augmenting the work of Saussure, Derrida describes the nature of the discourse of the Occident, metaphysics, or ontotheology, as such: "Very schematically: an opposition of metaphysical concepts (for example, speech/writing, presence/absence, etc.) is never the face-to-face of two terms, but a hierarchy and an order of subordination."[57] All metaphysical terms, or at least all of the kind under analysis here, come as corollaries: *Geist/Natur*, consciousness/perception, a priori/a posteriori, etc. The terms are not of the same value; there is a relation of dominance in all cases; supremacy, at least in most cases between the paired elements. Even so, the meaning of each individual term is irrevocably tied to its binary opposite. They mutually constitute one another.

Moreover, such pairs and such individual concepts do not stand alone: "Each concept, moreover, belongs to a systematic chain, and itself constitutes a system of predicates."[58] The explication of any one term, or any pair of terms, leads and/or bleeds into another pair of terms, or even a whole series of such structured terms. Mark Taylor nicely summarizes this aspect of the issue:

> Concepts are not isolated entities. Rather, they form intricate networks or complex webs of interrelations and co-implication. As a result of this interconnection, notions mutually condition and reciprocally define each other. Such thoroughgoing correlativity implies that no single concept is either absolutely primary or exclusively foundational. Clusters of coordinated notions form the matrix of any coherent conceptual system.[59]

What this procedure entails is that, as all meaning is constituted by the specific series of relations in a text, these terms assume structural positions relative to one another. These relations are rarely, if ever, homologous, as Taylor notes: "Invariably one term is privileged through the divestment of its relative. The resultant *economy of privilege* sustains an asymmetrical hierarchy in which one member governs or rules the other throughout the theological, logical, axiological, and even political domains."[60] We have already seen that the distinction between *Geist* and *Natur* is one such binary distinction, and reading these texts in light of the play of this binary pair will shed yet another vector of light on the historical discursive formation known as *the* phenomenology of religion.

It is this "economy of privilege" that is at the heart of the politics of *Geist*. The phenomenological tradition in modern philosophy generally, and the appropriation of phenomenological discourse by *Religionswissenschaft* more specifically, constructed a series of cultural representations which give scientific/scholarly credibility to that series of hierarchies we have now come to call by the name *colonialism*. Furthermore, in a classic case of power/knowledge, this system of representations still undergirds the structure of knowledge known as "comparative religion," "world religions," "history of religions," and, to the extent that it has been informed by this discursive formation, even "Religious Studies." As such, they are of crucial importance for both understanding—*and changing*—the body of "knowledge" and the system of representations with which it is so closely associated. As Charles Long argues, "for these dichotomies and binaries are most important for the assessment of the programs and hermeneutics of modernity."[61] This undertaking, which is the principal task of the body of this work, will be taken up in the last chapters after all the evidence in support of this claim is laid out.

Put another way, the binary "colonizer/colonized" is yet another structural binary pair of philosophemes, *latent* in this instance (i.e., not manifest or very rarely), which function to produce the meaning of "religion" in the discourse of the phenomenology of religion. That it maps onto the *Geist/Natur* binary is no accident: that mapping is the central element of the politics of *Geist*, a legacy which, I believe, haunts the human sciences to this day.[62] This major binary term is itself (along with the others) embedded within a larger discursive formation, namely, the Occident. The ideational element of that discursive formation has been dubbed "ontotheology." As such, it is necessary to discuss how the politics of *Geist* correlates to ontotheology. In brief, I will argue that the presence of elements of ontotheology are not incidental to the phenomenology of religion; rather, it is constitutive of it as a meaning-making or discursive formation. The discourse of the phenomenology of religion, then, is a subset of the discourse of ontotheology.

## Ontotheology

Within and between these texts there is a finite set of terms or philosophemes which are constantly activated in and into different roles, different scenes, and nuanced meanings. Terms such as "essence," "*Geist*," "nature" run throughout the discourse of the phenomenology of religion, from Hegel to Eliade. Moreover, they preexist Hegel and have a history that reaches back (arguably) to the Pre-Socratics. For the purposes of this study, I accept the historical argument of poststructuralism that these terms are derived from a specific Western discursive formation given the illuminating name of "ontotheology." That is, intellectuals of various persuasions have come to the scholarly consensus that the various philosophical, theological, axiological, metaphysical, political, and epistemological systems[63]—Platonism, Aristotelianism, Thomism, Nominalism, Realism, Rationalism, Empiricism, Critical Idealism, Absolute Idealism, Materialism, Atomism, Holism, Humanism, etc.—*structurally* have more in common than they differ. Derrida describes this ontotheology tradition (also referred to as the history of metaphysics) in the following way:

> [T]he history of (the only) *metaphysics*, which has in spite of all difference, not only from Plato to Hegel . . . but also beyond these apparent limits, from the Pre-Socratics to Heidegger, always assigned the origin of truth in general to the logos: the history of truth, the truth of truth, has always been . . . the debasement of writing, and its repression outside "full" speech.[64]

This perspective on Western intellectual history came about through the application of structuralism to philosophical and theological texts and discourse: "Saussure contributed greatly to turning against the metaphysical tradition of the concept of the sign that he borrowed from it."[65] It was the product of a radically new method for reading a group of texts that form a school or an intellectual tradition. The structuralist ideas of *langue* and *parole*, language (as an abstract system) and specific uses of language in concrete acts of speech, were used to show that, despite the many, many permutations of the system (*parole*), the various texts, schools, positions, and movements in philosophy, metaphysics in a broad sense, and theology were only permutations of an underlying structure (*langue*). In other words, specific texts are dependent on the structure in the way that statements in a language are dependent upon the grammar and lexicon of that language. A competent user of a language can make and understand perfectly many, many different statements. The grammar and lexicon of the language, by contrast, are quite fixed and stable. There is, then, both a structure to discourse and play within the discourse. The structure of this discourse revolves around the problematic of: Being-Becoming-Nothingness, form and matter, mind/soul and body, universal and particular, and so forth. Each individual text is a permutation or play of the finite yet vast possibilities within ontotheology. *The langue of the discourse of the phenomenology of religion is ontotheology.* This is the case whether it takes the form of a developmental diachronic scheme, that is, a history of consciousness or a static taxonomy of an ahistorical, a priori, unchanging structure consciousness.

## Postcolonial Discourse Theory

"How has travel and exploration writing *produced* 'the rest of the world' for European readerships at particular points in Europe's expansionist trajectory?"[66] *Mutatis mutandis*, we may ask: How has the discourse of the phenomenology of religion produced, via its representations, "the rest of the world," that is, non-Christian religions and/or the religions/religiosity of non-European peoples, for and in the readership of the scholarly world? It is a major argument of this study that use of this heuristic will illuminate the relationship—*nota bene*: not a causal one—between the image-repertoire and/or information-base of the texts of these European scholars and the world their governments and fellow citizens were rapidly colonizing.

*Overview*

At the same time the *Geisteswissenschaften* were emerging within Europe, the ramped colonization of vast segments of the globe was occurring outside of Europe. *I do not make any causal argument about the relationship between these two sets of events.* I am not arguing that colonialism caused the phenomenology of religion (in a base-superstructure manner) or that the phenomenology of religion caused colonialism (by creating an ideology which reinforced the impetus toward colonizing). However, one need not rely upon such a causal argument to see that something of interest about the nature of both may be learned by explicitly juxtaposing them. From the time of Hegel's *Phänomenologie* in 1807 to the time of Otto's *Das Heilige* published in 1917, Europeans had aggressively expanded both the scope and the nature of their conquest of the globe, for example, in the "race for Africa." For many European states there was a shift from colonialism to imperialism. The British adage, "The sun never sets on Queen Victoria's empire," was a reality which came into being at precisely this time.

From the period of 1800 to 1900, the world witnessed the "raw realities of Euro-expansionism, white supremacy, class domination, and heterosexism."[67] Euro-imperialism literally came to dominate the entire world. That is, it was most manifestly a form of *domination*. Guns, armies, and arms of war in all their forms were the sine qua non of colonialism/imperialism, and so were the murders, rapes, blunders, tortures, and enslavements that were made possible by those arms.[68] We must never, as scholars, allow ourselves the privilege of imperial *amnesia*: the business of colonization was a brutal, criminal enterprise, and it was "we" Euro-Americans ourselves who did it. And, it was a *global* phenomenon. This period produced, as Mary Louise Pratt, puts it, "a Euro-centered form of global, or, as I call it, 'planetary' consciousness."[69] Rather than this, that or the other religion, now *Religionswissenschaft* could employ the category, "world religions." This made possible a new episteme, a new paradigm within which it was now possible to rank and classify religions in a way that we will see throughout this study. Such rankings and classifications constitute a major element in what I am calling "the politics of *Geist*," discussed below.

Colonialism and imperialism were not, however, only physical realities. There was an entire apparatus for the colonization of the mind, so to speak, a cultural imperialism, a whole set of "representational practices of Europeans,"[70] which, as Pratt noted above, "produced 'the rest of the world.' " The *Geisteswissenschaften* were deeply informed by both elements of the colonial context. Charles Long speaks of

> [a]nother part of the late modern ideology [which] has to do with the subjugation of vast areas of the globe through the technological, economic, and military power of the West. I do not mean to imply that the human sciences were simply and merely the ideological counterpart to this subjugation. *I should, however, make the case that these sciences came into being presupposing this situation*. A great deal of the practical and theoretical meaning of the "others" is related to this colonial situation.[71]

From out of the colonial situation developed a division of academic labor but also an implicit ontological schema of human reality: "European cultures were studied through the established disciplines of the humanities, but non-Europeans were studied by anthropologists. In other words, Europe had civilization (history and the arts) while 'they' had culture (kinship structures and primitive religions)."[72] In similar vein, yet extended radically, Leela Gandhi describes colonialism as follows: "Colonialism, then, to put it simply, marks the historical process whereby the 'West' attempts systematically to cancel or negate the cultural difference and value of the 'non-West.' "[73] As noted above, I will argue that the metaphysics underlying the ranking and classification of religions, especially religions of people of color, is the means by which this canceling and negation occur in *Religionswissenschaft* (and Religious Studies?).[74]

Collections from colonial countries had a major, material impact on the *Religionswissenschaft* and other emergent "social sciences":

> The Royal Museum of Ethnography opened in Berlin in 1886, featuring massive collections of non-European artifacts, and the Berlin Anthropological Society was founded. An observer explained that social science had been impossible "until modern voyages of discovery had brought the necessary comparative materials from the newly opened regions of the world." This process generated distinctions between *Naturvölker* ("nature peoples"), non-Europeans, and Europeans, *Kulturvölker*.[75]

We will return to the issue of collections later in this study. Besides collections, colonial documents such as travel letters and administrative reports were used as sources for the study of religion—without which "comparative religion" would not have been possible. For example see Hegel, where he says of Eskimos: "The religion of magic is still found today among wholly crude and barbarous peoples such as the Eskimos. The Captain Ross—and others, such as Parry—discovered Eskimos who knew no other world than their icy rocks."[76] This quote shows us that Hegel is explicit in describing a people of color in pejorative terms, and, that he bases this description on the accounts made by men engaged in colonizing North America. When describing both the history and the religion of "the Hindoos," Hegel is very reliant upon both the sources and the point of view of British colonial administrators. As such, there is not just an affinity of ideas between the two, colonial representations were formative sources for *Religionswissenschaft* and the phenomenology of religion.

Direct travel was another material means by which the colonial situation enters into the texts and discourse of the phenomenology of religion. Consider Otto and the relationship between his travels abroad the writing of *Das Heilige*:

> The significant year for the development of his own distinctive contribution to religious thinking was, I suspect, 1910, when set out on a long journey to the East which was to take him round the world ... the long sojourn in the East in 1910 must have meant much more to him [than his travels in Europe]. He visited North Africa, Egypt and Palestine, India, China, and Japan.[77]

—all places where empire and colony had "visited" before him. Ergo, these colonial documents were, to some extent at least, constitutive of the field of early *Religionswissenschaft* and/or the phenomenology of religion. There is therefore a direct, material relation between the two.

There is, however, a deeper sense to this relation. Again, the problematic of *Geist/Natur* demonstrates how a genealogy of the discourse of the phenomenology of religion necessarily leads us to the problematics of colonial discourse theory. One need not accept the politics of colonial/postcolonial theory and theorists *in toto* to see that such a type of analysis can shed light on the discourse of the phenomenology of religion. Postcolonial theory shows, to anticipate, that the dictum of the phenomenology of religion, "the believer is always right" (Kristensen), that is, the goal is to examine phenomena as they appear in consciousness, turns out not to apply, at least not in the same way, to non-European religions, most often those of peoples of color. There is, in other words, a systematic ordering, an "economy of privilege," or a "violent hierarchy of opposition" that is, in my view, constitutive of the discourse of the phenomenology of religion. Where this discourse does not denigrate the religions of peoples of color, it elides it. A reading of this discourse informed by postcolonial theory will bring forth a new, if not absolute, set of truths that can only be illuminated by this specific heuristic. It will invert the narrative in Religious Studies, which holds up these phenomenologists as the "heroes" of that discipline in that they defended religion from reductionist methods, methods which they claimed denigrated these very same peoples. A rereading of these texts shows that they are *not* heroes. They are, *so to speak* (and I mean that qualification seriously), "villains." This narrative of Religious Studies breaks down when viewed from the perspective of postcolonial theory: the phenomenologists of religion, it turns out, are engaged in the symbolic cultural subordination of peoples of color by their metaphysical, teleological, and taxonomic views—unwittingly, in most cases I would add, but not all. The distinction *Geist/Natur* is not simply a metaphysical claim, it is a taxonomy of human beings. Some are more *Geist*, some are more *Natur*. Some are more self-conscious, some are less self-conscious. Even in allegedly static taxonomies such as those constructed by Kristensen, van der Leeuw, and Eliade, this is the case *despite* their protests to the contrary. W. B. Kristensen (discussed in depth later), the author of the "believer is always right" statement, uses the macro-distinction to found his classification of religious phenomena: Christian and non-Christian religions. A postcolonial reading will bring out the full significance of such an operation, the way it pervades the discourse of the phenomenology of religion's discourse and texts, and shows how they are, finally, not the work of some neutral "science of experience" but a system of colonial representations. It turns out that the structures of the discourse of the phenomenology of religion are remarkably similar to the system of colonial representations as described by postcolonial theory.

*Post/Colonial Discourse Theory*

There is something of a confusion of names in the realm of postcolonial theory. On the one hand, there is some confusion at the level of conceptualization concerning the difference between postcolonial discourse theory and colonial discourse theory. In addition, there is some difficulty in defining the differences between the geopolitical conditions, "colonialism" "imperialism," and "postcolonialism." Untangling these distinctions is beyond the scope of this study.[78] However, as this study is a genealogical analysis of a discourse, including the discourses of colonialism and postcolonialism, it is necessary to clarify some of these distinctions.

Mills explains the distinction between "colonial discourse theory" and "postcolonial discourse theory"[79] but concludes that "colonial discourse theory and post-colonial theory have both found *the notion of discourse* useful in characterizing the systematic nature of representations about colonized countries."[80] She further notes that, despite the proliferation of distinctions: "The study of colonial discourse does not generally make a distinction between these relations."[81]

I define my own approach as an analysis of that colonial and/or imperialist condition whereby Euro-Americans have dominated non-Europeans and the system of representations produced in and by that condition, by means of the heuristic of that strand of postcolonial discourse theory that identifies with and makes use of poststructuralism (again, in my sense of the term; see discussion above). I agree with Leela Gandhi's assessment of the relationship between poststructuralism and postcolonial theory:

> Poststructuralist thought has provided a somewhat more substantial impetus to the postcolonial studies project through its clear and confidently theorized proposal for a Western critique of Western civilization. In pursuing the terms of this critique, postcolonialism has also inherited a very specific understanding of Western domination as the symptom of an unwholesome alliance between power and knowledge.[82]

My critique is a critique of the West from within the West. It is aimed precisely at the way in which the phenomenology of religion is implicated in the kind of power/knowledge Gandhi describes. Robert Young explains how and why such a poststructuralist-postcolonial theory is not simply an ethics, a moral outcry, or a theory that is an accessory to more "fundamental" disciplines such as history or economics. Rather:

> The politics of poststructuralism forces the recognition that all knowledge may be variously contaminated, implicated in its very formal or "objective" structures. This means that in particular colonial discourse analysis is not merely a marginal adjunct to more mainstream studies, a specialized activity only for minorities or for historians of imperialism and colonialism, but itself forms the point of questioning of Western knowledge's categories and assumptions.[83]

For the last several centuries Europe has approached its "others" with the dual interests of politico-economic exploitation and potential objects of knowledge. Insofar as the patterns of knowledge in the West, most dramatically in Hegel's philosophy of history (and religion), replicate in important ways the colonial situation, poststructural-postcolonial discourse theory is a *necessary element* in the self-understanding of the West, an understanding of what its structure of knowledge *does*. The aim of this study is to perform this critique within a specific domain of knowledge, to wit, the phenomenology of religion. This is an internal critique, that is, a "Western critique of Western civilization."

Just as with "discourse" above, there is a weaker and stronger sense to the notion "post/colonial discourse." On the one hand, it literally refers to those discourses—letters, reports, collections, etc.—generated in and by various colonial contexts. On the other hand, as discourse produces its object, the discourses of the colonizers have played a historical role in reproducing their objects: "[D]uring the colonial period large parts of the non-European world were *produced* for Europe through a discourse that imbricated sets of questions and assumptions, methods of procedure and analysis, and kinds of writing and imagery."[84] As such, the object and method of post/colonial discourse theory, as well as that of the colonizers, does not "therefore simply refer to a body of texts with similar subject-matter, but rather refers to a set of practices and rules which produced those texts and the methodological organization of the thinking underlying those texts."[85] As these discourses were and are produced by authorized sources, governmental agencies, subcontracted civilian corporations, and universities, the images in colonial discourse "accrued truth-value to themselves through usage and familiarity,"[86] but also through exclusion. The unchallenged set of representations-*cum*-truth is a consequence of the fact that the colonized are unvoiced—even when spoken for "empathetically."

It is also important to note that the representations of colonists and imperialists are not simply monolithic, no more so than the on-the-ground realities of each individual colonized context. Mary Louise Pratt captures the continuity and plurality of such representations nicely, noting that: "Redundancy, discontinuity, and unreality. These are some of the chief coordinates of the text of Euroimperialism" and also noting that "the vast, discontinuous, and overdetermined history of imperial meaning-making"[87] is just that: vast, yet with repetitive themes throughout. My analysis only claims to capture a slice of those patterns, a trope or two or three, a few of its elements at best. I make no claim to analyzing the totality of *either* colonial representations and the phenomenology of religion.

*Orientalism*

A colonial discourse reading the texts of phenomenology of religion must include Edward Said's groundbreaking insight concerning "Orientalism," which I treat as species of colonial discourse critique. As such, it is useful in that it illuminates, *mutatis mutandis*, the way in which the phenomenology of religion produces representations of religion. Said argues that "Orientalism is a style of thought based upon an ontological and epistemological distinction made between 'the Orient' and (most of the time) 'the Occident.'"[88] In the *Geisteswissenschaften*, there is a kind of translation from empirically real entities such as India, Arabia, Africa, Hinduism, etc., into a "white mythology" in Derrida's terms, that is, a metaphysical taxonomy. Social-political-cultural entities become metaphysical substances. As essences, rather than messy agglomerations of empirical particulars,[89] the structuring of binary relations becomes possible. As Taylor described above, these binaries then come to define each other in a reciprocal, almost moietic fashion. Said has expressed this point regarding Orientalism:

> [I]s there any way of avoiding the hostility expressed by the division, say, of men into "us" (Westerners) and "they" (Orientals)? For such divisions are generalities whose use historically and actually has been to press the importance of the distinction between some men and some other men, usually towards not especially admirable ends... the result [of such a distinction] is usually to polarize the distinction—the Oriental becomes more Oriental, the Westerner more western...[90]

Orientalism, then, establishes an economy of privilege out of these essentialized binaries. Understood in this way, I take Orientalism to be a subspecies of Eurocentrism. While the two are not interchangeable, the dynamics in each are quite similar. To explain Orientalism is to grasp the pathological dynamics of Eurocentrism.

Ania Loomba has made a very salient point about Said's analysis, one that shows the profound implications of the method described by Taylor above. In the system of representations created by Western scholars, a hierarchy of correlative concepts emerges:

> Said shows that this opposition [between the West and the Orient, as described above] is crucial *to European self-conception*: if colonized people are irrational, Europeans are rational; if the former are barbaric, sensual, and lazy, Europe is civilization itself, with its sexual appetites under control and its dominant ethic that of hard work; if the Orient is static, Europe can be seen as developing

and marching ahead; the Orient has to be feminine so that Europe can be masculine.[91]

We will see, in a variety of ways, how these kinds of interdependent binary oppositions construct the meaning of "religion" in phenomenological discursive structures. The result is a kind of "power/knowledge" correlation that literally maps out the world we, to this day, variously refer to as "religion" or "world religions." As Said, again, claims: "My contention is that without examining Orientalism as a discourse one cannot possibly understand the enormously systematic discipline by which European culture was able to manage—and even produce—the Orient politically, sociologically, militarily, ideologically, scientifically, and imaginatively during the post-Enlightenment period."[92] *Mutatis mutandis*, substitute "Religious Studies" for "Orientalism as a discourse" and the point holds the same, if to a lesser degree.[93]

There is more than one way to be orientalist. Said distinguishes between "latent" versus "manifest" Orientalism.[94] He gives the following example of latent Orientalism: "The Oriental was linked thus to elements in Western society (delinquents, the insane, women, the poor) having in common an identity best described as lamentably alien."[95] Alien, yes, but also sub-ordinate and subordinated. We will see throughout this study many instance of manifest orientalism, for instance, Hegel's treatment of Indians and Tiele's treatment of the Chinese. However, the dominant form of Orientalism and/or Eurocentric colonialist representation in the discourse of the phenomenology of religion is the *latent* form. In the latent form, we have produced and are producing a reality which then reflects back to the discourses that produced that reality, in a circular, self-confirming manner. For example, we extract from "world religions"—itself already a colonial product—the Euro-Christian concept of *"the* sacred"; we then organize this data around that postulate; the data then confirm the fabricated concept. "World religions" and religion itself, is about *"the* sacred." Postcolonial theory is the attempt to disrupt this solipsistic circle of self-confirming representations.

## The Politics of *Geist*

How should one understand the notion of "politics" as used in this study? To some extent this should already be clear but the term is far too general to leave undefined. I am not interested in the on-the-ground politics of colonialism. I am also not interested in the involvement, if there is any, of these writers in colonial politics. I am also not interested in "academic politics" as this is generally understood. In one sense, I am not interested in "politics" at all. I am interested in "the political" by which I, following Richard Beardsworth, mean:

> I understand the term "politics" as designating the domain or practice of human behavior which normativizes the relations between a subject and its others (other human subjects, nature, technics, or the divine). I understand the term the "political" as the instance that gathers or founds such practice as a practice.... [it is] the trait that allows us to describe/recognize a gesture of thought or action as political.... [R]eligion also constitutes a politics—in the sense that I consider religion, as a specific determination of what is and is not of the domain of the political, to be itself of the domain and practice of politics. I am therefore using the terms politics and the political in a larger sense than a pragmatic definition would allow. [96]

"The political" is the discursive condition for the possibility of understanding *politics*. As such, one of the most important s/cites of contestation at the level of "the political," is metaphysics:

> Derrida's reflection upon the political is articulated through his reading of metaphysics. Following Heidegger and Derrida, I understand metaphysical thought as a specific organization of time; one that "disavows" time by casting an opposition between the atemporal and the temporal, the eternal and the transitory, the infinite and the finite, the transcendental and the empirical. It is well known that Derrida relates all his thoughts on the political to what he calls the "closure" of metaphysics.[97]

As we will see, this is a near-perfect description of the politics of *Geist*: it establishes a violent hierarch of subordination of its Others: matter, *Natur*, *Naturvölker*, etc. There is a systematic play to this subordination and nearly all of the philosophemes in the discourse of the phenomenology of religion participate in this play. "Inner experience," for example, will be adamantly differentiated from "sensation," in that it is autonomous and not caused—therefore subordinate—by "external" forces. Being dominates becoming, presence, absence, and the a priori the a posteriori.

This is also a metaphysics of the subject: note the Cartesian structure in the notion of "inner experience" (Dilthey), in Otto's idea of the holy as an a priori category, and Eliade's claim that the sacred is a structure of consciousness. Each of these propositions, in its own way, sets up a hierarchy where the subject and the subjective (broadly understood) is set above the object and the objective realm. This subject goes by many names: "a thing that thinks" (Descartes), Spirit/*Geist* (Hegel et al.), mind, consciousness, and finally "Man." The critique of the political is a critique, not of this or that implication (per se) of these categories, but of their global effect: to produce a nonempirical, nonpolitical, place of power in a version of the political that is rooted in metaphysics. Within this discourse only certain options, many as they are, are possible. The political circumscribes and determines the play of politics by eliding the fact that it is itself the will to power. "To render Becoming as Being: this is the supreme act of the will to power," quipped Nietzsche. Metaphysics defines reality; only certain options are possible within these reality definitions, one of them being "Man." To think otherwise, to understand the political aegis of phenomenology otherwise, is the form of "politics" at play in this study. My intervention is to explicate the political embedded in Spirit, consciousness, (inner) experience, "Man," etc., and lift it out of the texts of the phenomenology of religion so that it can be evaluated, as an epistemological, methodological, scholarly, and political pathology. While I do not presume that we have access to the "things themselves"—but rather precisely the opposite—I do not believe it is too strong a claim that this discursive structure and the politics, or symbolic power relations, that it constructs are a serious distortion of the world, the world that is, as it can be better explained by better theories and better analyses of the data.[98]

Such is my argument. As I have argued elsewhere, scholarly research, or "science" in an extended sense of the term, is heuristic in nature not ontological. As such, I am not claiming that this study is the direct, empirical apprehension of an "object," a "truth," understood in positivistic terms. Ergo: "We are no longer confronted with an ontological problem of being but with the discursive strategy of the moment of interrogation."[99]

Part II

# Readings in the Discourse of the Phenomenology of Religion

# 3

## *Geist*, History, Religion

### Hegel and the Structure of Phenomenology and *Religionswissenschaft*

"We will never be finished with the reading or rereading of Hegel, and, in a certain way, I do nothing other than attempt to explain myself on this point."[1] Foucault describes "this great, slightly phantomlike shadow that was Hegel, prowling through the nineteenth century..."[2] Hegel is not just a "creature of his time" in that we still exist "within the order of Hegelian discourse, which still holds together the language of our era by so many threads."[3] Nietzsche's quip that "[w]e Germans are Hegelians even if there never had been any Hegel"[4] applies broadly to the Germanic world and to the problematics of Continental thought generally.

It is not, of course, only postmodernists and poststructuralists that see Hegel as massively influential. Stanley Rosen argues that Hegel is of decisive importance in understanding Euro-American Modernity:

> One would not go too far in suggesting that Descartes marks the beginning of the modern age, or its philosophical articulation, whereas Hegel marks its end... there is an ambiguity at the beginning and the end of this age concerning the significance of religion. This ambiguity is inseparable from the question of the significance of the modern age.[5]

The Hegelian paradigm becomes the dominant paradigm of the nineteenth century and, as such, deeply informs the project(s) of both the *Geisteswissenschaften* and *Religionswissenschaft*. It arguably still dominates Western perceptions of history generally, "world history," and the West's own history. Poststructuralism is, in many ways, an attempt to "de-Hegelianize" contemporary thought. And, as Rosen notes, the question of religion is central to his thought and central to the problematic of Modernity. Hegelianism, religion, and Modernity all also impinge upon the problem of colonialism: religion, especially as understood in an Hegelian manner, reinforces the supremacy of Europe over non-Europe, and the reality of colonialism calls into question the meaning of Modernity.

Hegel's philosophy of religion was actually a philosophy of *religion*, that is, of actual historical religions, as opposed to working only within the confines of rational theology, to wit, arguments for the existence of God and so forth. As Merklinger explains, this reflects the radical change in the way religion was discussed in a post-Kantian context:

> Hegel knows that he, as a post-Kantian philosopher, cannot consider God as an object for Philosophical contemplation without first contemplating that aspect of being human in which the thought of God first arises, that is, human religious experience. Therefore, Hegel shifts his attention away from God as solely an object of thought as found in natural theology to God as an objective correlate of the religious experience of human subjects. Thus, for the first time in the history of the development of the philosophical inquiry into the content of religion, a philosopher undertook a conceptual grasp of religion as a *complete modality of human experience in itself*, the inner horizon of which is a concatenation of both "nonrational" human feeling and reason.[6]

Hegel, then, is forced to take the historical and experiential content of religion seriously, not simply analyze arguments. It is in this respect that he lays a foundation for subsequent *Religionswissenschaft*, which, *pace* Hegel, later takes the name "History of Religion." A treatment of religion in the manner described by Merklinger relies on a fully developed conception of history and of historical development or change. In order to understand Hegel's influence upon subsequent *Religionswissenschaft*, and to see how the politics of *Geist*, of which he is clearly the chief architect, are worked out in the scientific and philosophical analysis of religion, it will be necessary to look at his view of history, Spirit in history, and the relationship between the state, morality, and reason. A full treatment of all of these is clearly not possible here, but even a short look at how Hegel treats them will illuminate how the discursive structures of both phenomenology and *Religionswissenschaft* took the shape they eventually came to have in such thinkers as Tiele, Otto, and Eliade.

## The Nature of Historical Change: Hegel's Articulation of the Concept of *Entwicklung* ("Development")

Hegel's articulation of the concept of *Entwicklung*, or "development," is a classic piece of Hegelian dialectical analysis in that development is a process with three stages: the being that develops in the true sense of the term is first in itself, then being as *Dasein*, or existence (or, being as out of itself), and, finally, being as for itself.

It is interesting to note, however, that in his analysis of the term *Entwicklung*, Hegel claims only to be explicating the common meaning of the term: "These distinctions come out, even when we stop simply at the familiar notion of development; it is merely a question of reflecting on the notion of development."[7] Given that the literal, root meaning of the term can be roughly paraphrased as "to wind [*wickeln*] or spin out," as from within something, this claim is not far-fetched.[8]

The first stage of *Entwicklung*, or development, then, is being in itself. Hegel explains this as: "With regard to development, what immediately comes to our attention is that there must be something there that develops, which is to say something hidden—the seed, the tendency, the capacity, what Aristotle calls δυναμις."[9]

In the tradition of Aristotle, he uses the example of the seed to illustrate the difference between essential development and mere quantitative increase. The seed is an example of essential development, because, as he says: "With Aristotle we can say that in the simple, which is in itself, in the δυναμις, *potentia*, in the tendency, all that develops is contained. In development no more comes out than what is already there in itself."[10] The essence of the thing that develops is present at the origin. There is, thus, an essential continuity to the development of the object; contingency, irruption, or loss are not part of *essential* development. It is, as Derrida would say, fully present to itself at both the moment of origin and at the moment of fulfillment.

The next phase of *Entwicklung* is the phase of self-differentiation from its in-itselfness, whereby it comes to ex-sist:[11] "What follows is that the in-itself, the simple, the hidden, develops and unfolds. For it to develop means to posit itself, to enter into existence, to be as something distinct."[12] However, even in this act of self-differentiation (or self-alienation), the entity does not lose its essential identity: "Whether it is in-itself and hidden, or whether it is revealed and, as such, exists, it is one and the same thing."[13] The entity is essentially continuous, even if apparently—or empirically—not so. We can see how Hegel is forming a response to the problematic of change and identity posed by Seiwert at the beginning of this study.

Finally, in the third phase of *Entwicklung* the entity, by virtue of its self-estrangement in ex-sisting, comes to fully comprehend itself as itself. The manner in which Hegel describes this process is telling for the subsequent use of the concept of development:

> The third determination is that what is in-itself and what exists and is for itself are one and the same. This is precisely what is meant by development. If the in-itself were no longer the in-itself, then something else would be there, and a complete change would have taken place. In this [the latter] case there is something and it becomes something else. In regard to development, it is true, we can also speak of change, *but the change must be such that the other which results is nevertheless still identical with the first*, such that the simple, the in-itself, is not annihilated. It is something concrete, something differentiated, but still maintained in the unity of the original in-itself.[14]

Two points in summation. First, the key point in the process of development is the self-estrangement of the entity and its going out of itself into Otherness. This is what Hegel calls "mediation": "[D]evelopment involves mediation; the one *is* only to the extent to which it is related to the *other*."[15] Secondly, the *true* fruit of development is none other than "the being-for-itself of man, of spirit itself, since a plant does not have being-for-itself, if we speak in a language which has reference to consciousness. Only Spirit becomes truly for itself, identical with itself."[16] The example of the seed, then, is finally not sufficient; *Natur* cannot comprehend itself, only *Geist* can, but only through its self-externalizations. The τελος, the goal of *Geist*, of history, and by implication of the whole of Creation, is nothing less than *Geist's* self-realization: "The goal of Spirit is, if we may employ the expression, to comprehend itself, to remain no longer hidden to itself. The road to this is its development, and the series of developments form the levels of its development."[17]

## Geist and the Unity and Stages of History

### Geist and the Unity of History

Recall that in the discussion with which we began this study, Seiwert had laid out two options for the possibility of formulating historical identity: "either there is no identity of Buddhism or that Buddhism is not an empirical phenomenon."[18] The function of "Spirit" in Hegel's philosophy of history is precisely to answer this problem, clearly by taking the latter option. Given that, in the course of time, everything empirical changes or passes away, what is the identity, that is, what remains the same, between the moments of time which are continually passing? Or, again, what constitutes historical identity? As Julian Roberts has pointed out about Hegel's philosophy: "The philosophical problem at its center is the problem of change: how can change be made intelligible?"[19]

In the "Introduction" to his *Philosophy of History*, Hegel makes a triadic distinction between the pure notion of "mere change," the Asiatic notion of the "rise of new life," and, finally, the notion—the Occidental notion—of Spirit unfolding itself in the activity of historical destruction and rejuvenation.[20] It is Spirit's unfolding in particular historical events that gives events identity, that makes One out of the Many. In slightly varying ways, this was also the answer to both of Seiwert's questions—What constitutes historical identity? and What is a religion?—of the early history of *Religionswissenschaft* and of the "classical" exponents of the phenomenology of religion. As such, it needs to be examined closely.

In his philosophy of history, the notion of Spirit is the basis for Hegel arguing for a very strong concept of identity in and through time. Hegel's philosophy, then, is a philosophy of identity; its motto is *"das Wahre ist das Ganze"*—"the truth is the whole." The truth can only be found in the Whole because all of the parts contain the truth, that is, stand in a relationship of identity to one another; the Whole is present in the parts. Historical events are not simply contingent, random, unrelated occurrences. Behind the sheer flux of events, or "mere change," is the ongoing process of the Absolute Spirit's unfolding itself through negation. The permanent presence of Spirit is what gives significance (Rosen's term) and identity to the otherwise raw flux of occurrences in time. He announces this eschatological metaphysic in the conclusion of the above mentioned "Introduction":

> The principles of the successive phases of Spirit [*Volkgeister*] that animate the Nations in a necessitated gradation, are themselves only steps in the development [*Entwicklung*] of the one universal Spirit [*allgemeinen Geistes*], which through them elevates and completes itself to a self-comprehending totality [*Totalität*]. While we are thus concerned exclusively with the Idea of Spirit, and in the History of the World

regard everything as only its manifestation [*Erscheinung*], we have, in traversing the past—however extensive its periods—only to do with what is present; for philosophy, as occupying itself with the True, has to do with the eternally present. . . . [for] Spirit is immortal; with it there is no past, no future, but an essential [*wesentlich*] now. . . . [W]hat Spirit is what it has always essentially [*gewesen*] been; distinctions are only the development of this essential nature [*Wesen*].[21]

The immateriality, universality and immortality of Spirit allow the "distinctions" of historical development to be taken up as moments in the unfolding of Spirit. It is in relation to this overarching Spirit that the "moments" of history have their identity: "[W]hat Spirit is it has always essentially been," and, each finite mode of creation, that is, each human cultural form, is nothing more than a manifestation of Spirit at work.

The philosophical underpinning for this notion of Spirit is the primacy of the category of "Unity," which Hegel describes as: "[T]he essential category is unity, the inner connection of all these different manifestations. Here we must keep hold of the fact that it is only one spirit, one principle, which is stamped on the political situation and manifested in religion, art, moral and social life, trade, and industry, so that all these different forms are but branches of one main trunk."[22] The logical principle of Identity, of Oneness, is the basis for the understanding of all historical manifestations as manifestations of Spirit, of essence. "Distinctions," differences, or plurality are all purely derivative. Therefore, "continuity is essentially the notion that Being is One."[23]

The *Beisichselbstsein*, or "being-to-itself," of Spirit culminates in its own self-comprehension in Science: "The Spirit that, so developed, knows itself as Spirit, is Science."[24] The task of a phenomenology of Spirit is to describe the coming-to-be of this Science, the "ground and soil" of which gives us Hegel's ultimate statement of identity, namely, that Phenomenology is the "pure self-recognition in absolute otherness."[25]

The passage from the "Introduction" to *The Philosophy of History* introduces us to the central terminology, not only for Hegel's philosophy, but for the early history of *Religionswissenschaft*, viz.: *Geist, Totalität, Wesen und Erscheinung*, and *Entwicklung* (Spirit, totality, essence and manifestation, and development). What this terminology allows the hermeneute who employs it to do is to read historically and geographically distinct phenomena as forms of a common, unified, underlying essence (*Erscheinungen und Wesen*, or "essence and manifestation").[26] This life can be seen either as a dynamic process in development, which is how Tiele and Otto see them, or as a static taxonomy of self-generating, unchanging "manifestations of the sacred," which is how Kristensen, van der Leeuw, and Eliade see them.

## Geist and the Stages of History

We saw above how Hegel articulates the unity of history as manifestations of "the one universal Spirit [*allgemeinen Geistes*]." At the same time, however, he also describes these manifestations as "the successive phases of Spirit that animate the Nations in a necessitated gradation."[27] While the notion of Spirit sees history as a unity, the notion of *Weltgeschichte* as the unfolding of the *necessary gradations* of nations, or peoples or cultures, emphasizes differentiation. It is to this notion of differentiation to which we now turn, as it forms the basic structure for much of what will be taken as "knowledge" in the science of religion throughout much of its history. To refer back to our discussion in chapter 2 about this structure of knowledge, while Hegel's use of Spirit in the articulation of the idea of unity is manifestly logocentric in its evaluative priority on the universal and the rational (and his insistence on the connection of the moral to both), his notion of necessary gradations is manifestly Eurocentric and ethnocentric, and, as we shall see, overtly Christocentric. The course of world history follows the path of the natural sun:

> The History of the World travels from East to West, for Europe is absolutely the end of History, Asia the beginning. The History of the world has an East κατ εξοχην ... for although the Earth forms a sphere, History performs no circle round it, but has on the contrary a determinate East, viz., Asia. Here rises the outward physical Sun, and in the West it sinks down: here consentaneously rises the Sun of self-consciousness, which diffuses a nobler brilliance.[28]

China, the East, "is the childhood of History,"[29] while the end of the West, the German world, is its old age, and, contrary to nature: "Old Age of Nature is weakness; both that of Spirit is its perfect maturity and strength."[30] Unlike the physical sun, Spirit is linear in its development: what is past is incorporated into the present, but also left behind and transcended. The supremacy of the West, Hegel will argue throughout his entire corpus, is shown by Nature, by History, by the phenomenology of consciousness itself, by logical necessity, and by the object of religion, viz., God.

We need not discuss the issue completely but may note in passing that Hegel divides the basic stages of *Weltgeschichte*, which he also calls *Allgemeinen Geschichte*, or Universal History,[31] into four divisions: (1) the Oriental, (2) the Greek, (3) the Roman, (4) the Germanic.[32] Each stage, whether treated in philosophy, history, culture, or especially religion, has multiple substages.[33] For our purposes, we will briefly look at his characterization of the first and the last stages.

Of the "Oriental realm," Hegel says:

> The world-view of this first realm is substantial, without inward division, and it arises in natural communities patriarchically governed.... A still substantial, natural, mentality is a moment in the development of the state, and the point at which any state takes this form is the absolute beginning of its history. This has been emphasized and demonstrated with learning and profound insight in connection with the history of particular states by Dr. Stuhr in his book *Der Untergang. der Naturstaaten*.[34]

The "substantial" is the stage of the in-itself, of conceptually and objectively lacking outward distinctions. Oriental consciousness lacks differentiation within itself, especially differentiation from nature. This is what Hegel implies by the term *patriarchy* here: civil rule is not fully nor clearly differentiated from natural, family ties.[35] Consequently, the state, the structuring principle of morality, is lacking: "To the Chinese their moral laws are just like natural laws—external, positive commands—claims established by force."[36] The "oriental mind" lacks a sense of freedom bought by a sense of individuality through the separation of Spirit from nature. In a famous statement repeated throughout his corpus, Hegel argues:

> Orientals do not yet know that Spirit—Man as such—is free. And because they do not know it, they are not free. They only know that *one* is free; but for this very reason such freedom is mere caprice, ferocity, dullness of passion, or, perhaps, softness and tameness of desire—which again is nothing but an accident of nature and thus, again, caprice. This one is therefore only a despot, not a free man. The

consciousness of freedom first arose among the Greeks, and therefore they were free.[37]

Hegel takes the correlation between natural instinct on the one hand, and arbitrariness of action on the hand as creating the conditions of the essential passivity, which he takes as characteristic of the "Oriental mind."

By contrast, Hegel says the Christian-European-Germanic world, born of the initial formation of Christianity, is the realization of the principle of freedom:

> Spirit and its world are thus both alike lost and plunged in the infinite grief of that fate for which a people, the Jewish people, was held in readiness. Spirit is here pressed back upon itself in the extreme of its absolute negativity. This is the absolute turning point; mind rises out of this situation and grasps the infinite positivity of this its inward character, i.e. it grasps the principle of the unity of the divine nature and the human, the reconciliation of objective truth and freedom as the truth and freedom appearing within self-consciousness and subjectivity, a reconciliation with the fulfillment of which the principle of the north, the principle of the Germanic peoples, has been entrusted.[38]

The Germanic world, Hegel's own ethnic identity, is the fulfillment of *Allgemeinen Geschichte*. In the "principle of the north,"[39] Hegel asserts the supremacy of Germanic, Lutheran Christendom over Africa, Asia, Native Americans, Greeks, Romans, Jews, and Catholics: "[T]he Germans were predestined to be the bearers of the Christian principle, and to carry out the Idea as the absolutely Rational aim."[40] The rational logos, the ethnic Germanic, and the religious Christian notions of supremacy, each predicated on the distinction between *Geist* and *Natur*, here all come together.

For Hegel, the idea of freedom is not a purely political, secular idea. It is not incidental to the course of history, even, as we saw in chapter 1, in the very nature of reality. Freedom is the secular equivalent of God's providence, and is the goal and aim of history itself:

> Freedom is itself its own object of attainment and the sole purpose of Spirit. It is the ultimate purpose toward which all world history has continually aimed. To this end all the

> sacrifices have been offered on the vast altar of the earth throughout the long lapse of ages. Freedom alone is the purpose which realizes and fulfills itself, the only enduring pole in the change of events and conditions, the only truly efficient principle that pervades the whole. This final aim is God's purpose with the world. But God is the absolutely perfect Being and can, therefore, will nothing but Himself, His own will. The nature of His own will, His own nature, is what we here call the Idea of freedom.[41]

The "necessary gradations of the nations," as degrees of the emancipation of *Geist* from *Natur*, that is, freedom, then, do not represent, in Hegel's view, an arbitrary human viewpoint. It is God's will on earth, it is rooted in the divine nature itself.

Finally, in his view of history and the exploration of the globe by Europeans, Hegel makes the identification of Spirit and humanity with Europe and Christianity explicit when he says:

> that urging of Spirit *outwards*—that desire on the part of man to become acquainted with *his* world. The chivalrous spirit of the maritime heroes of Portugal and Spain opened a new way to the East Indies and discovered America. This progressive step also, involved no transgression limits of ecclesiastical principles or feeling. The aim of Columbus was by no means a merely secular one: it presented also a distinctly religious aspect; the treasures of those rich Indian lands which awaited his discovery were destined in his intention to be expended in a new Crusade, and the heathen inhabitants of the countries themselves were to be converted to Christianity.[42]

"Man's" discovery of "his world," the colonization of the non-European world, is here represented as part of those "necessary gradations of Nations," that is, of Spirit, to wit, European "Man's," inevitable triumph over his Other. The conversion of the heathen nations exports Spirit to the world and makes Spirit concretely universal—but Spirit is Europe. It is clear from the distinction that he makes here when he says "man" discovers his world. As we will see, this Eurocentrism is pervasive throughout the discourse of the phenomenology of religion.

Hegel is completely unapologetic about the fact that this process takes place by force. He describes "history as the slaughter-bench at which the happiness of peoples, the wisdom of states, and the virtue of individuals have been sacrificed,"[43] and argues that, as History is the realization of Reason, of Logos, it is right that some of its contents are merely *means* to Reason's, that is, God's, ultimate ends: "Reason governs the world and has consequently governed its history. In relation to this Reason, which is universal and substantial, in and for itself, all else is subordinate, subservient, and the means for its actualization."[44] That this is no abstract consideration, but a legitimation of real violence, again, Hegel makes completely explicit:

> The same consideration justifies civilized nations in regarding and treating as barbarians those who lag behind them in institutions which are the essential moments of the state. Thus a pastoral people may treat hunters as barbarians, and both of these are barbarians from the point of view of agriculturists, etc. The civilized nation is conscious that the rights of barbarians are unequal to its own and treats their autonomy as only a formality.[45]

As we shall see in the next section, Hegel has a distinct theory of what or who is "in" history or not in history. It is clear from the above statement that the consequence of his view is the legitimation of the subordination of peoples who are not "developed" in the manner he believes defines Spirit, that is, humanity—but, again, specifically European humanity, which culminates in "the principle of the north."

### "In" History: Reason, Morality, and the State

Hegel has a distinct concept of what counts as "history." Not all eventuation in the world is "historical." Following the dialectics of *Entwicklung*, only that which is out-of-itself can become an object of realization. So structured externalization of Spirit is necessary for its progressive self-realization and the highest form of this self-externalization of Spirit is the state:

> In the history of the World, only those peoples can come under our notice which form a state. For it must be understood that this latter is the realization of Freedom, i.e., of the absolute final aim, and that it exists for its own sake. It must further be understood that all the worth which the human being possesses—all spiritual reality, he possesses

only through the state. For his spiritual reality consists in this, that his own essence—Reason—is objectively present to him, that it possesses objective immediate existence for him. Thus only is he fully conscious; thus only is he a partaker of morality . . . [46]

"History" is a history of human beings forming the state, or an objective rational structure, and moving toward the self-conscious realization of freedom. As such, there is an "inside" and an "outside" to history: some peoples are "in" history and some lack the sufficient development of *Geist* to contribute to the progressive realization of history and so are not "in" history—or have a deficient conception of themselves as moral beings or as beings having or being in a state. The taxonomic distinction between "ethnographic" studies of peoples "who have no history"[47] and "history" as peoples who have formed a civilization is a direct reflection of this conception of history—which is predicated on the *qualitative* distinction between *Geist* and *Natur*. This is an idea, formulated in different ways, that runs throughout the discourse of the phenomenology of religion. Dilthey will say that "structure is everything," and Eliade will sharply differentiate between hierophanies that are more local and therefore less significant, and those which are more universal.

For Hegel, the state is a manifestation of the dialectical essence of reality itself, that is, it is the embodiment of and precondition for truth: "For Truth is the Unity of the universal and subjective Will; and the Universal is to be found in the State, in its laws, it universal and rational arrangements. The State is the Divine Idea as it exists on Earth."[48] Like the "divine idea" in Christianity, it is a reconciliation of the elements of existence, specifically the subjective and objective elements: "This essential being is the union of the *subjective* with the *rational* Will: it is the moral Whole, the *State* . . ."[49] The state unifies individual impulse with universal principle, and, besides being inherently rational, it is, as such, identical with the moral: "[T]he State is the actually existing, realized moral life. For it is the Unity of the universal, essential Will, with that of the individual; and this is 'Morality.' "[50] Bringing the argument full circle, the state is identified with both reason and morality, morality itself is not arbitrary and subjective (that would be a contradiction in terms for Hegel), but morality is itself a manifestation of Reason: "The laws of morality are not accidental, but are the essentially Rational."[51] Morality, the state, and reason are overlapping and essentially mutually implicated categories: morality is essentially rational, the state is a necessary condition for morality and is itself the rational reconciliation of dialectically defined opposites (individual/whole; particular/universal; subjective/objective; abstract/concrete).

Hegel also discusses the idea of "state" in a more limited sense, viz., in the sense of "objective spirit." Besides the secular concept of state:

> But when we speak of the manifestation [*Erscheinung*] of the spiritual we understand the term "state"in a more comprehensive sense, similar to the term *Reich* (empire, realm). For us, then, a people is primarily a spiritual individual. We do not emphasize the external aspects but concentrate on what has been called the spirit of a people. We mean its consciousness of itself, of its own truth, its own essence, the spiritual powers which live and rule in it . . . that which constitutes the culture of a nation.[52]

The idea of "objective spirit," or that a people constitute a "spiritual individual," or have an essential nature, becomes, as we saw in chapter 1, a fundamental premise of *Geisteswissenschaften* generally, but *Religionswissenschaft* as well. It is the empirical correlative of the paradigmatic notion of "*Wesen und Erscheinung*," essence and manifestation, so typical of this research tradition. This notion of historical research survives even when and where Hegel's more overt teleological arguments do not. It is the intellectual means by which it is possible to describe "Buddhism," "Christianity," "Hinduism," etc., as abstract wholes. There is no other way to unify the vast concrete emperia that make up these ostensive totalities. But it is a form of essentializing that leads to the positing of a distinct nature to groups of people, such as, "the African mind," the "Asiatic form of production," the "Indian character," and so forth. The phenomenology of religion, and to some degree, Religious Studies, has been dependent on this intellectual operation to posit its most fundamental objects of analysis and description, most especially the ideal abstract, "religion" in the singular.

Hegel explicitly ties these ideas of the state and objective spirit (or essential character) to religion. Religion, he argues, forms the most fundamental *Idee* of a people and, as such, is the ideal, that is, spiritual, basis of its sense of unity as a people:

> The objective existence of this unity is the State. The State, thus, is the foundation and center of the other concrete

aspects of national life, of art, law, morality, religion, science. All spiritual activity, then, has the aim of becoming conscious of this union, that is, of its freedom. Among the forms of these conscious unions religion is the highest. In it the spirit existing in the world becomes conscious of absolute Spirit.... The idea of God thus is the general fundament of a people.[53]

We will see ways in which the correlation of these elements informs the idea of "history" in "history of religions," a term for *Religionswissenschaft* or phenomenology of religion. This set of correlations defines what will count as data for that field as there is an inside and an outside to history. It will also serve as the criteria set for defining types of religion: "natural," "ethnic," "universal," and so forth. As articulated in this specific research tradition, in many ways these terms are simply a reiteration of Hegel's set of correlations of state (or structured whole), reason, and morality. The conception of *Geist*—i.e., "mind," "consciousness," "structure of consciousness," "man," "mental life," "psychic unity of mankind"—as the structuring principle of "history" becomes a constant, even constitutive set of philosophemes of the discourse of the phenomenology of religion even in a thinker such as van der Leeuw, who will say that the phenomenology of religions "does not know of the 'development' of religion,"[54] that is, who rejects, at least overtly, the notion of the progressive realization of *Geist*. The study of religion for him will still be about "meaning," and meaning is inseparable from "structure." It is structure which makes reality comprehensible. The basic template of Hegel's theory of history remains a constant in the discourse of the phenomenology of religion, even in those who *appear* to reject it.

## *Geist* and the Stages of Religious Self-Consciousness

Hegel's philosophy of religion operates on the same principle as his philosophy of history: the Notion of Religion is made "determinate" by its historical manifestations at various stages of human development and fully realizes itself in "the consummate religion," Christianity. In his description of determinate religions his notion of "essence and manifestation" can clearly be seen at work: "It is in determinate religion that determinations first enter into that universal essence; this is where cognition of God begins.... In determinate religion, spirit is determinate both as absolute spirit or object and as the subjective spirit that has its essence or absoluteness as its object."[55] Virtually all the thinkers treated in this study appropriate this view of "determinate religion," and the underlying theory of history that goes with it, in their formulations of a science of religion. It is what Eliade will famously and influentially call a "hierophany" or manifestation of *the* sacred.

## The Religion of Nature and the Nature of Religion

### NATURE OF RELIGION

Hegel defines religion as follows: "Religion possesses its object within itself—and that object is God, for religion is the relation of human consciousness to God."[56] As human consciousness is finite and God is infinite, religion is the relationship of the finite to the infinite, or consciousness of the infinite. As the infinite is, at least at the level of abstraction, the lack of limitation, religion "is the consciousness of freedom and truth."[57] As this relation occurs *within* consciousness, religion is also "therefore Spirit that realizes itself in consciousness."[58] Religion, then, is fundamentally "*geistig*," that is, mental or spiritual. It is influenced by external factors (at times; Hegel and others are quite inconsistent on this point). However, he is adamant that as consciousness is "free," that is, essentially independent, neither it nor religion can be reduced to external conditions. We see here an early version of an idea that is, again, constitutive of the discourse of the phenomenology of religion, viz., the sui generis nature of religion.

The coming-to-consciousness of God in the human spirit involves the separation and reconciliation of the finite from the infinite, of consciousness and *Geist* from the immediacy of *Natur*: "The human being is essentially spirit, and spirit is essentially this: to be for oneself, to be free, setting oneself over against the natural, withdrawing oneself from immersion in nature, severing oneself from nature and only reconciling oneself with nature for the first time through this severance and on the basis of it; and not only with nature but with one's own essence too, or with one's truth."[59] The self-alienation of Spirit or consciousness is necessary in order to have the object of consciousness, God, for-itself, and the reconciliation of this for-itself is a qualitatively different state than the original in-itselfness of "natural" consciousness: "This oneness brought forth by way of severance is the first spiritual or true oneness, that which comes forth out of reconciliation; it is not the unity of nature. The stone or the plant is immediately in this unity, but in a oneness that is not a unity worthy of spirit, it is not spiritual oneness. Spiritual oneness comes forth out of severed being."[60]

The self-objectification of Spirit entails that the "object" of comprehension, that "severed being," is a reflection of the subject that objectifies it: there is a dialectical, qualitative correlation between a subject and *its* object. Consequently, says Hegel, we can read off the nature or stage of a human being or human group from their conception of the object of religion, namely, God:

> Even as the content, God, determines itself, so on the other side subjective human spirit that has this knowledge determines itself. The principle by which God is defined for human beings is also the principle for how humanity defines itself inwardly, or for humanity in its own spirit. *An inferior god or a nature god has inferior, natural and unfree human beings as its correlates;* the pure concept of God or the spiritual God has as its correlate spirit that is free and spiritual, that actually knows God.[61]

In a move that we will find consistent throughout this literature, on the one hand the idea of Spirit seems to make humans equal with each other in that they participate in a universal nature. Of religion, Hegel famously says, "all religions have some share in the truth." On the other hand, this very same principle is used to differentiate human groups radically. Nowhere is this more obvious in *Religionswissenschaft*, the "history of religion," or phenomenology of religion, than in the idea of "nature religion." The phenomenology of religion shares Hegel's valuation of the relation, a "violent hierarchy" of an essentially binary term, between *Geist* and *Natur*. This valuation is embedded in one of phenomenology's most basic concepts: consciousness.

RELIGION OF NATURE

For Hegel, nature religion is "defined as the unity of the spirit and the natural, where the spirit still is in unity with nature. In being this way, spirit is not yet free, is not yet actual as spirit."[62] He is at pains to show that by the phrase "nature religion" he does not mean the worship of natural phenomena or physical objects. As he argues:

> [N]ature religion is not a religion in which external, physical objects are taken to be God and are revered as God; instead

> it is a religion in which the noblest element for human beings is what is spiritual, but the spiritual is [recognized] first in its immediate and natural mode.... [T]herefore, nature religion has the natural within it, but not sheer external or physical naturalness; it has a spiritual side at the same time, but what is *naturally* spiritual, his human being here present and sensibly facing us.[63]

"Nature religion," as Hegel means it, is the state of human conceptuality as *in*-itself, as not yet severed its immediate relation from nature such that it can have nature as an object *for* itself. As with the triadic pattern of *Entwicklung*, the pattern of religious consciousness, as well as the pattern of the history of religion, will begin with the in-itself stage. This is the stage of "nature religion," and the growth or emergence out of this is the work of Spirit in the domain of religion.

Given this sense of "nature religion," and given his dialectical, developmental view of *Geist*, Hegel goes to some pains to indicate that, while a necessary stage of consciousness, the "original state" of humanity is not, *pace* Rousseau, a natural goodness. Quite the opposite:

> As a state of existence, that initial natural oneness is in actuality not a state of innocence but the state of savagery, an animal state, of (natural) desire or general wildness. The animal in such a state is neither good nor evil; but human beings in the animal state are wild, are evil, are not as they ought to be. Humanity as it is by nature is not what it ought to be; human beings ought to be what they are through spirit, to which end they mold themselves by inner illumination, by knowing and willing what is right and proper.[64]

The opposition, again, between *Geist* and *Natur* is used as a qualitative and normative differentiation between human beings of different cultures and different historical periods. Hegel will characterize humans in whom *Geist* is insufficiently developed as "wild," "barbarous," "unfree," "superstitious," and "fearful." Every positive achievement they attain or characteristic they possess is qualified, even cancelled out, due to their placement in the overarching metanarrative of the development of religious consciousness and its place within the metanarrative of *Geist*.

This metanarrative is the structural principle for Hegel's history of religion, a structure that has so influenced the constitution of the idea of "world religions" that many textbooks on the subject published in the twenty-first century still implicitly follow this basic pattern. As we saw, "history begins in the East and ends in the West." So also with the history of religion: "So far as historical development [*Entwicklung*] is concerned, nature religion is the religion of the East."[65] It is to that history we shall now turn.

*"The Sun Rises in the East": Geist, Buddhism, and Hinduism*

BUDDHISM

Since, for Hegel, all cultural manifestations are necessary phases for the *Entwicklung* of *Geist*, the question that must be asked of any specific religion is: What contribution does it make to the τελος of *Geist's* self-realization? This is precisely the manner in which Hegel treats Buddhism and Hinduism.

Hegel understands Buddhism as a transitional phase of religious consciousness, wherein consciousness moves out of the sheer notion of dominion over nature,[66] and into an intensified relationship to itself. This is the movement of "going-into-self." This determination of religious consciousness "is the human being as *being within self*, or *self-contained* [*in sich seiend*]."[67]

This being-within-self is still a form of "nature religion" in that the self is grasped in immediacy as sheer substance. It is in terms of this dialectical tension between substance and individual that Hegel understands what he takes to be a key feature of this religion, viz., the veneration of the Buddhas: "In the religion of Lamaism the view is that definite individuals are God, that they are the divine substance as living, as sensibly present here. This sensible presence is the abiding, principle feature of this religion."[68] In the metanarrative of *Geist*, what this veneration represents is the advance of consciousness from sheer immediacy of magic. Here: "The highest power or the absolute is grasped not in this immediacy of self-consciousness but as substance, as an essence which, however, at the same time still retains this immediacy, so that it exists in one or more individuals."[69]

"Substance," however, is a merely negative determination of spirit and it is this negative determination that defines the essential character of this religion, both theoretically and practically. Theoretically, the idea that God, or ultimate reality, is nothing, Hegel says, "means nothing other than that God purely and simply is nothing determinate, is the indeterminate."[70]

In the practical domain, this theoretical notion represents the character of the adherents of this religion: "The image of the Buddha is in the thinking posture, with feet and arms intertwined so that a toe extends into the mouth—this is the withdrawal of self, this absorption in oneself. Hence the character of the peoples who adhere to this religion is one of tranquility, gentleness, and obedience, a character that stands above the wildness of desire and is the cessation of desire."[71] As a religious practice, "one has to make nothingness of oneself. Within one's being one has to behave in this negative way, to resist not what is external but only oneself."[72] The ultimate realization of this state is, of course, what Buddhists refer to as Nirvana which is often understood and misunderstood as a state of ultimate nothingness.

Hegel notes that the concepts of Buddhism may sound absurd to his audience, but he insists that this "is a definite and necessary stage of religious representation: God as the indeterminate, as indeterminacy, as this total void in which the initial mode of immediacy is superseded, has disappeared."[73] This, he argues, is an advance of the religious consciousness, and is the contribution that this determination makes to the final realization of spirit itself.

## HINDUISM

Hinduism is a related yet separate form of religious consciousness. Unlike Buddhism, which is simply going-into-self, Hinduism "is defined in such a way that here the substantiality is found in the totality of its externality; it is represented and known in and by this externality, by the totality of the world."[74] Since being-out-of-itself, *Da-sein*, is a necessary phase for Spirit, it comes as no surprise that Hegel would say of Hinduism, "here, therefore, the horizon is enlarged; we have here the totality. The viewpoint is concrete; that is the necessary progress."[75] Recall that to ex-sist is the second stage in the process of *Entwicklung*. While Buddhism is "in-itself," Hinduism is "out-of-itself," or an externalization of consciousness.

Hegel understands the dialectic of Hindu religion to be an unstable oscillation between the One Substance and what he calls the multiplicity of powers. The One Substance is "present as pure thinking, pure being-within-self, and this self-containment is distinguished from the multiplicity of things; it is external to particularization, so that it does not have its existence or its reality as such in the particular powers."[76]

The second aspect of this dialectic is the multiplicity of powers represented as a plurality of deities: "These are the particular powers that maintain themselves externally to self-contained being, so that they are not yet taken up into spirit, are not posited as truly ideal, but also are not yet distinct from spirit. The substance is not yet spiritual, for the powers are not yet posited outside of spirit."[77] Hegel uses the example of the *Trimurti* to illustrate this. Each of the three gods, Brahma, Vishnu, and Shiva, is, on the one hand, an absolute and eternal being. Yet, on the other hand, each is a transitory manifestation of the One, which is reabsorbed into the unity without becoming a determination of that unity.[78]

This indeterminacy of being/beings forms the basis of Hindu practice and character: "The absolute or highest *cultus* is that most complete emptying out of the human, the renunciation in which the Hindus relinquish all consciousness and willing, all passions and needs.... [T]he Hindus make this abstraction into the character of their consciousness, and of their entire existence."[79] This universal, abstract negation of differentiation into unity is the basis for those deficiencies of the Hindu character which Hegel variously terms "wild and unruly," "fanciful polytheism," "confused dreams," and so forth. The surrender of the particular into the abstract totality means that "human life has no higher worth than the being of natural objects or the life of a natural being.... Here one cannot ascribe worth to self in an affirmative way, but only negatively: life gains worth only through negation of self. Everything concrete is only negative when measured against this abstraction."[80]

Hegel draws three conclusions from this "fact." First, he says that without a concrete appreciation of reality, the true concept of history is impossible for a people. He explains the importance of this as follows:

> History is always of great importance to a people; since by means of that it becomes conscious of the path of development taken by its Spirit.... History presents a people with their own image in a condition which thereby becomes objective to them.... History fixes and imparts consistency to this fortuitous current—gives it the form of Universality, and by so doing posits a directive and restrictive rule for it ... that is, a rational political condition.[81]

The Hindus have only fancy, wild imagination, and confused dreams—a mythology in the pejorative sense—not history. The form of the Universal, that is, the apprehension of the particular as the self-differentiation of the universal, or "reason" is lacking.

From this, the second consequence follows: "[I]t follows that there is no ethics to be found, no determinate from of rational freedom, no right, no duty. The Hindu people are utterly sunk in the depths of an unethical life"; "[T]heir humanity does not yet have within it the content of freedom." [82]

Finally, these deficiencies have a bearing on the political existence of the Hindus: "The proper basis of the State, the principle of freedom is altogether absent: there cannot therefore be any State in the true sense of the term."[83] Lacking the freedom resultant from the rational determinations of the Whole, India's political existence is a state of "despotism without a principle."[84] Even among the nations of Asia, which are all characterized by despotism ("the East only knows that one is free"), India is unusually corrupt in this regard: "Asia generally is the scene of despotism ... but in India it is normal: for here there is no sense of personal independence with which a state of despotism could be compared, and which would raise revolt in the soul."[85] In a sweeping, poetic summary of the nature of the Hindu Spirit, Hegel compares it with a person in a debilitated condition: "[A]s a man who is quite reduced in body and spirit finds his existence altogether stupid and intolerable, and is driven to the creation of a dream-world and a delirious bliss in Opium."[86] Hinduism is the opiate of the Indian people. As noted above, the condition of the natural is "evil" in the sense that it is antithetical to the human spirit and so is a debased condition. As such, Hinduism is an "evil," debased religion.

### Elevation of the Spiritual over the Natural: The Nature and World-Historical Significance of Judaism

Hegel's view of the relation between Christianity and Judaism reflects the overarching scheme of his *Religionsphilosophie*. This scheme has three main parts: the concept of religion, determinate religion, and the consummate religion. Within the stage of determinate religion, there are three sub-phases: immediate religion, the (partial) elevation of the spiritual above the natural, and the religion of expediency. Judaism is the second part of the second phase of determinate religion, which Hegel calls "the religion of sublimity."

Hegel's metanarratological principle of the stage of religion to which Judaism belongs is the partial separation of *Geist* from *Natur*: "This is the stage where the spiritual elevates itself above the natural, to a freedom that is partly beyond natural life, and partly within it, so that the [simple] blending of the spiritual and the natural ceases.

It is the second stage of the ethnic religions."[87] The key characteristic of this religion is its emphasis on an ethical relationship to God: "God is known as a spirit whose determinations are rational and ethical. But this God still has a particular content, i.e., is still only his ethical power."[88] Characteristically, it is the purported restriction of ethics to ethnicity that is seen as the limitation of Judaism, its defining feature over and against the (at least implicit) universalism of Christianity: "[A] limitation is present in [this] religion, insofar as it is consciousness of God, a limitation understood partly in terms of the fact that the Jewish God is only a national God, has restricted himself to this nation."[89] By contrast, although Christianity may be national in its outward form, it represents a stage "when religion grasps itself, its content and object is this whole—*consciousness relating itself to its essence*, knowing itself as its essence and knowing its essence as its own."[90] Christianity and Judaism then, are finally different *in essentia*, that is, in their relationship to essence, to the essence of religion.

## Christianity: The Consummate Religion

Just as many before him and many after him, Hegel argues that there is a strict correlation between the nonrelative, non–culturally specific definition of "Spirit" and the view that Christianity is the supreme manifestation of Spirit in all of human history. This is an argument that scholars such as Tiele, Otto, and van der Leeuw will make, so while a complete analysis of Hegel's view of Christianity is neither necessary nor possible for our purposes here, several of its main themes must be examined rather carefully.

"Spirit's knowing of itself as it is implicitly is the *being-in-and-for-self* of Spirit, the consummate, the absolute religion in which it is manifest what Spirit is, what God is; and this religion is the Christian religion."[91] Such are the terms in which Hegel describes the essential nature of Christianity. He variously refers to Christianity as "the consummate religion" (*vollendete Religion*), the "absolute religion" and the "revealed religion" (*geoffenbarte Religion*). The word *voll* means *full* or *complete* and the connotation of the phrase "*vollendete Religion*" is that, in Christianity, completion, even perfection (*Vollkommenheit*), has been attained. Hegel sees this in terms of his dialectics of externalization: "consummate religion, the religion that is for itself, that is objective to itself."[92] This is religion that has *itself*, and not its other, for its objective content. "Revealed religion" has a similar meaning, namely, the self-positing of a content that becomes objective for itself and to itself. As this occurs within consciousness, which is finite Spirit, it is the "fulfillment" of Spirit's quest for itself: "Here, for the first time, spirit is as such the object, the content of religion, and spirit is only for spirit. Since it is content or object, it is, as spirit, this self-knowing or self-differentiating, and it itself furnishes the other side, that of subjective consciousness, which appears as finite. It is the religion whose fulfillment is itself."[93] This, again, is Spirit's coming to know itself through the positing of itself as its own content: "But when religion grasps itself, its content and object is this whole—consciousness relating itself to its essence, knowing itself as its essence and knowing its essence as its own—and that is spiritual religion. This means that Spirit is the object of religion, and the object of the latter—essence knows itself—is Spirit."[94]

Besides being the unique nature of Christianity, Hegel argues that there is complete conformity between this inner dynamic of the Christian religion and the nature of scientific understanding, or reason itself: "This is always the pattern in scientific knowledge; first the concept; then the particularity of the concept—reality, objectivity; and finally the stage in which the original concept is an object to itself, is for itself, becomes objective to itself is, related to itself."[95] In Christianity, so to speak, the "secular" logos of science and reason coincide with the divine logos.[96] As such, Christianity is objectively true and truth is its objective content. This objective content is also the δυναμις, the fundamental driving force of *Weltgeschichte*: "This is a fundamental fact in our science and must be kept constantly in mind just as we noted it in the Christian principle of self-consciousness and freedom, so it shows itself in the principle of freedom in general. World history is the progress of the consciousness of freedom."[97] In Christianity, Spirit, Reason, and Freedom all unite in perfect (ideal) realization. Christianity is the "end" of the history of religion: "Spirit must have been educated, must have traversed this circuit [of the history of religion, but also the history of consciousness and "secular" history].... This is the path and the goal by which Spirit has attained its proper concept, the concept of itself.... The Christian religion appeared when the time had come. This time is not a contingent time... it is a time determined in the eternal reason and wisdom of God."[98] World history, science, and Christianity all converge in a *parousia* of Spirit; Spirit's long journey into self-alienation ends in a homecoming, the home being "the principle of the north." Finally, the idea of "consummate" religion entails Spirit's transition from substance to subject:

> We have to consider this content as it exists in its consciousness. Absolute Spirit is content; that is how it exists in the

shape of its truth. But its truth consists not merely in being the substance or the inherent reality of the religious communion [in-itselfness, or nature religion]; nor again in coming out of this inwardness into the objectivity of imaginative thought [out-of-itselfness, or determinate religion]; but in becoming concrete actual self, reflecting itself into self, and being *Subject*. This, then, is the process which spirit realizes in its communion; this is its *life*.[99]

Given the correlation discussed earlier between the subject that apprehends a religious content and the object of religion apprehended, what Hegel is arguing is that only in "consummate" religion does humanity fully enter subjectivity. "Natural" humanity, as discussed above, confuses self with substance, that is, passive, dependent nature.[100] The realization of the Absolute content of religion makes humans subjects rather than substances, and this makes them free beings: "[T]hat Substance is essentially Subject, is expressed in the representation of the Absolute as *Spirit*—the most sublime Notion and the one which belongs to the modern age and its religion."[101] Christianity and Modernity merge: the metanarrative is a narrative of the progress of Spirit's self-consciousness. This is a point that will be taken up again later at the end of this section.

## TRINITARIAN PRINCIPLE

Hegel sees the divine life as the dialectical play of the three parts within itself: "[T]he eternal idea is expressed in terms of the holy Trinity: it is God himself, eternally triune. Sprit is this process, movement, life. This life is self-differentiation, self-determination."[102] As noted above, he sees this pattern as identical with reason, history, and consciousness. As such, the consciousness which has the Trinity as its object is fully self-conscious, that is, has itself as its object. This identification of the Persons of the Trinity with the stages of consciousness and the structures of logic is seen in the way he articulates the deeper meaning of the Father, Son, and Spirit: "Of these three, the first is the realm of universality; the second, the realm of particularity; the third, that of singularity."[103] In the first, the "idea of God is first as it is for thinking or in itself. This is the eternal idea of God for itself,"[104] or God the Father. The second is predicated on representation, and is present for sensible intuition: "that God is present for finite spirit as finite spirit."[105] In the "Holy Spirit," "God comes to be for sensibility, for subjectivity and in the subjectivity of spirit, in the innermost being of subjective spirit. Here reconciliation, the sublation of that separation, is made actual."[106] Father, Son, and Spirit are the same principles as the in-itself, the out-of-itself, and the in-and-for-itself that we have seen in Hegel's analyses of consciousness, reason, and the pattern of *Entwicklung*, which is the underlying pattern of history and of the history of religion.

This full-fledged trinitarianism sets Christianity apart from all other religions. While some semblance of Trinitarian principles can be found in other religions, they are not complete: "Apart from those already mentioned above, one can point to a countless number of forms in which the content of the Trinity appeared distinctly and in various religions. But this properly belongs to the history of the church."[107] Not only was it the "proper" work of the Christian, European church to elaborate fully the meaning of Trinitarian principles; it was the Germans who realized it most fully: "Jacob Boehme was the first to recognize the Trinity in another manner, as universal."[108] While Hegel has a qualified acceptance of Boehme's religious thought, he nevertheless sees Boehme, a German thinker, as a pivotal figure in the self-understanding of Christianity.

Other, non-Christian philosophies and religions have only a partial understanding of the true nature of the Trinitarian principles: "The Trinity played an essential role for the Pythagoreans and Plato, but its determinate characteristics are left entirely in a state of abstraction."[109] The abstract structure of logic is, indeed, Trinitarian, but only abstractly. Without the Incarnation, Trinitarian principles cannot be concrete. Similarly with the Hindu notion of the Trimurti: "[It] is not the Spirit, not genuine reconciliation, but rather origin and passing away."[110] Vishnu and Shiva represent the natural, cyclical process of change, not the inner, self-objectification, or "revelation" of Spirit to itself. As we shall see below, the self-alienation of Spirit is a necessary component of Hegel's idea of reconciliation. In the substantial mode of thinking of "the East," Spirit has not yet come to see itself as Spirit.

Finally, the Trinitarian impulse in God is directly linked to the logos as its essential expression: "The second moment, other being, the action of determining, self-determining activity as a whole, is, according to the broadest designation, λογος—rationally determinative activity, or precisely the word."[111] "Word" is mind expressing itself, making itself an external object to itself. The logos as universal reason and the logos as Christ incarnate, here merge. We will see how the phenomenologists of religion appropriate the concept of expression and of Spirit as underlying, or found within, the concretia of history. Dilthey is the main architect of this methodological principle and we will review his appropriation and modification of it in chapter 5.

RECONCILIATION

The dénouement of the history of religion *as such*, is the sacrifice of Christ on the cross. In that event a double movement occurs: the realization of the unity between God and humanity from the side of human consciousness, that is, a new consciousness, arises, and the self-alienation and reconciliation within the divine life itself, that is, the necessary separation between Father and Son, is overcome, thus fully actualizing Spirit, the third (Trinitarian) term, for the first time in history. As our concern is with *religion*, the human side of this equation, and not with theology per se, the former aspect will be discussed below.

The contradictory concept of Christ's death, that is, "God is dead," is given its full dialectical treatment by Hegel. The death of the divine being is a sacrifice, and: " 'To sacrifice' means to sublate the natural, to sublate otherness."[112] Here we have the famous Hegelian *aufheben*, with its simultaneous meanings of "sublate, transcend, supersede, and annul."[113] So "nature" is not simply done away with, but realized fully as Spirit's Other. As such, "when it is comprehended spiritually, this very death becomes the means of salvation, the focal point of reconciliation."[114] The full consciousness of the unity of the duality of *Geist* and *Natur* is now a possibility.

With Christ's death human consciousness is put on a new, higher footing. While the death of Christ was the death of a single human individual, it was also a moment in the *Allgemeine Geschichte*, the Universal History of Spirit: "But the suffering and death of Christ superseded his human relationships, and it is precisely in his death that *the transition into the religious sphere occurs*. On the one hand it is a natural death, brought about by injustice, hatred, and violence," while on the other hand, "what is of interest is an infinite relationship to God, to the present God, the certainty of the kingdom of God—finding satisfaction not in morality, ethics, or conscience, but rather in that than which nothing is higher, the relationship to God himself."[115] The sublation of the natural standpoint, not merely its otherworldly rejection, here creates the conditions for a higher message, the message of reconciliation. The condition for the possibility of this reconciliation is none other than the Trinitarian principle: "The reconciliation in Christ, in which one believes, make no sense if God is not known as the triune God [if it is not recognized] that God is, but also is as the other, as self-distinguishing, so that this other is God himself, having implicitly the divine nature in it, and that the sublation of this difference, this otherness, and the return of love, are the Spirit."[116] The difference for Hegel between this and any other notion of reconciliation is the fact that, in Christ, God was fully human, so the antithesis between the finite and the infinite could be sublated, not merely overcome from the outside in some form of a *deus ex machina* action: "It is the Son of Man who speaks thus, in whom this expression, this activity of what subsists in and for itself, is essentially the work of God—not as something suprahuman that appears in the shape of an external revelation, but rather as [God's] working in a human being, so that the divine presence is essentially identical with this human being."[117] As such, it is, for Hegel, authentic reconciliation.

The death of Christ opens a new era in human history and gives birth to a new possibility: "Since what is at issue is the consciousness of absolute reconciliation, we are here in the presence of a new consciousness of humanity, or a new religion. Through it a new world is constituted, a new actuality, a different world-condition, because [humanity's] outward determinate being, [its] natural existence, now has religion as its substantiality."[118] As we shall see others treated in this study claim, Christ and Christianity give humanity true religion, the full realization of religion. Above we noted that for Hegel, "religion is the relation of human consciousness of God"; religion is also "therefore Spirit that realizes itself in consciousness."[119] In the previous "necessary gradations of the nations" or, in this case, religions, humanity was still only substantial, that is, natural immediacy, or, the vain attempts at the mere cancellation of the natural standpoint. Now, in Christ and in Christianity, true religion has become the substance of the human standpoint, as "God was in Christ," so the *aufheben* of the difference between *Geist* and *Natur*, between finite spirit and infinite Spirit, between substance and subject, has been overcome in such a way that both are preserved and fully realized, that is, reconciliation has occurred: "The new religion expresses itself precisely as a new consciousness, the consciousness of a reconciliation of humanity with God."[120] This is the "good news" of the Gospel in and to *Weltgeschichte*. This particular act, the death of one man, gives birth to a universal possibility, and from it issues forth a new realization of Spirit. With this new Spirit, a new people, as its concrete manifestation, arises.

## Spirit as Life and as Community

Hegel's view of Spirit, of *Geist*, informs the history of the study of religion, which was often understood as the study of "objective spirit." As such, we must look at it in light of the discussion of the consummate religion, for here Hegel asserts the specificity of his concept of Spirit, a concept he, and those who follow him, will use to differentiate sharply between "nature religions" and "world religions," or between savages, semi-savages, and fully civilized peoples.

The key to this differentiating concept of Spirit is the idea that Spirit is life. It is not static substantiality, that is only Spirit apprehended as in-itself and not fully realized. Spirit is the inner life of God and that which separates humans from animals and nature. Hegel gives as description of the former notion as the inner life of God: "This is the life, the deed, the activity of God; his absolute activity, creative energy, and his activity is to posit himself in contradiction, but eternally to resolve and reconcile this contradiction: God himself is the resolving of these contradictions."[121] Put another way, "God" is not eternally static substance, but the eternal δυναμις, the eternal drive and energy of existence. This energy is *life*.

Key to Hegel's notion is the idea of differentiation. This is virtually his definition of "spirit" and/or "consciousness": "Consciousness is precisely the mode of finitude of Spirit: distinction is present here. One thing is on one side, another on the other side; something has its limit or end in something else, and in this way they are limited. Finitude is this distinguishing, which in Spirit takes the form of consciousness. Spirit must have consciousness, distinction, otherwise it is not Spirit."[122] Differentiating self and world, one object from another, one species of objects from other species or classes or objects, is what makes humans human and not merely animals: "For cognition or consciousness means in general a judging or dividing, a self-distinguishing within oneself. Animals have no consciousness, they are unable to make distinctions within themselves, they have no free being-for-self."[123] We will return to the issue of freedom later, as it is central to our overall argument, but it will be no surprise at this point that inner dynamic of Spirit, of consciousness itself turns out to be Trinitarian:

> Spirit is content of its consciousness to begin with in the form of pure substance; in other words, it is content of its pure consciousness. This element of thought is the process of descending into existence, or individuality. The middle

term between these two is their synthetic connection, the consciousness of passing into otherness, the process of imaginative presentation as such. The third stage is the return from this presentation and from that otherness; in other words, it is the element of self-consciousness itself. These three moments constitute the life of Spirit.[124]

Spirit has life, it is the triune movement of self-activity (not passive necessity). Spirit is life: it is this dynamic, differentiating activity of ever-positing and ever-resolving contradictions. The full realization of this life, this activity is the Absolute: "This, then, is the Absolute Idea. The Idea is the unity of concept [in-itselfness] and reality [out-of-itselfness]."[125] This, then is the realization of Truth: the unity of subject and object. As this concrete, actualized reality, its history is a necessary component. Spirit is only truly spirit

as that which dirempts itself and returns into itself again—i.e., only after traversing this circuit. What we have traversed in our treatment is the becoming, the bringing forth of Sprit by itself and only as such, or as eternally bringing itself forth, is it Sprit. This course is, therefore, the grasping or comprehension of Spirit. It is the concept that determines itself, and takes these determinations back into itself, as the concept; in this way the concept is infinite subjectivity.[126]

The life of Spirit, then, is not lived in abstract ideality. It must live in concrete, actualized history, to wit, in a community. "The community itself is the existing Sprit, the Spirit in its existence [*Existenz*], God existing as community.... The third element, then, is this consciousness—God as the Spirit. This Spirit as existing and realizing itself is the community."[127] While Hegel is here speaking specifically of the birth of the "holy Spirit," the third person of the Trinity, he is also speaking of the realization of Spirit in actuality—the identification of the two being no accident, of course. Spirit lives via a community; the community's life is Spirit realized. In Christ, a new spiritual communion is possible, and so a new form of its realization, a new people, will issue forth as its actualization in history.

In a discussion of the sonship of Jesus, which ties many of these themes together, Hegel argues that Otherness is a necessary presupposition of truth, or the actualization of the life of Spirit: "Otherness is requisite in order that there may be difference; it is necessary that what is distinguished should be the otherness as an entity. Only the absolute idea determines itself and is certain of itself as absolutely free within itself because of this self-determination. For this reason its self-determination involves letting this determinate entity exist as something free, something independent, or as an independent object. It is only for the being that is free that freedom is; it is only for the free human being that an other has freedom, too."[128] Know the truth and the truth shall set you free, indeed. Christ brings freedom into the world. It is the world-historical destiny of one people, one community, one nation, however, to realize fully this principle of freedom. This *Volk* is Hegel's *Volk*, the Germans.

### *The "Principle of the North": The World-Historical Destiny of the Germanic People*

Spirit, Truth, Freedom, and Religion must be concretely realized in actual history. The course of history is not mere fortuitousness, it is the workings of the Logos, of Reason, as Providence, and has a particular τελο, goal or destiny: "History is Spirit clothing itself with the form of events or the immediate actuality of nature."[129] The German people are the embodiment of this destiny of Spirit. In a series of statements that summarize many of the ideas we have reviewed, Hegel makes explicit these connections between religion, freedom, reason, and the Germanic people. "Reason," he says, "in general is the positive existence [*Wesen*] of Spirit, divine as well as human.... Religion as such, is Reason in the soul and heart."[130] Both Reason and religion are manifestations of Spirit, and as such, they have an inner connection. Reason is objective Spirit, while religion is inner Spirit, *Gemüt*, or heart. The state is a mediation between both: "Freedom in the state is preserved and established by religion.... The process displayed in history is only the manifestation of religion as human reason—the production of the religious principle which dwells in the heart of man, under the form of secular freedom. Thus the discord between the inner life of the heart and the actual world is removed. To realize is, however, the vocation of another people—or other peoples—viz., the German."[131] Although Christianity came to birth in the Roman world (the world under discussion in the immediate context of this passage), it is not the destiny of Rome to bring universal freedom to humanity. This, argues Hegel, constitutes the natural division of historical periods, that is, the course of Spirit's path to self-realization: "The preliminary statement given above of the various grades in the consciousness of freedom—that the Orientals knew only that *one is* free, the Greeks and Romans that some are free, while we [Europeans-German-Christian-moderns] know that all men absolutely, that is, as men, are free—is at the same time the natural division of world history."[132] Speaking of the Crusades, which Hegel takes to be a uniquely German-Christian undertaking, he says: "The West bade an eternal farewell to the East at the Holy Sepulcher, and gained a comprehension of its own principle of subjective finite freedom."[133] With the Germans, *Weltgeschichte* realizes that "new consciousness" which was incipient in the event of Christ's death and resurrection. The *Aufhebung* of the abstract objective structure of the Roman state and the merely substantial, natural standpoint of "the East" results in a new, higher synthesis of Spirit.

This freedom and knowledge comes about as a result of the combination of the unique content of the Christian religion and the German "nature": "Only the Germanic peoples came, through Christianity, to realize that man as man is free and that freedom of Spirit is the very essence of man's nature. This realization first arose in religion, in the innermost region of spirit; but to introduce it in the secular world was a further task which could only be solved and fulfilled by a long and severe effort of civilization."[134] Hegel gives a complex and nuanced history of the German peoples and states, and insists that, while some Germanic peoples had mixed ethnic origins, "*Germany proper* kept itself pure from any admixture."[135] The essential character of this properly German nation is the presence of *Gemüt*: "The German nation was characterized by the sense of natural totality—an idiosyncrasy which we may call Heart [*Gemüt*]."[136] In itself, *Gemüt* is simply subjectivity, and, as such, not the full objectification necessary for Spirit's full self-realization. However, in combination with Christianity, the objective and the subjective form a higher synthesis: " 'Heart' has no particular object; in Christianity we have the Absolute Object."[137] In the German-Christian nature, Spirit knows itself: "The absolutely universal is that which contains in it all determinations, and in virtue of this is itself indeterminate. Subject [individual personality] is the absolutely determinate; and these two are identical."[138]

The result of this combination is a higher stage of freedom. Subjective freedom, Hegel argues, has always been an essential trait of the German nature: "The ancient Germans were famed for their love of freedom.... Freedom has been the watchword in Germany down to the most recent times."[139] This subjective freedom comes to a higher stage of realization in that uniquely German form of Christianity, Protestantism: "This is the essence of the Reformation: Man is in his very nature destined to be free."[140] Luther, who is regarded as a great

*German,* brings about a new version of "the Good News," a renewal and furthering of both the German and the Christian Spirit. At the level of the individual, this occurs within the human being: "Truth with Lutherans is not a finished and complete thing; the subject himself must be imbued with Truth, surrendering his particular being in exchange for the substantial Truth, and making that Truth his own."[141] At the level of the state, due to the elimination of a separate religious sphere (e.g., monks and nuns), a greater reconciliation is possible: "[I]n the Protestant Church the reconciliation of Religion with Legal Right has taken place. In the Protestant world there is no sacred, no religious conscience in a state of separation from, or perhaps even hostility to secular right."[142] Again, in this way, subject and object, heart and state, are reconciled: "Thus Christian freedom is actualized."[143]

Hegel is the architect of the politics of *Geist*. Spirit's ontological status as distinct from and superior to *Natur* is tied directly to peoples, cultures, and religions: "nature religion" and *Naturvölker* are *lower* than fully realized Spirit. The inner, Trinitarian dialectics of Spirit, its self-differentiating and-self-reconciling life, are seen as identical the inner dynamics of the Logos, of Reason and of *Wissenschaft*. All of these are explicitly seen as directly correlative to the nature of Christianity. History is the progressive realization of this idea and culminates in European-German-Christian freedom. In Hegel, then, we see the pathologies of the "power-knowledge" correlation discussed in chapter 2: a logocentrism that is also a Euro- and ethnocentrism; both explicitly correlated with a Christocentrism. The history of phenomenological discourse will, in various ways, even by way of denial, reiterate many of these themes and perpetuate this structure of "knowledge." This is most clearly seen in one of the founding figures of *Religionswissenschaft*, C. P. Tiele. It is to him we now turn.

# 4

# Religion in Essence and Development

## C. P. Tiele, Early *Religionswissenschaft*, and the Phenomenology of Religion

Cornelius Petronus Tiele was one of the most important early practitioners of *Religionswissenschaft*. He is "a figure who deserves, in many respects, to be considered the founder of the science of religion."[1] As noted in chapter 1, he was the first scholar to hold a chair in History of Religions. He is also an important link between Hegel and the phenomenology of religion. While classic phenomenologists of religion would reject his notion of development, they would retain many of the structural features of his view of the history of religion. Furthermore, as discussed previously, both share a view of science as a combination of empirical ("historical") elements and ideal elements, as well as its important correlative notion of the separation of Spirit ("consciousness") from Nature. Tiele will articulate the latter in terms of his concepts of the essence of religion as unfolding through its development, a process for which he employs the "kernel/husk" metaphor in a quite literal and explicit way.

The exposition of Tiele that follows will rely upon two major sources. One is his history of religion, *Outlines of the History of Religion to the Spread of Universal Religions*, of which Jonathan Z. Smith tells us: "This influential monograph appeared in Dutch in 1876, with two subsequent editions, and was rapidly translated into English in (1877), French (1880), German (1880), Danish (1884), and Swedish (1887)—with the English and German versions going through as many as five or six later editions."[2] It was, in fact, one of the first "world religions" textbooks and, as can be seen from its many translations and editions, played an important role in the dissemination of the idea of "religion" as being articulated by this intellectual tradition as well as a dissemination of the idea of *Religionswissenschaft*.

The other main source used in this exposition is Tiele's *Elements of the Science of Religion*. This is a two volume work delivered in 1896 and 1898 as the Gifford Lectures.[3] This work is divided into two parts: the first is "morphological," and the second is "ontological." By the morphological, Tiele means that part "which is concerned with the constant changes of form resulting from an ever-progressing evolution."[4] By the ontological, he means that part "which treats of the permanent elements in what is changing, the unalterable element in transient and ever-altering forms—in a word, the origin and the very nature and essence of religion."[5] The structure of Tiele's science, then, corresponds very closely to Hegel's Science of Wisdom: what he is looking for in historical instances of religion is the development of forms, forms that are forms of some underlying, unchanging being, viz. the essence of religion and forms that progressively culminate in "higher" and higher stages.

The exposition that follows will focus on his view of the "development" of religion and notion of the essence of religion, as these are correlative concepts. An analysis of his treatment of the history of religion will show how all of these issues coalesce into a concrete representation of "religion" as a mental, that is, "spiritual" (*geistig*) human reality, fundamentally structured by an opposition between spirit and nature.

## The Concept of *"Entwicklung"* (Development)

The first volume of Tiele's *Elements of the Science of Religion* is devoted entirely to the concept of "development" (*Entwicklung* in German, *Ontkwikkeling* in Dutch), a concept which he there refers to as an "indispensable working hypothesis."[6] In his articulation of the concept of development, Tiele makes two broad, definitional points, and the terms he uses to make these points are instructive:

> What do we imply when we speak of development? In the first place, we imply that the object undergoing development is a unity; that the changes we observe are not like those that proceed from the caprices of fickle man, as the clothes we wear change with the freaks of fashion; that the oak already potentially exists in the acorn, and the man in the child. The one does not merely succeed or supersede the other, but the one grows out of the other.... Development... is growth from a germ, in which lies latent everything that afterwards springs from it.[7]

As we have seen and shall see, this essentialist notion of development is a central philosopheme which circulates throughout the discourse of the phenomenology of religion.

Secondly, as regards the *stages* of evolutionary change, the very concept of Development itself implies that

> each phase of the evolution has its value, importance, and right of existence, and that it is necessary to give birth to a higher phase, and continues to act in that higher phase. If I uproot an oak and plant a beech in its place, I cannot say that this beech has developed out of the oak ... [W]hen certain positivists say that morality, or when Strauss teaches that art, must supersede religion, they have no right to call this development.[8]

He describes the historical development of religion as "the evolution of the religious idea in history,"[9] and further claims that: "All genuine development is mental, and even the development which is called material is simply that of the human mind applied to material aims."[10] The mentalism or Idealism of Tiele's concept of development is further indicated by the answer he gives to the question of what it is that provides the essential continuity between the successive stages of development: "What is it, then, that we can characterize as the abiding, the unchanging, the essential element, as distinguished from the ever-varying phenomena in which it is revealed? 'The spirit,' everyone will of course reply, or, perhaps, 'the idea.' "[11] He describes "spirit" as "what may indeed develop, yet remains essentially the same, and retains the selfsame individuality throughout all changes."[12] This is the manner in which Tiele will describe the essence, or kernel, of religion, a point that shall be developed further in the next section.

"All development, including that of religion, takes place by means of assimilation."[13] The process of assimilation takes place by what he calls the "one-sided elaboration of a single root-idea to its utmost consequences" but, "at the same time, by its very one-sidedness, it awakens the need for other, and not less essential, elements of religion."[14] Two things, then, are of note here. First, as assimilation, development takes place by the incorporation of otherness into the selfsame. Although this is not identical to Hegel's notion of the self-alienation of Spirit, it is quite similar. Second, it is one, essential root-idea, which develops first in one direction, then in its opposite. This description of the mechanism of development is clearly similar to Hegel's notion of the dialectics of reconciliation.

Although there are many cases where it appears as if one religion has simply replaced or superseded another, according to Tiele, this is often only apparent (as he uses the example of the development of Iranian religion to show).[15] This insistence on the denial of "mere" supersession and on logical progression is characteristic of the use of the concept of *Entwicklung*—as opposed to Darwinian "natural selection."

Furthermore, in terms that sound much like Hegel, Tiele characterizes the process of assimilation as one of conflictual differentiation: "All growth, all development, all life is a battle..."[16] The oppositional structure of the elements of development are key: the self becomes itself in and through the other, the not-self.

This becomes clear in Tiele's description of the course religious development takes: "If we carefully trace the course of religious development we shall at once observe a continual movement from uniformity to ever greater diversity."[17] But this movement is not the only aspect of development: there is a second moment, the drive toward unity. His final description of the course of development is that of "ever-increasing differentiation, coupled with efforts for reconciliation and unity."[18]

It will be no surprise from the foregoing, to find that for Tiele, development is not merely a random process, but one that has a quite definite τελο or goal, and that this goal is the increase of human self-consciousness. As he puts it::

> [T]he double phenomenon... of development [i.e., of differentiation and unity], can, as it seems to me, only be accounted for by the fact that man becomes ever more clearly conscious of what he is and what he requires as a religious being, and of the nature and demands of the religion within him.... [A]ll spiritual development is at bottom simply progress in self-consciousness.... And when we ask why religious man cannot rest content with existing forms of religion, but ever strives to create new forms; why he tries to make his religion ever more self-contained and independent of all the external authority which so long controlled it... —I believe that this one answer applies to all these questions: Because he grows up in religious self-consciousness. Herein, therefore, consists the essence of religious development.[19]

Not only is self-consciousness the goal of development, religion is its crown: "[T]he development of religion is the necessary consummation of all human development, and is at once demanded and promoted by it."[20] Very much as with Hegel, in religion (with the constant aid of reason) spirit recognizes itself as spirit, and this coming to intellectual self-consciousness is the fulfillment of "man's" destiny.

In the course of his exposition of the concept of development, Tiele makes several important side-points, points that recur many times in the text, and which are relevant to the issues discussed here.

First, he claims that the foundation of the science of religion rests on the fact of the unity of the human mind. He makes this point repeatedly, but in particular in describing the relationship between the development of civilization generally and of religion in particular: "Progress in the intellectual, aesthetic, ethical, and even in the social and political spheres, has an educative influence on religion; and religion is sure in the end to assimilate thence all that makes its creed clearer and deeper.... This must take place. And why? Because the human spirit is one."[21] This is, of course, an essential premise underlying the notion of development as development out of an inherent potential.

Secondly, that the science of religion is a "fond illusion" if there are no laws of development, and:

> If such laws—or call them the rules, forms, necessary conditions, if you will, by which spiritual development is bound—did not exist, and if we were unable to form some idea of them corresponding with reality, it would be better to give up the science of religion altogether as a fond illusion. We should not even be entitled to speak of development at all, for this idea necessarily involves that of rules and laws.[22]

Furthermore, these laws are clearly based upon the aforementioned unity of the human mind: "And I would ask whether we are going too far, or assuming too much, in believing that we here discern a supreme law of development in its application to religion, the law of the *unity of mind*?"[23]

Tiele goes to considerable pains to indicate that the Laws of Development, as he understands them, are categorically different from *either* the laws of history or natural laws. The science of religion, as a mental science or *Geisteswissenschaft*, is clearly distinct from sciences founded on materialism, naturalism, or positivism—a Continental term that really means empiricism.[24] He states this point repeatedly, always along the following lines: "Let us, however, distinctly understand each other. The science of religion is not a natural but a mental science, and therefore there is no question here about natural laws. The mechanical element is entirely excluded"; "Nor, above all, must it be forgotten that laws of history are quite a different thing from laws of development."[25]

Finally, we must look at how Tiele articulates the notion of the development of religion by way of the metaphor of the "kernel and husk" of religion. This metaphor has been philosophically expressed as the relation between the "essence and manifestation" (*Wesen und Erscheinung*) of religion, and has been widely used throughout the history of the study of religion as a basis for speaking of "religion" in the singular. As such, it is an important philosopheme in the history of the study of religion and the manner in which it is articulated by Tiele will be telling for the thesis being advanced here.

First, we must note that Tiele defines the relation between kernel and husk in a binary, yet hierarchical manner: "[T]he husks in which the priceless treasure has been preserved throughout the ages have themselves been indispensable, but they have had their day; and in the fullness of time, just when the spiritual fruit they protect begins to run the risk of being choked by them they require to be removed and replaced by others. The husk is therefore invaluable, though only for the sake of the kernel. Our concern is now with the kernel. The kernel alone gives its value to the fruit, and alone affords us sustenance."[26] The husk is valuable, but only as a vehicle for the kernel. If it takes on a life of its own or makes its own demands, it begins to obstruct its original purpose, and thus begins that conflictual process of differentiation which propels the development of religious consciousness.

Second, the husk/kernel has a necessary relationship, but a relationship that is structurally analogous to the concrete/abstract, real/ideal, or, body/soul relationships:

> [T]he external manifestations of religious consciousness are not mere unimportant incidents, and that their study should by no means be neglected; above all, I consider it wrong to maintain that it does not matter what a man believes and teaches, or how he worships, provided only he believes something and worships in some fashion or other. But while I hold that the content of the doctrine and the forms of worship are by no means matters of indifference in religion, I can no more admit that they pertain to the essence of religion than I can regard my body as pertaining to the essence of my human nature, or suppose that the

loss of one of my limbs or organs would really impair my personality or true humanity.[27]

"Nature," that is, *wesen*, essence ("true humanity") must not be confused with *Natur*, mere nature. Again, while kernel and husk are interdependent, they are not of equal value. This structural relationship, as we shall see below, is the basis by which Tiele emplots the history of the development of religion: "lower religion," that is to say, lower races, have their value as "husk," but must be overcome—an act inherently and necessarily violent—when they threaten to choke out the kernel, that is, the true, spiritual essence of religion. Furthermore, we again see how the kernel/husk or essence/manifestation paradigm is a structural methodological principle: this will be the precise mode of research used in what is later called "the History of Religions," that is, to examine historical concretia in order to find essential, spiritual realities.

Tiele makes a point that will inform much of later phenomenology of religion, and one with which Dilthey and Wach will especially agree. He argues that the inner core of religious consciousness *must* seek its expression, that there is a pre-expressive reality, which is literally ex-pressed (*Ausdruk*) into an external form. The function of this external form is to convey an understanding of the internal content. We have, then, a model of religion that goes: essence-expression-understanding, a pattern that is virtually synonymous with the methodology of later phenomenology of religion.

> It is one of the conditions of the life of religion that its internal elements should be reflected in its external, that the subjective should constantly be objectivised. It is indeed of the utmost importance that the outward form should as faithfully as possible index the inward essence, and that the objective should agree as far as possible with the subjective—as far as possible, I say, because there are many cases in which images and symbols can only approximately express the thought that underlies them. Yet, for the very purpose of maintaining this agreement, they must constantly undergo change, because the subjective or inward essence is perpetually developing.[28]

"What is it, then, that we can characterize as the abiding, the unchanging, the essential element, as distinguished from the ever-lasting phenomena in which it is revealed?" Tiele asks. His answer, as we saw, though with qualifications, was: " 'The spirit,' everyone will of course reply, or, perhaps, 'the idea.' "[29] This answer forms the transition from his discussion of the morphological, or changing aspect of religion, the husk, to its kernel, that is, the unchanging essence of religion.

## Ontology, or the Essence of Religion

Tiele frames the question of essence in two distinct, yet related ways. First, he sees it as the abiding element, which underlies changing manifestations: "We have hitherto been occupied with the ever-changing forms and varying manifestations of religion throughout human history, but we must now inquire as to what is permanent in the forms arising out of each other, and superseding each other, and as to the elements they all possess in common. This alone will enable us, so far as our limited knowledge permits, to determine the essence of religion and ascend to its origin."[30] In this regard, he is, again, very much employing the "essence-manifestation" model typical of the Hegelian or Idealist view of history.

Second, he makes the classical argument for a specific difference of religion as a distinct category: "Does religion contain any constant elements, none of which it can lack without injuring it and rendering it imperfect, and which therefore belong to every sound and normal religion?"[31] He is looking for those universal characteristics that differentiate religion as a category from other categories. As we shall see below, he very much subscribes to the notion that, as a reflection of human nature, culture has distinct, perhaps even ontologically grounded, spheres, namely, morality, science, art, and so forth—a deployment of what is known as a faculty psychology, that is, that humans think, feel, and will. As with all thinkers who make this species of argument, and, typical of arguments in the history of the study of religion, he will want to find those characteristics that make religion an autonomous sphere, with a place of its own among these other spheres.

His answers, as well as the way in which he qualifies these answers, to both these questions are instructive. First, let us look at how he describes the abiding element, the "husk" or *wesen*, essence, from its changing, outward manifestations. This point will take us back to a previous point on the issue of development, as the two issues are inextricably and correlatively interrelated. The abiding element, it will be no surprise, is spirit: "What is it, then, that we can characterize as the abiding, the unchanging, the essential element, as distinguished from the ever-varying phenomena in which it is revealed? 'The spirit,' everyone will of course reply, or, perhaps, 'the idea.'"[32] He describes "spirit" as "what may indeed develop, yet remains essentially the same, and retains the self-same individuality throughout all changes."[33] As such, this sounds very much like Hegel and the Idealist paradigm for history.

Tiele does not accept the term *spirit* without qualification, however. He goes on to say: "In this it [the term *spirit*] might be here employed; but, to prevent mistake, I prefer to use the word 'being.'"[34] The problem with the term *spirit* seems to be that it is too vague:

> But I cannot accept this answer without some further definition. The terms used in the so-called mental sciences are apt to be so uncertain and arbitrary that, as we are concerned with a question of fundamental importance, we are bound to determine the precise meaning we assign to them. The term "spirit," in particular, is apt to be the least definite of all. When we speak of spiritual kindred in the domain of religion, we denote persons of the same way of thinking, advocates of the same principles; yet we cannot deny that men of totally different views sometimes act more in accordance with the spirit of our principles than others who belong to our own party.... As a rule, we here use the word "spirit" to signify a certain sentiment or frame of mind, but we also include the idea of a direction both of thought and life.[35]

It is unclear here what the possible mistake might be, or, what the change in terminology, given his definition of it, actually effects. My guess would be that he is here, as appropriators of Hegel often did, trying to have the benefit of the concept, but at the same time wants to distance himself from Hegelianism so as to ensure that the science of religion is regarded as truly scientific.

In place of the term *spirit* Tiele prefers the word *being*: "In this sense it [the term *spirit*] might be here employed; but, to prevent mistake, I prefer to use the word "being"—that which is, as distinguished from that which grows or becomes, the οὐσία as distinguished from the ever-changing μορφαί; and I have therefore called this part of our course the ontological, though it might perhaps have better been described as the physiological."[36] I can only assume that when he qualifies "ontological" with "physiological," he means the latter in terms of its root meaning as φύσις, or "nature." That is perfectly in keeping both with his argument, viz., an attempt to find the quiddity of religion, its nature (φυσις, *Wesen*, or essence) and with his appeal to the Greek etymology of his technical vocabulary. It would be quite misleading to assume that here he is making some kind of gesture to a materialist, reductive, explanatory view of either religion or of the science of religion. He clearly does *not* reject the concept of "spirit" or *Geist* outright, but merely qualifies it. It is at least arguable that his qualification of the term *spirit* here is simply an attempt to be more precise. As he understands the term, it means both the abiding and the changing element. His attempt at find the unchanging, specific difference of the source and nature of religion differentiates, in classical terms, the *ens* from the *esse*, the existence from the essence, or being. "Spirit," as a term, he claims, combines that which must be teased out—and, as we have seen, there is good reason to argue that in post-Hegelian discourse that is indeed the case. He will use the term rather liberally thought the *Elements* (as well as elsewhere), and especially in the last chapter, titled "The Place of Religion in Spiritual Life." He is, in short, in no way shy about the term in general. Here, he is simply trying to make a more precise distinction. This attempt is, in all likelihood, an attempt to distance himself somewhat from a more overt Hegelianism, and, to be more scientifically precise. As we discussed in chapter 1, this is the exact means by which the appropriation of Hegel's major motifs were retained in the *Geisteswissenschaften* in the nineteenth century.

However we determine the precise meaning of the concept of "spirit" in Tiele, it is clear that the "abiding element" of religion of which he speaks is and will be a feature of the human mind: "Religion therefore, which is a mental condition, manifests itself in all kinds of words and deeds."[37] In terms that sound very much like Schleiermacher and Hegel, and which Otto in particular will use, he articulates this constant element in opposition to its more external manifestations:

> In order, therefore, to determine the true essence of religion, we must mount from the visible to the invisible, from the phenomena of external nature to the source whence they spring. We need not seek for that essence, that abiding element, in religion as an anthropological phenomenon; for, as such, religion is subject to continual changes; but we must seek for it in the religiosity, or religious frame of mind, in which it has originated. Although in reality the two things are inseparable, we must try to distinguish between the

ever-changing manifestations of religion and the sentiment which underlies them.[38]

The language here is rather vague but it is a fair rendition to say that "anthropological" means outward behavior of human beings, while "religious frame of mind," as we shall see below, means something like what later thinkers will call the religious a priori, i.e., that essential, spiritual, structure of "Mind" that is immaterial, invariant, and which is the underlying, expressive agent in all religious history.

So much for the way in which Tiele answers that part of the question of the essence of religion having to do with the unchanging, underlying kernel that is manifest in history. If Tiele is more like Hegel on that issue, when it comes to the issue of delineating the specific difference of religion, the other aspect of defining the essence of religion, Tiele is much more like Schleiermacher. He argues that the core of religion, that which makes it different from other aspects of human spiritual or cultural activity, is not singular, but triune: "The true constituents of religion are emotions, conceptions, and sentiments, of which words and deeds are at once the offspring and the index. To describe these constituents as manifestations seems to me a misuse of the term."[39] These, again, are not that which is manifest, but that which does the manifesting, so to speak. Tiele is clear on this point: "In order to understand the essence of religion we must study these three root-ideas of all religion in succession. They may fairly, though not quite fully, be summed up in the favorite watchword of religion, 'faith, charity, and hope,' and they also coincide, though not quite exactly, with the three constituents of religion, conceptions, sentiments, and actions."[40] That is to say, when Tiele makes his case for what may be called the structural essence of religion, that is, the conditions for the possibility of religion appearing in history as a human phenomenon, he resorts to a very traditional faculty psychology, viz., that the human mind is composed of three (sometimes four) "faculties," emotion, reason, and will (aesthetic sensibility sometimes being the fourth area), and that these manifest themselves in distinct, autonomous cultural regions: religion, science, and ethics (art sometimes, again, being the fourth realm). Here, Tiele is clearly thinking in the same general vein as Kant and Schleiermacher.

The actual specific difference, that which separates "religion" from other spheres or either objective reality or compartments of the human mind is *piety*. Drawing upon an old, traditional line of argument, Tiele argues that the essence of religion is piety: "It [the specific difference of religion] must be sought for in a certain sentiment or disposition—in religiosity. Religion is essentially a frame of mind in which all its various elements have their source. Religion is piety, manifesting itself in word and deed, in conceptions and observances, in doctrine and in life."[41] After reviewing a rather lengthy etymology of the word *piety* in various languages,[42] he concludes further that the essence of piety is adoration: "I maintain that its [piety's] essence, and therefore the essence of religion itself, is adoration. In adoration are united those two phases of religion which are termed by the schools 'transcendent' and 'immanent' respectively."[43] This covers both the object of adoration and the subject of adoration, that is, the human being who adores his or her god.

The basis for this notion of adoration is an innate sense of the infinite. The way in which he frames this issue is telling both for what he means by "mind" or "spirit," and, as to how and why he will deal with various religions in history. The core of "man" is his innate sense of that which is unlimited:

> It is man's original, unconscious, innate sense of infinity that gives rise to his first stammering utterances of that sense [of adoration], and to all his beautiful dreams of the past and the future. These utterances and these dreams may have long since passed away, but the sense of infinity from which they proceed remains a constant quantity. It is inherent in the human soul. It lies at the root of man's whole spiritual life. It is revealed in his intellectual, his æsthetic, and his moral life.[44]

This sense of the infinite is, to a certain extent, derived negatively, that is, in opposition to the finite: "Mere animal, selfish enjoyment cannot satisfy him permanently, because he feels that, as a man, he has an inward impulse which constrains him to overstep the boundaries of the finite and to strive after an infinite perfection, though he knows it to be unattainable for him as an earthly being. The Infinite, the Absolute, very Being, as opposed to continual becoming and perishing—or call it as you will—that is the principle which gives him constant unrest, because it dwells within him."[45]

Like others who have so argued, Tiele claims that this sense of the infinite is the peculiar essence of "man," of that which distinguishes "man" from animals and from nature: "Whatever name we give it—instinct, or an innate, original, and unconscious form of thought, or form of conception—it is the specifically human element in man, the idea which dominates him."[46] Haunted, as it were, by the idea of the infinite, "man" can never find satisfaction in "mere animal, selfish enjoyment," that is to say, in his merely natural, bodily aspect. The implication, again scientific (i.e., "psychological"), not theological, is that non-nature is the essence of "man," and non-nature, in this tradition, is nothing other than *Geist*, even if it is not explicitly named as such.

The basis for this innatist argument about the infinitely within "man" rests on a cleavage between sense and reason. That is, in a manner similar to Schleiermacher and Otto, he argues against the idea that the perception of the infinite causes religion, but rather, that the sense of the infinite is a priori, and *not* derived from sense: "I do not, however, assert that religion emanates from a perception of the Infinite within us, because such perception requires a considerable measure of self-knowledge and reflection, which is only attainable long after religion has come into existence, long after the religious spirit has revealed itself. The origin of religion consists in the fact that man has the Infinite within him, even before he is himself conscious of it, and whether he recognizes it or not."[47]

In point of fact, Tiele suggests that it is the other way around: "We must inquire whether the results of sensuous perception are not rather supplemented by those of inward perception than irreconcilably opposed to it."[48] As we discussed in chapter 1, Tiele's epistemology is not the same as British Empiricism. Typical of the Continental tradition, he argues for the "cooperation" of sense and reason, of percepts and the a priori mind, which organizes them into a meaningful reality: "But it is neither by perception nor by reflection that he acquires the idea of the Infinite, although that idea finds support in psychological perceptions, and becomes an object of reflection."[49] The awareness of the finite and the infinite have, in fact, distinct origins in human consciousness, origins that imply an important qualitative distinction in the realities in question: "He gives it [the innate concept of the Infinite] precedence over the Finite; for with this he only becomes acquainted by means of the perception of his senses, and it is only later that he converts it, by means of reasoning, into a general idea."[50] This is another way of saying that nature, that is, sense perception, is lower than spirit, and, that earlier, "*prima*," primitive "man," is less spiritual-rational-ethical than later, developed "man." His narrative of religion, just as was Hegel's, is a narrative of progressive self-realization. Later stages of development are "higher" in that they are fuller apprehensions of the Infinite, apprehensions that have come about through the cooperation of intellect with sense. The growth in intellect, the nonmaterial in "Man," is directly proportionate to the growth of spirit and the every purifying of religion in history.

The separation of reason from sense is crucial to his understanding of ethics. We saw the same argument in Hegel: reason is the universal while sense is the particular. When Tiele actually deals with the history of religions he will classify them as "nature religions" and "ethical religions." This taxonomy is rooted in his view of the nature of "man," of mind, of spirit, and of the relationship between spirit and nature. As such, it is a constitutive principle for Tiele's scientific treatment of the history of religion, a treatment that, as we shall see, conforms rather closely (if not exactly) to Hegel's treatment of the history of religion. It is to that treatment of the history of religion/s to which we now turn.

## History of Religion/s

Tiele's actual history of religion reflects these more abstract principles rather directly. His treatment of the materials of the history of religions is predicated on a categorical distinction between *kinds* of religions, a distinction he goes to some pains to emphasize. This distinction is drawn in both the tone and the content of the language of the following passage:

> What a difference between the Hera of Argos, who was little more than a fetish, and the goddess full of majesty, worthily chosen to be the consort of the greatest of the gods, to be united with him in chaste though not always peaceful marriage! What a gulf between the rude boorish religion of the ancient Romans and the worship of Jupiter Capitolinus, to whose temple the noble Scipio Africanus went up every morning in order to prepare himself for his daily tasks, and who for a long period beheld the whole civilized world at his feet![51]

The great Roman, a master of civilization, who stands at the origin of "us," of "that project called 'Europe,' " worships in a categorically different way than do the "rude," the "boorish," the fetishists, the polydaemonists, the worshipers of magic, of merely tribal religions (as opposed to higher, national religions; see below).

This is no passing issue for Tiele. It constitutes the definition of religion and the core of his typology of religions, a typology that is at once synchronic and diachronic. He articulates this in reference to a series of similar definitions and/or typologies proposed by other writers: "I mean those described by Whitney as unconsciously growing, and distinguished by him from those instituted by individual founders, which are not materially different from those called naturalistic and supra-naturalistic by the well-known German philosopher Eduard von Hartmann, and which I prefer to characterize as the nature religions and the ethical religions."[52]

Another defining feature of this categorical distinction between kinds of religions is the idea of history. Tiele demarcates both the first order material of the history of religion and the second order discipline of the History of Religion as follows: "A description of the so-called nature-religions, which belongs to ethnology, is excluded from our design for obvious reasons. *They have no history*; and in the historic chain they only serve to enable us to form an idea of the ancient prehistoric animistic religions of which they are the remains, or, it may be said, the ruins."[53] As we saw earlier with Hegel, there is a direct correlation between the *Entwicklung* of *Geist* and being "inside" or "outside" of History—with a capital "H." Tiele will argue, as we will see below, that nature religions and/or animism, is an undifferentiated whole, without context, cultural specificity, or individuality. Just as a birch tree, an object of nature, partakes of the same nature (essence, *Wesen*) in America as it does in Asia or Africa, so nature religions are not differentiated by the work of human labor and spirit: "they have no history." This echoes, though it is not identical with, Dilthey's dictum: "Nature is explained, culture is understood." Nature does not have a history in the proper sense of "history."

The structure of oppositions, then, which constitute both the second order discourse of the science of religion and the first order data religion, here is: unconscious (undifferentiated collective?) versus individuation ("founding" is an explicit act of an individualized subject/agent), nature versus supra-nature (with clear implications of an "above" and a "below"), and natural versus ethical, with the obvious implication that the "merely" natural is less than (Tiele calls nature religions "lower religions") ethical religions, and "ethnography," that is, race, that is, nature, and "history," that is, culture, that is, spirit. The division, then, between nature and spirit, is a structural principal of the history of religions, a fact about which Tiele is adamant: "It is *one of the most certain facts established by historical investigation* that there is nowhere in the whole history of the development of religion so distinct a cleavage, so sharp a demarcation, as between what we have called the nature and the ethical religions."[54] *Science*, not theology, not morality, not *Kultur*, not ethnic identity, draws this conclusion, so Tiele argues. The argument is, again, a fortiori, not ad hoc.

Similarly, Tiele draws a sharp contrast between the mode of development (*Entwicklung*, again, "unfolding" from within) of nature religions and ethical religions:

> In the case of the latter [ethical religions] we feel at once that there has been a new departure, that an entirely new order of things supersedes the old. Wherever one nature religion or one ethical religion (as we shall meanwhile continue to call them) merges in another of like kind, the transition is generally gradual, sometimes hardly perceptible, and only noticeable in the later development, or at all events it is not the result of a violent change. But the substitution of ethical religions for nature religions is, as a rule, the result of a revolution, or at least of an intentional reform. Yet the former have undoubtedly developed out of the latter. They have long, in embryonic condition, slumbered in the bosom of the nature-religions, where they have gradually matured before they saw the light; but their birth comes as a surprise, a catastrophe. And as soon as they come into existence they assume an attitude of opposition to the prevailing religion.[55]

Again, the difference is not one of degree, nor is it one of particular circumstance ("genealogical," in his terms); it is, rather, a difference *in kind*. Nature religions grow smoothly out of one another, as they are essentially of the same species or kind, as a new branch grows off the same tree without a violent break, but simply in continuity with the essential nature of the tree. The growth of an ethical religion out of a nature religion, though an admitted fact (if a somewhat begrudged fact, from the tone of the text), comes as a violent, oppositional disruption. The ethical and the natural are not the same *kinds* of phenomena; they are, in fact, inherently opposed. The relationship between them, then, is always marked by violence.

*Stages in the History of Religion*

Tiele's view of the development of what he calls the religious idea, though not as thoroughly articulated as is Hegel's, is nevertheless quite similar. The driving engine is a process of rationalization:

It is on various grounds probable that the earliest religion, which has left but faint traces behind it, was followed by a period in which Animism generally prevailed. This stage, which is still represented by the so-called Nature-religions, or rather by the polydaemonistic magic tribal religions, early developed among civilized nations into polytheistic national religions resting upon a traditional doctrine. Not until a later period did polytheism give place here and there to nomistic religions, or religious communities founded on a law or holy scripture, and subduing polytheism more or less completely beneath pantheism or monotheism. These last, again, contain the roots of the Universal or world religions, which start from principles and maxims. Were we to confine ourselves to a sketch of the abstract development of the religious idea in humanity, we should have to follow this order.[56]

While there is an *Ur*-religion, animism, or "nature religion" is the earliest form of religion known to us. It is "prima," then in both a diachronic and an ontological sense: first in history, but first in that it is closest to nature. It is also, we should note, held by Tiele to be still present in the form of "tribal" religions. These "tribal" peoples are, of course, by and large, peoples dominated by European colonization. The pattern of development is *away* from nature *toward* reason/spirit. This nature religion is "subdued" by the development of the nation out of the tribe, and by the formation of laws and of the idea of the holy—all of which are logocentric philosophemes which imply rationalization, that is, "spiritualization," or humanization, over and against nature. There is a categorical break between religions that precede the "Universal" religions, in that the older religions develop out of animism, or nature religion, while Universal religions are founded on a rational basis, that is, upon "principles and maxims." Thus, we have the unfolding of the religious idea throughout the stages of humanity.

Such is the theoretical conceptualization of the development—*Entwicklung*—of religions. Tiele's "empirical" narrative in of the history of religion in *Outlines* divides religion up into the following successive stages:

1. From the polydaemonistic magic tribal religions of the present day we shall endeavor to become acquainted

with Animism, this being the form of religion that must have preceded the religions known to us by history, and served as their foundation (of which the Mexicans and Peruvians and the Finns will be an example)

2. Religion among the Chinese;

3. Among the Egyptians, the Semites proper, and the northern Semites or Mesopotamians, in connection with whom the Akkadian religion, which dominates all the north Semitic religions, will be discussed;

4. Among the Indo-Germans who came little, or not at all, into contact with the Semites, the Aryans, Hindus, Eranians, Letto-Slavs, and Germans;

5. Among the Indo-Germans in whose religion the national elements were supplemented and blended with others of north Semitic or Hamitic origin, viz., the Greeks and Romans.[57]

While not completely conforming to Hegel's more elaborate metanarrative of *Geist*, Tiele's metanarrative does not differ significantly from it. We start in "nature" and in "pre-history" (again, a term loaded with important connotations), then we move to "the East," viz., China, then to the "Middle East," onto the Aryans (Indo-Germans—*not* Indo-Europeans) and end in the West, viz., the "cradle" of European civilization, Greece and Rome. History, with a capital "H," culminates with "us."

*Animism (aka, Race)*

In order to fully explicate the politics of *Geist* and the power/knowledge correlation it sets up, it will be instructive to look at the ways in which Tiele deals with two primary pieces of data: animism, or "nature religions," and "the East," especially China. For brevity's sake, the following discussion will be confined to these areas of the history of religions. We have seen how these are critical sites in the construction of the logo- and Eurocentric metanarrative of *Geist*, so his treatment of these will be telling for our thesis.

Tiele offers the following definition of animism: "Animism is not itself a religion, but a sort of primitive philosophy, which not only controls religion, but rules the whole life of the natural man. It is the belief in the existence of souls or spirits, of which only the powerful—those on which man feels himself dependent, and before which he stands in awe—acquire, the rank, of divine beings, and become objects of worship."[58] By "philosophy," of course, Tiele means an "idea" or conception. His methodological idealism is consistent in that regard. Although it is a "philosophy," it is nevertheless primitive, that is, part of the life of the "natural man" as opposed to the more spiritualized, rational, national, and ethical "man" of the higher stages of civilization.

This primitive and nonrational "idea" begets a similar kind of religion: "The religions controlled by Animism are characterized, first of all, by a varied, confused, and indeterminate doctrine, an unorganized polydaemonism, which does not, however, exclude the belief in a supreme spirit, though in practice this commonly bears but little fruit... and in the next place, by magic, which but rarely rises to real worship."[59] Lacking the rational determination of spirit or mind to form a true moral fiber, the peoples and religions of nature are predicated on a base sensualism and hedonistic imperative: "In the animistic religions fear is more powerful than any other feeling, such as gratitude or trust. The spirits and their worshippers are alike selfish. The evil spirits receive, as a rule, more homage than the good, the lower more than the higher, the local more than the remote, the special more than the general. The allotment of their rewards or punishments depends not on men's good or bad actions, but on the sacrifices and gifts which are offered to them or withheld."[60] This is, of course, an image of an irrational, even "inverted world": evil prevails over good, the specific prevails over the general, the pecuniary over moral principle. Clearly, with animism, "man" has *not* "grown up in religious self-consciousness." As Hegel noted, when humans exist in a state of nature, they are evil, that is, they live in an ethically inverted world. This is further evident in the lack of moral principles in animism: "With morality this religion has little or no connection."[61] In this scheme, "moral" is synonymous with "spiritual," that which differentiates "man" from "nature," (as well as its correlates, "rational," "national," etc.).

Tiele closely associates animism with race and is not shy about naming names. In a typical passage, he invokes a concatenation of peoples whose defining characteristic is their natural/racial "character": "Moreover, among races the most widely separated, the Negroes, Polynesians, and Americans, there exist certain secret associations, types of the later mysteries and sacred orders, which exercise a most formidable influence."[62] Unlike historical religions, animism is an undifferentiated mass which is the same everywhere, but for detail and nuance: the "animistic religion is, in its nature [i.e., *Wesen*, essence], and even in its ideas and usages, with slight modification everywhere the same."[63] This is, of course, in keeping with the Idealist/Hegelian view of the difference between *Natur* and *Geist*: *Geist* self-differentiates and acts back upon itself, while *Natur* is a uniform, ahistorical, atemporal passive substance—rather than a self-conscious, self-actualizing, self-differentiating subject.

His characterization of race and of specific races is instructive for our thesis. In a sweeping statement, he makes essentialist characterizations of several different ethnic-cultural groups: "The joyous careless disposition of the sensual Negro is reflected in his religion as clearly as the somber melancholy character of the American Indian in his. If the latter is endowed with much more poetic feeling than the former, whose mythology is of the poorest order, and in this resembles that of the Semites, he is surpassed by the poetic genius of, the Polynesian, which displays itself in his rich mythology."[64] Each race is, stereotypically, endowed with its unique gifts. Underlying this uniqueness is, at the very least, a complete homogeneity of in-group features, that is, an essential nature.

He does not say much about Africans or Polynesians that is instructive, but his characterization of Native Americans is interesting. He ties them to nature and, in keeping with the Hegelian view of *Natur* as uniform and indistinct, he argues for an essential homogeneity—and deficiency—in all Native American societies:

> The original religions of America exhibit religious Animism at every stage of development. In one and the same race, whose religions possess everywhere the same distinctive character, and have certain peculiar usages in common.... Among some tribes, such as the Shoshonee and Comanches in North America, the Botokuds and Ototmaks, the Pampas Indians, some of the Brazilian savages, and the Terra-del-Fuegians of South America, hardly anything more than the first germs of a *cultus* is to be traced.[65]

Lacking fully developed *Geist*, the Native American mostly lacks true religion. That they lack *Geist* and are closer to *Natur* is a point about which Tiele is quite explicit. Speaking of the Shoshone and Comanche, he cites a government document—a colonial source—as evidence of this fact: "the Shoshonee and Comanches, tribes which stand 'nearer to the brutes than probably any other portion of the human race' (*Report of the Comm. of Indian Affairs*, 1854, p. 209)."[66]

One would think that Tiele would see the urban civilizations of Native, Meso-America in a different light. However, this is not the case. Speaking of even the most "advanced" nations of the Amerindians, the Aztecs and the Mayans, Tiele argues that: "The beings whom these nations worship, are as yet no gods in the strict sense, i.e., supernatural beings, they are hardly more than spirits: they are, however, the representatives of the higher powers and phenomena of nature."[67] He does note that: "Yet in their conception of the higher powers, and in the relation in which they imagined themselves to stand to them, it is impossible not to recognize the beginnings of a purer and more rational view."[68] The contrast, however, is telling: by claiming the "beginnings" of a purer and more rational view, he is clearly claiming that this is not typical of these peoples. What is typical, by implication—and explicit statement—is that they are, by contrast, impure and irrational.

He does not only treat non-Europeans in this manner. He extends this analysis to the Finns, which, although "European" in contemporary geographic terms, are not Aryans, a point he goes to some length to make: "Over a large extent of Asia and Europe the Aryans, and perhaps also the Semites, were preceded by Turanian peoples."[69] The religion of these non-Aryans is also a nature religion in Tiele's specific sense, and, as such, lacking moralization: "All the spirits which they [the Finns] worship, even the highest, are nature-beings of more or less might, but chiefly eminent for their magical power, and rarely endowed with moral qualities."[70] Tiele discusses their chief deity, Ukko, as high god and creator, and describes him as follows: "The ethical element is almost entirely deficient. Even in the representation of Ukko I have not succeeded in discovering it. Evil spirits and good cry to him for help, and he grants it, alike"[71] Although literate, this does not raise them above *Natur*. About their epic poems, collected under the name of Kalevala, he says: "the subject of which is not a moral or national conflict, but simply the contest of the powers of nature personified."[72] His final, summary statement about these non-Aryans connects them back with the other non-European racial groups discussed above: "The worship of spirits (the chief of whom are called *Haltia*) and the doctrine of immortality are not developed any further among the Finns than among the Nature-peoples."[73]

Finally, an interesting methodological feature develops here. While much of *Religionswissenschaft* and phenomenology of religion have been well-nigh obsessed with advocating a nonreductive argument for religion, Tiele here rather readily employs reductive, or quasi-reductive arguments for the variations of animism throughout the races:

> The influence of the locality and the occupation of the different peoples must also be taken into account. Lowest in the scale stands the religion of the root-digging Australians, who do, indeed, engage in hunting, but show little skill in it, and that of the Bosjesmans, who live largely by plunder. The religion of the Koikoin or Hottentots, and of the Kaffirs, who are both for the most part pastoral tribes, is mild, that of some of the war-loving Negro tribes sanguinary and cruel; while among those Negroes who are engaged chiefly in industry and commerce, without neglecting cattle-breeding and agriculture, a much more humane and civilized worship prevails; in which however the spirit of trade shows itself in a certain cunning towards the spirits. The myths of the Polynesians at once betray that they have sprung up among a people of husbandmen and fishermen, and their religious customs correspond entirely to the beneficent nature which surrounds them.[74]

The reason for this seems relatively clear (if not defensible): these races have not yet emancipated themselves fully from nature, and so are more susceptible to its influence. True spirit, true mind, namely, *Geist*, will come along at a later stage of history and then religion/s will be sui generis, autonomous, and fully other than *Natur*. The qualitative difference between these groups of people, between *Naturvölker* and later civilized "man," requires qualitatively different scientific principles of explanation. While this may be objectionable as a scientific approach, it is *completely consistent* with the fundamental assumptions of an Idealist conception of "History," rooted as it is in the radical difference between "mind," "consciousness," or *Geist*, and "body," "sense-perception," or *Natur*.

## "The East": China

So much for those peoples explicitly labeled as *Naturvölker*. One would think that ancient, literate civilizations with established states, even empires, would be treated differently. Not necessarily. In a move both quite consistent with his own methodology and with the Hegelian metanarrative of *Geist*, Tiele claims that the distinctive feature of Chinese religion is, again, its relative proximity to *Natur*: "The religion of the old Chinese Empire, as it existed certainly from the twelfth century B.C., and probably at a much earlier period, is best described as a purified and organized worship of spirits, with a predominant fetishist tendency, combined into a system.... The sole objects of worship are the spirits (*shin*)."[75] For Tiele, the distinction between "gods" and "spirits," as was seen above in a discussion of the Aztecs and Mayans, is a distinction between more and less developed, between the emergence of personality out of nature. This is further borne out by his assessment of ancient Chinese ideas of immortality: "The doctrine of continued existence after death among the Chinese entirely accords with that of the Nature-peoples."[76] Spirit, personality, has not yet emerged from the germ in the East; only blind nature is found here.

As he will with Hinduism, Tiele sees China as a mixed form of religion, residing somewhere between a full-blown ethical religion and a backward nature religion. While he says above that Chinese religion barely rises above the level of spirit worship, he qualifies this in a positive (if somewhat backhanded) way: "It may be regarded as a great advance that there is no mention of essentially evil spirits, that all spirits are exalted servants of Shang-ti, and in their intercourse with men esteem moral qualities above everything else."[77] We saw above in his description of the Finns and other *Naturvölker* that they did not differentiate between the worship of good spirits and evil spirits. A sensuous hedonism prevails in their religiosity at the expense of a higher moral conception of deity. Not so with the Chinese; there is at least a minimal conception of morality in their religious conceptions.

The ambiguity Tiele finds in the Chinese shows itself in the way in which he contrasts Confucius and Confucianism with Lao Tzu and Taoism. Although he makes some qualifications on the issue, he counts Confucianism as an ethical religion.[78] In so doing, however, Tiele is quick to include an argument for inferiority of Taoism:

> The question whether Taoism, the other great Chinese religion, can be deemed an ethical religion has yet to undergo an investigation for which I do not consider myself qualified; but judging from its historical development I suspect that it has no such claim. For, although it appeals to Lao-tse, the other great Chinese sage, an older contemporary of Kong, and highly revered but not followed by the latter, and to his *Tao-te-King*, the book of the *Way and the Virtue*, as a sacred writ, I fear that it can just as little claim such a title as it is possible to find relationship between the silly superstitions and dreary magic arts in which it delights, and the gloomy but profound speculations of the master.[79]

So we see that, despite what many feel is a religion of tremendous philosophical sophistication, Tiele sees Taoism as a crude nature religion and the lofty thought of Lao Tzu as "profound" but "gloomy."[80] The terms of denigration are, again, the predominance of the natural, despite the presence of "sacred writ" (a consistently logocentric criterion of valuation) over the *geistig*, over those "departments" of spirit that make religions higher.

In this contrast Tiele seems to be implying two things, both interrelated and both consistent with the Hegelian notion of the relationship between nature, form, ethics, and development. On the one hand, he seems to imply that Taoism is a religion of the people, and so represents the majority of Chinese, their character, their *Wesen*, and their relative stage of *Entwicklung*, more accurately than does Confucianism. He says of Taoism: "The often obscure system developed in the *Tao-te-King* is purely Chinese."[81] Taoism, he seems to be arguing, is the "real" ethnic and religious context of China. He argues that it is both primitive and ancient: "This religious community [the Taoists] represents rather the spiritist side of Animism. As a religious tendency it existed from the earliest times, and even tried to derive its origin from the ancient Emperor Hoang-ti."[82] He argues further that, as a religion, Taoism "is marked by a morbid asceticism, and takes up an attitude of hostility toward civilization and progress, but it is distinguished by a pure and sometimes elevated morality."[83]

Confucianism, by contrast, seems to be a religion of the literati, of the elite,[84] and, more importantly, of the state. In this discursive universe, a state religion is by definition more formal, more abstract, less tied to passion, to the senses, interests, and so to nature. China, then, although emerging into *Geist*, into freedom, is still mostly tied to *Natur*. This is a point further supported by Tiele's view that the spheres of religion and politics have yet achieved autonomy in China. Speaking of a series of persecutions, Tiele notes: "The occasion of the persecution was political rather than religious, although between these two spheres no sharp distinction can be made in China."[85] As Hegel said and Tiele confirmed in his view of the oppositional nature of *Entwicklung*, full separation and individuation are the prerequisites for real reconciliation, which leads to self-consciousness.

While Confucius represents an advance from the gloomy, confused nature mysticism of Lao Tzu, Tiele clearly qualifies even this view. On the one hand, Tiele describes Confucius as having had "a high sense of calling, and attached great value to purity of morals," and he also notes that he was "inordinately punctilious about all forms, and perhaps not wholly free from superstition."[86] This is explained by his milieu: "If he thus appears somewhat narrow-minded, whoever judges him by the age in which he lived and the nation to which he belonged, notes the powerful impression he made upon friends and foes."[87] His unique and distinctive personality stands out from the milieu in which history finds him.

Finally, Confucius's teachings are also tied to *Natur*, making the seeming escape from *Natur* limited, even in this "ethical" religion: "The religious doctrine of Kong-tse is ethical naturalism, founded on the state religion of the Tshow."[88] In the discursive context I have elaborated throughout this book, the term *ethical naturalism* must strike the ear in a rather definite way. It is quite clearly a lefthanded compliment, almost an oxymoron, a way of staking Confucianism, which Tiele clearly regards as the highest development of Chinese religion, to a backward nature religion.

China, then, in Tiele's scheme, will play no large part in *Weltgeschichte* because it is too bound up with its own peculiar ethnicity. As such, neither Taoism nor Confucianism can rise to the level of universal religions, "yet they prove too national for either of them to become a universal religion. It was only when Chinese civilization made its way complete, as in Corea [sic] or Japan, that the Chinese religion, especially the doctrine and worship of Kong-tse, was adopted with it."[89] Tiele seems to be agreeing with Hegel when Hegel says that "[t]he existence of a national spirit is broken when it has used up and exhausted itself. World history, the World Spirit, continues on its course."[90] Tiele's idea of development and his correlative notion of the relationship between spirit and nature would further seem to force him to concur with Hegel's assessment of the state of a nation or people when they have lost their place in *Weltgeschichte*:

> After this period, the declining nation has lost the interest of the absolute; it may indeed absorb the higher principle positively and begin building its life on it, but the principle is only like an adopted child, not like a relative to whom its ties are immanently vital and vigorous. Perhaps it loses its autonomy, or it may still exist, or drag out its existence, as a particular state or a group of states and involve itself without rhyme or reason in manifold enterprises at home and battles abroad.[91]

China and the Chinese live on, but they will not be part of the modern era. As we shall see, that era belongs to a different religion, viz., Christianity.

### Christianity, the Consummate Religion

"[I]f therefore we place Christianity as a form of religion among the most highly developed ethical religions, it will be on purely scientific grounds. And if we place it in the same category as others, such as Buddhism, we by no means imply that it is of equal religious value."[92] Citing Eduard von Hartmann's view that there are two poles in religion, an objective pole and a subjective one, and that in Christianity these two poles are reconciled, Tiele argues that "this forms, indeed, the foundation of Christianity, but is only now beginning to realize itself in that religion as the only one possible for the modern world. This is one of the subtle observations, so suggestive, so profitable for further investigation, in which his book abounds."[93] Christianity is not only a religion of reconciliation, it is moment of reconciliation of religion with the other domains of spirit. All of this follows from the scientific presuppositions which Tiele has previously articulated.

As "man grows up in religious self-consciousness," he comes to realize himself as distinct from nature, he has himself for himself as an object of contemplation. Religion, as the most "spiritual" element of Spirit, plays a central role in this process: "[T]he development of religion is the necessary consummation of all human development, and is at once demanded and promoted by it."[94] Tiele makes this point repeatedly, always along the same lines: "that religion, though not the mother of civilization, exerts the profoundest and mightiest influence over it, while in turn it gains sustenance from civilization, borrowing from it, and assimilating, whatever may conduce to its own growth. Religion is so intimately bound up with man's personality that it wields a kind of central authority over all the other activities of his spiritual life. It is, in fact, the great motive power of all higher development and progress."[95] Without religion, "man" (Tiele's term) is lost and tend to degenerate toward his lower element.

If religion is, as it were, the essence of the essence of "man," then Christianity is the highest point in the development of religion, a point that shall be addressed later. After noting that it may appear to compromise his scientific and impartial position, he nevertheless claims that: "even from this point of view [i.e., the scientific investigation of religion], and as the result of historic and philosophic investigation, I maintain that the appearance of Christianity inaugurated an entirely new epoch in the development of religion; that all the streams of the religious life of man, once separate, unite in it; and that religious development will henceforth consist in an ever higher realization of the principles of that religion."[96] The inner τελος of *Entwicklung* then is the increase in self-consciousness, of which religion is the consummation; and the consummation of religion is the arrival of Christianity. Tiele makes this claim, it should be noted, *not* as a theologian, but as a *Religionswissenschaftler*, as a scientist whose duty it is to trace out the laws of the *Entwicklung* of Spirit.[97] One may judge as to whether Tiele's Christocentrism is derived from his logocentrism, or his logocentrism is derived from his Christocentrism. However, what is clear is that *the two are intimately correlated*. We witness this in the way *Religionswissenschaft* crowns Christianity as the highest development of religion.

Tiele makes this argument on the basis of his developmental morphology of both the object of religion, conceptions of God, and the subject of religion, believing human beings. Speaking of the object of religion, Tiele asks:

> What then, it may be asked, has the only, eternal, all-wise and powerful, omnipresent and omniscient, holy, just, merciful, and gracious God, whom Christians, Jews, and Mohammedans alike worship, albeit in different ways—the God whom the Gospel proclaims as the Perfect one, the loving, all-attracting, all-reconciling heavenly Father—what has He in common with even the highest of the nature-gods, the Zeus-Jupiter of Hellas and Rome, not to speak of the bloodthirsty beings in whose honour Canaanites and Moabites, Accadians, Celts, Mexicans, and many others slaughtered their fellow-men and even their own children? What has He in common with the gods (not to descend to the lowest stage) whose power extends over a limited domain only, who have been born and who die, who are swayed by the lower passions and are subject to human weaknesses?[98]

While there is an affirmative to this series of questions—all conceptions of deity do have something in common—the rhetorical framing of it clearly indicates a hierarchical view of the value of various peoples' conceptions of their gods. As with Hegel, though not as explicitly stated: you know a people by their god. This is even more explicit when he turns to the subjective side of religion, the human beings who hold such conceptions:

> Have we ourselves nothing in common with the people who worshipped these beings? Is not the difference between

their gods and ours essentially the same as the difference which separates them from us, though they were men of the same mould as ourselves? We need not at present inquire into the causes of that difference, as we have investigated them already. It is a difference of capacity and of circumstances, but still more a difference in development—the difference between the grain of mustard-seed and the tree in whose branches lodge the fowls of the air, the difference between the stammering child and the mighty orator, between the unbridled fancy of the youth and the ripe wisdom of the experienced thinker.[99]

Again, while there is an essential kernel, there is all the difference between the impotent kernel and the fully realized oak tree. On both the objective and subjective sides of the study of religion, then, it is clear that Tiele sees Christianity as the superior religion (always only a small step away from seeing it as the religion of the superior: you know a people by their god).

Tiele also makes the argument for the supremacy of Christianity on the grounds that it is the only truly universal religion. As we have seen, Tiele devotes a considerable amount of time and intellectual capital in distinguishing ethical religions from nature religions. He makes a similar, though not as drastic distinction between ethical religions and universal religions, of which there are three: "I shall not select for the purpose one of the two great world-religions, Buddhism and Christianity, which, having sprung up within limited circles, and having been rejected, after a longer or shorter struggle, by the very peoples from which they emanated, now count their adherents by many millions; nor shall I select their mighty rival Mohammedanism, which can only be called a world-religion with certain reservations."[100] In asserting the supremacy of Christianity, he argues that it is the only truly universal religion. He does this, in part, by arguing that the other two contenders are each flawed in a particular way. Islam's flaw is, according to Tiele, and this is an argument about Islam which we will see repeated numerous times, is too "ethnic," or, in Tiele's terms, "particularistic." He makes this contrast as follows:

> In short, Buddhism as well as Christianity are universalistic in character, while all the other ethical religions are in the main particularistic. Of these Mohammedanism is the least particularistic. This religion also extends to all nationalities, and makes no distinction between Arabian believers and

converts of other nations. But its sacred language, its obligatory pilgrimage to Mecca and Medina, and its minutely detailed legal ceremonial, render it far more particularistic than either Buddhism or Christianity, to which it is inferior in other respects also. Born of a combination of Judaism with an ill-understood and degenerate Christianity, and grafted on the Arabian religion at a time when the highest religious development was making itself felt, it was in fact compelled, if it would vie with Christianity, to adopt the form of a universalistic religion; but it remained much more Semitic and even Arabic than Buddhism was Aryan or Indian; while it entirely lacks the *general human element of Christianity* and its marvelous adaptability to the most divergent of human needs.[101]

Again, "Christian" is equated with "human" in the most universal sense. Islam, however, still mixes its ethical element (i.e., universal, rational principles) with its ethnicity. Its transitory, temporal dimensions or "husk" has not yet been shed (and there is no indication that it will be).

The problem with Buddhism as a truly universal religion is quite different in character. It is not that it is too "ethnic"; it is too rational, having gone so far in its "one-sided development" in that direction that it is no longer really a "religion" at all. In a statement that captures all elements of his separatist and supremacist argument for Christianity, Tiele says:

> Professor von Siebeck has therefore called Islâm a *Rückbildung*, a decline to a lower plane; and when I formerly classed it with Buddhism and Christianity among the so-called World-religions, several scholars protested. And I admit that there is a material difference between Islâm and these two great religions, inasmuch as Islâm did not spontaneously produce the universalistic principle as a necessary corollary of its fundamental conceptions, but borrowed it from Christianity, and accepted it in a political more than in a religious sense. In fact the universalism of Islâm differs little from, and is but an extension of, the proselytism of Judaism. It is a world-religion in the same sense as we speak of a world-monarchy, a religion essentially national and in so far particularistic, yet striving to subjugate the world and to substitute Mecca for Jerusalem as its religious

> capital. Further study and reflection, however, have led me to take a somewhat different view of this subject, especially as regards Buddhism and Christianity, from that which I formerly held in common with others. Have we not, by ranking these two religions with the other ethical religions, though on a higher platform, unwittingly coordinated what is really heterogeneous? Can we—and this is the chief question—call them religions in the same sense as the Jewish, the Parsee, or any other? It is not on the ground that Buddhism might originally be called atheistic, and therefore not a religion at all . . .[102]

Christianity, then, stands alone among even the three most universal religions. Unlike Islam, it is *allgemein*, general, universal, and human, and has transcended its ethnic particularity. Unlike Buddhism, which becomes so rationalistic, that is, so abstractly universal, it remains truly religious. As the modern is to the developed, and the past is to the undeveloped, as the developed is the rational, and the rational is the *geistig*, the truly human, Christianity is, a fortiori from the findings of the science of religion, the most universal expression of the human spirit and therefore the religion for Modernity. History, science, reason, culture and religion all find their consummation in essential principles of the Christian religion.

Tiele ends with a definite note of triumphalism by evoking the theme of reconciliation of Spirit with itself, of science with culture and with religion—*all based on the facts* of the history of religion. Religion is central to History: "Nothing can be more absurd, or rather nothing sadder, than an attempt to ignore religion in the writing of history."[103] Although he rejects the idea that the science of religion will inaugurate a new religion or new era in religion, as science is an expression of Spirit, he does argue that it will be the handmaiden of Spirit in a "homecoming" scenario played out in the house of the Father:

> Our science cannot call forth such a manifestation [of religion], but it may pave the way for it by tracing the evolution of religion, explaining its essentials, and showing where its origin is to be sought for. Let it do its own duty in throwing light upon the part that religion has ever played in the history of mankind, and still plays in every human soul. And then, without preaching, or special pleading, or apologetic argument, *but solely by means of the actual facts it*

*reveals*, our beloved science will help to bring home to the restless spirits of our time the truth that there is no rest for them unless "they arise and go to their Father."[104]

As we shall see, later *Religionswissenschaftlichers*, especially Rudolf Otto and Mircea Eliade, will make similar evocations.

# 5

# "Experience, Expression, Understanding"
## Wilhelm Dilthey on *Geist* and the Methodology of the *Geisteswissenschaft*

David Palmer refers to what he calls "Dilthey's hermeneutical formula" as having three major components, viz., "experience, expression, understanding,"[1] or, in German, *Erlebnis, Ausdruck, Verstehen*. Palmer also quite rightly notes that, despite the widespread use of, and conventionally assumed correlation between these terms, "this formula of 'experience-expression-understanding' is far from self-explanatory."[2] These three categories will form the structure of this discussion of Dilthey and the principal task will be to explicate the meaning and play of these terms.

### Experience *(Erlebnis)*

The first of the terms of this "hermeneutical formula," *Erlebnis*, is a term unique to Dilthey and is directly associated with his philosophy: "*Erlebnis* as a singular noun was virtually nonexistent in German before Dilthey's use of it in a highly specific sense."[3] The distinctness of this term stems from the fact that there are two words in German for "experience": "*Erfahrung* and the more technical and recent *Erlebnis*. The former refers to experience in general, as when one refers to his "experience" in life. Dilthey uses the more specific and limited term *Erlebnis*, coined from the verb *erleben* (to experience, especially in individual instances)."[4]

*Inner Experience*

"All science is a science of experience; but all experience has its original constitution and validity in the conditions of consciousness, in which it takes place—in the totality of our nature. We call this standpoint ... the epistemological standpoint; modern science can recognize no other."[5] With this statement Dilthey lays out his entire agenda for the human sciences. Science is based upon experience, not rational "construction" (as metaphysics is often referred to in this period), but experience is not simply a "bundle of percepts" as radical empiricists had argued. Experience is the manifestation of the totality of human nature and this human nature can be read off of its manifestations in history, that is, all forms of human self-expression in politics, society, economics, and culture—including religion.

As such, Dilthey's approach can be described as working from the inside out; from inner human experience and its "conditions of consciousness" to outer manifestations in cultural products—which, in turn, can be read back "into" this originating inner experience. Therefore, in order correctly and fully to understand the unique aspects of human experience, as opposed to mere perception, it is necessary to separate the purely inner, purely human element of "experience," or *Erlebnis*, from external components of that experience. In this vein, Dilthey argues: "[T]hose events the mind links together out of material supplied exclusively by the sense [must] be separated as a special class from facts given primarily in inner experience (i.e., without any cooperation of the senses) and are then formed out of the original stuff of inner experience.... Thus a special realm of experiences emerges, which has its independent origin and its content in inner experience and accordingly is naturally the object of a special science of experience."[6] Dilthey here is making an important point, which, although it is couched in the language of phenomenality, is, and is meant to stand, in sharp contrast to classical forms of empiricist arguments. "Inner experience" is precisely *not* "perception." Perceptions are stimuli that come from outside consciousness. Inner experiences (*Innerwerden*) are those actions of consciousness upon, to, and for itself. Willing and imagination are prime examples of the action of consciousness upon itself. Objects of perception are formed by the interaction, or "cooperation," between inner experience and externally derived sense stimuli. But objects of experience, or their mental representations (*Vorstellungen*), are a qualitatively distinct class of experiential events according to Dilthey.

This inner experience is apodictic and is, as such, the foundation for a science of experience: "[E]very object, as well as every feeling, is given as a fact of consciousness, or more succinctly, *is* a fact of consciousness [*Bewußtseintatsachen*]. This entails that existence is attributed to anything and everything that I experience in this way. In fact, the certainty with which existence is asserted here is as immediate as it can be: This knowing [*Wissens*] is not only immediate, but unshakeable."[7] Its immediacy is rooted in the fact that it is consciousness's own, direct relationship to itself.[8] The very meaning of the idea of an "external world," argues Dilthey, is dependent upon the existence of inner experience and its structure: "[W]e can conceive of no way in which something could stand opposed as something outer to something inner other than its being a fact of consciousness. The object is there only for a subject; what stands over against [*Gegenstand*], only for a consciousness."[9] Object and subject are completely correlative terms, a point which phenomenologists (such as Husserl) take as a basic axiom. Consequently, for any science that takes experience as its starting point, interiority or subjectivity must be taken into account.

The difference between Dilthey and this strand of thought in German intellectual history and typical Anglo-American Empiricism is that the key issue is *not* a matter of finding a "correlation" between the mental representation of an object and the extramental object, but on the logical, experiential, even dialectical correlation between the subject and its object. The empiricist theory of correlation results in putting the emphasis on the side of the object. Dilthey is concerned to return the emphasis, even primacy, to the side of the subject. It is not, finally, the subject's relation to an external object that is of primary concern, it is the *subject's relation to itself* that forms the foundation for both life and for science. This is, of course, another way of asserting the ultimate autonomy, or freedom of consciousness: it is even free from sensation, that is, that which is outside itself, not itself, or is other than itself.

The key characteristic of this inner experience, which separates it from perception, is its reflexivity. What Dilthey calls "reflexive awareness"

> is a consciousness that does not place a content over against the subject of consciousness (it does not re-present it); rather, a content is present in it without any differentiation. That which constitutes its content is in no way distinguished from the act in which it occurs. That which has reflexive awareness is not separated from that which constitutes the content of the awareness. What constitutes the content of consciousness is not distinguished from the consciousness itself.[10]

Again, in this sense, "inner experience" can be seen as the primordial moment of consciousness, underivable from subsequent causes, effects, or events. The editors of Dilthey's text, in a footnote, put the point very clearly: "The reflexive (self-given) is to be distinguished from the reflective (given to thought). Reflexive awareness in its most basic sense is an immediate pre-reflective mode of self-givenness in which the dichotomies of form and content, subject and object characteristic of reflective consciousness do not yet exist."[11] For both the foundationalist point and for the issue of freedom, the distinction between the *self*-given and the given-*to*-self are crucial.

The locus, of course, of this inner experience is consciousness. It is with the concept of consciousness proper that a transition between sheer internality and selfhood proper starts to emerge: "The expression 'consciousness' (*conscientia*) cannot be defined; we can only exhibit what it denotes as an ultimate datum incapable of further analysis. I experience in myself the way in which something (a series of facts) is there for me. No matter how diverse these facts may be that exist in me, what they have in common and what results in their being-there-for-me [*für-mich-da-sein*] I call 'consciousness.' "[12] The being of the object is relative to the subject. The objects of perception constantly change; the subject does not. This "me," which is necessarily attached to every percept, is the ground of their being, and, as such, emerges as something separable.

Although in reflexive awareness there is no full separation between the subject of experience and the object of experience, at the level of consciousness this separation begins to emerge: "Thus I only appear to live among things that exist independent of my consciousness; in reality, my self distinguishes itself from facts of my own consciousness, formations whose locus is in me. *My consciousness is the locus which encompasses this seemingly immeasurable external world.*"[13] Because inner experience is generated internally and is free, it exists separately from the data of sense experience, and hence, as sense of a self that is not identical, as in Hume with a "bundle of percepts," emerges. Selfhood, at least as the correlative structure of objects, is essential, that is, an ever-present unity underlying the flux of stimuli. This self is the foundation of thought, experience, and, as we shall see below, science—at least the human sciences.

Consequently, this self is for Dilthey what Tillich following Heidegger referred to as "the relational center" of the world. Dilthey does not claim that the ego actually *is* the center of the world, or that there is no world outside the self; he resists the claims of Absolute Idealism. More on the model of Husserl and later phenomenologists, this is what he means by "lived-experience," *Erlebnis*: this is how humans *experience* the world. As will be discussed below, the concept of a universal selfhood is the basis for Dilthey's theory of *Verstehen*, which he takes to be the process by which a self comes to know another self. And that point is one of the major methodological concepts of the phenomenology of religion.

A final point on this principle of phenomenality. In contrast to classical epistemological models of the subject (which Dilthey famously described as "bloodless"), the constitution of inner experience is not a matter of a purely rational faculty. It involves the whole human being: "[S]ince whatever is-there-for-us exists by virtue of this inner experience... whatever constitutes a value or purpose for us is so given to us only in the lived experience of our feeling and our will."[14] Once the move to take facts of consciousness as apodictic givens is made, all facts of consciousness are put on an equal footing. We are no longer concerned with the realist or positivist problem of establishing a correlation between inner representations (*Vorstellungen*) and outer objects—because inner experience has been sharply differentiated from representation. So, all those faculties that contribute to the constitution of inner experience are now necessarily part of the analysis of experience which is the basis for the human sciences. As we shall see later in this chapter, this opens the door for a *scientific treatment*—rather than a skeptical, scientific dismissal—of acts and products of imagination (mostly art) and will (politics and morality).

> The most important elements of our image and knowledge of reality—such as the unity of life in the person, the outer world, individuals apart from us, their life in time, and their influence on each other—are all things we can explain from this totality of human nature, whose real life process [*Lebensprozess*] manifests itself in its various aspects through willing, feeling, and imagining. It is not the assumption of a rigid a priori of our cognitive capacity, but only the history of the development alone, proceeding from the totality of our being, which can answer the questions we all have to address to philosophy.[15]

"Values," "purposes," and "goals" now have scientific respectability, a respectability they did not have in rival, positivistic theories of science. Dilthey hopes here to have put the human sciences on a firm, nonmetaphysical basis, to wit, in experience, but not to have surrendered core human values which were so intrinsic to Idealism, yet defended by faulty, nonscientific arguments. In subsequent chapters, it will be clear that this move is basic to phenomenology of religion because, on its basis, religion, too, gains respectability as a scientific object.

On the basis of this line of argument in Dilthey, Andre Bowie makes a point that not only further illuminates Dilthey's argument, but helps connect it to issues that shall be discussed in later in this study:

> Dilthey's ground is precisely "experience" (*Erlebnis*), which, given that it is generally conceived of in pre-propositional terms, puts him in the camp of those whom Derrida regards as seeking "to decipher . . . a truth or an origin that escapes the play and order of the sign." The distinction between *Erlebnis* and *Erfahrung*, both of which can be translated as "experience," lies in the former being an immediate given, an "origin" in Derrida's sense, and the latter, as it is generally in Kant, being the result of a judgment in which a concept is applied to an intuition.[16]

This is an enormously important point for the history we are reviewing here. This separation between inner experience and experience derived from stimuli entails two, correlative points. First, it means that important aspects of consciousness are not caused by forces outside the mind. These free, underivable, internal "facts of consciousness" form a foundation for thought that is apodictic: "Only in inner experience, in facts of consciousness [*Bewußtseintatsachen*], have I found a firm anchor for my thinking, and I am confident that no reader will evade the proof on this point."[17] The reader cannot evade the proof on this point because, following Descartes, Dilthey holds that it is logically impossible for consciousness to deny its own existence. The object of consciousness can always be doubted, but consciousness's relation to itself is, as Husserl (also following Descartes) claimed, is apodictic. As Bowie pointed out above, this is an "origin," or a foundation upon which Dilthey can set the *Geisteswissenschaften*.

Second, and consequently, this separation means there is a "special realm" of mental activity that is sui generis and free. As shall be discussed below and as has been seen from the foregoing, the correlation between freedom and consciousness is a vital issue, arguably the core issue, in this intellectual tradition. In Hegel it is formulated quite explicitly in the definitions of *Natur* and *Geist* discussed previously. In phenomenologists of religion such as Otto and Eliade, this very point of Dilthey's will become the basis for arguing that religious experience must be studied on its own terms, namely, as a "special realm" of experience, and can only be properly understood if understood as originating sui generis in the primordial act/s of consciousness. We shall return to this issue later in our discussion of Dilthey.

## Structure/Nexus (Zusammenhang)

"*Struktur ist alles.*"[18] Another serious difference between Dilthey and classical Anglophonic Empiricism is that, like most Germanic, continental thinkers, Dilthey rejects the idea of the mind as a *tabula rasa*. Such a model is too passive and ignores the mind's active role in shaping the materials it draws from the senses. Dilthey's reliance upon the notions of "structure" and "nexus" are his counterarguments to the *tabula rasa* theory. Experience is never "raw," it is not merely a stream of percepts chaotically floating through consciousness. Rather, it is structured in its very process of apprehension, thus giving the self an inherent "integrity" in a very literal sense of the term. Because of the consistency and coherence supplied by structure, there is a basis, despite the flux of percepts, for an enduring self, and hence, a universal, human nature.

Although he occasionally uses the term *Struktur*, Dilthey much prefers the term *der Zusammenhang*, to describe this structuring activity of consciousness. In Dilthey's texts, this term is most often translated as "nexus,"[19] though it can mean such related things as "coherence," "continuity," or "connection." Both terms indicate the notion of a series of things that are joined together and, as a result of being so joined or connected, become a kind of unity unto themselves.

If the principle of phenomenality, reviewed above, is the first principle of philosophy, what he calls "the second principle of philosophy," is the notion that "the nexus that encompasses the facts of consciousness—including perceptions, memories, objects and representations of them, and finally concepts—is psychological, i.e., it is contained in the totality of psychic life."[20] Percepts and the material of inner experience do not exist in isolation as a mere "bundle of percepts" the way Hume had described them. "Because whatever exists for me—things, persons, axioms, concepts, feelings, acts of will—is apprehended in the psychological nexus of the totality of my consciousness, where it primordially and originally exists..."[21] The nexus, or connections, or joining together of all internal events is absolutely basic for Dilthey. There is no going behind it or underneath it to get to a more primordial ground. As Rodi argues, "Dilthey would claim that his own concept of 'structure' and 'differentiation' was gained solely through the immediate inner experience of 'life itself.'"[22] This is, Dilthey claims, what separates his view from the "constructivism" or a priorism of Hegel and other metaphysicians. Dilthey's science is based on the actual facts of the human mind, taken as a whole, on "lived experience," not merely on rational, deductive categories superimposed upon experience—at least that is his claim.

Rodi also quite rightly argues that the concept of nexus is not a secondary attribute and that it is conceived as a direct corollary to the principle of phenomenality, which he claimed was apodictic: "Dilthey's concept of the structural quality of the life of spirit corresponds to the theory of the intentionality of consciousness in that structure is not merely a psychological fact but the phenomenological description of an essential quality of consciousness."[23]

It is in this "soup" of the nexus of the facts of consciousness that inner experience is shaped into something more than a chaotic flux: "Inner experience arises when inner perceptions are linked together reflectively in the nexus of self-consciousness, and are thus apprehended by means of their characteristics or relations with the self."[24] And not only is this true of inner experience, it is also true of outer experience: "When outer experience is integrated into inner experience as a fact of consciousness, that comprehensive nexus of experience comes into being which is constituted by the facts of consciousness and embraces every state of affairs."[25] Even for external objects, Dilthey argues that "each state of affairs exists *realiter* in the nexus of consciousness."[26] The nexus is the interweaving and integration of all elements of perception. It is through this interweaving process that it becomes "experience."

This experience, as Andre Bowie has noted, in this way the " 'mental nexus (*der seelische Zusammenhang*) forms the ground beneath (*Untergrund*) the process of cognition' of the Kantian subject."[27] As shall be shown with Otto, this is a crucial trope throughout this discourse. That there is an immediate, direct experience, which is not subject to the process of schematization, either of language or of the Kantian categories, was an absolutely foundational claim for this whole approach. Since one of the major Kantian categories was "causality" it became, among other things, possible by means of this move to argue that religious experience was sui generis, that is, not subject to the laws of causation because it arises prior to them. Gadamer confirms this point:

> Even in his ideas on "descriptive and analytical psychology," Dilthey was trying to explain "how one's inner life is woven into continuity" (*Zusammenhang*) in a way that is different from explaining the knowledge of nature by

appeal to the categories. He used the concept of structure to distinguish the experiential character of psychological continuity from the causal continuity of natural processes. Logically "structure" is distinguished by its referring to a totality of relationships that do not depend on a temporal, causal succession but on intrinsic connections.[28]

Just as Dilthey's phenomenalism turns out to be radically different than Anglophonic Empiricism, Dilthey's concept of "psychology" is not a science based on causality, on finding the laws of mental operations, but a "structural" and descriptive psychology which sees the origins of experience as rooted in the mind.[29]

It is on the basis of this concept of a nexus or structure to consciousness that a reconstruction of the "mental world" is made possible: "Accordingly, the explanation of this nexus, in which perceptions and other mental processes are found, must be based on the analysis of psychic life as a whole";[30] "the nexus of the facts of consciousness is thus contained in the totality of psychic life and is to be developed from that totality to whatever extent analysis permits."[31] Given that the meaning of ideas, experiences, and the like are going to be found in the psychic nexus, the reconstruction of the thought of a person, the basic goal of the hermeneutical approach to the human sciences, which Dilthey is here championing, is done by reconstructing that nexus insofar as there are materials available. The more of the nexus that can be recovered the greater the likelihood of correct understanding. So, we move from inner to outer, from the primordial to the structured, and so to the possibility of recovering *meaning*. Commenting on Dilthey's notion of structure, Gadamer makes the following astute point: "Like the coherence of a text, the structural coherence of life is defined as a relation between the whole and the parts."[32] The issue of structure, then, leads to the issue of meaning.

*Meaning (Bedeutung)*

"Thus we come face to face with the category of meaning." [33] The "payoff" for the *Geisteswissenschaften* of the related categories of structure and nexus (or connection, coherence) is that the flux of experience as formed by those categories is meaningful. This is a major point for Dilthey of his articulation of the hermeneutical nature of the *Geisteswissenschaften* hangs on it.

Meaning is *not* something retroactively imposed upon the flux of experience. Rather: "Experience in its concrete reality is made coherent by the category of meaning. This is the unity which, through memory, joins together what has been experienced either directly or through empathy. *Its meaning does not lie in something outside the experiences which gives them unity but is contained in them and constitutes the connections between them.*"[34] Because the content of experience is apodictically given in consciousness and because experience comes to be what is the structuring activity of consciousness itself, experience is, according to Dilthey, inherently meaningful. "Meaning" is an act by which consciousness connects disparate elements of the materials of inner and outer experience and conjoins them into larger wholes. Thus, Gadamer notes: "Experience has a definite immediacy which eludes every opinion about its meaning. Everything that is experienced is experienced by oneself, and part of its meaning is that it belongs to the unity of this self and thus contains an unmistakable and irreplaceable relation to the whole of this one life."[35]

This issue of the "whole" is crucial. Following an ancient hermeneutical tradition, Dilthey holds that, in the interpretations of texts, "meaning" is the result of the part-whole relationship. So also with experience:

> The relation contained in it [the category of meaning] defines and clarifies the conception we have of our lives; it is also the point of view from which we grasp and describe the coexistence and sequence of lives in history, emphasizing what is significant and meaningful and thus shaping every event; it is, quite generally, the category which is peculiar to life and to the historical world; indeed, it is inherent in life because it is the particular relationship which exists between its parts; all life contains this relationship which is essential for describing it.[36]

As was noted above, in the process of reconstructing the thought of another person, the more of the overall nexus, or set of psychic connections, the researcher has, the better the reconstruction. So also with meaning. Individual percepts, events, etc., are made meaningful by their relation to the totality to which they belong. Like most hermeneuticists, Dilthey sees "the whole" on the model of ever larger concentric circles in which each unit is subsumed by larger units. So, in the life of a self, the complete biography of the individual is the whole of which individual events, thoughts, etc., are given meaning. The life of that individual, on the other hand, takes place in a distinct historical and cultural period, and so that larger totality must be understood as completely as possible. Finally, all of these are events within the totality of human experience, and so "world-history" is the final whole of which the life of each individual, each nature, each cultural epoch is but a part—and, as such is meaningful.

This, of course, is how Dilthey came to embrace, with all it philosophical problems, historicism and contextualism; those concepts are very much a part of his legacy and very much a part of the legacy that later phenomenologists of religion, especially van der Leeuw and Eliade would appropriate from him, especially the latter concept. We may note in passing how similar Dilthey's theory of meaning is to Hegel's philosophy of history. As Raymond Betanzos notes: "As in Hegel's *Phenomenology*, so here too, 'the truth is in the whole.' "[37]

The foundation of the category of meaning in experience opens the door to scientific consideration of issues of value: "Meaning, value, purpose, development, ideal, are such categories. But they all depend on the fact that the connectedness of a life can only be understood through the meaning the individual parts have for understanding the whole and that every part of the life of mankind can only be understood in the same way. Meaning is the comprehensive category through which life becomes comprehensible."[38] As noted before, this point was championed by phenomenologists of religion and other scholars because it was seen as a bulwark against a growing tendency to "explain away" values, or simply see discussions of values and purposes as "soft," not part of "hard" science. If values and purposes are inherent, given elements of experience, then they are legitimate subjects of scientific inquiry, and, they can be seen as having a valid ontological status of their own.

Meaning for Dilthey is closely related to memory, and hence to historical reconstruction:

> Because remembering involves recognition everything past is structurally related to a former experience by being a reproduction of it. Future possibilities are also linked to the sequence because of the range of potentialities mapped out by it. Thus, in this process, there arises a view of the continuity of mental life in time which constitutes the course of a life. In this every single experience is related to the whole. This connectedness of life is not a sum or quintessence of successive moments but a unity constituted by relationships which link all the parts.[39]

To understand is to see things as part of a whole; this is intrinsic to the functioning of consciousness and not something foisted onto experience. In this way Dilthey believed he had struck a middle-ground between an overly reductive empiricism and an overly speculative idealism.

The category of "meaning" is also intimately related to the possibility of understanding through reconstruction, and so, in the final section on Dilthey, we shall return to it. What is "understood," according to Dilthey's famous hermeneutical formula, "experience-expression-understanding," is the ex-pression of this apodictically given, inner, structured, and inherently meaningful experience. So, it is to the concept of "expression" (*Ausdruck*) we now turn.

## Expression *(Ausdruck)*

*Reconstruction*

As Dilthey sets up the problem, the basis of our knowledge of human beings, the central task of the human sciences, is to get at the inner content of *Erlebnis*, that is, to reconstruct experience. In his famous work on poetry, *Dichtung und Erlebnis* (*Poetry and Experience*),[40] this is how Dilthey frames the central question of poetics: "How do we overcome the difficulty, which all the human sciences must face, of deriving universally valid principles from inner experiences, which are personally limited, composite, and yet incapable of analysis?"[41] The function of Dilthey's emphasis on the interiority of experience was to make it an apodictic foundation for a science of human behavior based on experience, and this was framed in direct opposition to speculative metaphysics which simply posited dogmatically the existence of a human essence. The problem this very move creates is, once the key to understanding human beings is "locked away," so to speak, inside them, how is it possible for scholars to access it? In a far-reaching, programmatic statement, a statement that will find clear echoes in van der Leeuw and Eliade, Dilthey re-poses the issue: "Can we come to know how processes grounded in human nature and, consequently, of universal scope yield these various kinds of poetry, which are separated according to nations and periods? Here we touch on the most fundamental fact of the human sciences: the historicity of psychic life as it is manifested in every system of culture produced by man. How is the sameness of our human nature, as expressed in uniformities, related to its variability, its historical character?"[42]

## EXPERIENCE AS THAT WHICH IS BEING RECONSTRUCTED

The answer for Dilthey lies in his analysis of how to reconstruct the meaning of literature: "The poet's imagination and his attitude toward the world of experience provide the point of departure for every theory seriously directed to explaining the manifold world of poetry and literature in the succession of its manifestations."[43] In literature, a prime example, but only an example, of cultural products in general, what is to be reconstructed is the *Erlebnis* along with the entire life-nexus, or *Lebenszusammenhang*, of the poet, that is, of the creator of the cultural product. Works of art, especially literature, are especially useful for this purpose because they manifest this inner experience to a greater degree than other kinds of cultural products: "Throughout history a living, active, creative and responsive soul is present at all times and places. Every first class document is an expression of such a soul."[44] Consequently, "the substratum of all true poetry is a lived or living experience [*Erlebnis, lebendige Erfahrung*] and whatever psychic constituents are related to it."[45]

### Expressions

Fortunately, there is a solution to this problem and this solution is the basis for the method of the *Geisteswissenschaften*. The solution lies in the fact that this inner experience receives "expression" (*Ausdruck*) in outward form: "What is given are always expressions of life; occurring in the world of the senses they are always expressions of a mind which they help us understand."[46] In "world of the senses," that is, as objectifications of this inner world, which are therefore accessible to the inner world of others. It is through these expressions that we come to know and understand the experience of others: "A significant complement to experience, through which alone, we can know the abundance and continuity of mental life, lies in the fact that inner states find outward expressions and that the latter can be understood by going back to the former. An outer manifestation [*Erscheinung*] is the expression of an inner state by means of an artificial convention or a natural, ordered relationship between expression and what is expressed. In both cases it is the outward sign of a fact."[47]

Speaking specifically of the process of the formation of poetic style, Dilthey gives a virtual definition of "expression." It occurs through a process "by which *something outer is enlivened by something inner or something inner is made visible and intuitable by something outer.* . . .

Contents and relations acquired in inner experience are transferred to outer experience."[48] Dilthey is interestingly silent about the details of this "transference." He has a large agenda before him, and never really gave this issue much careful consideration. He seems to have thought that it was simply quite evident that the mind expresses itself, and, that media for this expression, such as language, were simply means to this end.

Similarly, Dilthey does not say much about language. What he does say tells us much about how he understands the relationship between inner and outer: "Because it is in language alone human inwardness finds its complete, exhaustive and objectively comprehensible expression that literature is immeasurably significant for our understanding of intellectual life and history. *The art of understanding therefore centers on the interpretation of written records of human existence.*"[49] One can comb Dilthey's corpus and not find much more than such asides on the rather significant issue of language. This is especially problematic given the tremendous emphasis placed on the role of language in the structuring of subjectivity in the twentieth century. As such, we can concur with Bowie's argument that one of the clear weaknesses with Dilthey's theories of interpretation, psychology, and culture "is that in his reflections on these matters language plays a relatively subordinate role."[50] If the issue is really the mind that expresses itself and the not the "medium" used in that expression, then this is understandable.

The key features of expressions, which allow scholars to use them as reliable sources for the reconstruction of the life-nexus of their expressers, are their objectivity and (relative) permanence: "Actions and their permanent, outward results constantly help us to reconstruct the mental content from which they arose. The civil law was created in the order to regulate the life of a certain period but the student of the age of Frederick uses it to understand the spirit [*Geist*] of that age; he goes back from the laws to the intentions of the legislators and from there back to the spirit from which they arose."[51] As noted above, written documents, or writing, are a superior form of expression due to their relative permanence. It makes for a higher kind of society. Per the discussion of religion in Hegel and Tiele, religions that possessed writing, or sacred writ, were characteristically "higher religions."

*Objective Spirit*

Given the kinds of cultural objects or realities which Dilthey, following the Historical School, wants to study, namely, things such as "culture," "religion," "art," etc., that is, macro-scaled objects that exist over long periods of time, the question arises: When we speak of "expressions" in this way, what is being expressed? Or, who or what is *doing* the expressing? Dilthey's answer is unequivocal on this point: "The great outer reality of the mind [*Geist*] always surrounds us. It is a manifestation of the mind in the world of senses—from the fleeting expression to the century-long rule of a constitution or code of law. *Every single expression of life represents a common feature in the realm of this objective mind [objektiver Geist]*."[52]

As Gadamer points out, there is a transition from *Erlebnis* as the inner reality of individuals to the problem of objective spirit, which is bound up with the problem of understanding and recreating past, *collective* experience. This involves "the transition from the structure of coherence in an individual's experience to *historical coherence*, which is *not experienced by any individual at all*."[53] "Life," as the milieu and presuppositions of experience, is experienced by no one in particular. The question then arises: How can it be known? If the postulate of historical knowledge was the homogeneity of the known and the knower, how can something that is not experienced be known?

The answer lies in Dilthey's reappropriation of Hegel's concept of objective spirit. The unity that forms collectivities is analogous to the structure that forms coherence in individual experience: "The way individuals belong together—as in the solidarity of a generation or one nation—represents a spiritual reality which must be recognized as such..."[54]—it is "*geistig*," i.e., spiritual or "mental," *not* causal. Gadamer points out that, in his later works, Dilthey shifts from the foundational concept of "Life," so closely bound to the concept of *Erlebnis*, to a "teleological interpretive schema is imposed on life and it is conceived as *spirit*. Accordingly, we find that in his later years Dilthey draws closer and closer to Hegel and speaks of *spirit* where he used to say 'life.'"[55]

By "objective mind" (*objektiver Geist*), Dilthey means: "the manifold forms in which what individuals hold in common have objectified themselves in the world of the senses. In this objective mind [*Geist*] the past is a permanently enduring present for us. Its realm extends from the style of life and the forms of social intercourse, to the system of purposes which society has created for itself, to custom, law, state, religion, art, science and philosophy."[56] Objective spirit, then, is the formal, collective, externalized, and enduring repository of myriads of individual expressions from the past. Melded together, these individual expressions are the objective, external inherited milieu within which new expressions will be formed. And, as a congealment of the past, as with Hegel so for Dilthey, the past is enduringly made into a presence (precisely as Derrida would argue with his notion of the "metaphysics of presence," which he also calls logocentrism).

Although Dilthey is famous for his alleged "irrationalism," this certainly does not apply to the realm of objective spirit. Spirit expresses itself in an ordered form: "This placing of the individual expressions of life into a common context is facilitated by the articulate order in the objective mind [*Geist*]. It embraces particular homogenous systems like law or religion, and these have a firm and regular structure."[57] Dilthey never goes to far as to equate this "articulate order in the objective mind" with Reason as did Hegel, but his emphasis on the homogeneity of cultural systems and the rather smooth, nonviolent integration of individual elements in the collectivity creates a sense of the cultural world, if not guided by a providential Reason, at least as a harmonious whole.

Finally, the analysis of objective spirit is a key methodological principle for Dilthey and is the basis, as shall be shown in the next section, for his hermeneutical approach to history: "The extension of our knowledge of what is given in experience takes place through the interpretation of the objectifications of life and this interpretation, in turn, is only made possible by plumbing the depths of subjective experience."[58] The oscillation between inner, private subjectivity and outer collective objectivity, an oscillation between Schleiermacher and Hegel, at least to some degree marks the course of methodology in the human sciences as understood by Dilthey. Looking upon this structure overall, and especially on how, once the question of meaning and subjectivity is put in these kinds of terms, Gadamer draws the only conclusion possible, and a conclusion that is characteristic of the entire philosophical-intellectual-methodological movement being analyzed in this book: "Without a doubt this is an adaptation of Hegel."[59]

## Understanding *(Verstehen)*

### The Nature of Understanding

Inner experience expresses itself outwardly; such is Dilthey's model. Again, this creates a specific kind of problematic, viz., the inherent subjectivity of reconstruction: "Everyone is enclosed within his own consciousness which is unique and makes all apprehension subjective.... The possibility of apprehending something alien is one of the most difficult problems of epistemology. How can an individual understand another person's expressions objectively and validly?"[60] The answer to this problem turns out to be that, finally, the expresser and the interpreter of expressions, the object of knowledge and the knowing subject, are not, in fact, alien at all:

> Understanding [*Verstehen*] is the rediscovery of the I in the Thou; the mind rediscovers itself at ever higher levels of connectedness;[61] this sameness of the mind in the I and the Thou and in every subject of a community, in every system of culture and, finally, in the totality of mind and universal history, makes the working together of the different processes in the human studies possible. In these the knowing subject is one with its object, which is the same at all stages of its objectification.[62]

Dilthey argues for this correlation between knower and known, between hermeneute and object of interpretation, along two main lines: what I shall call the "maker thesis" and the identity thesis. The maker thesis holds that one human can understand the expressions of another human because both are "makers" of cultural meanings: "The fact that the investigator of history is the same as the one who makes it, is the first condition which makes scientific history possible."[63] Or, as he says elsewhere: "[O]nly that which the mind has made can it fully understand."[64] Bambach notes that Dilthey follows Vico's famous dictum: *"verum et factum convertuntur."*[65] Vico argued that the world of nations, of civil society (i.e., what in contemporary terms would be called "culture") can be understood because, "since men had made it, men could come to know it."[66] So, humans understand history, religion, culture, texts, art, poetry, etc., because they themselves have made these. As we shall see later and as we saw in chapter 1, this does not apply to nature; Dilthey draws a sharp contrast between nature and culture and the modes of knowing either.

The identity thesis is a similar argument, but entails a stronger claim, viz.: "What makes historical knowledge possible [for Dilthey] is the homogeneity of subject and object."[67] It is from the interiority and homogenous nature of that interior life that "understanding" springs: "For life is given to me directly only as my own. And only from this, my own life, do I understand the life around me."[68] Not only individual human experience, understood in either a phenomenalist manner or an empiricist manner, but universal human nature, which lives both within us and without us, is the basis for understanding social, historical, or cultural reality: "I am involved in the interactions of society because its various systems intersect in my life. These systems have sprung from the same human nature as I experience in myself and understand in others."[69] Gadamer makes an interesting commentary on the identity thesis, viz., that: "For Dilthey the ultimate presupposition for knowledge of the historical world is experience (*Erlebnis*). In it the identity between consciousness and object—that postulate of speculative idealism—is still demonstrable reality."[70]

"The category of meaning has obviously a particularly close *connection with understanding*."[71] We saw earlier that meaning is related to the structure that Dilthey took to be innate to experience. As such, meaning is part of the interior aspect of Dilthey's analysis. It reconnects to the external aspect of his analysis with the problematics of understanding. The hermeneute stands outside the interiority of the expresser of art, religion, poetry, or cultural meaning and must connect with that interiority. "Meaning" is part of the connection, as it is rooted in life: "The category of meaning designates the relation, rooted in life itself, of parts to whole."[72] In classic Romantic fashion, Dilthey sees meaning as a relation of part to whole: "In all these and other cases the single moment derives its meaning from its connection with the whole, from the relation between future and past, between the individual and mankind."[73] Dilthey summarizes the three "moments" of interpretation, "experience, expression, understanding," in a description of the nature of the act of understanding meaning:

> Thus the concept of meaning arises, first of all, in relation to the process of understanding. It contains the relation of something outward, something given to the senses, to something inward, of which it is the expression. But this relation is essentially different from the grammatical one. The expression of mental content in the parts of life is different from the expression of meaning by a word. Hence such words as meaning, comprehension, significance (of a life or of history) are only pointers to the relation between events and an inner connection, contained in understanding and required by it.[74]

As "only pointers," it is clear that understanding for Dilthey, as it will be for all phenomenologists of religion, is something more than linguistic. It is the intuition of one subjectivity by another subjectivity. While this is not quite the same as Hegel's statement about Spirit's coming "self-recognition through absolute otherness," there is some similarity. One self understands another self via their common subjectivity. There is a moment of "self-recognition," then, but it is grounded more in commonality than in otherness, let alone absolute otherness. Yet, if they were not two, that is, in some way other to one another, the need for understanding would not arise: "Interpretation would be impossible if expressions of life were completely strange. It would be unnecessary if nothing strange were in them."[75] This commonality is, again, an aspect of "objective mind," or the commonality of human nature: "Just as the objective mind contains a structural order of types so does mankind and this leads from the regularity and structure of general human nature to the types through which understanding grasps individuals."[76] The identity thesis holds, then, that although concrete humans are different and stand in a relationship of exteriority to one another, this exteriority is overcome by a common nature, or what Derrida earlier described as the idea of "philosophy as presence" and "the self-proximity of subjectivity."[77]

*Hermeneutics*

The combined problems of meaning and reconstruction raise the issue of hermeneutics. Hermeneutics is, in Dilthey's view, an essential component of "understanding": "We call the process by which we recognize some inner content from signs received by the senses *understanding* [*Verstehen*]."[78] Debate over the meaning of Dilthey's hermeneutics is a complex problem, as Bowie notes: "Dilthey is sometimes, with a degree of justification, seen as giving too much scope to the experience of the individual subject as a criterion of textual meaning."[79] As was discussed in chapter 1, this study is not concerned with an exposition of the historical development of Dilthey's hermeneutic theory *an sich*, but rather with the way in which it has been appropriated in the history of phenomenological discourse in the study of religion. In this respect, Dilthey's "psychologizing" of the hermeneutic problematic was very much the way he was read, whether or not that is the best rendition of his more final or mature position.

The basic structure of Dilthey's analysis of experience, expression, and understanding is that his analysis of experience starts from the inside and moves out to the expressions of interiority, while his analysis of understanding starts from the outside, with those expressions of interiority and "moves" them inward back to the interiority of the hermeneute. Ergo, given the alterity, the externality of the inner world of the author, in order to understand, "we have to reconstruct the inner source of the signs which strike our senses. Everything: material, structure, even the most individual features of this reconstruction, have to be supplied by transferring them from our own lives. How, then, can an individually structured consciousness reconstruct—and thereby know objectively—the distinct individuality of another?"[80]

Dilthey's answer to this problem lies in his view of the nature of the act of understanding: "Understanding is the process of recognizing a mental state from a sense-given sign by which it is expressed."[81] The "mental state" is what is signified by the sign and it is the ultimate target of understanding. Such understanding is possible because "[t]he same human spirit speaks to us from stone, marble, musical compositions, gestures, words and writings, from actions, economic arrangements and constitutions, and has to be interpreted."[82] By contrast: "Understanding of nature—*interpretatito naturae*—is a figurative expression."[83] Humans are neither of the same kind nor do they make natural objects, ergo, they cannot understand nature.

There is an ambiguity of emphasis in Dilthey's view of hermeneutics. On the one hand, it is clearly concerned with written texts: "hermeneutics, which is the methodology of the interpretation of written records."[84] On the other hand, these texts reveal an inner consciousness which is pre- or nonverbal. Although Dilthey does not offer much in the way of a theory language, he does describe it as having an intimate relation to interiority: "Because it is in language alone human inwardness finds its complete, exhaustive and objectively comprehensible expression that literature is immeasurably significant for our understanding of intellectual life and history. The art of understanding therefore centers on the interpretation of written records of human existence."[85] The advantage of written records as opposed to introspection—the other pole of analysis of consciousness—is that it provides the possibility for an objective science of the mind: "But even the most strenuous attention can only give rise to a systematic process with a controllable degree of objectivity if the expression has been given permanent form so that we can repeatedly return to it. Such systematic understanding of recorded expressions we call exegesis or interpretation."[86] As a fixed objectification of mind, writing is a controllable factor of research. It can be returned to again and again, whereas the flux of internal experience, wherein ideas originate, is too fleeting to be scientifically objective.

As is well known, Dilthey appeals to Schleiermacher's hermeneutics, another major influence on the history of the phenomenology of religion, in the formulation of his own views. In a summary of Schleiermacher's view, Dilthey notes the two poles of "understanding" and the role that the concept of subjectivity plays in both: "The possibility of valid interpretation can be deduced from the nature of understanding. There the personalities of the interpreter and his author do not confront each other as two facts which cannot be compared: both have been formed by a common human nature and this makes common speech and understanding among men possible. Here Schleiermacher's formal expressions can be further explained psychologically. All individual differences are, in the last resort, conditioned not by qualitative differences between people but by differences of degree in their mental processes."[87] In a manner similar to what we have seen before, the idea of the homogeneity of subjectivity is directly connected with the idea of degrees of development. While the notion of *Entwicklung* is not as strong in Dilthey as it is in Hegel, it is certainly not absent.[88]

## Dilthey and Hegel/*Geist* und *Natur*

*Dilthey and Hegel*

The move from interiority to exteriority, and the broader, historical contextualization of this exteriority, forces Dilthey to move beyond— though never completely reject--Schleiermacher's psychologistic notion of understanding to the more Hegelian notion of objective spirit. As Bowie notes: "[I]n his later work Dilthey moved closer to Hegel's notion of 'objective spirit.' "[89] Bambach concurs: "An exegete of *Geist*, Dilthey attempted to see all methodological access to history as something grounded in the part-to-whole interplay of self and world."[90] Unlike those that wanted to appease Positivism completely, Dilthey's "attitude was in no sense typically antimetaphysical, like the historicists. Dilthey held Hegel in high regard and believed that metaphysics could not be dismissed offhand as an unscientific aberration of the human spirit."[91] Dilthey did not think of the division of the sciences to be merely "methodological,"; it is rooted in the structure of reality itself: "He even claimed that the actual division of the sciences according to nature and spirit was based on these metaphysical principles of first philosophy."[92] While it may be true that in his later work, Dilthey modified his more individualistic and psychologistic views, he nevertheless does not abandon the subject-oriented perspective. Rather, as Makkreel and Rodi note, he collectivizes and externalizes the subject of "inner experience" into that of "objective spirit": "Here we see Dilthey renounce his own earlier procedure of beginning with an aesthetics of genius. But he does not replace it with a reception-aesthetics. . . . Instead, poetics must start with an examination of the work as part of objective spirit."[93] Dilthey, then, is very much a "Hegelian" in the sense described in chapter 1: a critical appropriator a larger paradigm for the human sciences. As he was deeply influential on the history of the structure of the discourse of the phenomenology of religion, we can see the way in which it, too, was "Hegelian" in this qualified sense.

Gadamer also makes a strong case for the presence of a strong Hegelian bent in Dilthey: "His critique of 'positivity,' the concept of self-alienation, the definition of mind as recognition of oneself in other being..."[94] all are indications of it. Gadamer even argues that one can find the concept of "absolute spirit" in Dilthey's understanding of historical consciousness. Dilthey does claim that, in historical consciousness, "here, life is understood by life."[95] Gadamer points out that, contrary to Hegel's view: "It is not in the speculative knowledge of the concept, but in historical consciousness that spirit's knowledge of itself is consummated."[96] This is no insignificant difference from Hegel, but the larger point should not be lost: the paradigm of science is still that of a subject coming to know itself through its objectifications. As we shall see later on, this paradigm is very much the structure of classical phenomenology of religion.

### Geist versus Natur

Finally, like Hegel (and Tiele), Dilthey sees Spirit and nature as incommensurable realities. He makes this case from his analysis of inner experience, with which we began: "Because we encounter reality, as the correlative of experience, through the cooperation of our senses with inner experience, the difference in the provenance of the elements which comprise our experience results in an incommensurability in the elements of our scientific calculation. And this incommensurability does not permit us to derive the reality of either particular source from the other."[97] Spirit is, as phenomenologists of religion will often claim about religion, sui generis. It is not "caused" by something outside itself, and so cannot be "explained." Again, it must be "understood": only Spirit can know Spirit.

The opposition between *Geist* and *Natur* in Dilthey becomes the basis for separate sciences and characterizes humanity's relation to nature generally:

> The motivation behind the habit of seeing these sciences as a unity in contrast with those of nature derives from the depth and fullness of human self-consciousness... a

man finds in this self-consciousness a sovereignty of will, a responsibility for actions, a capacity for subordinating everything to thought and for resisting any foreign elements in the citadel of freedom in his person: by these things he distinguishes himself from nature. He finds himself with respect to nature an *imperium in imperio*, to use Spinoza's expression. And because for him only data of his own consciousness exist, a result is that every value and every goal in life has its locus in this independently functioning intellectual world within him, and every goal of his activities consists in producing intellectual results. And so he distinguishes nature from history, in which, surrounded though it is by that structure of objective necessity which nature consists of, freedom flashes forth at innumerable points in the whole.[98]

Nature is the Other of Spirit, just as much for Dilthey as for Hegel and for Tiele. And it is the subordination of nature to Spirit that informs not only the "values" of Dilthey, but his very conception of what the human sciences are and can and must do. The subordination of this other is, however, simply an instance of the general theme here: the subordination of otherness itself—either by absorbing it into the other's other, the self, or by establishing a hierarchy of "higher" and "lower," of "sovereign" or "subaltern," of master over slave. The critical question then becomes: What counts as nature? Or, even more critically still: *Who* counts as nature? We saw in Hegel's history of religion that some peoples are considered closer to nature, farther from Spirit, less free, and consequently, less human. Dilthey masks this trajectory in his thinking by a universalism of mind, but this is at best a limited (*sic*!) universal; at worst, a false universal. As we shall see, these same divisions will not only constantly recur in the phenomenology of religion, they are *constitutive* of it.

These same general tendencies will be much more explicit in one of the arch phenomenologists of religion, Rudolf Otto. It is his work to which we now turn.

# 6

# *Geist*, Nature, and History
## The Phenomenology of Rudolf Otto

"No consideration of the development of the phenomenological approach would be complete if it did not note the influence of Rudolph [sic] Otto. His *The Idea of the Holy* [*Das Heilige*] (1923) was of the greatest importance in providing a direction for future development in the field, and acted as a seminal work for later authors on a par with van der Leeuw's."[1] Perhaps the most important influence Otto had was on Mircea Eliade. Eliade begins his most famous work, *The Sacred and the Profane* (published in 1957), by referring to Otto's work: "The extraordinary interest aroused all over the world by Rudolf Otto's *Das Heilige* (*The Sacred* [sic]), published in 1917, still persists.... After forty years, Otto's analyses have not lost their value; readers of this book will profit by reading and reflecting on them."[2] Otto's influence on the study of religion generally and the phenomenology of religion specifically is hard to overstate. As Thomas Ryba, a historian of the phenomenology of religion states: "Those influenced by Rudolf Otto's exposition of the holy read like a twentieth-century Who's Who. The later works of Nelson, Heiler, Wach, van der Leeuw, Nygren, and Eliade all show a marked debt to this exposition."[3] Otto, then, is clearly a seminal figure in the phenomenology of religion, and any genealogy of it must include his work. This chapter will review the discursive structure of Otto's approach, exemplified most clearly in his celebrated and oft-cited work, *The Idea of the Holy*.[4] This book is routinely cited in introductory textbooks to the field, world religion books, by members of the field of Religious Studies, and by scholars in related disciplines such as philosophy and history. Other of his works will be used in support of the basic arguments of *The Idea of the Holy*. Given this wide dissemination, Otto's work is a convenient site (or cite) for the review of a discursive field which is authenticated as "knowledge" by academic institutions, societies, presses, and the whole professional apparatus of the university system. As we shall see, his work is a classic instantiation of the "power/knowledge" correlation discussed in chapter 2.

Otto is a transitional figure between the nineteenth- and twentieth-century approaches in *Religionswissenschaft*. While nineteenth-century figures such as Hegel and Tiele focused on the historical development (*Entwicklung*) of religion, with a strong emphasis on its teleological culmination in Christianity, twentieth-century phenomenologists would, for the most part, locate religion theoretically in a transhistorical, static concept of consciousness, an idea that would come to be called the "religious a priori." Otto combines both approaches. He accepts the idea of the religion as the development of Spirit in history. However, his work is also the *locus classicus* for the argument that religion, or "the holy," is an a priori category of consciousness. While Tiele clearly reflects the more overtly historical approach of Hegel, Otto, like Dilthey, combines the more subjective (i.e., internal to consciousness) approach of Kant and Schleiermacher. Eliade's statement that "the sacred is a structure of consciousness, not a stage of history,"[5] reflects the subjective side of Otto's approach. For Otto, "the holy" is *both* a category of consciousness *and* manifest by "degrees of gradation" at different stages of history. As the *Receptionsgeschichte* of Otto's work was determined by van der Leeuw and Eliade, most scholars emphasize his a priori, structural analytic of consciousness at the cost of his view of the history of religion and the philosophy of history that underlies that view. Thus, scholars overemphasize his relationship to Kant and Schleiermacher and fail to see his very close connection to Hegel and Dilthey. Such a reading also sees Otto as closer to Husserl, and thus makes it easier to read the phenomenology of religion as a quasi-Husserlian project. By contrast, the analysis presented here will attempt to show the deep correlation between *both* elements: the history of religion is for Otto, just as it was for Hegel and Tiele, the gradual manifestation of the holy in and to consciousness. Otto's paradigm, then, is predicated upon the notion of the "essence and manifestation" of religion in history.[6] Just as with Hegel and Tiele, the plot of the narrative of the appearance of the holy in history is its progressive purification, that is, its emancipation from nature and natural elements of consciousness (sense, emotion, and natural, physical objects of perception).

What we shall do in this chapter, then, is look at the way in which Otto establishes the a priori nature of religion or the holy. In so doing, it will become immediately obvious that much of both the method and purpose by and for which he accomplishes this is to claim a radical separation between mind and matter, or, again, *Geist* und *Natur*.

The a priori nature of religion becomes the basis of a philosophy of history that sees the manifestations of religion as expressions of the universal, essential religious consciousness. The plot of the history of religions, then, follows the same pattern as that of Hegel and Tiele: it is the gradual separation of *Geist* from *Natur*, that is, the movement of Spirit toward freedom. The progressive movement of Spirit will mean that its manifestations become more moral and more rational, again, just as with Hegel and Tiele. Finally, the geo-global pattern will also be similar: the "primitives" are overcome by "Eastern" religion, which is then seen as inferior both to Christianity in general and to Christianity's Gothic expression in figures such as Meister Eckhart and Martin Luther. The universal, rational, essential movement of all religion, of Spirit itself, culminates in the "us" of Otto's religious, national, cultural, and ethnic identity.

## *Geist* versus *Natur*: The Structure of the Religious A Priori

Recall that the basic, constitutive concepts which ground the discursive play of the phenomenology of religion are the radical qualitative distinction Hegel posits between *Geist* and *Natur*: "Freedom is the sole truth of Spirit. Matter possesses gravity in virtue of its tendency toward a central point.... Spirit, on the contrary, may be defined as that which has its center in itself. It has not a unity outside itself, but has already found it; it exists in and with itself. Matter has its essence out of itself; Spirit is self contained existence (*Bei-sich-selbst-seyn*).[7] Otto completely agrees, arguing that: "The direct experience that spirit has of itself, of its individuality and freedom, of its incomparability with all that is beneath it, is far too constant and genuine to admit of its being put into a difficulty by a doctrine which it has itself established."[8] Nature/Matter, as such, cannot attain true selfhood or subjectivity as the essence of subjectivity is to be "in-and-for-itself." Matter's ontological determination is to have its being as "out-of-itself." Otto changes the discourse of Religious Studies by elevating this notion to a methodological principle. This is the basis of his famous definition of "the holy" as an a priori category. This is well known. However, what has not been discussed in the literature (either of appropriation or critique) is that this distinction is predicated upon and meant to reinforce the *Geist/Natur* distinction. This distinction underlies Otto's entire approach both to religion and the study of religion. It will be our task to analyze carefully the implications of the idea of the a priori.

## The Holy as A Priori

In Otto's famous assertion of the holy as an a priori category, he explicitly argues for the separation of Spirit (or mind, as Harvey tends to translate "*Geist*") and nature: "the 'holy' in the fullest sense of the word is a combined, complex category.... But in both—and the assertion must be strictly maintained against all sensationalism and naturalism—it a *purely a priori* category," and with it "we are referred away from all sense-experience back to an original and underivable capacity of the mind implanted in the 'pure reason' independently of all perception."[9] There are two components to this claim: the separation of mind of nature and the distinction between "pure reason" and sense perception.

When Otto states that the a priori nature of the holy must be maintained "against all sensationalism and naturalism," he is, again, arguing for the radical distinction between Spirit and nature or mind and matter. Otto, in fact, wrote an entire book on the subject (translated as *Naturalism and Religion*), a work that is a lengthy polemic against all forms "sensationalism and naturalism." In many ways, this work laid the foundation for *The Idea of the Holy*, and it is instructive to read the two in relation to one another. In that work, Otto goes to great pains to show that the human thought is not, as empiricists, materialists, and some Darwinians claimed, based upon physical, that is, natural, bodily sensation, but is independent, that is, free, as Dilthey had also argued, from natural stimuli:

> External nature is nothing more than the stimulus, the pressure upon the mind, which liberates from its depths the peculiar reactions and responses to this stimulus, and calls them forth from its own treasure-stores. Certainly in this creating the consciousness is entirely dependent on the impressions stamped on it from outside, and to that extent upon "experience." But it is by no means a *tabula rasa*, and a merely passive mirror of the outer world, for it translates the stimulus thus received into quite a different language, and builds up from it a new reality, which is quite unlike the mathematical and qualityless reality without.[10]

The language Otto uses strongly asserts an oppositional contrast between the active, self-possessing, self-creating aspects of "mind" and the passivity, externality, and naturalness of sense impressions.

Mind is other than nature and stands above it. As with Dilthey, he argues that, while experience is drawn from sensation, it is by no means identical with it. The natural world, which is "different," "without" (i.e., external), and "quite unlike" the world of the mind, is quality-less. Mind or Spirit is the domain of "quality," meaning, moral values and/or the holy, while nature is merely quantity. These distinctions are restated in the terms of post-Cartesian physics. The a priori's social, cultural, moral, and religious function is clearly to preserve the domain of values or "quality" over and against a "quality-less" and literally nonpersonal world of mere nature: "All these [values, thoughts, qualities] are of a psychical [*geistig*] nature, immaterial, and underivable from the material. And it is difficult to see, for instance, why the forming of judgments should be regarded as more durable and indestructible than sensation and desire. The difference lies higher than this,—not in the fact that man has a few 'capacities' more than the animal, but in the difference in principle, that the psychical in man can be developed to spirit, and that this is impossible anywhere else."[11] This is because "[c]onsciousness, thought, even the commonest sensation of pleasure and pain, or the simplest sense-perception, cannot be compared with 'matter and energy,' with the movements of masses, molecules, and elements."[12]

While these comments are in many ways directed at an eighteenth-century post-Cartesian physics, Otto is also concerned to counter the growing influence of 1nineteenth-century Darwinian evolution. Given the independent nature of thought and consciousness described above, it follows that "man" is not simply another kind of "animal" (i.e., "merely" a natural being): "What is implicit in him as *homo sapiens*, a member of a zoological order, is nothing more than the natural basis upon which, in human and individual history, he may build up an entirely unique and new creation, an upper story: the world and life of the spirit."[13] Again, this is because "[w]hat Eckhart means by the ground of the soul [*Seelengrund*] does indeed exist"[14] "Man" lives in a different world, a world created by mind or spirit. This notion, which in phenomenology would come to be called the *Lebenswelt* and would be arrived at by "bracketing" the natural world, is the true world of "man." It is a world of qualities, of values, and, of course, of religion.

Besides the strict separation between mind and nature or the human and the animal, Otto defines the a priori-ness of the holy by differentiating sense and reason, stating, in his articulation of the holy that "away from all sense-experience" and that it resides in " 'pure reason' independently of all perception."[15] In this way of articulating the concept of the a priori nature of the holy, Otto follows Kant and Dilthey and a host of others in differentiating between sense impressions, whose only role even in empirical knowledge consists of "giving merely the occasion" for the formation of concepts and "our own faculty of cognition"[16] which is innate and part of the a priori structure of consciousness as such. "The numinous is of the latter kind. It issues from the deepest foundation of cognitive apprehension that the soul possesses."[17] As such: "We find ... involved in the numinous experience, beliefs and feelings qualitatively different from anything that 'natural' sense-perception is capable of giving us.... [T]here is never any question of the transformation of *one* class of percepts into a class of [mental/conceptual] entities qualitatively *other*."[18]

From the analysis of the language Otto himself uses in his articulation of the a priori nature of the holy it becomes quite evident that he is obsessed with "purity" and with what Heidegger called (in quite a different context) "own-mostness," *Einheit*, or self-possession. While this is framed in abstract, philosophical language, given that he clearly associates nonwhite, non-European, non-Christians with "nature" and white, European (especially Germanic), Christians with "spirit," it is rather evident that the structure of Otto's discourse on "purity" is also a discourse on racial purity. We shall return to this point later.

These correlative notions that reason and sense, Spirit and nature, mind and body are distinct, form the basis for Otto's methodological principle of "empathy": "For the Spirit knows and recognizes what is of the Spirit."[19] Given that natural sensations and causations are categorically different than mental acts, states, and objects, only mind can understand mind. As Dilthey had argued, "Nature is explained, culture is understood." Otto completely agrees: "To *know* and to *understand conceptually* are two different things, are often even mutually exclusive and contrasted."[20] This is the basis for Otto's famous/infamous statement about the role of religious experience in the study of religion:

> The reader is invited to direct his mind to a moment of deeply-felt religious experience, as little as possible qualified by other forms of consciousness. Whoever cannot do this, whoever knows no such moments in his experience, is requested to read no farther; for it is not easy to discuss questions of religious psychology with one who can recollect the emotions of his adolescence, the discomforts of

indigestion, or, say, social feelings, but cannot recall any intrinsically religious feelings.[21]

As only Spirit can know Spirit, and, as the universal structure of consciousness separates the religious sphere from both the natural sphere on the one hand and other spheres of consciousness on the other hand, only the religious can understand religion. Also, religious experience is not to be reduced to or confused with mere emotions, physical sensations, or "social feelings." Religion is, as shall be discussed below, sui generis, and so neither dependent upon nor derived from the nonreligious. The study of religion cannot, therefore, employ reductive methods for a phenomenon that is qualitatively other than external causes.

As Adina Davidovich argues, there is a close correlation between the empathetic understanding argument and the a priori argument:

> Otto's "sympathy" is based on the assumption that in so far as others are rational beings like us, their experience reflects the same ultimate organizing principles. The study of the experience of others becomes therefore the attempt to see how this superstructure of organizing principles is manifest in their experience. Being exposed to texts, stories, monuments, artifacts, etc., I reflect on my informed experience which previous analysis had established. Once an a priori element of reason is identified, it is a moot question whether we can find it in other people or in other cultures. If we accept a principle as an a priori principle of reason we necessarily accept it as a principle of every manifestation of reason.[22]

While "spiritual" (*geistig*) might be a better term than rational, the point holds either way: as a priori, the *structures* of consciousness are apodictically and necessarily universal. As universal, all humans participate in it—albeit to varying degrees of realization.

Finally, this a priori realm of "pure reason," then, in turn becomes the criterion by which the value of religions is measured. He defines "rational" as: "An object that can thus be thought conceptually may be termed *rational* . . . and a religion which recognizes and maintains such a view of God is in so far a 'rational' religion. Only on such terms is *belief* possible in contrast to mere *feeling*."[23] Put bluntly, *Geist* thinks; *Natur* feels, "feeling" being derived from the senses, that is, the body, that is, nature.

## Freedom, Dependence, and Lordship over Nature: The Ontological Basis of the Sui Generis Argument

We saw in Hegel that one of the consequences of separating Spirit from nature was a way of conceiving the freedom and lordship of Spirit over nature. We also saw how this notion formed the inner logic of his narrative of the history of religion. So also with Otto. Otto asserts that freedom is metaphysically grounded in this separation between mind or Spirit and nature (or sensation, feeling, etc.):

> In maintaining freedom of the mind it is asserted that it can preserve its own nature and laws in face of external compulsion or laws, and in face of the merely psychological compulsion of the "lower courses of thought," even from the "half-natural" laws of the association of ideas. Thus "freedom" is pre-eminently freedom of thought. And in speaking thus we are presupposing that the mind has a nature of its own, distinguished even from the purely psychological nature, and has a code of laws of its own, lying beyond the scope of all natural laws, which psychical motives and physical conditions may prevent it following, but which they can never suspend or pull down to their own level.[24]

Mind or Spirit is here asserted as causally independent and ontologically superior in a hierarchy of substances that constitute the universe as we know it. All reductive arguments, whether social, cultural, or biological, even psychological, are, Otto claims, simply and totally mistaken: mind is *qualitatively* distinct and above matter and cannot be explained on the same terms as natural phenomena. Otto invokes Kant to argue that the body is dependent on the mind, and not simply the other way around: "But if the dependence of the mind upon the body be great, that of the body upon the mind is greater still. Even Kant wrote tersely and dryly about 'the power of our mind through mere will to be master over our morbid feelings.'"[25] It is not surprising that Kant would describe feelings as "morbid" and see them as "lower" than reason. In this Otto mostly concurs. More to the point, Otto sees in mind or reason mastery over nature. This is a theme that runs throughout his articulation of the a priori and of the holy: it is qualitatively, even metaphysically superior to nature and should differentiate itself from it by exercising its lordship over it.

When contrasted with matter or nature, mind or Spirit takes on the sense of a metaphysical substance, an almost abstract character.

However, this is not, as we saw with Hegel, the real differentiating quality between humans and animals. That quality is what Otto calls "personality," or personhood: "Personality is a word which gives us an inward thrill. It expresses what is most individual in us, what is set before us, our highest task and the inmost tendency of our being. What is personality?"[26] He argues, in typical Romantic fashion, that personality is a nebulous thing that does not admit of clear definitions or descriptions. Nonetheless: "But one thing at any rate we can affirm about it with certainty: it is absolutely bounded off from the whole world and all existence as a self-contained and independent world in itself. The more we become persons, the more clearly, definitely, and indissolubly we raise ourselves with our spiritual life and spiritual possessions out of all the currents of natural phenomena."[27] Our "own-mostness" or "the inmost tendency of our being," that is, that which is "us" most and least not-us, is personality, which is in turn founded upon mind, soul, or Spirit. This "raises" us out of nature. As we shall see, this is precisely the way in which Otto will emplot his narrative of the history of religion.

Finally, along with reason, mind, and Spirit, morality, too, is a domain of freedom:

> Freedom of thought is also the most obvious example of that freedom of the spirit in morally "willing," which it is the business of ethical science to teach and defend. As in the one case thought shows itself superior to the physiologically or psychologically conditioned sequence of its concepts, so the free spirit, in the uniqueness of its moral laws, reveals itself as lord over all the motives, the lower feelings of pleasure and pain that have their play within us.[28]

Again, part of the function of the a priori argument, as well as the insistence upon religion, is to protect that "own-most" domain of the specifically human, viz., values, from its others. This is what "freedom" means in this Hegelian discourse. Freedom necessarily entails the exercise of lordship. For there to be true, "pure" morality, *Geist*, the moral agent, must exercise "lord over all the motives."

## The Sui Generis Argument

This translates directly into the radical independence of the holy or religion generally from all other causal factors. Since mind cannot be reduced to feelings or sensations and Spirit is qualitatively distinct from nature, religion is independent from any other domain. It is unique (*Einheit*, "own-mostness"): "For if there be any single domain of human experience that presents us with something unmistakably specific and unique, peculiar to itself, assuredly it is that of the religious life"[29]; " 'Holiness'—'the holy'—is a category of interpretation and valuations peculiar to the sphere of religion."[30] The holy, or religion, as Otto understands it is not a cultural construct, is not a mere concept, or a culturally specific institution, practice, or set of values. The holy is "a unique 'numinous' category of value and of a definitely 'numinous' state of mind, which is always found wherever the category is applied. This mental state is perfectly sui generis and irreducible to any other; and therefore, like every absolutely primary and elementary datum, while it admits of being discussed, it cannot be strictly defined."[31] The holy, or religion, is part of the furniture of the universe.

## Philosophy of History

Otto makes the distinction between Spirit and nature an explicit part of his conception of the science of religion. He argues that an Idealist concept of history is necessary for there to be a science of religion, and history can *only* be understood if it possesses an underlying unity. In the human domain, this unity must be Spirit:

> There is something presupposed by history as such—not only the history of mind or spirit, with which we are here concerned—which alone makes it history, and this is the existence of a *quale*, something with a potentiality of its own, capable of *becoming, in the special sense of coming to be that to which it was predisposed and predetermined*. . . . [I]t must already *be something* if it is to really *become* anything. . . . In short, to propose a history of mind is to presuppose a mind or spirit determinately qualified; to profess to give a history of religion is to presuppose a spirit specifically qualified for religion.[32]

For Otto, as for Hegel and Tiele, Spirit is the substance and subject of history, the "it" that makes any history a history *of* something. For there to be a history of religion, the subject of that history must be something, that is, have a determinate nature (*Wesen*), which can be the subject of such a history. In terms of our discussion of Seiwert's problematic with which we began, "religion" is either not a unified thing or it is not an empirical entity. Like Hegel, Otto takes the latter option. For Otto, without the concept of an essence to history, only "mere aggregation" is possible: "An oak-tree can *become*, and thus have a sort of 'history'; whereas a heap of stones cannot. The random addition and subtraction, displacement and rearrangement, of elements in a mere aggregation can certainly be followed in narrative form, but this is not in the deeper sense an historical narrative."[33] There must be an "it" which is the subject of the process of becoming, and this "it" is that which gives the process of becoming identity rather than being "mere aggregation." For human beings, clearly this "it" cannot be an empirical entity—that would make it a "mere aggregation," and not the development of an essential nature. It must be something that is not bound to a specific time, place, or human production, that is, it must be nonmaterial and transcendental in nature. This, of course, is exactly what Otto claimed in his definition of the holy as "a *purely a priori* category."[34]

In another critique of Darwinian evolutionary theory, Otto claims that underlying substance of developing consciousness cannot be explained in biological terms: "[T]he whole idea of 'explaining' in terms of 'evolution' is a futile one. The process of becoming is pictured as a simple process of culmination, a gradual increase of intensities, while the business is really one of change in quality and the introduction of what is new."[35] Spirit is radically distinct from matter and so to compare the two is to change the subject, so to speak. Recall that Tiele said if you replace an oak tree with a beech tree, you cannot call this "development."

## Criteriology for the History of Religions

The notion of the holy as an a priori—and therefore universal—feature of consciousness as such plays a critical role in Otto's view of religion. As Phillip Almond explains: "The relative value of religions can be measured according to the extent to which they actualize the religious *a priori*. The criteria for this evaluation are determined from 'within' religion, that is, by the degree to which the Holy is *revealed* in each tradition. The religious *a priori* thus affords an 'objective' standard against which its various manifestations can be measured; consequently, the history and comparison of religions can be a theology of religions"[36]—but also a science of religion, or *Religionswissenschaft*.

The dichotomies of Spirit and nature, a priori and a posteriori, reason and sense (or reason and feeling), allow Otto to emplot a history of religion (which is also a history of consciousness or Spirit) from "primitives," for whom genuine spiritual experience is "confounded with 'natural' feelings,"[37] to "a rational religion like Christianity."[38] The movement of *Religionsgeschichte* then, is the same as in Hegel's metanarrative of *Geist*: Spirit moves *away* from *Natur* and comes to pure self-recognition by means of its own externalizations. Otto's history of religion traces out these stages as Spirit and the holy move from its "confused" involvement in natural objects and sensations to externalizations that are purer expressions of Spirit's own emancipated character. In the exposition that follows, I will trace Otto's plot of the history of religion, which, as it turns out, is virtually identical to Hegel's plot for the history of Spirit. It starts with "primitive" religion, moves to and through the "East" and pagan antiquity, and literally culminates in the "us" to which Otto and Hegel belonged, namely, Germanic-European Christianity. Each stage of the *Entwicklung* or development of religious consciousness will be described.

## "The Deficient Rationalization and Moralization of Experience": "Primitive" Religion

Otto's narrative of the history of the development of Spirit in the realm of religion begins by looking at how he describes the early phases of the appearance of the holy in history. The holy, or numinous, appears gradually in the prehistory of "man": the "numinous only unfolds its full content by slow degrees, as one by one the series of requisite stimuli or incitements becomes operative."[39] As noted before, external, that is, natural stimuli are the occasion, not the source or origin, for mind or Spirit to become operative. At first, the holy is "mixed" with things external to its essence.

"In the second place, the 'primitiveness' of the cruder phases is due to the abrupt, capricious, and desultory character which marks the earliest form of numinous emotion; and, in consequence, to its indistinctness, which causes it to be merged and confounded with 'natural' feelings."[40] Otto, like Hegel, is not shy about describing "primitive" religion in derogatory terms. A mind not freed from nature is a barbaric mind, and, while it may potentially claim that which is true of all religion or the true essence of mind as such, it does not begin to actualize this abstract potential. Historical science indicates that the manifestations of the holy at this stage of human history are crude and lack a fully developed moral consciousness.

"Finally, and most important, there is the deficient rationalization and moralization of the experience, for it is only gradually that the numinous feeling becomes charged with progressively rational, moral, and cultural significance."[41] Like Hegel, Otto closely associates rationality with Spirit. Reason is that part of mind which is truly different from nature and cannot be reduced to nature in any way. Early humanity, though potentially rational, was not actually so, and, as such, religion at this stage lacks both a moral consciousness and sufficient rationality to differentiate itself from mere nature. So Otto concludes: "These considerations account for the primitive and savage character of the numinous consciousness at its outset"[42]—"the numinous consciousness" and the *human beings* at this stage of development or of history. The plot, then, of Otto's story is the same as Hegel's: Spirit moves away from nature.

## The (Feminine) Passivity of the East versus the (Masculine) Vitality of the Gothic West

### Śankara versus Eckhart: Otto's Orientalism

Otto makes a similar argument about the "East" as he does about "primitives." In his book, *Mysticism East and West*, he goes to great pains to differentiate rather than identify, the mysticisms of the "East" and that of the "West." He uses Śankara as the main representative of the former and Eckhart as the main representative of the latter. He is clear from the first that these two types of religious experiences must be sharply differentiated: "[I]n spite of 'convergence of types' between East and West, the inner spirit yet differs, and that the very different ground upon which mysticism rose in Europe also colors the highest mystical experience in a way which is Christian and not Indian."[43] There are many kinds of differences. For purposes here we will look at only two. First, we will look at the passivity and "coolness" of temperament of Śankara versus the dynamic and active nature of Eckhart's mysticism. Second, we will look at Otto's view of the differences between Śankara's and Eckhart's views of the godhead. In both cases we will see Otto's use of supposedly rational, scientific, *wissenschaftlich* methods to assert a quasi-derogatory view of "the East" and assert the supremacy of his own religion and ethnicity.

Otto says many, many things about the vital activism of Eckhart in contrast to the passivity of Śankara. We cannot detail all of them, but we will start with the issue of "abstraction." In response to a charge that mysticism in general and Eckhart in particular traffic in empty abstractions, Otto argues that: "To say that this 'Gothic' personality, absolutely permeated and glowing with the urge of a tremendous new life-impulse, lived in abstractions is absurd."[44] On the contrary, this "Gothic personality" espouses a view that celebrates the vital strength of the living will: "Eckhart's position is neither mystical quietism nor secular activity, but an identity of the deepest unity and the most vivid multiplicity, and therefore of the most profound quiet and most vital motion. It is therefore both a complete inward composure and a most powerful actualization and exercise of the will."[45] Eckhart is, therefore, a "voluntarist": "Thus Eckhart becomes the panegyrist of the strong and active will, and the powerful act—of a voluntarism which alone truly deserves this name."[46]

Entailed in this is the argument that Śankara's Indian view is world-denying while Eckhart's Gothic view is life-affirming: "For Śankara, the world remains world, painful and miserable, to be fled from, and denied. As we have already seen the result of this attitude is peculiar art of painting the world in pessimistic colors."[47] By contrast, the "Gothic personality," Eckhart, in at least partial agreement with that arch Gothic personality Luther, is world-, and life-affirming: "But Eckhart says: 'I would gladly remain here until the last day.' For him samsāra is already nirvāna, and both become one; he finds joy in the world, radiant with God's light. It is characteristic that with him there are no mournful plaints or lamentations over the world and the body, which play so great a role in Francis, occasionally disfigure Luther's preaching, and are so frequent in Indian philosophy, both in Buddhism and in Hinduism."[48]

In contrast to Śankara's world-denying view, this "Gothic personality" espouses a kind of *Lebensphilosophie*: "His mysticism is quiveringly *alive* and of powerful vitality, and therefore far removed from 'Abstraction.' It is therefore also very far from Śankara and Indian mysticism, and the reason for that difference lies in the foundation from which it rises. In spite of great formal equalities, the inner core of Eckhart is as different from that of Śankara as the soil of Palestine and of Christian Gothic Germany in the thirteenth century is different from that of India."[49] As Otto makes clear, the differences described here are not merely a matter of individual idiosyncrasies, but are a matter of "soil," that is, of differences in national, cultural, and religious *character*. This is very much the same kind of argument about the differences between India and Europe made by Hegel, discussed earlier.[50]

We have seen how Otto, *pace* Hegel, argues for a correlation between the stages of human development and their conceptions of divinity. If Otto argues that India is essentially passive and the Gothic West is essentially active, it is not surprising that he will also argue that Śankara's god is passive and inferior and Eckhart's god is active, vital, and superior. Again, Otto says many things in this regard and it will not be possible to detail them all.

One point which Otto makes again and again is that vital activity is essential to the Gothic conception of deity while it is an objection to the Indian conception of deity. Using an old philosophical notion as a point of entry into this discussion he argues: "The Deity of Eckhart is *causa sui*, but this is not in the merely exclusive sense, that every foreign *causa* is shut out, but in the most positive sense of a ceaseless self-production of Himself."[51] As with Hegel, the outgoing, externalizing moment is an essential component of Spirit, of that which differentiates Spirit from mere substance, of that which gives Spirit an inner life, namely, personality.

By contrast, Śankara finds this inner differentiation and external creativity of the godhead a defect, a falling away from an eternal, immutable perfection:

> This [the notion of *causa sui*] is indeed the case with Śankara, for whom the coming forth of God and the world from the primeval oneness of Brahman is the great "mistake" of Avidyā. But it is not so with Eckhart. God is the wheel rolling out of itself, which, rolling on, not rolling back, reaches its first position again. That it rolls from inward, outward, and inward again is of deep significance.[52] God is, in Himself, tremendous life movement. Out of undifferentiated unity He enters into the multiplicity of personal life and persons, in whom the world and therewith the multiplicity of the world is contained.[53]

The contrast is clear: "Is this Brahman a *living* God? 'I am the living God'—that is more than a God who lives."[54] Insofar as Eckhart's god is mystical it is not because this conception is abstract, passive, mere substance. Rather: "This God becomes a mystical God because He is a stream of glowing vitality."[55]

In a statement that captures both his argument for the superiority of the Western conception of God and the inferiority of the merely natural, Otto again differentiates the Brahmanic conception of God from the Teutonic: "This God is in Himself a living *process*, not a static Being. We may here use the word 'process' but only for want of a better, for it has nothing of the nature of any ordinary process. A process is a natural event, but this is no event; it is activity, mighty self-positing, a procreation not under the compulsion of laws or blind impulse but in the creative power and freedom of sublime wonder."[56]

What clearly emerges from this exercise in "comparative religion" is a replication of the structure of relations as conveyed classic image of "the Orient" as described by Edward Said and others. Again, my argument here is not simply that Otto's exposition of texts is in error, but that his hermeneutical assumptions, whether conscious or unconscious, are predicated upon a hierarchical structural relationship that nearly mirrors perfectly the structure of European colonial relations. He first essentializes "the East," reducing it to a single character, and then shows it to be passive, feminine, and inferior to an essentialized Gothic West in every sense. While others have claimed that Otto is primarily a normative, theological thinker, I am arguing that he does this on the basis of *Wissenschaft* and that this was a standard practice and almost universally accepted view in the *Geisteswissenschaften* in general and in *Religionswissenschaft* in particular.

*Plotinus versus Eckhart: Pagan versus Christian*

Although he does not develop the theme thoroughly, Otto also insists that, in a manner similar to his critique of Śankara, the Gothic-Christian mysticism of Eckhart transcends the best representative of mysticism in Greco-Roman antiquity, viz., Plotinus: "Here again Eckhart differs completely from Plotinus though he is always represented as his pupil. Plotinus also is the publisher of a mystical love, but his love is throughout not the Christian *agápē* but the Greek *erōs*, which is enjoyment, and enjoyment of a sensual and supersensual beauty, arising from an aesthetic experience almost unknown to Eckhart."[57] Again, by contrast, while the aesthetically and sensual orientation of Plotinus lends itself to a wild emotionalism, which, as we saw, is the mark of a less-developed spirituality, Eckhart is more like another arch Gothic personality, Kant, in effacing emotion even in mystical experience: "Eckhart knows nothing of such emotional orgies or such 'pathological' love (as Kant calls it). For him love is not *erōs* but the Christian virtue of *agápē*, strong as death but no paroxysm, inward but of deep humility, at once active in willing and doing as Kant's 'practical' love."[58]

The *differentia* between Christian *agápē* and Greek *erōs* are reason-morality-Spirit. Sensuality is the mark of the less emancipated, less fully realized stage of Spirit or manifestation of the numen. On that basis, as well as on the basis of his own exegesis of Plotinus and Eckhart, Otto positively bristles at the idea that Eckhart would be dependent upon the sensualistic pagan. The Hegelian-Idealist correlations hold true, even *within* the West: as Spirit is to nature, as developed is to primitive, as West is to East, so also is Modern to Ancient (and Christian to Pagan) within the West. Just as in Hegel's metanarrative of Spirit, Otto sees the Gothic West as the culmination of *Religionsweltgeschichte*.

## The Stage of Monotheism: Judaism and Islam versus Christianity

### The Case of Judaism

Just as with Hegel and many others, Otto saw the "arrival" of Spirit at the stage of monotheism as a tremendous advance in its emancipation from nature, its rationalization, and its coming to full self-consciousness. One would think, then, that all monotheisms would receive a different kind of treatment than has "primitive" religion, "Eastern" religion, or paganism. However, this is not the case. Otto sees deep and basic differences between the three "major" monotheistic religions, Judaism, Islam, and Christianity. As these differences add significant weight to the thesis that Otto's history of religion mirrors the European colonial situation, a close look at it will be necessary, starting with Judaism.

Like most Christians, Otto had a somewhat ambivalent view of Judaism. On the one hand, it represents a definite stage of progress in the *Entwicklung* or development of religious consciousness: "[W]hile the feelings of the non-rational and numinous constitute a vital factor in every form religion may take, they are pre-eminently in evidence in Semitic religion and most of all in the religion of the Bible."[59] Semitic monotheism constitutes a radical break with nature religion by holding the divine to be outside nature and its transcendent source. The numinous, however, is both rational and nonrational. With Biblical religion, the emergence of a purer form of the numinous can be detected: "The lower stage of numinous consciousness, viz. daemonic dread, has already been long superseded by the time we reach the Prophets and Psalmists."[60]

On the other hand, he is quick to make the classic Christian supracessionist argument, that is, that Christianity both transcends and completes Judaism, albeit in somewhat new terms. Speaking of Jesus, Otto argues as follows: "What of the Lord of this kingdom, the 'heavenly Father'? As its Lord He is not less, but far more 'holy,' 'numinous,' mysterious ... and *sanctus* than His kingdom. He is all these in an absolute degree, and in this aspect of his nature He represents the sublimation and the consummation of all that the old covenant had grasped by way of 'creature-consciousness,' 'holy awe,' and the like. Not to realize this is to turn the gospel of Jesus into a mere idyll."[61] We saw earlier the value Otto places on the philosophical concept of "personality," that is, Spirit's inner life and self-reflective nature (as opposed to the Indian and pagan notion of mere substance). That concept seems to be what defines the superiority of Christ and Christianity over Judaism: "Christ had rather to teach and to proclaim what was *not* self-evident to the Jews, but His own original discovery and revelation, that this very 'Holy One' is a 'heavenly Father.' "[62] Fatherhood represents a higher stage of the development of personality than the image of "lawgiver," so prominent in Mosaic religion, as he argues elsewhere: "On the one hand was Pharisaism, with its servitude to Law; on the other, John the Baptist, with his harsh, ascetic interpretation of God."[63] Jesus represents the *via media*, a synthesis of these extremes that transcends the limits of both.

## The Case of Islam

If Otto held a somewhat ambivalent view of Judaism, he is unequivocal in his view of Islam. Speaking of the process by which the numinous is made more rational throughout religious development, he sharply contrasts both Judaic monotheism and Christian personalism with the irrational and retrograde monotheism of Islam: "The culmination of the process [of rationalization] is found in the prophets and in the Gospels. And it is in this that the special nobility of the religion revealed to us in the Bible is to be found, which, when the stage represented by the 'deutero-Isaiah' is reached, justifies its claim to be a universal world-religion. Here is to be found its manifest superiority over, e.g. Islam, in which Allah is a mere 'numen,' and is in fact precisely Yahweh in His pre-Mosaic form and upon a larger scale."[64] Rather than being the teleological, progressive development of the rationalization of the numinous, which one would expect from his theory of history, for reasons hard to understand from a logical point of view, Otto saw Arabic monotheism as a regression, and to him, Islam represents a desultory mixing of sensuous and numinous elements. Contrasting the Quranic notion of predestination with that of Luther, Otto employs rather striking language for a practitioner of *Religionswissenschaft*:

> If it be really true that the consciousness of the numinous, as "creature-feeling," is the root of the predestination idea,

then we should expect that the form of religious faith marked by an undue and exaggerated insistence on the non-rational elements in the idea of God would also lean most markedly to predestination. And such is obviously the case. No religion has such a leaning to predestination as Islam; and the special quality of Islam is just that in it, from its commencement onwards, the rational and specifically moral aspect of the idea of God was unable to acquire a firm and clear impress that it won, e.g., in Christianity or Judaism. In Allah the numinous is absolutely preponderant over everything else. So that, when Islam is criticized for giving a merely "fortuitous" character to the claim of morality, as though the moral law were only valid through the chance of caprice of the deity, the criticism is well justified, only "chance" and fortuitousness have nothing to do with the matter. The explanation is rather that the numinous in Allah, nay, even his uncanny daemonic character, outweighs what is rational in him. And this will account for what is commonly called the "fanatical" character of this religion. Strongly excited feelings of the numen, that runs to frenzy, untempered by the more rational elements of religious experience—that is everywhere the very essence of fanaticism.[65]

Otto, again, seems here to be reiterating Hegel's theo-anthropogenic thesis: "An inferior god or a nature god has inferior, natural and unfree human beings as its correlates; the pure concept of God or the spiritual God has as its correlate spirit that is free and spiritual, that actually knows God."[66] The teleological "arrival" of the stage of monotheism does not, per se, automatically mean that a given group of human beings have emancipated themselves from nature. Otto's argument clearly indicates that the "Arab character" is more closely tied to emotion or passion, and so to *Natur*, and less tied to reason, and so to *Geist*, than is the "Hebrew character" or the "Christian character." So it is not, finally, a matter of a stage of history or of religious content that determines spirit. It is, apparently, a matter of race. It is not coincidental to this analysis of the structural relations between Judaism, Christianity, and Islam, which seems in many ways to defy Otto's own logic, that Judaism contributes to Christianity and Europe and so is valorized to a degree, while Islam and Arabic civilization have long been held to be the antagonists and rivals of both Christianity and Europe. To anticipate the conclusion of this essay a bit, the analyses of theorists such as Edward Said (e.g., in his work, *Orientalism*) describe the functioning of the system of representations created by Western scholars, including Otto and *Religionswissenschaft*, as a hierarchy of correlative concepts: Islam *must* be irrational if Christianity is to be rational. Judaism *must* be legalistic if Christianity is to be the consummate religion of love. We will return to these issues in the conclusion of this study.

## Supremacy of Christianity Thesis

By contrast, in its combination of elements of "pure reason" with outward expressions, the Christian religion, "with its peculiar and unique content of belief and feeling, standing in all its historical greatness and *supremacy* when measured against other religions,"[67] and thereby "shows its superiority over others. It is a more perfect religion and more perfectly religious than they, in so far as what is potential in religion in general becomes in Christianity a pure actuality."[68] Because, as argued above, "we count this the very mark and criterion of a religion's high rank and superior value—that it should have no lack of *conceptions* about God; that it should admit knowledge—the knowledge that comes by faith—of the transcendent in terms of conceptual thought.... Christianity not only possesses them in unique clarity and abundance, and this is, though not the sole or even the chief, yet a very real sign of its *superiority* over religions of other forms and at other levels."[69] As we saw with Hegel, Tiele, and Dilthey, "structure is everything," that is, the ability to give form to the unformed is a basic principle, which defines something as "higher" in the scale of "development." For Otto, Christianity is a synthesis of the numenal content with rational-ethical form. As such, Christianity is the consummation, or the "pure actualization" of religion. Otto's generic description of religion becomes the standard by which he ranks religions. As with Hegel and Tiele, Otto claims supremacy and superiority for the Christian religion. Given the criteria/description of religion he lays out, Christianity fulfills them to a greater degree, so the argument goes, than any other religion, whether tribal or primitive, whether "Eastern," or Greco-Roman. Otto's idea of the holy is a supremacist view of world religion. The colonialist's religion is the supreme religion, ergo, Christian civilization is the superior civilization.

The same point applied to moral concepts. Otto goes to great pains, as had Schleiermacher before him, to show that religion is not the same thing as morality. However, just as with Hegel, both are part of the rational, immaterial, non-natural essence of Spirit, and so advances in Spirit will correlate with advances in conceptions of the holy as well as moral concepts. In this, too, Christianity proves its supremacy over other religions: "No religion has brought the mystery of the need for atonement or expiation to so complete, so profound, or so powerful expression as Christianity."[70] The consciousness of atonement and sin is, for Otto, first a numinous quality, but, through the development of the idea, it gets progressively rationalized into ethics. As the Christian religion has attained the highest point of unity between *hyle* and *morphe*, between the numenal content and the structuration of rational conceptualization, so too is it the supreme religion in its articulation of the moral dimension of Spirit. It becomes possible, then, to measure and rank religions as to their development of morality. Some religions will be deemed "degenerate" religions while others will be considered ethical. None, however, rise to the level of the Christian religion.

## Conclusion

On the one hand, the very nature of the idea of an a priori category would seem to move in an egalitarian, universalistic, and inclusive direction, and Otto does famously state that "[t]here is no religion in which [the idea of the holy] does not live as the real innermost core, and without it no religion would be worthy of the name."[71] On the other hand, Otto draws the logical consequence of this sequence of claims, from his analysis of the "holy" as a "pure" a priori category (i.e., belonging to Spirit), to its manifestation throughout history, which also, as with Hegel, is the history of *Geist's* gradual emancipation from *Natur*: "For nothing is more clearly taught by a comparison of religions than this: the *qualitative* difference of religions in their higher stages. There is no single thing which marks the difference between man and man so penetratingly as his religion; neither race, nor climate, nor way of life can compare with it."[72] Comparing Hinduism with Christianity, he continues:

> There is an unlikeness in a human being who conceives and has an inward experience of the of the Eternal Being as an omnipotent Karma urging from birth to birth, with an ever-recurring agony of the lust for life, who finds salvation in a blissful cessation of the desire for existence; and in another who has experience of it as an official of the law, auditing one's own life in a debit and credit of "good works"; and an *absolute unlikeness* in another, who has experience of it as the "Father of Jesus Christ."[73]

While it would *seem* that the universalistic tendency of terms such as "*Geist,*" "man," "essence," "a priori," etc., would tend towards a more egalitarian view of religion, precisely the opposite is the case.

Such a colonialist-discourse reading of Otto's texts would seem to be all the more necessary given the dominant tendency in Religious Studies to valorize Otto and depoliticize him. One scholar, who describes herself as a Jewish feminist, argues in a recent book for "the inclusivity of The Idea of the Holy,"[74] claiming that "Otto's concept of holiness proposes an egalitarian anthropology"[75] and that *"The Idea of the Holy* is . . . socially and historically disengaged."[76] Moreover, "whilst Otto's concept of holiness is heavily dependent on Western philosophical categories and his own Lutheran tradition, it is never parochial. The close relation of his phenomenology and his theology entails that Otto imposes no obligation of choice between one's own tradition and another, or any . . . tests of spiritual loyalty."[77] Such are the kind of scholarly hermeneutics one encounters in the field Religious Studies, an academic field that, as we saw others charge, has arguably been more interested in "inter-faith dialogue" than in critical scholarship.

By contrast, the genealogical, poststructuralist-postcolonial reading of Otto offered here allows us translate the abstract, metaphysical conceptual dichotomies such as a priori/a posteriori, Spirit/Nature, sense/reason into a kind of veiled speech about historically real social groups: Indians, Chinese, Africans, Native Americans, and so forth. We can then see the logocentric, Eurocentric, and Christocentric tendencies of Religious Studies as a field of "knowledge" as these are expressed in Otto's famous and oft-cited work, *The Idea of the Holy*. What Otto articulates becomes the pattern for Religious Studies in all too many cases: the concept of essence is used, first to define one's own religion as the "pure" and "perfect" realization of the Idea; then, to arrange all others in relative gradation insofar as they approximate the Idea. In an abstract system of concepts, this would be one thing. Applied to real human groups as Otto does, the metanarrative of *Geist*, whether articulated diachronically or synchronically, is simply and factually a narrative of the *supremacy*—his term, not mine—of white, Christian Europe over black, "primitive" Africa and a movement away from brown or yellow, "despotic" Asia. While subsequent phenomenologist of religion will modify parts of this structure, to the extent that Otto and his work are still regularly cited in critical, even definitional places in the field, the politics of *Geist* still inform the structure of Religious Studies.

# 7

# Phenomenology as Empathetic Taxonomy

## The Phenomenological Approaches of Chantepie de la Saussaye and W. B. Kristensen

> The phenomenology of religion has as its ultimate end, the arrangement of sympathetically interpreted religious phenomena in taxonomies which reveal their common forms of development.
>
> —Thomas Ryba, *The Essence of Phenomenology*

Chantepie de la Saussaye was a Dutch contemporary of C. P. Teile's. He is widely regarded as the first scholar to use the term, "phenomenology of *religion*." As such, he is an important figure in the history of the development of phenomenology of religion and the study of religion generally: "He was one of the first to conceive of the phenomenology of religion as a scientific discipline."[1] Recall also van der Leeuw's remark (cited in chapter 1 of this study) in the preface to his *Religion in Essence and Manifestation* (originally published in 1933): "As regards Phenomenology itself, Chantepie's volume should be consulted."[2]

In 1878 Chantepie took the new chair at Amsterdam and held it until 1899. He then went to Leiden and held a chair there in Theological Encyclopedia, Doctrine of God, and Ethics until his retirement in 1916. Tiele's successor at Leiden was W. B. Kristensen, a Norwegian classicist who had studied with Tiele before receiving his PhD Kristensen assumed Tiele's former chair in 1900 and held it until 1937. Thus, as both were at Leiden, the careers of these two scholars of religion are closely connected, even if their work differs, and goes back to the origin of Religious Studies as an autonomous discipline.

W. B. Kristensen was part of the second generation of scholars who held a chair in History of Religions, and was one of the principal mentors of the succeeding generations of Dutch phenomenologists. His phenomenology is characterized by a decided lack of Husserlian *terminology* (e.g., "structure," "*epoché*," "eidetic vision," etc.). Its clearest source is Chantepie de la Saussaye's approach to phenomenological classification by structural parallels. If only in this respect, he follows Chantepie. Kristensen's approach to phenomenology sets the themes for many subsequent versions of phenomenology: the procedure of *simile in multis*, the role of empathy in research, the emphasis on meaning, and the ideal nature of representations of religion, and, clearly influenced by Chantepie, the tripartite nature of the science of religion.

The relationship between Chantepie and Kristensen, however, is complex and this complexity is important for the history of the study of religion. Speaking of contemporary phenomenologists of religion, Walter Capps notes that:

> When they trace their intellectual roots, the genealogy they offer tends to reach back not to Husserl ... but to such relatively obscure figures such as Cornelius Petrus Tiele ... and Pierre Daniel Chantepie de la Saussaye.... These two are credited as being the first phenomenologists of religion, if only because they employed a descriptive system of classification in coming to terms with the particulars of religion. This strain of phenomenology has moved from Tiele and Chantepie into the twentieth century under the influence of W. Brede Kristensen, Geraardus van der Leeuw, Geo Windengren, C. J. Bleeker, Mircea Eliade, their students, and a host of others, some of whom have eventually come to disclaim most associations with any philosophical founding fathers.[3]

It is clear then, that from Chantepie to Kristensen we have a generational transition. It is also clear that both men were central to the history of the phenomenology of religion. Finally, it is also clear that, as with Hegel in the nineteenth century, we have another case of appropriation via critique and ostensive rejection.[4]

Capps describes this generational shift by contrasting the treatment of the origins of religion: "Both Tiele and Chantepie engaged in phenomenology of religion while maintaining methodological interest in questions religion's origin and essence. However, by the time of W. Brede Kristensen (1867–1953), a Norwegian who, following Tiele's death, taught at the University of Leiden, phenomenology came to be understood as a clear alternative to the search for origins and essences."[5]

In analyzing the discursive formations of each of author, then, we shall look at the explanations, the metatheory, each has for both *Religionswissenschaft* and for *Religionsphänomenologie*. We will look at different issues surrounding this metatheory. Then, where possible, we will examine the actual treatment each offers on the concrete materials of the history of religions.

In both of their theories and in their treatment of the data, what we will find is, in one generation of phenomenologists of religion, a shift from a developmental, diachronic paradigm to a synchronic, taxonomic paradigm. Speaking historically, we move from the nineteenth to the twentieth century. Kristensen's critique of Otto is an important early moment in this transition, a transition from phenomenology's "formative" period to its "classical" period. Subsequent phenomenologists will *ostensibly* reject developmental schemes. Thus, in this chapter, the science of religion will take a new turn.

## Chantepie: *Religionswissenschaft* as a Tripart Science

### The Structure of Religionswissenschaft

In his major work, *Manual of the Science of Religion*, Chantepie is quite explicit about the role of Hegel's philosophy of religion in the development of *Religionswissenschaft*. Among the essential conditions for the development of a science of religion, Chantepie says that "the first is, that religion, as such, should become an object of philosophical knowledge."[6] He credits Kant and Schleiermacher for providing the foundations for this knowledge, but argues that "we must see Hegel as its true founder, because he first carried out the vast idea of realizing, as a whole, the various modes for studying religion (metaphysical, psychological, and historical), and made us see the harmony between the idea and the realization of religion [*zwischem dem Begriff und der Erscheinung der Religion zur Anschauung zu bringen*]."[7]

Furthermore, the structure of his science is built around this harmony between the idea and realization of religion: "The object of the science of religion is the study of religion, of its essence and its manifestations [*Die Religionswissenschaft hat die Erforschung der Religion, ihres Wesens und ihrer Erscheinungen zur Aufgabe*]"; "The *unity* of religion in the *variety* of its forms is what is presupposed by the science of religion."[8] The classic metaphysics of the "One and the Many" is at work here. In the discourse of the phenomenology of religion, this idea of unity in variety is usually expressed by "essence and manifestation," a term that is thoroughly Hegelian and clearly metaphysical. So the science of religion presupposes a metaphysics.

Chantepie divides up the labor of the science of religion into three parts. The philosophy of religion defines the idea, or essence of religion (*Idee*, or *Wesen*), and, as such, establishes the *specifica differentia* of the category. The history of religion collects the "actual facts" of religion. Chantepie divides the "historical part" into two sub-parts: "The ethnographical [part] gives us details of the religions of savage tribes, the so-called children of nature (*Naturvölker*), or *that part of mankind that has no history*. The second division gives us the historical development of the religions of civilized nations."[9] The third part is the properly phenomenological part: "The collecting and grouping of various religious phenomena forms the transition from the history to the phenomenology of religion. The latter treats religion according to its subjective and objective sides, and therefore consists of a psychological and a metaphysical part."[10]

The structure of this science, then, is as follows: there is an underlying essence of religion, "religion as such," which manifests itself in various historical instances. As these manifestations are manifestation *of* an essence, there is a deep identity underlying them. As such, it is possible to array the forms in which these manifestations present themselves in a nonhistorical taxonomy, or, in other words, a "phenomenology." As Chantepie conceives it, phenomenology is a technique of classification, of extracting formal elements from material instances. Such a conception is only possible, however, if one assumes an underlying unity to the multiplicity of historical materials. It is necessary to examine, then, how this phenomenological operation works.

## Phenomenology as Taxonomic Operation

Chantepie explains the basic structure of the phenomenological operation:

> The phenomenology of religion is most closely connected with psychology, in so far as it deals with facts of human consciousness. Even the outward forms of religion can only be explained from inward processes: religious acts, ideas, and sentiments are not distinguished from non-religious

acts, ideas, and sentiments by any outward mark, but only by a certain inward relation.[11]

The structure articulated here is consistent with the logic of the phenomenological project: it moves from the "inward," that is, "facts of human consciousness," to the "outward," which can only be understood as religious by their relation to the inward "sentiments." Essence precedes existence; this view is Idealist in that the "outer" is dependent upon consciousness. The following is an analysis of Chantepie's treatment of several areas of his phenomenological taxonomy of religion.

*Object of Worship*

Regarding the object of worship, the logic of phenomenology remains consistent: "Religion has in reality but one object, the living God who manifests Himself among all the nations as the only real God."[12] Here again, we find unity in the plurality. As with many other instances, phenomenology here is articulating what looks like an egalitarian, universalist notion: "all the nations." However, when it comes to the worship of nature, things are less clear: "[W]ith regard to the worship of nature, it is still difficult to say definitely what constitutes the real object of worship. . . . The worship of nature is so differently interpreted that it is impossible to discover a universal formula."[13] While it would be wrong to make too much of this, it is not without any significance that the contrast between the "real God" of "all the nations" is quite clear, while the "other nations?" who worship nature remain unclear, "it is still difficult say definitely what constitutes the real object of worship," and it also lacks the universality of the religion of the nations: "[I]t is impossible to discover a universal formula." Who are these people that worship an obscure object, who worship *nature*? They are the object, by and large, not of a phenomenological treatment, but an ethnographic treatment, as noted above.

*Idolatry*

Another object of phenomenological analysis is what Chantepie refers to as "idolatry," which "is the religious veneration of idols. But what is an idol?"[14] There is not a single essence to an idol, but two forms of its manifestation: that among people of "a lower stage of civilization" and that among "the more highly educated" strata of the same society.

They worship the same object, yet, for the lower class, "to them the essence and the power of the original are present in the image."[15] For the educated class, idols are looked "upon as a mere symbol and reminder of the deity."[16] Finally, the nature and origin of idols "cannot be traced back to one idea, but we must admit both views of the subject."[17] We will see how, in the larger science of religion, this plays out: the lower stages will be dealt with, by and large, in the "ethnographic" part, while the educated or civilized peoples will be treated in the "historical" part. As with Hegel, there is an inside and an outside to history. Some peoples do not (yet?) have the moral, intellectual, social, and spiritual development both facilitated by a history and necessary for there to be a history of a nation. Again, Chantepie locates this problem of the classification of idolatry in the phenomenological section of the science of religion, that is, the explanation of the outward forms by the inner processes.

The discussion of idols takes an interesting twist when the idols of India and Greece are implicitly compared: "But we must not delve too deeply for the hidden meaning [of idols], because many things, for instance in the idols of India, may be no more than the product of a thoughtless and tasteless imagination. In the Greek religion..." by contrast, the human form comes to be highly emphasized: "This development is of high importance not only for the history of art, but likewise for that of religion."[18]

The reason that it is of "high" importance is not *primarily* religious but aesthetic-moral: "the impressions made by a Zeus or an Athena of Phidias were rather of an aesthetic and morally elevating nature."[19] The exalted nature of these Greco-European models elevates the mind and soul above the mere sensuousness of their form and content to the contemplation of a higher ideal of beauty, which has as its correlate the idea of moral principle. Just as with Hegel, the Greeks represent something of a break with nature in the "religion of beauty."

## The Phenomenology of the Gods

After a review of the phenomenon of personification of the gods, or "outer form" of the gods, Chantepie treats the subjective side of the phenomenon: "Let us now pass from the outer form of the god to its meaning. Our attention is first called to the connection between gods and nature."[20] As one might expect after reviewing previous thinkers, the meaning of the gods lies in their relationship to nature: "[T]he connection between most of the deities of mythology and the life of nature cannot be mistaken. But besides this connection, their difference also from nature-beings [natural beings?] must be emphasized."[21] He rejects a simplistic notion of "spiritualization," arguing that it is not specific enough to explain the difference between the gods and nature. He cites, rather, three areas in which this differentiation occurs: the family, art, and thought.

The issue of the family is rather straightforward: he argues that the origin and meaning of the gods does not lie in natural phenomena, but in the gods themselves. They neither merely represent nature-beings (e.g., the sun—versus the son), nor are they derived therefrom. They are, as a species, *causa sui*; a god can only come from another god.

The differentiation of the gods from nature is more extensively realized in art: "[T]hrough aesthetic and ethic spiritualization, the gods were brought nearer to man both outwardly and inwardly, and raised into ideals of human perfection. With deities developed in this way we almost forget whatever of their natural character still clings to them." [22] The underlying premise is that the human is distinct from the natural and that aesthetics and ethics are themselves markers of the human. Again, in the phenomenological analysis of the gods, we have reiterated the *Geist/Natur* distinction. To be an ideal of perfection is to shed the connection to nature.

This process is intensified in the realm of "thought": "Both [personification and the connection to nature] are absent when the gods are transformed into intellectual ideas, but the result is nevertheless the same, namely, the loosening of the bond between gods and nature."[23] Thought, or "our thought," in the singular and therefore as universal, abstracts from "the world" and thereby raises its object above the concrete: "Our thought strives after the general and the abstract ... and is inclined to put the individual [aspect of the] gods in the background, for the general idea of the divine.... Thought realizes ... the idea of a world-unity."[24] Again, the abstract, *pace* Plato, is above the *hylé*, the material, and therefore the natural.

In his phenomenology of the gods, then, we have yet another micronarrative of the emergence of the *geistig* out of the natural. The concept of divine families indicates a non-natural origin and essence of the gods. Art anthropomorphizes them, thus making them more like "Man," and so less like nature—the underlying premises are quite obvious. Finally, it is thought, that realm least effected by and least resembling nature, that the gods are all but liberated from their bond to nature. Although he does not explicitly render this as an evolutionary process, he does use the word *developed* (*Entwicklung*). What is clear that this is a phenomenology which, qua phenomenology, entails the gradual separation of *Geist* from *Natur*. That this is a structural feature of Chantepie's *Religionswissenschaft* can be seen in greater clarity by looking at the other divisions of the science of religion, viz., ethnography and history.

## Ethnographic Part

In describing what he means by "ethnography," Chantepie makes the following distinction: "Anthropology occupies itself with the physical, ethnography with the social side of human life; the former treats of man as a natural being, the latter man as a rational social being."[25] We again have the division between the physical elements of humanity and the "inward" elements. This forms the very structure of the way this branch of the tripart science of religion works: "Although ethnography can include in the domain of its enquiries the whole mental development [*Entwicklung*] of man, yet people generally divide the ethnographic description of low races from the historical treatment of civilized nations, and thus place ethnography between anthropology and history."[26] Civilized nations have history, just as with Hegel, but: "Amongst savages, race is the only thing we can consider, but in higher stages of civilizations this is only the foundation on which the development of nations has been carried out."[27] Savages *are* race, that is, are defined by the body: "For the classification of mankind several criteria have been taken into account. First, the color of skin."[28] Skin color first; *prima*, the first to step away from nature, that is, the lower races, races at the bottom of a hierarchy of privilege, wherein "higher" means both farther from nature/skin/race, and also therefore better. Skin, race, *define* but only for the lower races or savages. This is the result of the anthropological, or physical side of the study of humanity.

The ethnographical study, by contrast looks at the "mental" development of humanity, and classifies humans according to the stage their society has reached. "Savages" are "races who do not cultivate the soil, or possess domestic animals" and use only "the roughest wood and stone implements."[29] "But as soon as the soil is tilled and flocks are kept, a higher stage of civilization is reached. Tylor calls the races on this middle stage, barbarians."[30] Finally, "the third stage, that of civilization, the use of writing is the condition with which an historical life begins, when the results of the past are consciously received into the life of the present."[31] Race, soil, logos, thus are the stages of civilization that are, at the same time, *types* of human beings. Whatever common essence humanity has, it is not realized in the same degree by different peoples. While it is not absolutely the case, by and large the lower races are peoples of color, the "barbarians," or intermediate stages are non-Europeans,[32] and Europe is taken as civilized without hesitation or qualification.

This classification is also, in the main, a classification of types of religions. "In the lowest stage we find everything, in theory as well as in practice, utterly unorganized" and the aims of these religio-magic religions "are connected with the special needs of daily life,"[33] or, with material concerns: food, shelter, health, income, etc. Even at the level of religion, at the level of Spirit, the concern with the material and bodily dominates. Spirit, then, is not conscious of itself as Spirit, it is "utterly unorganized," with no rational-moral structure to it.

The barbarian stage of religion has "no special effect in view, but are practiced because they belong to the system of the worship of God."[34] While savage religion is a means to an end, or has only extrinsic value, with barbarian religion a new stage is reached wherein religion becomes an end in itself, that is, it has intrinsic value. The highest stage is defined as "a consciously cared for, and developed religious teaching handed down in writings."[35] Consciousness, developed (*Entwicklung* again), and writing here *construct difference*. These logocentric elements compose the nature of religion and the nature of the peoples who practice these religions. For Chantepie holds that races have intrinsic characteristics, a point we must examine.

Chantepie forms his view of innate "dispositions" by arguing against the claim that humans are products of their environment, one version of which he explicitly names as materialism: "There is a school which explains everything by outward environments and circumstances; some consider this to be a materialistic and democratic prejudice."[36] Besides setting up this view for a critique, the significance of this statement is that materialism is labeled as a prejudice, which is not only dismissive, it sets materialism apart by implicitly labeling it as a "theory." The significance of this is that phenomenologists routinely deny that phenomenology is a theory. It is merely description, it is a return, a release from theory and a movement "back to the things themselves" as Husserl so often said. We have seen and will see further on two things. First, is that phenomenologists invariably deny they have a theory and invariably accuse any kind of reductive argument as a theory that *imposes* itself on the data. Second, we have and will see that phenomenology is not only a theory, it is a metaphysics. One central paired philosopheme/assumption of this metaphysics is the categorical difference between consciousness and embodiment or, at a higher level of generality, Spirit's difference from Matter/Nature. It is clear that these philosophemes underlie Chantepie's construction of the stages of civilization and his theory of race.[37]

In opposition to the argument predicated on environmental factors in the development of the "disposition" (by which I take him to mean a general moral and intellectual character), Chantepie makes a number of points. One is that there are clear limits to the capacity of some peoples, that is, "to the often proved incapability of races to overstep certain mental limits."[38]

He further argues that the proof of an innate disposition is that even if the environmental factors are changed, the disposition of a people would not: "If we compare the sanguine Negro with the melancholy Malay, we can hardly maintain that if these two races had exchanged their homes and circumstances, they would also possess inverted mental abilities. Such differences can only be accounted for by original disposition."[39] This is because "blood brings certain dispositions."[40]

## History of Religions

The History of Religion forms the third part of the science of religion. Space does not allow for a full treatment of the subject here; however, we can examine two "case studies," viz., China and India. We saw with Hegel and Tiele that these two religions occupied a strategic place as Europe's Other. As such, it will useful to examine them briefly.

### China

We have seen that China is a key touchstone for the formation of narratives of religious history in the discourse of the phenomenology of religion. There are three important points in the treatment of China. First is the order of treatment in his history. While his pattern does not follow Hegel's in detail, it is quite similar in a key point: it begins with China. Second, while he does not argue for a linear history of development from East to West, he does hold a developmental theory of religion and culture generally. Therefore, by putting China in the first of history, he has lifted it out of the realm of the savage, but as first, it is implicitly the least developed of the historical religions. Finally, in a very Eurocentric manner, not unlike Hegel's judgment on China, he argues: "Chinese civilization early reached a considerable height, both materially and intellectually.... It has spread over a large territory and civilized many savage tribes, but it has never had any important influence on the course of the world's history."[41] China, turned in upon itself, does not objectify itself, but is "lost" in pure subjectivity. Thus turned inward, she does not step out into history as understood by Europeans. In other words, China has no "influence" on Europe, therefore China has no influence on *world* history. Neither does China participate in *Weltgiest*, the World Spirit of which history is the unfolding. While he denies that China does not change, its change is locked as being-within-itself, not as the full realization of being-in-and-for-itself.

*Hinduism/India*

We saw with Hegel, Tiele, and Otto that India was an important contrast for Christianity and that Christianity would come to know itself as Spirit. Chantepie's treatment of Hinduism has some interesting points of contact with Hegel's. Two points shall be examined: the dream state of Hindus and the lack of a proper sense of history.

The dreamlike state is due to "an aversion to the reality of the outer world [which] forms an essential element" in the "uniformly developed character" of the Hindus, developed over thousands of years and through a tumultuous history.[42] The "theoretical" dimension of this dream state lies in the basic metaphysical assumptions of Hindus: "The belief in the unity of the world may be said to be the fundamental dogma of all Hindu conceptions."[43] Speaking of the Rig Veda: "The thought here prevails that the world forms one whole."[44] The fault in this view is that it does not allow Hindus to see particulars and to make clear distinctions between them: "The state of the perceptive soul is that of a sleep without dreams, in which hearing, thinking, and knowledge go on, but yet one cannot say that this or that is known.... [T]he world of phenomena, the individual existences, are only a dream."[45] Recall that this was the very same claim that Hegel had made about Hindus.

Something of a corollary to this dream state is "the abstruse character of Hindu thought."[46] In a discussion of one text, he makes just this point: "[T]he abstruse character of Hindu thought is clearly shown";[47] and speaking of another text, he remarks upon "its abstruse fantastic tone."[48] Speaking of the Upanishads, some of the greatest texts of Hindu religion, he says: "The thoughts are mostly abstruse, and the manner of presenting them in metaphors and comparisons makes them still more complicated. We can hardly realize them properly, not only because they are foreign to us, but rather because our language gives them a finish and precision which they do not possess in themselves."[49] They are completed, or at least, made intelligible by *us*. Only in our language is there any hope to render clarity, that is, reason, out of the dream state, which leads to abstruseness. By themselves, the Indians are a sorry lot.

This theme is amplified even more when the theme of history arises. Recall that Hegel had denied the Indians history, that is, they lacked the Spiritual conditions for it, and thus were crippled as a nation. In a similar fashion, Chantepie argues for "the total want of what may be called the historical sense" owing to the complete "absence of historical writings."[50] As he argued before, while Hindus have writing, an important maker of the stage of "civilized" development, a yet higher stage of development is to have a clearly defined history and therefore clearly defined states. As such: "For the development of mankind, the history of the small Greek states is of far greater importance than that of the vast country of India."[51] Consequently: "[W]e can hardly count them with the historical nations, for they are distinguished neither by noteworthy political formations, nor by the endeavor to assert and defend themselves against other nations."[52] Which is why "the history of the world . . . has so little to do with the Hindus."[53] Denying statehood to India on the basis of its lack of structure is tantamount to saying that it lacks the full imprint, if you will, of the Logos. No structure, no reason. It also legitimates the imposition of a structure on these people who, in their dreamlike, monistic state are incapable of forming one on their own. Colonization is good for the Hindus. Finally, the lack of a historical sense is yet another means by which the West triumphs over the East: the small Greek (European) states trump India's vast and ancient culture.

This also applies to both the study of the Hindus and to the study of religion. As Chantepie argues: "Although the history of religion as a whole treats of the inner phases of national life, yet the firm construction of external history with its clearly defined periods is necessary, as it forms the framework surrounding the growth of the history of religion. But this framework is utterly wanting here."[54] Two things are worth noting here. First, *incipit* the Logos: without structure, Spirit cannot properly objectify itself and so we have a deficient spirit. History is the proper, solid form of the realization of Spirit in the external, objective world. A people filled with abstruse meanings and lost in a dreamlike state. Second, Chantepie articulates an interesting methodological point: although the proper object of *Religionswissenschaft*, even when it is dealing with history, is the inner, the inward aspect, it needs the framework of solid history to study the development of religion. This is, again, the phenomenological concern with consciousness, interiority, and religious experience (individual or collective). However, this is now qualified: the study of consciousness presupposes the external, the outward, "the firm construction of external history." This is interesting on a number of levels, but recall his discussion on innate dispositions with the example of the "Negro" and the Malay. There, he denied that "environment" was a determinate factor. Perhaps there is no contradiction here. However, it seems to me that Europeans are concerned to show that India, with its grandeur and antiquity, its ancient textual traditions, which precede Europe's development by some length of time, perhaps a millennium or more, combined with the discovery that Sanskrit was an Indo-European (or "Indo-German") language, is a potential threat to Europe's cultural supremacy, that, at the very least, it could claim equal status with Europe. That would not only make the colonization of such a civilized nation a crime, it would destroy the study of religion's metanarrative, a narrative that completely hinges on the supremacy of Europe and the subordinate status of all other nations. In the structure of the discourse of the phenomenology of religion, both are unacceptable. This position is, again, a fortiori and not ad hoc.

Such is the work of Chantepie de la Saussaye. He introduced the taxonomic type of phenomenology, he described *Religionswissenschaft* as a tripart (or "Trinitarian") science, while maintaining that in any part of this science, the proper object of study is the inward, the inner states of persons and nations, of man to be sure. In many ways, he laid a structural foundation for what we have been calling "classic phenomenology." W. Brede Kristensen is an early, perhaps the first, representative of this phase of the history of phenomenology. We turn now to an analysis of his contribution.

## W. Brede Kristensen

During his lifetime Kristensen's published work did not earn him the notoriety that some of the other scholars studied here have attained. His influence came through his teaching rather than his writings, especially given that he did not publish work on methodology. What we have left are his unpublished (during his lifetime) course notes, compiled together in a large volume titled *The Meaning of Religion: Lectures in the Phenomenology of Religion*. Consequently, all citations concerning his views on methodology are taken from the English translation (the original version) of the "General Introduction" to *The Meaning of Religion*, his most complete statement of the aims and methods of phenomenology. Virtually all commentators on Kristensen draw from this work. Olaf Pettersson makes a typical justification for relying so heavily on this work: "As a source for the following survey (of Kristensen's approach) I use his book *The Meaning of Religion*, that was published in 1960—seven years after Kristensen's death."[55]

Kristensen, true to Chantepie's view of phenomenology as a taxonomic approach, offers no history of religion, but a vast amount of structural analyses. The second part of the book more resembles Eliade's *Patterns in Comparative Religion* than it does either Tiele's work or Chantepie's *Manual*. Our focus, then, will be on his statements about metatheory and methodology.

*Methodology*

"Phenomenology has as its objects to come as far as possible into contact with and to understand the extremely varied and divergent religious data."[56] The method of phenomenology, according to Kristensen, is that of finding the *simile in multis*; of bringing unity out of diversity. This task, he argues, is different from an older conception of "Comparative religion," which tries to compare religions as discreet wholes (more in the manner in which many nineteenth-century scholars did):

> Phenomenology does not try to compare the religions with one another as large units, but it takes out of their historical setting the similar facts and phenomena which it encounters in different religions, brings them together, and studies them in groups. The corresponding data, which are sometimes nearly identical, bring us automatically to comparative study.[57]

The operation of phenomenology, then, is to take what later phenomenologists will call "structures," namely, common elements found in historical instances of religion such as sacrifice, prayer, etc., isolate them from their specific place within that context, and group them together according to their "similarities." As such: "*It is not important in which religion we find them.*"[58]

There is, for Kristensen, a certain inductive quality to the notion of "commonality" or "similarity": "It is difficult to give an answer on the basis of data from one particular religion. We must have a general view based on observations gathered from as many religions as possible in order that we may achieve certainty."[59] That is, the preliminary stage of the delineation of the commonality of a spe-

cific "phenomenon" is the aggregation of prima facie similar types—
"Completely unique phenomena hardly ever occur"[60]—without any initial attempt to find a deeper sense of the commonality. We will return to this point shortly, to see what kind of account Kristensen does give for the "deeper" source of commonality between phenomena.

What this initial aggregation is supposed to show about the similarity between the phenomena is that it resides "not only in their historical context, but also in their ideal connection."[61] This is because "[p]henomenology is a systematic science, not just an historical discipline which considers the Greek, Roman, or Egyptian religion by itself. The problem is to determine what sacrifice itself is, not just what Greek, Roman, or Hebrew sacrifice is."[62] For Kristensen, phenomenology is the study of what other researchers call "ideal types." One of the questions we want to ask is: What does it mean to represent the other by means of ideal types?

Another crucial aspect of methodology for Kristensen is the empathetic understanding of others by means of one's own religious experience. In the same vein as Schleiermacher and Dilthey,[63] Kristensen argues: "By means of empathy he [the historian] tries to relive in his own experience that which is 'alien,' and that, too, he can only approximate. This imaginative re-experiencing of a situation strange to us is a form of representation and not reality itself, for that always asserts itself with sovereign authority."[64] This is the idea of *"Nachleben"* once again. It is the idea we have seen that consciousness can know consciousness, despite differences of historical/temporal context. The reason for this empathetic entering into the experience of others is twofold: methodologically, it is the means by which phenomenology is "objective," and therefore scientific (as opposed, in a specifically theological context, to particularistic and confessional); religiously, it promotes an ecumenical and tolerant relationship among the various confessions, a point many theologians and phenomenologists would make.

As with Otto, Kristensen argues that the means by which this empathy is achieved is our own religious experience: "We make use of our own religious experience in order to understand the experience of others.... There is an appeal made to the indefinable sympathy we must have for religious data which sometimes appear so alien to us."[65] Even though this would seem to align him with Otto, as we shall see below, he is very critical of Otto's theological intrusion into an ostensible science of religion (namely, in claiming, on the basis of his science of religion, that Christianity is the supreme religion). Against this, he asserts that:

> The historian and the student of Phenomenology must therefore be able to forget themselves, to be able to surrender themselves to others.... [otherwise] No justice is then done to the values which are alien to us, because they are not allowed to speak in their own language. If the historian tries to understand the religious data from a different viewpoint than that of the believers, he negates the religious reality. For there is no religious reality other than the faith of the believers.[66]

The goal of phenomenological research is the accurate, objectively factual representation of the data: "It is their religion that we want to understand, and not our own."[67] This cannot be achieved, he argues against Otto, if we take our own standpoint as the beginning and the criterion. We must "surrender ourselves" to the other in order to be both objective (an epistemological, veridical concern) and ecumenical (an ethical concern). After van der Leeuw this notion becomes the manner in which the Husserlian doctrine of the *epoché* gets appropriated. It is clear that, although Kristensen does regard the operation of phenomenology as a representation, he distinguishes between kinds of representations in such a way as to suggest that there are reasons and criteria that make some representations more veridical than others. That is, in saying the product of phenomenology is a representation, Kristensen is by no means a constructivist. In order for his methodological stipulations to make any sense, he must be arguing that there is at least some degree of veridicality via mimesis to the representations he proffers.

## The Representation of Religion

As we saw before, the representation of religion is based upon on ideal construction, which, however, is purported to be veridical. The question we must ask now is, What is the basis for the commonality upon which this ideal is constructed? Kristensen's preliminary answer gives us a hint: "The purpose of such study [i.e., phenomenology] is to become acquainted with the religious thought, idea or need which underlies the group of corresponding data."[68] That is, it is on the basis of such idealities as "religious thought, idea or need" that the specific, concrete instances of religious phenomena are to be associated into groups:

In order to understand particular (historical) data, we must frequently (and perhaps always) make use of the generalizations which are the results of comparative research. The sacredness of the Greek and Roman kings must be seen in the light of the ancient concept of kingship; particular sacrifices in the light of the religious essence of sacrifice.... [T]he religious essence of sacrifice is a concept and not historical reality (only the particular applications are reality), but we cannot dispense with those concepts. In historical research they are virtually considered as realities: to an important extent they give the research direction leading to the satisfying result of understanding the data.[69]

Two important points come out of this passage. First, he reiterates the notion that it is on the basis of the idealities that we relate discrete phenomena together. He elaborates this point further by means of two notions: the meaning of a phenomenon and the locus of that meaning in the nature of the human subject.

The ideal commonality of the groups of phenomena is based on their meaning: "Now to determine what is common is not so simple. It is certainly not to be sought in the outward traits which are held in common, in how the priests are clad and how the rites are divided among them. It is the common meaning of the sacrificial acts that is important, and that we must try to understand."[70] Reiterating a theme so prominent in Dilthey, and which will become a founding notion for all subsequent phenomenological approaches to religion, Kristensen relates essence, commonality, and ideality to the category of "meaning." He repeatedly uses phrases such as "common meaning," "religious significance," "religious meaning," "religious essence," "religious concept," and "ideal connection" in different yet very close ways, often even in synonymous ways. Although he does not articulate this explicitly, he is making the distinction between an "outward," specific instance, and a presumably "inward," common, general, even essential meaning. When it comes to the explanation or interpretation—either one; he uses both terms—of historical materials, Kristensen is clearly an idealist. He is also what we may call a "moderate essentialist," a point we shall return to below.

In order to understand this idealism, we must ask a further question: What is the basis or "grounding" of this common meaning? Kristensen himself puts the point thus: "[S]acrifices take place in almost all religions, although in different forms. This cannot be accidental. How is this fact to be explained? The sacrificial acts evidently issue from a religious need of a very universal nature."[71] So, we must ask, "What religious need has caused men, in all times and places, to present offerings to the gods?"[72] Immediately after this, he makes the point, quoted above, about meaning being the basis of commonality. This meaning is rooted in the nature of human beings, at least as that nature is expressed in religion. This notion of human nature is, in fact, basic to his most general characterization of the phenomenological enterprise: "Phenomenology's way of working (the grouping of characteristic data) and its task (the illustration of man's religious disposition) make is a systematic discipline."[73] That is, the meanings, idealities and their representations are based upon the nature of the human subject. Kristensen uses terms such as "religious need," "religious idea," "religious disposition," and "religious value" almost interchangeably. Whenever he does, he seems to be making an anthropological claim that such "manifestations" are expressions of a universal human nature. Religious values, he later claims in a different discussion, have "accurately expressed the religious consciousness."[74] Kristensen never makes the kind of strong statements of universality and subjectivity that we saw in the previous history of the study of religion. He is somewhat distinct from other phenomenologists in that, by and large, he more modest in what he claims than earlier—or, as will soon be seen, later—approaches were. However, as do all the theorists under study here, it is clear that Kristensen sees the representations of religion as veridical representations of the religious expressions of humanity that are grounded in the universal nature of human subjectivity or consciousness.

The second point to come out of the quote above[75] is the way in which Kristensen tries to qualify the nature of essence as an indispensable construct for the direction of research. This is based on his conception of the science of religion, a topic to which we must now turn.

### The Tripart Science: Philosophy, History, and Phenomenology in *Religionswissenschaft*

We saw earlier that Kristensen's notion of essence appears to be something on the order of an inductive generalization. He had earlier said that "we must have a general view based on observations gathered from as many religions as possible in order that we may achieve certainty."[76] However, farther on he criticizes just this notion of essence. If we confine ourselves to examining just the common forms of religious phenomena, "we are then left with empty concepts. The common element that we find in this way is so vague and fleeting that is gives no guidance in the research of Phenomenology."[77] The problem is how to determine the essence of a phenomenon, around which particular instances of that essence may be formed into groups and studied: "But if we must group the phenomena according to characteristics which correspond as far as possible to the essential and typical elements of religion, how do we then determine which data typically illustrate men's religious disposition, and how do we determine what are the essential elements of religion?"[78] Here again is the problem of the reconstruction of subjective expression posed in a similar manner, if also somewhat altered, as it was in Dilthey.

The answer he gives to this defines his conception of how the general science of religion is structured, what its divisions are, and how they relate to each other. As we just saw, an inductive generalization is not to Kristensen's liking. This is presumably because the function of the concept of essence is to give very strict and clear *differentia*, which will in turn guide research. Inductive generalizations do not give strict *differentia*, because further research (i.e., compiling of more cases) may change the *differentia*. To paraphrase Hume, there is no inductive guarantee that future instances of X will conform to, or have exactly the same characteristics as, past instances of X. The solution to this problem, Kristensen argues, is to resort to Philosophy:

> That which is really essential is shown by philosophical investigation. Essence is a philosophical concept, and it is the chief task of Philosophy of Religion to formulate that essence. The principal ideas in Phenomenology are borrowed from Philosophy of Religion. Philosophy must furnish the guiding principle in the research of Phenomenology. . . . It is the task of Philosophy of Religion to describe the essence of religion by determining the relation of religion to other spiritual realities—the intellectual, moral and aesthetic factors in our spiritual life—and thus to arrive at a definition of religion's distinctive nature.[79]

Just as did Schleiermacher and Otto, Kristensen sees the study of religion as predicated on the separation of religion from other "spiritual realities," for instance, art, morality, politics, and theoretical reason, that is, departments, so to speak, of *Geist*. Following Chantepie here, he holds that this is done by the deployment of the classical, logical-philosophical notion of essence, namely, as giving the *specifica differentia* of "religion" as an autonomous and distinct category.[80] Unlike Otto, he argues for neither an a priori nor a sui generis concept of religion or religious experience. The latter is, perhaps alluded to by the invocation of religion's specific difference, however. Thus, Philosophy, understood as the science of essence (i.e., logic, Logos), forms one part of the general science of religion.

Unlike Hegel, or most philosophers for that matter, Kristensen holds an odd view of how this philosophical essence is reached, one that echoes a theme we have seen before: "It is evident that in the philosophical determination of the essence of religion, we make use of data which lie outside the territory of philosophy, outside our knowledge. We make use of our own religious experience in order to understand the experience of other."[81] Similarly: "Yes, Philosophy presupposes personal religious experience; the theory of religion presupposes the practice of religion."[82] Essence is not separable from experience; both are "spiritual," or ideal phenomena. This is the subjective basis for the determination of essence.

History forms another part of the science of religion. The question is, however, what is the relationship between phenomenology and history? Or, to put the issue in more contemporary terms, what is the connection between "structure" and "event," or "genesis"? Phenomenology, after all, separates ideal types from their historical contexts, so what is the use of History? Kristensen answers: "Phenomenology of Religion is the systematic treatment of History of Religion. That is to say, its task is to classify and group the numerous and widely divergent data in such a way that an over-all view can be obtained of their religious content and the religious values they contain."[83] Phenomenology and History, then, are treated in a hylemorphic manner, related as form and matter: the ideal types established by the former (based upon the essence of the phenomena) give form to the *hylé* provided by the latter; the form is abstracted from the matter and it is on the basis of these forms that understanding (or, in the older hylemorphic tradition, "intelligibility") is achieved. Further, the abstracted forms are the basis by which the historian finds his or her way through the maze of material. Kristensen, without explicitly naming it, seems to be articulating something like a hermeneutical circle here: "The relationship between history and phenomenology thus becomes clear. The one assumes the presence of the other, and vice versa."[84]

Finally, what is the status of the three parts of the "general science of religion"? Kristensen gives his complete statement on the matter:

> Thus we see that anticipated concepts and principles are used in all the provinces of the general science of religion:

history, typology and philosophy.... None of the three is independent; the value and the accuracy of the results of one of them depend on the value and accuracy of the results of the other two. The place which the research of Phenomenology occupies between history and philosophy makes it extraordinarily interesting and important. The particular and the universal interpenetrate again and again; Phenomenology is at once systematic History of Religion and applied Philosophy of Religion.[85]

Here again, the resemblance between this and Chantepie's position is very strong. The importance, as noted earlier, of this fact is that it indicates the direction that classical phenomenology had taken before van der Leeuw's appropriation of Husserlian terminology. We can thus see more clearly what the structure of this discursive formation looks like.

## Phenomenological Limit

There are two principal points that serve to qualify Kristensen's position on phenomenology as a science of religion. First of all, he explicitly limits the claims that any science can make about religion. Secondly, he is critical of evolutionary theories, such as those of Hegel, Tiele, and Otto, and this characterizes and qualifies phenomenology's approach to history in a very important way.

### Limits of Religionswissenschaft

"Let us be completely aware of the limited validity of historical research. This limitation is imposed by the subject itself; namely, the absolute character of all faith. Every believer looks upon his own religion as a unique, autonomous and absolute reality. It is of absolute value and thus incomparable."[86] This sense of the absoluteness and the uniqueness of each believer's own "faith" mitigates the possibility of comparative, structural research. Following a philosophical and theological line standard at least since Kant, Kristensen holds that finite, temporal form of knowledge cannot comprehend the infinite, absolute experience which he assumes to be essential to religion. There is an inevitable and unbridgeable gulf, finally, between the faith of the believer and the work of scholarly reconstruction: "The historian's standpoint is a different one. There is a distance between him and the object of research, he cannot identify himself with it as the believer does. . . . The historian seeks to understand, and he is able to do that in an approximate way, approximate, but no more."[87] This recalls, if obliquely, Dilthey's dictum that "nature is explained, spirit is understood," if we see in the two varying degrees of precision in the analysis of religious data.

The science of religion, then, must be satisfied with such approximations. This is further evidenced by the way (as we have already seen) he qualifies the constructs used in research. Speaking specifically of the notion of essence he says: "[T]he religious essence of sacrifice is a concept and not historical reality" but "such fictitious realities and general formulations are assumed in all science."[88] Two things stand out about this remark, given what we will see in the subsequent history of the phenomenology of religion. First, he at once acknowledges the necessity of representation in the act of reconstruction and apologizes for it, as if it were some kind of fall from actuality. This implies that either religious experience itself, or some other realm of experience, could be or does in fact, have a more direct, immediate contact with reality: "The 'existential' nature of the religious datum is never disclosed by research. That cannot be defined."[89] There is, in the way this point is set, a trace of nostalgia for that kind of *unmittlebar Bewusstsein*, for a kind of contact with reality that is outside of representation, and therefore outside of all the historicity and contingency attendant upon all human conventions.

Secondly, he will be the last figure we see who has such a modest view of the possibilities of a science of religion. Eliade frequently lambasted scholars of religion for their "philosophical timidity" and held high hopes for phenomenology of religion as a central source of cultural renewal.[90] Van der Leeuw's occasional claims for phenomenology are of a similar kind, and both represent a radical departure from their predecessor's modesty.

Two points on Kristensen's view of history will conclude our discussion of his position. Despite his qualification of the representational character of historical science, he nevertheless ontologizes the act of historical retention. He contrasts the enduring with the passing, and explicitly correlates the former with the "essential" and the latter with the "inessential":

> The religious phenomena which primarily engage the attention of the historian and phenomenologist, however, are the formulations of belief and cultic practices which have endured for centuries and sometimes for thousands of years. They have proved themselves able to bear the life of numerous generations, because they have accurately expressed the

religious consciousness of an entire people.... The enduring existence of all these religious data proves their religious value: they have been felt to be as essential values of life, and they have indeed been just that.[91]

In light of Kristensen's critique of Otto and Hegel, which we are about to see, this is a remarkable claim. Historical survival, as depicted in this passage, is not a contingent, chance event, but based upon the essential—and by implication, ontological—character of such things as "values" and "consciousness." We cannot help but detect the classical Christian-Platonic scheme of a divided line between time and timelessness, correlated with a division between the essential and the derivative. Implicit and qualified with much personal humility as it may be, ontotheology is very much alive in this distinction.

This ontologizing of historical retention does not allow for either a "politics of memory," nor for the possibility that each generation appropriates and modifies what it takes from the past, such that there may not be any essential continuity between the past and the present. On the first point, he says, "[N]umerous passing fluctuations have undoubtedly disappeared from sight, and the principal lines indicating what is enduring and valuable come much more directly into focus."[92] The disappearance of things from history is attributed to their ontological character as "passing fluctuations." Kristensen does not entertain the possibility that, to paraphrase Foucault, history has known invasions, plunders, and reversals. Such disappearances are the result of human activity, often deliberate and violent policies of extermination. Religion, and not in the least Christianity, have often played a central role in such policies. Ontologizing retention depoliticizes history.

He also claims that those things retained by historical memory are "essential values," which "have accurately expressed the religious consciousness of an entire people." This asserts that that which has been retained has retained an essential identity, and that this identity is bound up with religious *consciousness*, that is, the human (perhaps even "transcendental") subject. Although Kristensen asserts these themes with the utmost circumspection, they nevertheless amount to a very distinct philosophy of history and, as such, play a *constitutive* role in his practice and articulation of phenomenology.

*Contra Entwicklung*

As was mentioned earlier, such a view of history is all the more remarkable when put next to Kristensen's critique of Otto and Hegel (which immediately follows the passages just cited). This is important because it is the basis for separating what I am calling "classical phenomenology of religion" from early *Religionswissenschaft*. My argument is that the latter has an evolutionary and teleological view of history, whereas the former is predicated upon (among other things) an *ostensive* rejection of such evolutionary views.

Kristensen makes this point in his discussion of Otto, arguing that "history and philosophy must work together; that is to say, the one may not lay down the law to the other. Each is equally autonomous in its own territory. But the autonomy is denied if a particular pattern of development, the evolutionary pattern, is forced on history."[93] And this is precisely what Otto and Hegel do: they impose a developmental pattern on history based upon their notions of the essence of religion, which, for Otto, was the idea of the holy: "Like Hegel, Otto believes that in the essence the germ of all phenomena is contained, that the phenomena have to be understood on the basis of that essence."[94] Hegel and Otto make the opposite mistake of Tiele, "who on the basis of historical data try to ascend to the formulation of the essence of religion."[95] The problem with evolutionary views is that they relativize the views of the believer, which, of course, Kristensen argues, must be understood as necessarily absolute. Reiterating the argument of the historian's "self-surrender" to the data and to the other, he says: "We must put the questions differently than Otto does. We should not take the concept 'holiness' as our starting point. . . . On the contrary, we should ask how the believer conceives the phenomena he calls 'holy.' "[96] And this, because "[t]he standpoint of Phenomenology is therefore the viewpoint of the believer, and not the concept 'holiness' in its elements or moment."[97] Evolutionary views relativize the view of the believer and impose an a priori (and therefore heteronymous) scheme on history by seeing one's own faith as the culmination of history, and thereby positing the other's as but a passing episode in the historical process. This position on evolution, and the priority of representing religion as "that which appears" to the believer, as it appears to the believer, along with a decidedly synchronic view of historical data, are all typical of the subsequent history of phenomenology.

## Classification of Religions

Although Kristensen does not, as noted earlier, compare *religions* as a whole with one another, he is not without a macro-structural comparison for *religion* as a whole:

> It is possible very roughly to speak of two types: the type represented by our European civilization, and especially Christianity, and the "Ancient" type—I don't know any better name for it—which the nations of antiquity represent and also, at least for the most part, those civilizations which are "foreign" to own. This distinction between our own and that which is foreign to us is at least of practical importance in our work.[98]

"Our own," especially Christianity and "the foreign" are structural principles, which form Kristensen's taxonomy. He will use this way of classifying religions and for classifying the "structural parallels" that will constitute the work of phenomenological analysis. Clearly, this is an important issue for both levels of this study, that is, elucidating his notion of the phenomenology of religion and looking for ways in which that notion reflects colonial discourse. As such, it is necessary to examine it thoroughly.

He describes the Ancient type of religion as having a more or less homogenous nature: "It is a remarkable fact that the peoples of Antiquity very often understood each other surprisingly well in religious matters, in spite of all of their differences in national character and religion . . . it is especially clear from the agreement of their basic religious ideas and institutions, notwithstanding the different ways they are expressed."[99] Once again, "it does not matter in which religion we find them." There is an essential character, quality, *Wesen* to the Ancients—all of them—and each is but a varying expression of that essence. The myriad ancient peoples then, all of them explicitly marked as non-European, are all of one kind and are thus denied any real, that is, essential (in his sense) identity of their own. In this discourse, their individuality is reduced to a particular instantiation of a general essence. In short: all of the non-European societies are lumped together without any concern for their historical specificity.

What then are these "basic religious ideas" which the Ancients had in common? "That which is characteristic of the Ancient civilizations and religions is the vivid consciousness of the cooperation between, indeed a fusion of, the finite and infinite factors in all phenomena connected with the essentials of life."[100] The finite and infinite translate rather easily, as we will see below, into divine phenomena and natural phenomena. As we have seen elsewhere, the claim of "fusion" of the two entails that there is not a clear differentiation between nature and the gods.

This sense of the fusion of the finite and the infinite was combined with a sense of mysticism/mystery. The Ancient man had

> an awareness of the mystical background of existence. In
> the man of Antiquity there was dominant just this sense of
> the mystery that surrounds us, a feeling of the spontaneous
> forces and energies whose meaning he always understood
> in the form of myth. He was, to be sure, also acquainted
> with rational relations of causality, but he attached primary
> significance to that which eluded conceptual understand-
> ing. It was this irrational factor which was most important
> to him.[101]

This awareness of the mystical "whose meaning he always understood in the form of myth,"[102] is a basic characteristic of the Ancients. That it is restricted to its expression in the form of myth could be the basis of a quite interesting opposition. For some time, it was a commonplace assumption that "they had myth, we have history."[103] Kristensen is on the verge of such a statement but never actually makes it. One could deduce from the rest of the structures of his discourse that he would agree with such an opposition and one would be on firm footing in doing so. However, as he does not explicitly state such an opposition one cannot make such a claim. It is interesting that he deploys the term *myth* in regard to the Ancients, and gives it an important place, and yet never attaches the term to the Moderns. We are "enlightened"; they are not. Ergo?

Another characteristic of the Ancients is that they hold a pluralistic view of the powers of the universe. As opposed to the unified view of nature that the West would eventually develop: "For the Ancients, on the contrary, the mystery of one phenomenon differed from that of another quite as much as the phenomena themselves differ; each case is new and special and points to a new 'numen.' "[104] As a consequence: "Autonomous substances differing from one another cannot be reduced to one and the same principle.... They point, therefore, to different gods."[105] This sense of the mysterious and the mystical expresses itself by attributing a god to every aspect of nature, each regarded as a separate, individual existence. He draws that conclusion that: "Rational differences (of size, weight, and force) are relative and can be comprehended in a generalization, but not so with irrational differences.... This is what polytheism is."[106] That is, polytheism is irrational. We are rational; they are irrational.

This contrast applies to the differing ways in which the Ancients and the Moderns regard nature as a whole: "This pluralistic notion of the mystery of life's expressions is induced by the religious sense of nature, a sense which the Ancients had very strongly but which we have lost."[107] The Ancients are close to nature; they understand and worship animals and animal spirits, venerate vegetative cycles of death and rebirth, while we Moderns stand apart from nature; they have left such a relationship to nature behind. Here again: they are *Natur*, "we" are *Geist*, that is, rational.

Regarding the basic phenomenological problem of a reconstruction of this Ancient form of religion based upon understanding (in the phenomenological/hermeneutical sense): "The only difficulty for us is to form an accurate conception of this reality and to understand it from within."[108]

What of the Moderns? What are their essential characteristics and what is the narrative of their history. Kristensen begins this discussion by remarking: "[B]ut it is useful beforehand to indicate that the differences exist."[109] This indicates that his narrative is a narrative of difference, not of commonality. This is one of the paradoxes of the phenomenology of religion: while it emphasizes essence and therefore unity, it nevertheless parses out difference, often in quite dramatic ways. Which aspect here is most basic to the discourse of the phenomenology of religion? The answer lies in the details.

The identity of the Moderns is constructed, to a large degree (to what degree is certainly debatable) by a series of oppositions. Modern versus Ancient is a temporal opposition, but it is more of a qualitative opposition. This opposition is coupled with a number of other oppositions, such as: rational/irrational, polytheism/monotheism, history/myth, *Geist*/*Natur*, and, quite explicitly, us/them. *We* are Moderns, Kristensen says quite explicitly, employing the italics himself. As noted above, Christianity is the best representative of the Modern type of religion. However, the theme that dominates his discussion of the Moderns is the opposition between the sovereign, conscious, and rational self and its relationship to nature.

We can elucidate these claims further by looking at the narrative of the Moderns' coming into being: "Our type of civilization came into being early in Greek history with the classical enlightenment. This rationalism in which the individual became conscious of his abilities won the leading position in Greece and Rome, but the Ancient type continued to live along side it."[110] This "rationalistic type" was pushed into the background by the *Ancient* form of Christianity:[111] "Then the mentality of the 'Enlightenment' won[112] back a great deal of lost ground by means of the Renaissance and especially by the revival of Aristotelian philosophy in Scholasticism. Since then it has characterized all of modern civilization. Our scientific and ethical orientation is preponderantly Aristotelian, that is to say, 'enlightened-classical.' "[113]

Furthermore, in differentiating this "enlightened-classical" civilization from the Ancient type, he argues:

> Since the time of the Greeks, however, the conviction has dominated in Modern man that the unknown can and must be more and more limited and that it proves to be not essentially different from that which is already known. That which inspires this line of thinking is the sense of the autonomous and dominating activity of the human mind in subjecting nature to itself.[114]

This recalls the statement from Dilthey to the effect that man "finds himself with respect to nature an *imperium in imperio*, to use Spinoza's expression."[115] While the Ancients' most basic belief is the *fusion* of the divine and the natural in an irrational manner, the Moderns have *autonomy* in relation to nature, they view nature rationally, they dominate nature and subjugate it to themselves.

Kristensen is, in many ways, as far from Hegel as one could imagine, especially given his outright rejection of evolutionary paradigms of any and all sorts. He is much more modest in his claims for what the science of consciousness can achieve. He denies that it has any underlying metaphysical or even theoretical basis. It even goes so far as to surrender to the believer and put the believer's point of view ahead of itself.

We are, then, unprepared for the way in which Kristensen classifies religion. While the arguments are, at least in some places subtle, they are obviously blatant in others. His entire taxonomy is divided up into as virulent (if not vitriolic) a Christocentrism and Logocentrism,[116] an Us/Them dichotomy, as we have seen in this study. All of this comes from and is consistent with the *structural* features of the discourse of the phenomenology of religion, articulated here in its "classical" form.

# 8

# Experience, Expression, Empathy

## Gerardus van der Leeuw's Phenomenological Program

Gerardus van der Leeuw's *magnum opus*, *Phänomenologie der Religion* was published in 1933. This work is widely regarded as the seminal statement of classical phenomenology of religion. Attached to the work was an "Epilogomena," which dealt primarily with methodological questions and with issues concerning the place of phenomenology within *Religionswissenschaft*. As these latter issues are the primary concern here, the bulk of this exposition will focus on the Epilogomena, although some issues entail looking at the body of the text and its structure as a whole.

### Subject/Object; Experience/Expression; Inward/Outward

Like most phenomenologists, van der Leeuw saw the conceptual structure of phenomenology both as a philosophy and as a method for the human sciences (*Geisteswissenschaften*), as grounded in what he claims are three "natural," or given, correlations: subject as correlated with an object; experience as correlated with an expression; and the "inward" as correlated with the "outward." These correlations, all of which are integrally related, form the conceptual foundation for phenomenology of religion as van der Leeuw understands and practices it.

*Phenomenon, Subject, Object*

The phenomenon is something that "appears" and appears *to* someone: "Phenomenology seeks the phenomenon, as such; the phenomenon, again, is what 'appears' [*was sich zeigt*]."[1] Unlike explanatory sciences, phenomenology does not try to explain *why* something appears, it merely starts from the given, from what "is there," from the "absolute givenness of the phenomenon itself," as Husserl's famous motto puts it. This assumption is the opening gesture for, and the conditions for the possibility of, specifically phenomenological research. Immediately implied in the notion of "appearance" is the correlative relationship of an object, a something that appears, and a subject, that to which the object appears. As such, the "phenomenon" is "neither pure object ... [nor] something purely subjective," but, rather must be understood as "an object related to a subject, and a subject related to an object."[2] The "phenomenon," then, exists within the structure of a relationship, a relationship defined by *two* givens: the subject and the object.

Avoiding, he believes, both reductionism and subjectivism, van der Leeuw repeatedly insists that the phenomenon "is not produced by the subject, and still less substantiated or demonstrated by it; its entire essence is given in its appearance, and its appearance to 'someone.' "[3] As the phenomenon is a correlative of the subject and object, it cannot be either a passive "impression" as empiricist psychology holds, nor a purely subjective projection or construction. The key for van der Leeuw to maintaining the middle ground of phenomenology is to insist on the givenness to consciousness of the "phenomenon itself." Van der Leeuw claims that this makes phenomenology different than other approaches to religion in that it has no theoretical orientation which it imposes on religious data, but is a pure description of that data:

> I have tried to avoid, above all else, any imperiously dominating theory, and in this Volume there will be found neither evolutionary, nor so-called anti-evolutionary, nor indeed any other theories.... What I myself consider may be opposed to theories, as the phenomenological comprehension of History [*als phänomenologisches Verständnis der Geschichte*], should be clear from the Epilogomena.[4]

Clearly, van der Leeuw regards phenomenology as a purely descriptive approach that is, as such, pre- or a-theoretical in nature. This, again, is based upon the sense of the absolute givenness of the phenomenon, as well as the naturalness of the correlations described above. This also entails, as shall be discussed below, that, at the level of what he calls *Urerlebnis*, that is, at the primal or original level of experience, the phenomenon is outside of any form of mediation, and therefore, outside of any form or system of representation. The phenomenon is that which is *immediately* given to a subject. This is the basis for the problematic of phenomenological reconstruction. It also places consciousness front and center as the given area, so to speak, within which objects appear (Daniel Dennett referred to it as the "Cartesian theater of consciousness").

Van der Leeuw so far gives all that is essential to his project: the appearance of a "something" that necessarily implies both the subject and the object of such an appearance. The structure of *Religion in Essence and Manifestation* corresponds to this essential structure: part one is entitled "The Object of Religion; The Subject of Religion; Object and Subject in their Reciprocal Operation." The notions of experience and expression, inward and outward, follow upon this structure, which is taken as the basic, foundational structure of van der Leeuw's notion of a science of religion.[5] Note too, that this is a Hegelian structure wherein two alterious phenomena are reconciled into a more complete, reciprocal unity.

So far, this notion of the necessary correlation between a subject and an object sounds very Husserlian. However, as will be discussed further below, van der Leeuw's notion of the subject is not at all the same as either Kant's or Husserl's notion of the transcendental ego. Like Schleiermacher and Otto, van der Leeuw slides easily from a logical analysis of the apodictic structure of experience into a religious or metaphysical notion of the subject as the primal interiority of human beings, or, as *Geist*, "spirit," or the soul (even *Seelengrund*, as with Otto).

*Erlebnis*

Van der Leeuw's analysis of experience is developed in the text in a circle of references from the Epilogomena to the section on "Religious Experience" (a subdivision of part two: "The Subject of Religion," section A: "Inward Action") and back to the Epilogomena. This circle must be followed in order to get it straight; each section qualifies and illuminates the other.

The appearance to someone is "experience," *Erlebnis*. In a note in the Epilogomena on this point he says: "The term 'experience' (*Erlebnis*) is itself objectively oriented (we always experience something) and designates a 'structure' [*Schön der Ausdruck, 'Erlebnis' ist gegenständlich gerichtet (man erlebt etwas) und bezeichnet eine, 'Stuktur'*]."[6] The key to his notion of experience is the phrase, *"man erlebt etwas"*: "one," the subject, always experiences a "something," an object, even if that something is only an illusion or phantasm. Again, although he does not cite it, he seems to be following Husserl's notion of the intentional nature of the object of experience. He also invokes the idea of structure, a key term in Dilthey's theory of historical reconstruction.

Added to the note just cited is a cross-reference to the section on "Religious Experience." There, he spells out his view of experience more fully and relates it to the other correlations we want to look at. He quotes Spranger, one of his favorite authorities, on just this point: " '[I]n the very expression *Er-leben* there already resounds some degree of objective orientation,' "[7] namely, the orientation of consciousness toward, or at, an object of experience. The question for van der Leeuw is, What part does each "term" play in the experience? That is, going back to the discussion earlier, is an "experience" constituted more by the object, as positivists hold, or by the subject, as Idealists hold? The dilemma here is as follows: if van der Leeuw says it is the object that gives experience, then he abandons the bracketing of the question of the reality of the object, that is, he cannot claim to be starting from the sheer givenness of the object to consciousness, which he must as he himself says, if he is doing "phenomenology." The science of religion then would be a "theoretical," that is, an explanatory science, not a pure phenomenological understanding of History.

On the other hand, if he says that experience is constructed only by (or in) the subject, then he is faced with several problems. First, he could be charged with Idealism, which, in the history of the study of religion (as well as science and philosophy), is generally seen as usurping the activity of empirical, factual description with, or by, philosophical (i.e., a priori, deductive) "construction" (per the discussion in chapter 1 concerning the critical rejection-appropriation of Hegel). Secondly, if the phenomenon were only a product of the subject, he would have to explain why the science of religion should not be a subdiscipline of psychology. This, in turn, raises the issue of a psychological reductive theory of religion—which the entire project of phenomenology was set up to resist. Finally, as a theologian, van der Leeuw wants very much to retain the independent reality of the intentional object of religious experience. God must not be handed over to Feuerbach.

How then, does van der Leeuw avoid these problems? In a long section of his discussion of "Religious Experience" he grapples with precisely this problem:

> What the nature of an experience is will be most clearly understood if it is compared with the "event." Event and experience, then, are the same "content," in the first place as

fact, and then as meaning also. A phenomenon therefore is always related to experience, since unless this is so it would not appear to us meaningfully. But outer phenomena also possess an element constituted by fact and event, a natural aspect, which cannot be understood as such. I understand the altar, for example, as a "locality" or "position"; but I cannot understand the stone of which it is made. Thus the experience is, *idealiter*, devoid of fact and event: it is meaning in its purity.[8]

Although the experience and the event are necessarily correlated, it is possible to give the specific difference of each, to account for what each contributes separately. As Dilthey had argued, so argues van der Leeuw: experience is always experience *of* something: it necessarily has an intentional object. However, what may be *understood* of experience is only its meaning. The meaning is not reducible to the "fact" or "event"; it is a supplement to it. The sheer facticity, or eventicity, if you will, or the natural aspect of the object is not a possible object of understanding. Ergo, the *meaning* of the experience must be what the subject brings. In a note to this section he says "objectively, this means that experience, apart from the world of events, does not exist; and subjectively, that there is no meaning which cannot be understood."[9] As shall be discussed further below, meaning is not simply the subject's, but is the correlative product of both subject and object: "Thus the sphere of meaning is a third realm, subsisting above mere subjectivity and mere objectivity."[10] However, if, for the purposes of analysis only, experience is viewed from the perspective of the subject, "meaning in its purity" can be isolated. The possibility of the recovery of meaning is, as will be discussed below, due to the common, universal nature of the subject.

In passing we should note that the separation between "a natural aspect, which cannot be understood as such" and "meaning in its purity," reiterates, once again, the division between inert nature and meaning-giving subjectivity which does not traffic in "facts and events." The opposition between *Geist* and *Natur* is once again in play; it is essentially interwoven in the very fabric of the way in which "experience" itself, the most basic datum of phenomenology, is described or put into discourse.

What is important in experience for phenomenological research, then, is its essence, structure, or meaning, which, "with respect to its [i.e., experience's] meaning, constitutes a unity. Experience, therefore, is not pure 'life,' since . . . it is inseparably connected with its interpretation as experience. 'Life' itself is incomprehensible: 'What the disciple of Sais unveils is form, not life' "; "its entire essence is given in its appearance, and its appearance to 'someone.' "[11] This move, again, seems to resemble Husserl's eidetic vision, that is, the extraction from experience, but is, in fact, indebted to Dilthey's general formulation of the problematics of *Verstehen*, or understanding, including, of course, the doctrine of the use of empathetic imagination in understanding. Meaning, essence, and structure, then, form the basis of the phenomenological reconstruction of experience.

*Expression, the Inward and the Outward*

In the section on "Religious Experience," van der Leeuw discusses the notion of experience in more detail and connects it to the other correlations mentioned above. To do so it is necessary to explain what it means to separate the inner from the outer:

> The division of our subject into Outward and Inward Action by no means implies a belief in the possibility of separating the inner from the outer:
>
>> Wouldst thou truly study Nature?
>> Seek the Whole in every feature.
>> Nought's within and nought' without,
>> For whatever's in will out.
>
> Everything external is closely connected with something internal; and, conversely, without the outer there is not inner, or if there were it would not appear.[12]

The separation of the two is, therefore, only a working fiction, a matter of method or approach. The difference is lies not in the objects, but in the mode in which it is apprehended: "[E]very experience without exception may be regarded from two quite different sides: from the point of view of its expression, or as it were its external aspect, and also from the angle of its impression, or in other words its internal aspect. I say advisedly 'as it were.' For the outer is always and simultaneously the inner, and conversely."[13] Precisely for the same reason that subject and object are correlates, then, inward and outward are also necessarily correlated. One can separate them only for the sake of analysis; in "life" they are never separate.

As with Dilthey, Kristensen, Wach, Eliade, as will be seen in the next chapters, the notion of the correlation between inward and outward is seen as directly correlated to the notions of experience and expression (*Ausdruck*): "It is therefore never permissible to place 'institutional' religion in antithesis to the inward experience of religion. For every dogma, every act of worship [and, by extension, every expression], can only become understood primarily as the reflection of some experience; every act, every idea, is the expression of a need or a release, of pain or bliss."[14] Ergo, although the pairs are correlated, experience is primary and expression follows from it. External forms are not separable from internal states because external forms are *derived* from those states. These states are *naturally* given to expression: "[T]o be articulately expressed pertains to experience."[15] This point will come up again when we look at how he understands writing and its relation to historical reconstruction. It is a model, as we saw, derived from Dilthey and one that becomes a structural principle in the discourse of the phenomenology of religion. Wach uses the same language, and what Eliade will call "hierophanies" are "expressions" in the sense used here.

## Structure, Meaning, and Phenomenological Reconstruction

### Meaning-as-Structure

Given the inherent inaccessibility to someone else's "primal experience," understood as essentially that which appears, as that which makes itself present to "someone," the only means of recovering the phenomenon is "reconstruction": "therefore every historian reconstructs. What then does this reconstruction imply?"[16]

This is the entry into the central problematic of phenomenology: given that the actual, historical instances of "primal experience" have irrevocably passed away, what is recoverable from that "appearance"? On the basis of what does the historian/phenomenologist reconstruct? The answer is, as suggested by Dilthey's characterization of the disciple of Sais, structure. Van der Leeuw argues that this reconstruction is an "outline" (*Grundrisse*, or "summary") of the "chaotic maze of so-called 'reality' ... called structure."[17] The concept of "structure," so crucial for Dilthey's program of reconstruction, reappears as van der Leeuw's basic philosopheme of identity-cum-meaning. He describes structure as

> a connection [*Zusammenhang*] which is neither merely experienced directly, nor abstracted logically or causally, but which is understood [*verstanden*]. It is an organic whole [*organisches Ganzes*] which cannot be analyzed into its own constituents, but which can from these be comprehended; or in other terms, a fabric of particulars, not to be compounded by the addition of these, nor the deduction of one from the others, but again only understood as a whole. ... Structure is reality significantly [*sinnvoll*] organized. ... It is always, therefore, both understanding and intelligibility [*Er ist immer sowohl das Verständnis als die Verständlichkeit*]: and this, indeed, in an unanalyzable, experienced connection.[18]

The possibility of the reconstruction then, resides in the connection, *der Zusammenhang*, of events in experience, which is understood. This connection is and must be purely formal: it is "reality significantly organized," that is, not the "chaotic maze" of particulars, or the "mere aggregation" of which Otto spoke. Subject and object are fused together into an unanalyzable "whole." The meaning, the truth, of the appearance-as-experience, represented in the reconstruction, is in the Whole. As a whole, in true Hegelian fashion, it cannot be separated into "cause" and "effect," or any other logical division. Not only is it the case that *"das Wahre ist das Ganze,"* that the truth is the whole, but *der Sinn ist das Ganze*—the meaning is the whole. The meaning resides only in the Whole, only in the totality of the connections, that is, in the structure. And it is the recovery of meaning, made possible by the presence of structure in experience, that is the possibility for reconstruction: "The entrance gate to the reality of primal experience, itself wholly inaccessible, is meaning [*Wirklichkeit des Urerlebnisses ist der Sinn*]: my meaning and its meaning, which have become irrevocably one in the act of understanding."[19]

This last point, viz., "my meaning and its meaning, which have become irrevocably one," demands further comment. However, such comment must be withheld for the moment because what this point does is introduce the transition from "structure" to "type." Understanding never comes about, he says, by means of single experiences, but by the unities of several experiential sequences. These unities present a similarity, which "manifests itself as a community of essential nature."[20] This understood connection, or *Wesensgemeinshaft*, forms the basis for comprehending an even wider "objective connection" in the phenomenon, which van der Leeuw calls "type": "[T]his is what we mean by speaking of types, together with structure."[21]

Van der Leeuw's articulation of the relation between structure and type is, frankly, quite vague. What he says about the type is, however, significant for the larger argument being made here. " 'Type' in itself, however, has no reality; nor is it a photograph of reality. Like structure, it is timeless and need not actually occur in history. But it possesses life, its own significance [*Sinn*], its own law."[22] Like structure, type is a purely formal entity, but its very formality is what makes sense out of the otherwise singular, unconnected, "chaotic" nature of experience. As with Hegel, van der Leeuw holds that the "type itself" is never conceived apart from some definite kind, for example, the soul: "[T]here is always and only some definite kind of soul which is believed in."[23] But the status of the type itself, which is what a λογοσ of the phenomenon must deal, presents the central question of phenomenological research: "The type itself (to repeat) is timeless: nor is it real. Nevertheless it is alive and appears to us," leaving us the central question of method, namely, "What then are we to do in order actually to observe it?"[24]

*Phenomenological Reconstruction*

The answer to this founding question, "We resort to phenomenology,"[25] entails the seven steps of phenomenology as a method, presented as points A-G of section two of the first section of the Epilogomena. Rather than review each point, only certain key points will be highlighted.

The first step, though they are not sequentially arranged, is to establish a taxonomy: "What has become manifest, in the first place, receives a name. . . . In giving names we separate phenomena and also associate them; in other words, we classify. We include or reject: this we call a 'sacrifice' and that a 'purification.' "[26] No attempt is made to connect these conventional categories to his theory of types or of structures. It is therefore unclear what relation they have to the things so named. Are they simply adequate to their objects? If so, what is the point of phenomenology? Are they merely conventional placeholders? If so, what is the point of using them, let alone "in the first place"?

In order for this to be more than an empty, pedantic exercise whereby the names take on a life of their own, the second step must be preformed, namely, "the interpolation of the phenomenon into our own lives."[27] This is an absolutely crucial turn, and his reasoning behind it demands careful attention. This maneuver is based upon a basic characteristic of "the phenomenon," namely, "that everything that appears to us does not submit itself to us directly and immediately, but only as a symbol of some meaning to be interpreted by us, as something which offers itself to us for interpretation."[28] The veracity of this interpretation, again, is neither empirical nor causal in nature, but has to do with the subject's relation to the object: " 'Reality' is always my reality, history my history," because (quoting Spranger), history is " 'the retrogressive prolongation of man now living.' "[29]

In extrapolating this basic idea of understanding as sympathetically entering into the experience of another, he makes explicit what can only be a necessary premise of such a methodological stipulation: *"homo sum, humani nil a me alienum puto*: this is no key to the deepest comprehension of the remotest experience, but is nevertheless the triumphant assertion that the essentially human always remains the essentially human, and is, as such, comprehensible [*dass Wesentlich-Menschliches immer Wesentlich-Menschliches bleibt und als solches verstandlich ist*]."[30] The essential sameness of human being is the ground of phenomenological reconstruction. We can understand the type, the structure created at some different time, by some other person precisely because such difference and such otherness are not essential, are not fundamental. As expressions of an inner, universal subjectivity, they are intelligible, that is, their difference from us is *bridgeable*: "Certainly the monuments of the first dynasty [of Egypt] are intelligible only with great difficulty, but as an expression, as a human statement, they are no harder than my colleague's letter."[31] This is because, qua human expression, "there is something that is intelligible in accord with our own experience."[32]

Again quoting Dilthey, van der Leeuw argues that the task of phenomenology is to interpret these expressions of experience; it is concerned with their meaning: " 'The sciences of the mind are based on the relations between experience, expression and understanding.' . . . The aim of science, therefore, is to understand this logos; essentially, science is hermeneutics."[33] The transcendental, transhistorical structure of human being "always remains"—as with Hegel, who earlier was quoted as saying, "What *Geist* is, it has always essentially been," so also with "Man." To be human is to participate in this structure, and, as such, is to be able to comprehend this structure: "Phenomenology, therefore, is not a method that has been reflectively elaborated, but is man's true vital activity," for in it, he argues, it is given to man "what is given to neither animal nor god: standing aside and understanding what appears into view."[34] The figure "Man," then, occupies a central and founding position in the method of phenomenology.

## Religion in History

*Structure versus "development"*

The by now familiar philosophemes of "structure," "Man," "essence," and "meaning" each play an important role in how van der Leeuw understands phenomenological treatment of religions in history. As previously noted before, in the preface to the 1933 German edition, he describes his phenomenology of religion as "the phenomenological apprehension of History." In that same preface, he says that work is intended for those "whose studies include some familiarity with the History of Religion [*Religionsgeschichte*]" and for them this work will be "a useful Introduction to the comprehension of the historical material [*Verständnis des historischen Materials*]."[35] He further describes the work as a "presentation of the manifestations of Religion [*die Erscheinungen der Religion*],"[36] thus echoing the previous notions of how *Religionswissenschaft* treats history. From the discussion just presented, we may now see that *das Wesen der Religion* means the essential *meaning* of religion, and that this meaning is recovered from and through "concrete" historical data by the delineation of its structure, subjectively apprehended.

It will be no surprise, then, when van der Leeuw begins his discussion of "Religions" (the first section of part five: "Forms") by connecting "religions" to "form," and doing so in the name of Schleiermacher: "Religion actually exists only in religions," as Heinrich Frick very justly asserts with reference to Schleiermacher's fifth Discourse upon Religion [in *Vergleichende Religion*]. This means that religion does not, as such, appear to us; what we can observe, therefore is always only one concrete religion: in other terms, only its prevailing historical form appears to us.[37]

As with Schleiermacher and Hegel, van der Leeuw holds that *die wirklich Religionen*, actual or concrete religions, are manifest as "concrete universals." The embellishment van der Leeuw provides is to limit the apprehension of this concrete universal to its form. What appears or is manifest, then, of a concrete religion is its formal character. Such forms, however, in strict opposition to "evolutionism," should "not be taken to involve stages or periods in the history of religion but eternal structures, and that they also serve to classify the historic religions according to the degree in which they participate in one or the other of these structures."[38] This is the sense in which van der Leeuw's "history" or method of dealing with concrete materials of religion is putatively synchronic and not diachronic. In this regard, he prefigures Eliade's theory of the "hierophany."

Here can be seen two typical features of classical phenomenology of religion's approach to history. First, it rejects the earlier, evolutionary conception of history as having distinct phases or stages. In a much-quoted passage, van der Leeuw says, "[P]henomenology knows nothing of any historical 'development' of religion, still less of an 'origin' of religion [*Von einer historischen 'Entwicklung' der Religion weiss die Phänomenologie nichts . . . von einem 'Ursprung' der Religion noch weniger*]."[39] The mention of the term "*Entwicklung*" there is a direct allusion to the Hegelian conception of the philosophy of history. It has broader application, however, and also encompasses any and all evolutionary theories. This is the central argument that separates phenomenologists such as van der Leeuw from earlier *Religionswissenschaftlichers* such as Tiele and Otto.

Secondly, it, again, indicates (implicitly) the role of form or structure in phenomenological reconstruction of history. In his discussion of "Religions" he describes the relationship between history and structure by appeal to the concept of "objective spirit": "There subsists a style, a consciousness proper to the period, an objective spirit" and "in my own experience religion receives a special form which is, however, merely one specific form of the vast historic formation [or, "objective spirit"] wherein I myself exist."[40] The task of a systematic science is to classify these forms: "But objective spirit, still further, is so infinitely differentiated that the necessity of a typology is absolutely imperative."[41]

The understanding of the forms of objective spirit that each religion manifests is attained by the use of ideal types (which, as we saw, are virtually indistinguishable from forms or structures). The ideal type "must then be the result of the closest cooperation between phenomenological comprehension and the investigation of all that has been historically given."[42] Form and matter must be integrally related; the form must be an apprehension of the structure of the form; the matter must express a particular *Wesen*, essence, or structure; it must be a manifestation of a determinate form of objective spirit. We will return to this issue in the final section, when we review the various ways in which van der Leeuw qualifies his position.

*Outline of van der Leeuw's History of Religion*

Van der Leeuw devotes an entire section of *Religion in Essence and Manifestation* to an account of the history of religion. Since he places so much emphasis on religion as the phenomenological comprehension of history, this would seem to the best place to look at how he both typologizes and narrativizes religion.

As with Hegel, Tiele, and Otto, van der Leeuw begins his narrative of the history of religion with that stratum of religion that is not "in" history, viz., "primitive religion." Van der Leeuw rejects the terms *higher* and *lower* as adequate descriptors of religious types. He prefers *primitive* and *modern*, "provided always that these are not taken to involve stages or periods in the history of religion but eternal structures."[43] However, he never gives any clear specific difference between the "primitive" and "modern" except that the latter is not "in" history:

> This typology [of world religions] excludes the non-historical and predominantly unhistorical (that is, the primitive) religions; and I need not repeat the contention that every religion is more or less primitive. Nevertheless there are religions which possess a sharply outlined historic from distinguishing them from all others. But this category does not include the religions of so-called primitive peoples.[44]

Why they do not "have" history is not explained. He goes to great lengths to say that the study of religion is the study of the historical religions, and yet, this form of religion has no history. He also goes to great pains to distinguish his view of primitive religion from that of Tiele and some others, overtly rejecting for instance, racial typologies of religion. And yet. The distinction between religions that have history and those that do not—we can only guess which actual religions they are as he does not name them—is a serious, structural distinction in his narrative of the history of religions, as we will see with the next religion.

In line with the Hegelian motifs in the history of religion, the analysis of specifically historical religion begins with and in China. As will be discussed below, van der Leeuw rejects the concept of historical stages and is looking for "eternal structures."[45] Given what many have claimed is a very important difference in approach, one would think there would be a correlative difference in results. This, however, is not the case.

"Historical form, then, is presented first of all by the religion of remoteness... it received its historic form first of all in China and predominantly, in fact, in Confucianism."[46] Like Hegel, the history of religion has its beginning in the East. However, although there are many, many structural similarities between Hegel's and van der Leeuw's metanarrative of religion, van der Leeuw does not follow the East to West orientation in nearly as strict a fashion as does Hegel.

Deism, for instance, is listed as another manifestation of the religion of remoteness.

His taxonomy-cum-narrative of history of religion proceeds as follows: Religions of Remoteness and of Flight; The Religion of Struggle; The Religion of Repose; The Religion of Unrest; (Interlude on the "dynamics of religions"); The Religion of Strain and Form; The Religion of Infinity and of Asceticism; The Religion of Nothingness and of Compassion; The Religion of Will and of Obedience; The Religion of Majesty and of Humility; The Religion of Love.

Each type corresponds to an historical instantiation. The typology-cum-narrative, as noted above, starts with the "East equals early" structure, albeit without perfect consistency, and continues that trajectory through the early types. So, the Religion of Struggle, which emphasizes dualism, is found in the "oriental" worlds of Egypt and Persia. The Religion of Unrest is primarily, though not exclusively, associated with Judaism. The Religion of Strain and Form is that of ancient Greece.

Up to this point the Hegelian paradigm for the history of religions (viz., history moves from the East to the West in incremental stages) has been followed quite faithfully. With the Religion of Infinity and of Asceticism and the Religion of Nothingness and of Compassion, however, the narrative reverses geographical course and returns to India in the form of Hinduism and Buddhism, respectively. The Religion of Will and of Obedience returns us to Israel, where much of the discussion is taken up with the differences between Judaism and ancient Greek religion—again, a prominent motif in the Hegelian history of religion/*Geist*.

Although the pattern of the Hegelian metanarrative is being followed here, at least in the round, van der Leeuw never claims that any of these types of religion represent a specific stage in the overall history of religion. Nor does he ever claim that each type is an advance over the other. Almost. While his essentialism forces him to make some dubious judgments about specific religions along the way, when it comes to the last two types of religion, the Religion of Majesty and of Humility and the Religion of Love, he makes some rather heavyhanded evaluative comments, which belie his purportedly neutral phenomenological stance.

*The Case of Islam*

The Religion of Majesty and of Humility is Islam. In his discussion of Islam, van der Leeuw cites a long passage from a letter sent to him by "a friend who has labored among Moslems for many years and who speaks the language."[47] The passage is worth citing in its entirety:

> Islam is in the first, second and third place a religio-social complex, in which equal emphasis is due to each factor of this combination.... Its motive power is the longing to be a kingdom of God: its weakness that, quite unsuspectingly, it wishes to realize this goal from a spirit that is not reborn and remains at bottom worldly.... Itself historically dependent, an offshoot of Semitic prophetism, Islam is comparatively poor in thought and feeling. Nevertheless it develops a colossal power which is rooted in its faith in God, or in other words, it takes god's sovereignty in absolute seriousness.[48]

It is important to note that van der Leeuw does not disavow this statement. In fact, he uses it as a template for his exposition of Islam, repeating the last phrase, as well as other parts of the letter, throughout this chapter. He argues, for instance, that "in Islam, then, the concept of Power reaches its loftiest peak,"[49] but that "God's mighty power is indeed 'unsuspectingly' believed in by the prophet's followers ... which certainly implies an intense faith, but at the same time a very feeble humanity."[50] Finally, the chapter on Islam concludes with the following summary observation: "Of God he knows only that He is, and that His Being is overpowering. This, undeniably, is very much: but on the other hand, when measured against the more sophisticated religions, it is very little."[51] So, although he denies that there are teleological, evolutionary stages in the history of religion, he nevertheless concurs with the judgment about Islam made by virtually all those Christian theologian, historians, and philosophers of religion who *do* argue for determinate stages of religion. This strongly suggests that the valuational scheme that structures these kinds of judgments is rooted in something other than the evolutionary framework, indeed, it suggests further that the evolutionary framework and the anti-evolutionary framework are both rooted in a valuational-cum-ontological framework that is more basic, more fundamental to each, at the root, so to speak, of each, than are the supposed oppositions of each of these camps.[52]

*Christian Supremacy,* noch einmal

This point is further compounded by van der Leeuw's treatment of Christianity. This problem is complex, and has two different sides to it, one heuristic and the other material. His heuristic argument for his treatment of Christianity is predicated on the idea of the specific religious, cultural, and historical location of the researching subject, that is, that the historian or phenomenologist of religion *exists* in a definite context: "But gradually it is being perceived that man exists in the world in some quite definite way and that—with all due respect to his own *Weltanschauung*—any 'unprejudiced' treatment is not merely impossible but positively fatal. For it prevents the investigator's complete personality becoming engaged in his scientific task."[53] The corollary of this heuristic approach is a certain relativity of perspective: "It would therefore be quite possible, in itself, for a Buddhist to set out the phenomenology of religion, with his own as the starting point; and then he would naturally discover the culmination of religion in Buddhism."[54] He adds to this that the issue for phenomenology qua phenomenology is not ontological truth, namely, whether the universe itself conforms to the dictates of Christianity or of Buddhism. Such decisions are matters for other disciplines, especially theology and metaphysics.

The material treatment of Christianity is developed by means of two related arguments. First, the idea that Christianity is the "fulfillment of religion in general," and second, that the essence of Christianity is love.

From a strictly phenomenological stance, however qualified by the phenomenologist's *Sitz im Leben*, van der Leeuw makes the claim, not unfamiliar (nor surprising) in this intellectual tradition:

> I myself regard Christianity, then, as the central form of historical religions; and in general the "comparison" of religions among themselves is possible only by thus beginning from one's own attitude to life.... Surveying the realm of historic religions, therefore, from the point of view of Christianity, I consider that we perceive that the Gospel appears as the fulfillment of religion in general. But whether this "appearance" has its roots in any ultimate "reality" is again an issue which theology must decide.[55]

As with Schleiermacher, Hegel, Otto, and others, van der Leeuw understands Christianity's place among "the religions" as one of consummation—recall Hegel's description of Christianity as "the Consummate Religion." Unlike Schleiermacher and Hegel, he does repeatedly say, as at the end of the quote above, that this is not necessarily an ontological reality, but only the outcome of a situated, phenomenological analysis. It would seem to be fair, however, to argue that the structure of concepts used to articulate, even construct, the phenomenology of religion *inevitably*, and, historically speaking, *invariably*, lead up to the idea that Christianity is the supreme religion.[56]

Van der Leeuw's material exposition of Christianity also follows a theme very familiar in this intellectual tradition: "[T]he typology of Christianity needs only *one* word: *Love*."[57] Christianity is the religion of love, a point Hegel had made in his early essays nearly a century and a half earlier. Furthermore, this notion of love as essential and Christianity as essentially love, is articulated by and through a kind of concept of reconciliation: "[T]his is because, in Christianity, God's activity and the reciprocal activity of man are essentially the same," the apotheosis of which is " 'the form Christ has taken in man.' "[58] Just as in the Hegelian philosophy of religion (and history), the Incarnation is the central, all-encompassing moment in the history of *Geist*. And, just as in this history, for van der Leeuw, the Incarnation reconciles the basic antinomies of existence in an exhaustive manner.

The essence of Christianity as love is the material basis for its consummation of all other (others'?) religions. Love forms the basis for the fulfillment or consummation of religion because it reconciles all the oppositions in "the religions":

> God: Father, Son and Holy Spirit—thus are consummated, equally, the religion of Will (Israel), of Form (Greece), and also of Infinity (India). The Father's Will is glorified as God's creative deed, whose essence is love of the world. The impetuous energy of Jahveh (and also of Allah) is experienced as an impetuous deed of love: "God so loved the world" that He gave Himself to the world in the Form of the Son.[59]

Here we can see the fruits of the essentialism of both the data of religions and of the subject, articulated by and through the scheme of onto-theology—of which phenomenology must be understood as a "subdivision." This articulation of the "phenomenological comprehension of the history of religion" re-encapsulates the triumphalist, Hegelian narrative of *Geist*: in the consummate religion, the Christian overcomes the Jew, modern Europe overcomes antiquity (Greece), the West overcomes the East (India), and the Occident overcomes the Orient (Islam). This is the logical structure and outcome of van der Leeuw's phenomenological treatment of the history of religions.

## Van der Leeuw's Relationship to Hegel

Another important aspect of van der Leeuw's view of history is his relationship to Hegel, specifically revolving around the issue of the "development" (or *Entwicklung*) of religion. By rejecting the notion of *Entwicklung*, and by the synchronic approach so characteristic of his phenomenological method, one would assume that van der Leeuw thoroughly rejects Hegel or Hegelianism. This is not, however, the case. In virtually every place in *Religion in Essence and Manifestation* where Hegel's name comes up, van der Leeuw marks it with a qualified approval. In his summation of the history of phenomenological approaches, he says of Hegel:

> Hegel is the first philosopher who treats history, including the history of religion, in its full seriousness: Absolute Spirit has its life in history as it is comprehended. Exceedingly fruitful for all history, and typical for all philosophy, the conclusion of the *Phenomenology* still remains [*sind noch immer*]: The "conservation (of spiritual forms), looked at from the side of their free existence appearing in the form of contingency, is History; looked at from the side of their intellectually comprehended organization [*begriffenen Organisation*], it is the Science of the ways in which knowledge appears" [*erscheinenden Wissens*].[60]

This is clearly not a condemnation of Hegel. The *"noch immer"* clearly states that this is the living part of the project of "phenomenology." The language of *"begriffen Organisation"* and *"erscheinended Wissens,"* although slightly different terminology, clearly echoes the remarks in the Preface to *Religion in Essence and Manifestation* about the "phenomenological comprehension of History," of the "manifestations of Religion" in history.

As discussed previously, the usual charge against Hegel by thinkers with a more strictly phenomenological bent is that he foregoes "description" by introducing philosophical "constructions." Van der Leeuw, in fact, raises this issue, but it is very interesting to note how he deals with it. In the section on "The Religions," in connection with the discussion of objective spirit and typology, he says: "The two classical typologies of this type, however, are Hegel's and Goethe's."[61] He raises the standard critique of Hegel's position: "It is true that the question may arise whether philosophic construction has not displaced phenomenological observation,"[62] yet, farther down, after discussing the problems with other typologies, he argues that: "Hegel's much derided classification... should be esteemed as a most necessary effort that well deserves consideration. Historical typology is a quite indispensable and essential subdivision of the phenomenology of religion. This typology excludes the non-historical and predominantly unhistorical (that is, the primitive) religions."[63]

In the context of the historical thesis being developed here, viz., that classical phenomenology is more heir to Hegelian phenomenology than it is to Husserlian phenomenology, this last passage is very significant—all the more when taken together with the previous one. First of all, it clearly does *not* distance van der Leeuw's conception of the project of a phenomenology of religion from Hegel; rather the reverse: Hegel is praised for, at least, his initial efforts here. Furthermore, this point clearly echoes Chantepie's argument on Hegel's place in a typology of religion, and the place of such typology in the whole of *Religionswissenschaft*. The argument is not that van der Leeuw is, therefore, a "Hegelian"; the issue is more complicated than that. But it is clear that van der Leeuw sees some important lines of continuity between his own project and that of Hegel and of Dilthey. This is significant because it forces us to change the traditional reading of van der Leeuw as a Husserlian, or quasi-Husserlian. This also forces a change in the reading of the pedigree of phenomenology, a reading in which the role that Husserl has played must be greatly diminished. The general approach of classical phenomenology of religion, especially when seen as a "phenomenological comprehension of History," is *much* closer to Hegel's model of phenomenology than it is to Husserl's, although, strictly speaking, it belongs to neither in its entirety.

*Writing*

While we are on the topic of van der Leeuw's view of history another, and final, point that needs to be addressed is his understanding of writing. In a section on "The Written Word," in the body of the text, he makes a few remarks about writing which are significant in relation to his notion of phenomenological reconstruction, and the ways in which he will qualify that notion.

He begins by making a connection between the written word and the fetish: "[W]hat we have in black and white we can safely take home with us—the tendency already discerned in Fetishism becomes evident also in the valuation of the written word."[64] What is characteristic of the fetish its ability to be a bearer of power: "Objects existing in intimate relation to soul-stuff possess indisputable potency.... This systematic reckoning with the power subsisting in things we call Fetishism."[65] The source of power is the "soul-stuff," however and not the mere fact of their being written down.

In discussing creeds, van der Leeuw makes some general remarks about writing and its relation to interiority: "Creeds are a special type of holy writ. Like all that is written, they too are derived from the living, spoken word.... To be written down implies far less for them than for genuine holy writ," because they "represent acts of trust, praise, adoration, etc."[66] Consistent with his view of the relation described earlier between experience and expression, van der Leeuw holds that writing is always subsequent to "original experience," always a representation of some nonwritten, perhaps even nonlinguistic "phenomenon." In a text already partially cited, he lays this out in full: "Certainly we can understand Schleiermacher's conclusion that all expression involves the stagnation of religious experience, so that the definition of doctrine as 'experience that has become torpid' would not be incorrect; still, to be articulately expressed pertains to experience, as does its utterance also"; so much so that "even in the most abstruse dogma the original experience of God may repeatedly be renewed."[67]

Van der Leeuw's affirmation of Schleiermacher allows him to retain the primacy of experience over expression/writing, while his qualification allows him to keep the two in the tight correlation he needs to maintain his theory of phenomenological reconstruction. Without the correlation between soul-stuff and text, reconstruction via interpolation would not be possible.

## Limits of *Religionsphänomenologie*

Van der Leeuw employs two explicit, methodological constraints in his articulation of phenomenology as a paradigm for the study of religion: the *epoché* and what I shall call the "philological restraint."

### *Epoché*

In a footnote, which he refers back to several times, van der Leeuw explains what he means by the *"epoché."* This footnote comes during the chapter of the work on "the Religion of Love" (namely, Christianity), discussed above. As noted above, he begins this section by arguing against a long-term trend in comparative religion to act as if one's own religious commitments had no bearing on one's view of the history of religion. He then goes on to treat Christianity, his "own religion," but says that, although he will "deliberately begin our survey of religious phenomena from the Christian viewpoint," as he does he will "retain the typical phenomenological intellectual suspense (*epoché*), while at the same time I bear in mind that this is only possible in the light of one's own experience."[68] He explains what he means by the *epoché*:

> It implies that no judgment is expressed concerning the objective world, which is thus placed "between brackets," as it were. All phenomena, therefore, are considered solely as they are presented to the mind, without any further aspects such as their real existence, or their value, being taken into account; in this way the observer restricts himself to pure description systematically pursued.[69]

This sounds very much like Husserl's statements about the *epoché*, such as (e.g.): "I use the 'phenomenological' *epoché*, which completely bars me from using any judgment that concerns spatio-temporal existence (*Dasein*)."[70] Here, there is no real difference between the two statements. However, as closer examination reveals, the resemblance is only very slight.

Van der Leeuw discusses the *epoché* in two places in the Epilogomena. His first discussion of it is as one of the steps in phenomenological procedure, which we looked at earlier. Phenomenology, he says, "is neither metaphysics, nor the comprehension of empirical reality. It observes restraint (the *epoché*), and its understanding of events depends upon its employing 'brackets.' Phenomenology is concerned only with 'phenomena' ... for it, there is nothing 'behind' the phenomenon."[71] So far, again, we seem to be in a Husserlian mode.

Van der Leeuw, however, completely parts with Husserl in the very next sentence: "This restraint, still further, implies no mere methodological device, no cautious procedure, but the distinctive characteristic of man's whole attitude to reality."[72] Recall that earlier he was quoted as saying that phenomenology is "man's true vital activity." He clarifies both of these statements by quoting a long passage from Scheler—with much approval—in which Scheler relates phenomenological restraint to the Buddha, Plato, and the human condition in general. Clearly, this sort of vitalistic conception of phenomenology is in complete contradiction to what Husserl understood by the term. Husserl explicitly contrasts the *epoché* with the "natural standpoint," which would include any psychological disposition.[73] He also adamantly opposes any psychological interpretation of phenomenology, repeatedly making statements such as: "Pure phenomenology ... is not psychology.... Great as is the importance which phenomenology must claim to possess for psychology n the matter of method ... it is itself ... as little identifiable with psychology as is geometry with natural science."[74] As such, we can only conclude that, although he does invoke the *epoché* as a restraint upon phenomenological activity, his conception of that restraint in no way, finally, resembles Husserl's. Van der Leeuw's is much closer to that of Schleiermacher's and Dilthey's *"Einfülung."*

*Philological Restraint*

The other restrain van der Leeuw invokes is a textual, philological one, arguing that "if phenomenology is to complete its own task, it imperatively requires perpetual correcting by the most conscientious philological and archaeological research."[75] Both phenomenology and traditional historical reconstruction require attention to material facts and careful explications of texts. Both, in other words, require interpretation—just as Dilthey had argued. The type of interpretation used by both is not, however, the same: "But this purely philological hermeneutics has a more restricted purpose than the purely phenomenological. For it is concerned in the first place with the Text, and then with the fact in the sense of what is concretely implied: of what can be translated in other words. This of course necessitates meaning, only it is a shallower and broader meaning than phenomenological understanding."[76] He reiterates this contrast in another place, when distinguishing phenomenology from history: "For the historian, everything is directed first of all to establishing what has actually happened; and in this he can never succeed unless he understands. But also, when he fails to understand, he must describe what he has found, even if he remains at the stage of mere cataloguing. But when the phenomenologist ceases to comprehend, he can have no more to say."[77]

Given that he has claimed that, "subjectively, there is no meaning which cannot be understood" by means of the interpolation of our own, common, universal, *Wesentlich-Menschlich,* or essentially human subjectivity, this contrast undermines, if not completely abolishes, the underlying logic of the "philological restraint." It is subsumed by his notion of the primacy of experience to expression and by his notion that an expression is intelligible because it is an expression of human subjectivity. He would agree with what we shall see both Wach and Eliade say, when they claim that what we are interested in when we study a text is that universal subjectivity known as "Man."

9

# Overcoming the Foreign through Experience, Expression, Understanding

## The Method/ology of Joachim Wach

"Questions have often been raised as to the nature of *Religionswissenschaft*.... On this question, Wach had an unshakable conviction that it was truly and properly a *Geisteswissenschaft*."[1] More than any other author surveyed in this study, Joachim Wach was explicit, open, and relatively self-conscious about the nature of his discipline and its relation to other disciplines. He was also versed in its history: "He lived in the twentieth century, but he was more at home in the nineteenth, academically speaking... and his intellectual gaze never wandered very far from Dilthey's *Erlebnis* (experience), *Ausdruck* (expression), and *Verstehen* (understanding)."[2] As such, Wach fits very much within the genealogy traced out in this study. He is, in a sense, a pivotal point in that, like Otto, he can be seen as a bridge between the nineteenth-century approach and the more synchronic (he will call it systematic) approach of the post-Husserlian phenomenology of religion. As can be seen by the quote above and even a casual survey of his terminology, he is, like van der Leeuw, more of a Diltheian than a Husserlian—which puts him closer to Hegel than Husserl. While he does not write any extended history of religion, his works are rife with micronarratives by means of which he locates religions, "Christian and Non-Christian," as the title of one of his books has it, in a historical scheme that is more nineteenth century than the synchronic approach of a post-Husserlian phenomenology. It is in these micronarratives, which emerge in his treatment of society, culture, philosophy, etc., that, despite his protestations to the contrary, he places religions in a diachronic scheme that is both temporal and qualitative. This allows him to rank religions in terms of their degree of apprehension, and expression, of ultimate reality. "Primitive religions" will be, for the most part, found wanting in many areas while Christianity will *always* be characterized in the most positive terms. Thus, the scholar who seeks to understand the phenomenologists, ends up, by using a set of philosophemes, with a structured discourse built on a series of abstract concepts (e.g., essence, meaning, universal, *Geist*, etc.) that are profoundly logocentric, Eurocentric, and Christocentric. How does this happen? To answer this question, we will have look at his major categories, those named above, namely, experience-expression-understanding, *noch einmal*. Then we will examine the ways in which he puts these concepts into practice in his treatment of various aspect of the history of religions.

## Experience

*Religious Experience*

As we shall see, for Wach experience and essence are closely related. Religious experience is the *primum datum* of *Religionswissenschaft*, and, it is the inner core, the origin of religion. However, it must be understood as *religious* experience. Therefore, Wach uses four criteria as the specific difference of the category "religious experience," which differentiates the religious from the nonreligious in the plethora of all human experience. This is one way in which religious experience is closely tied to the essence of religion.

What, then, differentiates religious from nonreligious experience? The first criterion is the object or content of religious experience:

> Religious experience is a response to what is experienced as ultimate reality; that is, in religious experiences we react not to any single or finite phenomenon, material or otherwise, but to what we realize as undergirding and conditioning all that constitutes our world of experiences. We agree with Paul Tillich when he says that "the presence of the demand of 'ultimacy' in the structure of our existence is the basis of religious experience."[3]

Ultimacy, then, is the dividing line, the specific difference between the religious and the nonreligious. This is a well-known definition, not without problems, but interesting for our purposes in that he goes out of his way to mention the material, a subset of the finite. As the ultimate is higher in value than the finite, and the material, or matter, is a subset of the finite, the ultimate is also higher than the material.

We see a wedge here, however slight, in the very definition of religion for the introduction of the distinction between *Geist* and *Natur*. Wach does not use those terms here; that is not what I am arguing. While he uses both terms elsewhere, especially Spirit, he does not do so in direct conjunction with and opposition to *Natur*, a term he rarely, if ever, uses. However, he does use the terms *finite* and *material* quite often, and these terms will turn out to have the same structural place in his discourse as do *Geist/Natur* in the broader discourse of the phenomenology of religion.

As with other authors we have reviewed, the determination of essence is the major goal of the history/phenomenology of religion. While Wach, to my knowledge, never claims that religion is an a priori category or a structure of consciousness, he does argue that it is universal among humans and this universality is rooted in human nature (he does not elaborate on this concept but seems to assume its general meaning). This is found in religion's "own-most-ness": "A historical study of religions (*Religionshistorie*) must understand *the development* [*Entwicklung*] of a religion first of all from that *religion's own principle*. Here again we encounter a great danger to which many historians of religions succumb: preoccupied with the history of forms, they forget the essence."[4] *Morphé* gets lost in *hylè*. We see a familiar form of relating historical change to essential continuity, the problem Seiwert posed at the very beginning of this study. The unchanging element in the *Entwicklung* of a religion is its principle. The principle, which elsewhere he calls the "idea," is clearly a *mental* construct; it is an *idea* that drives the historical movement of religions, not any material or sociopolitical condition. Ergo, there is a kernel, an essence that unfolds in and through time. This not only defines his understanding of what religion is, its *ens* and *esse* (it is an ideal object), but what history itself is: the bearer, if you will, of essence.

The determination of essence in experience, *as* experience, is the novel move of the phenomenology of religion. Wach argues for the separation, but interdependence of philosophy and phenomenology, but the separation is based on the difference between an a priori and an a posteriori approach to definition. Philosophy gives a logical specific difference; phenomenology finds a universally typical specific difference. Hegel sought to conjoin the two. Wach separates them, but only to a degree. The philosopher's determination of essence is a necessary corollary he will argue, as do other phenomenologists, and his categories and methods are clearly concepts derived from the history of metaphysics. Also, as we will see later, Wach evokes "objective spirit" at crucial moments.

The second factor in religious experience is: "Religious experience is a total response of the total being to what is apprehended as ultimate reality... we are involved... as integral persons."[5] Religion is not just a matter of the intellect, that is, a system of "beliefs," as Rationalists claim. Nor is it a matter of mere "feeling," as in the tradition of Schleiermacher and Otto. Finally, while it is practical, and therefore connected to morality, "[m]oral judgment, however, does not necessarily represent a reaction to ultimate reality."[6] The traditional faculty psychology, then, does not help us locate the essence or origin of religious experience: it differentiates itself from intellect (belief), emotion (or aesthetics), and will (morality). This separation of religious experience from these traditional categories is one of the major achievements of the phenomenology of religion. It did, in some respects, relative to more traditional forms of treatment at the time, represent a return to "the things themselves," or, at least, to experience in its own right. However, "experience" is a subcategory of "consciousness," and the locus of religion in experience/consciousness marks the presence/return/retrieval of "Man."

The third mark of religious experience is that it "is the most intense experience of which man is capable.... The modern term 'existential' designates the profound concern and the utter seriousness of this experience."[7] In one sense, this is an obvious corollary of the first criterion. On another level, however, it is a kind of braggadocio on the part of the phenomenology of religion. The claim is that "no greater can be conceived," that is, that the object of analysis of the discourse of the phenomenology of religion is the most important, fundamental aspect of human existence. Ergo, the science of Religion should be given its rightful place as the Queen of the sciences.

The fourth and final criterion of true religious experience is that it "is practical, that is to say it involves an imperative, a commitment which impels man to act."[8] It must, however, be separated from morality, another realm defined by the imperative, as discussed above.

We see then that Wach uses a multifactoral strategy for defining the specific difference of religious experience. This, in and of itself, is a sophisticated strategy for several reasons. One, he is arguing that these criteria are derived from experience; they are generalizations made from the data. He is also not tied to one single criterion upon which all others rest; these are typical cases found in all genuine religious experience. It also allows him to achieve a separate domain for both religion and the study of religion. However, it sets up a scheme that allows him to call some things pseudo-, semi-, or false religion, a point to be discussed below.

## Homo Religiosous (Again)

"Humanity, by nature, is attuned to religion."[9] While arguing against overstating the commonalities of human nature this much can be said on the matter: "When speaking about the content of universal human nature, one cannot be too cautious. Still, perhaps we may say that the greatest degree of universality is found in feeling and the will, which are likely to be more constant than human understanding and practical activity."[10] While he suggests caution, he himself is bold in stating this: "[T]here cannot be any doubt that religious experience is constitutive in the nature of man."[11] This is true also at the level of religious experience: "[R]eligious experience as we have defined it ... is *universal*. The empirical proof of this statement can be found in the testimonies of explorers and investigators. 'There are no peoples, however primitive, without religion and magic,'" Wach argues, citing Malinowski.[12] While employing no invocation of the idea of religion as a category of the mind or of consciousness, he does make it perfectly synonymous with humanity as a whole. It is worthy of note that his data for this universality is "the testimonies of explorers and investigators," that is, those involved in the colonization of the globe and thereby creating what Mary Louise Pratt earlier referred to as a "planetary consciousness." Once the globe has been surveyed it is possible, at least theoretically, to make non–a priori statements about the universality of religion. Right in the definition of religion's universality, then, we find the touch of the colonialist's hand.

At least for the founded religions, but, from what we have seen above, in all likelihood all religions, experience is their origin: "The founded religions, as distinct from those whose beginnings are lost in a dim past, trace their origin back to such creative religious experiences and impulses. The new religion starts from a specific experience."[13] Experience, then, lies at the origin of religion. A fundamentally new experience brings about a new religion. Experience is primordial, ergo, the origins of religion reside in the consciousness that "contains" that experience, so to speak. Consciousness, that is to say, "Man," stands at the origin of religion. His existence and religion's existence are coeval.

Note that we have also added "origin" to the "universal" described above, thus putting religious experience at the center of religion, the science of religion, the study of "Man," and, arguably, at the center of the life of "Man." As an experience that "undergirds all that constitutes our world of experience," the experience of ultimate reality is the study of religion as the study of the foundations of experience and/or consciousness. Essence, universality, origin, and human nature all converge on a single point. The metaphysics underlying this scheme brings home the fullness of presence, in Derrida's sense.

*Essence*

Because universality and essence are not technically the same concepts, it will be useful, imperative even, to discuss this topic. To understand Wach's hermeneutics we must understand his view of essence. Wach et al., do not subscribe to a positivistic view of the empirical contents of religion or of history. They see these contents as an *Erscheinung*, as manifestations (*heirophanies* in Eliade's term): "We have spoken above of what is generally representative of spiritual, and therefore also of religious expressions. The expression then becomes transparent; it allows something to shine through of the specific and perhaps unique spirit (*Geist*) of a certain religious context. Thus it is that views into the depths (*Tiefenblicke*) become possible. Not always and not to everybody do they open themselves."[14] Historical recovery, then, means sifting out essence and meaning from the concretia found in the empirical data. While they agree that verification of these details is important, they consider it a preliminary task, preparatory for the real task, finding meaning or essence. This is why the "history of religions" is also "the phenomenology of religion": the determination of structure/essence/meaning surpasses in importance for the work of the discipline. Without this underlying kernel, historical facts are, as Otto said, "mere aggregation" (as opposed to a genuine unity); merely dead husks.

Wach, as do others surveyed, has a running polemic against approaches to the study of religion that are reductive and/or do not acknowledge the sui generis nature of religion: "If we wish to determine the nature of religious experience, where shall we begin? In opposition to the popular preoccupation with the quest for the function of religion, it is necessary to stress the search for the nature of religion."[15] The essence of religion, its nature, cannot be found by analyzing its function. Function may be considered as an attribute ("accident" in older philosophical terms) of religion, but not its essence. Phenomenologists tend, rightly in the main, to associate functional views of religion with empiricist approaches to gathering the data of religion and reductive theories about the nature of religion.

The autonomy of religion, understood as an essence, is a foundational notion for the phenomenological method, a method that is contrasted with other approaches: "It is obvious that a preconceived notion of the (nonautonomous) nature of religion will of necessity endanger the discipline that studies religions. The phenomenology is 'innocent of theory;'" by contrast to reductive approaches, "accepting the autonomy of religion implies no prejudice."¹⁶ Because, as Bleeker said, phenomenology renders religious phenomena "clear and transparent," in the Husserlian sense of going "back to the things themselves," it is not a *theory* of religion. It is the eidetic apprehension of what is, of what is manifest in human consciousness. Fact: humans have religion, ergo it is studied as such. By contrast (and by implication) all other theories are *theories*, that is, not pure science, not pure description, but science contaminated by a priori assumptions and prejudices. This assertion that phenomenology is not a theory is a major plank in the elision of its own operations as being operations embedded in a complex network of historical and structural concepts. As we saw with Kristensen, this results in the belief that phenomenologists have direct access to "the things themselves," while functionalists, et al., have only a mediated access. Since religion is a given element of human nature, the phenomenology of religion, as that science which has direct access to that element, can become a vehicle for cultural (*Geistesleben*) renewal: "To combine all this into a complete theory, into a theory that would, indeed, contribute to the great, universal symbolism of the human spirit, will be a task for the future."¹⁷ Eliade will call this the "New Humanism" and will set a similar, even more grandiose agenda for the phenomenology of religion. This is possible, again, because of the direct intuition of Spirit, that is, of human nature, that is, of "Man."

Wach is adamant that the history of religions cannot be critiqued by, and certainly is not subordinated to, either positivist empiricism or materialism. "We no longer need to defend the delimitation of an autonomous realm known as religion within human cultural life (*Geistesleben*). Earlier, it was necessary to maintain the autonomy of religion against the onslaught of English and French positivism and above all against the many shades of materialism."¹⁸ Given his emphasis on Spirit, on *Geistesleben*, and on inner experience *pace* Dilthey, it is fair to say that his rejection of materialism, first, sets up a binary, Spirit/matter, and second, by extension, *Geist/Natur*. In his narratives and structural analyses Wach does not *explicitly* rank religions according to their proximity to *Natur* or to *Geist*. However, in all of his listings of religions, he places non-European religions, most often of people of color, as the *"prima,"* primitive and lists Christianity in the category, "highest." He does explicitly say that "in the course of historical development, definite tendencies toward *systematization* may be discerned. . . . The role played by reason and reflection is significant, being an important factor in continued development [*Entwicklung*]."¹⁹

"*Prima*" can, of course, mean temporally first. However, in the discourse of the phenomenology of religion it has meant first in the differentiation of Spirit from nature, just as Hegel had argued in his discussion of "nature religion." Primitives take the initial step out of nature and into humanhood, but it is only a first step. The first, in this discourse, is the least developed.[20] Ergo, we again have the binary, *Geist/Natur*, however *implicit* it is in Wach.

There is yet another way to determine essence: distinguish between the genuine and the false in religion: "We do not come to know Christ better by denigrating the non-Christian religions instead of distinguishing carefully between the genuine and the false."[21] How might one go about this? He gives a nuanced example of what criteria can be used to do this by looking at the "amount of religious productivity and vitality which speaks from within the specific phenomenon. If, for example, we consider the faith in a god (*Gottesglauben*) of a certain African tribe, we must determine *the degree of perfection* to which this belief in a god is expressed by this particular community; then we must honor the level of theistic experience which appears attained therein."[22] The emphasis is added because the main work of this distinction is done by a somewhat vague criterion in relation to which we may measure "the faith in a god of a certain African tribe." While I would not give it too much significance, the fact that he uses "a certain African tribe" in the discussion of the potential falsity of religion is not merely incidental, either. Later he will say that Native Americans are incapable of making the distinctions between moral categories that are a core element of civilized societies. Both, of course, are characterized at a macro-level as non-Christian versus *the* Christian religion—it is in the title of one of his main works, *Types of Religious Experience: Christian and Non-Christian*. We have again, albeit implicitly—but quite consistently—a set of binaries that define and categorize peoples of the world by classifying their religions in this manner. Again, what do Native Americans and "tribal" Africans have in common? That they are non-European. This, again, pertains, albeit indirectly, to the definition of the essence of religion and religious experience.

## Expression

*Inside, Out*

"Scheler has defined the dividing line between man and animals by attributing to man *Geist*, the ability to reflect on his own nature and to become a moral being, capable of renunciation and self-sacrifice. I would prefer to draw the line between those beings which are and those which are not able to create permanent expressions for their internal experience, which may be understood independently of subjective life."[23] Expressions then, are an anthropological fact, indeed, even the very definition of "Man." As with Dilthey and van der Leeuw, it is a matter of *life*. It belongs to the human itself; it is not a derivative reality. The issue of permanence is also important (as it was with Kristensen). While only spirit can comprehend spirit, inner experience must be objectified for it to be an enduring, as opposed to a fleeting, moment in the life of Spirit. Experience is by nature fleeting; objectifications remain long after the experience—and the experiencer—have passed. Thus, we have "objective spirit" as a corollary anthropological fact and hermeneutical necessity.

Expression provides access to the inner experience of the other: "[R]eligious experience tends towards expression. This tendency is universal. Only in and through its expression does any of our experiences exist for others, does any religious experience exist for us, the students of the history of religion. The religious experience of another person can never become the object of direct observation."[24] He indicates that this is a basic aspect of religion, but also an aspect that calls for a particular kind of study: "The basic, genuine experience which we call 'religious' tends to express or objectify itself in various ways. We need a phenomenology of the expressions of religious experience, a 'grammar' of religious language, based on a comprehensive empirical, phenomenological, and comparative study."[25] In the same vein as with Dilthey and van der Leeuw, Wach argues that "between soul and soul": "The expression of religious life is a bridge to its understanding. But this bridge would be impassable if there were no certainty that somehow one soul can understand another."[26] The materials of these expressions are the *emperia* of the History of Religions and its *necessary* hermeneutical dimension. To study religion is not simply to acquire facts, but to interpret them. This form of interpretation leads to "understanding," in a very distinct sense. Reading religion data as an expression—or a "manifestation"; *Erscheinung*—necessitates a different kind of operation performed upon those data than if one reads them as "representations," that is, purely external kinds of signs: "The idea of representation (*Vertretung*) is also of no help when we are concerned ... with understanding the inner processes of others."[27] A stop sign is a representation; a *churinga* is a manifestation of Spirit, or a religious expression. This is because "[t]he possibilities of human experience are not exhausted with the sum total of an individual's external experiences (*äussere Lebensfahrung*).... There is an internal experience (*inneres Erleben*) in which external experiences (*Erfahrungen*) can be anticipated."[28] The inner is basic; from it we derive the external. Essence precedes existence.

In "our search for universals in religion": "A comparative study of the *forms* of the expression of religious experience, the world over, shows an amazing similarity in structure."[29] While historically situated, "the forms of this expression, though conditioned by the environment within which it originated, show similarities in structure; there are universal themes in religious thought, the universal is always embedded in the particular."[30] We return to one of the classic principles of metaphysics and ontotheology: that the finite is in and of itself insignificant (literally); time and space are the enemies of the universal, yet it can overcome them through expression of the inner life, that is, the "eternally human," as Wach often refers to it. We see yet another way metaphysics offers a solution for the hermeneutic problem generally, and the question posed by Seiwert at the beginning: the identity of a religion spread out over time and geography. The truly religious in the expression so spread out is, first, an anthropological fact, and as such, second, it is the universal dimension of the finite reality. The finite, time and historical-geographical dispersion—or, the Other of the universal—is denied by the idealist, logocentric, Platonic-scholastic universal. This universal is rooted in "Man" (as "Man" is himself both universal and *a* universal), both in the original expressor and in the hermeneute who reads these expressions. The universal overcomes the disruption of presence; the Other is, finally, reduced to and subsumed in the Same.

Living in specific circumstances means that the husk, of the expression as opposed to its kernel, will be drawn from the immediate world in which "Man" finds himself: "Man always finds himself situationally conditioned: whatever he experiences, he experiences in *time* and *space* ... he cannot but give expression to what he has seen, felt, etc.,... but by means of analogy from what is known and familiar to him,"[31] because "a good deal of what is called religion belongs to the category of culture and custom. But it is the conviction of the author of the following essays [Wach himself] that we must carefully distinguish between religious *experience* and its *expression*,"[32] or, again, the external husk and the internal kernel. Ergo, whatever the content of religious experience, its expression will be drawn from the symbolic resources within which it resides. Wach explicitly ranks religions as "primitive," "lower," and "higher." One of the factors underlying this ranking system is the spiritual, sometimes also the material and political, conditions in which an experience and its expression take place. "Lower" religions take place in relatively less developed conditions, ergo, their content does not represent the universal as clearly as do those of the "higher" religions. As we shall see, Eliade makes a similar argument, often contrasting something like village Christianity with institutional Christianity, claiming that the latter is a more universal, therefore complete manifestation of the sacred. The metaphysical category, "the Universal," again, supplies the reassurance of presence.

*Symbols*

As the expression uses a "local" vehicle, if you will, to convey its universal truth, that vehicle must itself be examined: "The symbol is the primary means of expressing the content of any experience which we call religious. The use of symbolic expression is universal. By symbol a meaning is conveyed . . ."[33] In other words, as did Dilthey, Wach holds to an *expressive theory* of symbolism. While he does believe that they have common, universal structures (at least some of them), the key thing about symbols is that they express an inner experience. There is, of course, a necessary individualizing of this experience so described—it occurs "inside" the individual, albeit a common, universal inner experience. As such, there is an individuation in the notion of symbols and how they get their meaning. As expressions, they must be tied to those individual moments of inner experience. Again, while they are structured, the concept of structure here is isomorphic: the individual unit has a ideal and continuous Being. As such, it would be difficult, if possible, to explain how they could be elements of a system. This means that Wach's theory of symbolism is subjectivist, in a broad sense of the term (e.g., Cartesian). It is "Man" and his inner meanings, that is, those most removed from external, natural causation that are *ex*-pressed in religious expression. The autonomy of systems of symbols would threaten the literal sanctity of "Man's" inner realm. The symbol then, would stand aside and apart from "Man" and would not issue from within him. The threat of the disruption of presence, again, is thwarted.

Note also, that he does not say that *religion* is expressed in human experience. It is, so to speak, religion that *does* the expressing. This is in keeping with his "essence precedes existence" stance and his view that religion is sui generis, that is, nothing causes religion itself to be expressed. That would lead to the dangerous notion that religion is not sui generis but rather that it is caused by some underlying phenomenon (society, function, material base). Religious expressions express only *religious* experience, however, muddled up with nonreligious elements they may be. When one knows how to distinguish the essential from the inessential, the universal from the particular, then one can find the religious in the expression and separate it out.

## Understanding

A major component of Wach's hermeneutics is the idea of understanding, or *Verstehen*. Recall Dilthey's maxim: "Nature is explained, spirit is understood." Wach subscribes to this program of methodology completely. In many ways, he reiterates much of what Dilthey had already said. Wach will reiterate the concatenation of: expression-understanding-structure-essence and the subjective aspect of Dilthey's theory of apprehension of the other: "In the human understanding, as the excellent hermeneutics of Wilhelm Dilthey have shown, the totality of the mind and soul (*Totalität des Gemüts*) is effective."[34] Understanding is a very specific concept with multiple components, so it must be examined carefully.

### Affinity

The basis of understanding is the common human nature, soul, or spirit, between human and human: "[N]ot everything can, in principle, be understood, but only that in whose nature (*Wesen*) I can somehow 'take part.' Thus it is possible to say: you comprehend only what is like yourself, no more."[35] Wach takes this principle of affinity to extremes that we do not find in other phenomenologists. He quotes Goethe on the matter with approval: "*In jedem Menschen liegen alle Formen des Menschlichen*" ("In every man all forms of human character are potentially present")[36] and Droysen to the same end: " '*So sollst Du sein, denn so verstehe isch Dich.*' (Droysen) ('Thus shalt thou be, for thus do I know thee or thy true nature.')."[37] Participation, *methexis*, or affinity is rooted, again, not only in a common human nature, but in the *intelligibility* of things "like me." Much as van der Leeuw had argued that "nothing human is alien to me," Wach is claiming that the inner experience of which Dilthey spoke is the site and the condition for the possibility of true *methexis*, not merely rational comprehension. As such, the intelligibility of the other is neither fully rational nor is it fully empirical:

> The possibilities of human experience are not exhausted with the sum total of an individual's external experiences (*äussere Lebensfahrung*). A person does not need to have actu-

ally been in love to understand a lover. He does not need to have waged battles in order to understand a general, nor does he need to grow old to understand the aged. There is an internal experience (*inneres Erleben*) in which external experiences (*Erfahrungen*) can be anticipated.[38]

One of the reasons that positivism and empiricism will not suffice for the study of religion is due to the nature of experience itself. Empiricism (typically) takes sensation to be the sum and substance of experience. Dilthey, Otto, and Wach argue that there is an inner experience, to wit, the self acting upon itself, and this inner experience is not affected by sensation. Recall that Otto was adamant on this point. The mystery of religious experience occurs in this inner realm. As inner, it can only be reached by a kind of psychological analogy: my inner experience is like your inner experience. These inner experiences are the kernel, the essence of religion.

As such, *methexis* is a radically subjective method. It is not a completely rational process: "The primary task of scholarship—fathoming meaning—does not fall to reason alone. Whoever understands, understands with his whole heart (*mit der 'Totaltät des Gemütes'*)."[39] Wach explicitly states that understanding in his sense involves a mysterious connection: "This spirit, however, can be comprehended only when an interest is present that we can conceive of as the expression of a mysterious, inner *methexis*."[40] One's life experience plays an important part in understanding. The broader its range, the more one can understand: "Experience significantly increases a person's ability to comprehend. The hermeneutical theorists have repeatedly stressed this point, and correctly so."[41] He quotes the famous phrase, which Dilthey also used: "*Interpres non fir sed nascitur* [An interpreter is not made but born]."[42] This inner *methexis* drives the hermeneute to a transformational experience: "Given the inner affinity discussed above, the person who wishes to understand enters into a mysterious communication with the object of study that allows him to penetrate to its core. One side of his being (*Wesen*) is touched. The anticipation of related life drives him on."[43] By "related life" I take him to mean something similar to van der Leeuw's notion that understanding is a fully human act. The related life, or connected (nexus, in Dilthey's terms), or integral life is a quest that can be fulfilled, at least in part, by the scholarly study of religion. The academic, methodological study of religion has the potential to *transform* the scholar.

This notion stems from Dilthey's notion of the difference between explaining and understanding. At one level the condition for the possibility of this is the Platonic notion of participation and the logos:

"We come back, therefore, to the Platonic principle that if any rational understanding is to be possible, the *logos* in us must be akin to the *logos* in things. This hermeneutical principle proves to be valid for the understanding of religion, too."[44] However, as a sui generis thing, there are limits to the degree that reason can *understand* religion: "The structure (*Gestzlichkeit*) of religious life—and I must emphasize this point here—is original, and thus in the end it cannot be comprehended from the point of view of philosophy, science, or ethics."[45]

## Sympathy

"How, in fact, is sympathy (*Nachfühlen*) possible at all?"[46] Wach poses this question and immediately gives its answer: "Once the inner relationship has been defined, the rest is not so problematic."[47] Again, if the real locus of inner experience is in that sub- or pre-empirical realm, it can only be accessed by means of its expressions. However: "What is decisive is what is *made* of experience. To external experiences is added the inner power of the imagination. It is by imagination that experiences first bear fruit for understanding religion."[48] Wach distinguishes between a representation and an expression. A representation expresses external forms of experience (derived from sense perception) and an expression is the outer manifestation of the "inner process" of pre- or sub-empirical experience. "The idea of representation (*Vertretung*) is also of no help when we are concerned . . . with understanding the inner processes of others."[49] The target is the latter, not the former and this misunderstanding is, Wach et al., would argue, how empiricists both misunderstand religion and the phenomenology of religion. It is reached by many objective methods; Wach is at pains to make that clear (e.g., historical context and philology), but finally it is imagination that allows one to sympathetically enter into, or "feel with" (*Nach-fülhlen*; to feel after, by implication what has been felt before by another in another (past) time).

What must happen is that a bridge must be formed from one inner self to another inner self, which raises a question (as we shall see below) that Wach is constantly asking: "Is it possible to conceive of a study of religions apart from the possibility of an inner relationship with what is *foreign*? How could we understand the Buddha or Muhammad?"[50] Notice that Christ is missing from the list. Despite the differences of almost two millennia, there is no consciousness on Wach's part that understanding Christ or Christianity is problematic. That Buddha and Muhammad represent the foreign is telling of a Eurocentric perspective. In most cases where the issue of sympathy comes up, it arises in relation to the problem of understanding "the foreign," that is, non-European religions. He takes Christianity—with no mention of Judaism—that is, Europe, as the unmarked, unproblematic basis from which any interpretative comparison is made. We have seen, and will to continue to see, that this is a common trend in the discourse of the phenomenology of religion.

Imaginative sympathy combines with other elements of the nature of the data to produce "understanding":

> [Sympathetic] Understanding possesses the power needed to penetrate the depths, for it is nourished from within. In this way, not only do the activity, the feeling, and the thought of human beings, the character and wills of the great personalities—of religious heroes—become understandable; so, too, does the entire world of expression, the simplest sentence, the smallest utterance, the apparently insignificant fact.[51]

> This spirit, however, can be comprehended only when an interest is present that we can conceive of as the expression of a mysterious, inner *methexis*.[52]

Only spirit knows spirit *as* spirit, Hegel had said. This idea leads to a discussion of objective Spirit, which will be taken up shortly. There is an intermediary term, between inner *methexis* and objective spirit, that is a necessary component of understanding: structure.

## Structure and History

"What is important is the context; in Dilthey's words, 'structure is everything.' "[53] Not all of the process of understanding is subjective. The objective side of understanding is rooted in an apprehension of structure: "Hermeneutical theory aims at understanding these structures and forms."[54]

The means by which these structures are understood entails a complex relation between history and structure, because: "Research in a historical study of religions repeatedly demands a holistic or systematic ordering (*Zusammenordnung*)."[55] This systematic ordering is rescued from empty a priori concepts because of its relationship to empirical content: "There are in theory very close connections between the historical and systematic branches of this as of every other discipline."[56]

Many philosophers and historians see a conflict between what each does. Wach, however, denies that the conflict is necessary:

> It is easy to see that we are here not really confronted with an alternative because the empiricist cannot wholly dispense with categories with which to organize his facts, nor can his opponent forego documentation and illustration of ideas by empirical (historical) facts. Flesh and bones—both are indispensable, neither an unorganized mass nor a mere skeleton would be satisfactory.[57]

Wach seems to argue that, although different kinds of operations, they are both essential parts of a humanistic study of religion and cannot be fully separated: " '[H]istorical' in this sense does not contrast with 'systematic'; rather, systematic treatment is included in the historical."[58]

While on the one hand asserting the complementary nature of their relationship, Wach also describes the different roles each part plays: "What is it that interests the historian? Development; 'Becoming.' His work is characterized by a genetic point of view. The systematician, by contrast, turns his attention to cross-sections; his is interested not in Becoming but in what has become (*das Gewordene*)."[59] In other words: "[T]he historical study of religion is in the end possible only after systematics has isolated and identified useful categories."[60] Both *hyle* and *morphe* are necessary; the ideal and the material elements.

How then are structural concepts defined? How does the researcher discover them? This question returns us to the issue of structure. First of all, Wach rejects the idea that categories of the systematic approach are reached a priori, arguing that "categories supplied by the philosopher of religion can never satisfy the scholar who works empirically"[61]—including the scholar working in a systematic manner.

Wach makes a claim that recalls Kristensen's statement about the experiential dimension of the determination of essence: "Let me make clear once more the logical nature of these 'systematic' concepts. They are derived from experience."[62] It is uncertain what "experience" here means. It could mean "empirical," per the discussion above about the extraction of structures from historical data. Or, as with Kristensen, and, per the discussion above about empathetic understanding, it could mean one's own religious experience. Evidence for the latter view can easily be found. Consider this rather extreme statement:

> [T]he conviction that religion is not dead but alive, that more or less innately, more or less purely actualized, ... lives in

all of us; that the soul's final attitudes, experiences, and decisions are "eternally human," and that this "eternally human" includes not only the general attitudes toward life that are expressed in particular religions but also the modalities in which they express themselves.[63]

It is clear that Wach cannot disassociate subjective experience from "understanding" in the technical, hermeneutical sense. This is quite typical of the discourse of the phenomenology of religion, being structured so heavily by the "inner/outer" binary as it is.

The other interesting and related claim concerns the "eternally human." It recalls van der Leeuw's statement that "nothing human is foreign to me." The basis for hermeneutical understanding, then, is the fact that both the hermeneute and the believer share a common nature. By delving into the depths of this common nature one can arrive at a sameness rooted there, a sameness that overcomes all differences found in expressions (i.e., empirical historical research). The paradigm of the "transcendental subject" is a basic philosopheme that makes understanding, in the hermeneutical sense, possible. This subject is held to be universal and, ultimately, homogenous.

However, access to this "eternally human" is also made through the structural method so central, as we saw with Chantepie and Kristensen, to the phenomenological method. How, then, does this structural approach work as a *method*? Rather than being a priori categories, as positivists would claim, these categories are reached by "a kind of abstraction" in which the scholar "looks for what is similar."[64] Again, the trope of "the Same" shows itself to be a major term within the discourse of the phenomenology of religion. This trope is the basis of the structural method.

The process by which the structures are found first entails that structural parallels be found in the *hyle*, the historical matter: "What methods must the systematic study of religions employ? One method above all: comparison. . . . [F]or the formal systematization it [comparison] is essential."[65] Comparison starts with a description: "It would seem obvious that when a scholar becomes interested in studying a particular historical phenomenon systematically, he will want to isolate it from its historical context and understand and describe it first of on its own terms."[66] As we have seen before, phenomenology is taken to be an atheoretical method of description. Ergo, it is possible, with the right training of course, to describe a religious phenomenon "on its own terms." Structure is *derived*, not *imposed*.

Extracting structure from data involves two steps: "First, it must formulate abstract, ideal-typical concepts, and second, it must identify the regularities and principles that appear in the historical development."[67] The first is accomplished thusly: "We drop whatever characteristic are not common to all; and from the total picture of the common characteristics provide we obtain our concept"[68] or structure. Underlying the multiplicity is "the unity of what occurs in individual patterns and groups of forms—or structures."[69] This first step is the systematic or phenomenological part of the approach. The second is the historical part and will be dealt with later in this chapter. However, even there the trope of the Same, the drive to find unity in multiplicity and meaning out of matter is still in the forefront of this method: "Any historical study of religions that does not wish to limit itself to superficial appearances and does not see the mere compilation of facts and data as its goal must seek a unifying and organizing principle that holds the individual phenomena together."[70] Structure, history, and experience come together in the following manner:

> Some would question the identity and unity of the far-flung studies which together make up the work in our field. This unity is, indeed, difficult to conceive as long as single data are seen—be they philological, archaeological, anthropological, historical, or sociological. In order to relate these data and to interpret them as expressions of religious experiences, some notions of the *nature* of this *experience* are necessary. In other words the narrowly historical quest has to be supplemented by a systematic (phenomenological) one.[71]

It is possible to find the "nature" of religious experiences because, again, there is a nature, which ultimately provides a unity, to religious experience: "The formal shape of cultus, dogma, and other forms ... are grounded in the total religious life [and] are all determined by the basic attitude (*Grundhaltung*) of which the entire religion is an expression."[72] All of the structures of the components of a religion will be intelligible, both as religious, as elements of a particular religion, and as structures, if they are understood as manifestations or expressions of the idea of that religion. That is, the *Grundhaltung* is an essence of which these structures are manifestations. Another word for this attitude or idea: objective Spirit.

## Objective Spirit and the Philosophy of Religion

The more fully objective manner by which one understands the object of interpretation is to study it through its *expressions*:

> For everything spiritual (*alles Seelische*) and everything cultural (*alles Geistige*) in the expression of a certain inner attitude (*Haltung*) or spirit (*Geist*) that is, to be sure, often very complex and difficult to interpret or comprehend. It is necessary to 'understand' this spirit, to relate to it even those expressions that are most objective and appear to be most independent, and to interpret those expressions from the "spirit."[73]

We understand the expressions as expressions of spirit; we understand the spirit (of a religion) through its expressions. Expression, then, as with Dilthey, is a key hermeneutical concept for it is only by these expressions that we can retrieve and reconstruct these inner experiences: "The expression of religious life is a bridge to its understanding. But this bridge would be impassable if there were no certainty that somehow one soul can understand another."[74]

This procedure of reaching "understanding" is not, as noted before, purely subjective. It is also the product of a disciplined approach of the Humanities: "Their [the humanities] object is "historical" (*historisch*): the objectification of the spirit (*Geist*). Their method is research; it begins with interpretation (*Auslegung*) and ends with understanding (*Verstehen*)."[75] The three components, then, are history understood as the objectification of spirit, interpretation, and finally *Verstehen*.

It is clear that Wach is relying on the philosophical program of Dilthey here. However, Dilthey alone is not the only source; Hegel is also a source. In the articulation of both its method and its metatheory, the History of Religions draws upon, is even dependent upon, philosophy:

> My specific attempt to point out the significance of objective religion is in harmony with a more general tendency in related humanistic disciplines. Philosophy seems to have taken the lead here. Its interests were for a long time dominated by purely epistemological and logical problems, but now once again it is energetically pursuing problems of culture; it is becoming, once again, a philosophy of the historical world. In the process, a concept has come to the fore that it is of the utmost importance for all the humanistic studies to study and clarify: the concept of the objective spirit.[76]

Wach identifies this philosophy which takes up the problems of culture: "Ever since Hegel's philosophy of religion there has been a lively interchange between the history of religions and the philosophy of religion."[77] While Hegel's significance is crucial, it is, as I have argued throughout, mediated by the work of Dilthey: "Hegel was the first to formulate the concept of the objective spirit, which he placed within the immense system of his philosophy of spirit. When his mighty structure collapsed, Dilthey took up this most important concept and sought to reestablish it apart from metaphysics."[78] What was this most important concept? What is it that *Religionswissenschaft* has taken from Dilthey's work? Wach argues: "One of the most important themes of Dilthey's work was the connection between the psychological world and objective reality. He treated this theme repeatedly from the points of view of psychology, logic, and epistemology, whether he has drawn to it by a concern for connections between the collective soul and the objective spirit."[79]

There are two specific issues in *Religionswissenschaft* for which it needs philosophy. First is the determination of the essence of religion: "Should historians of religions explore the essential nature (*Wesen*) of religion? Should they identify typical regularities and evaluate various religious forms? Clearly such questions lead more or less directly into philosophy, so that here the history of religions shades into the philosophy of religion."[80]

Second, and finally, the idea of objective spirit is a key aspect of hermeneutical theory and practice:

> Every hermeneutics that goes beyond a theory of techniques and methods is grounded in certain metaphysical convictions, for example, the convictions of a philosophy of life or of spirit, according to which the idea of participation, based on an essential commonality (*Wesensgemeinsamkeit*) is the presupposition of all understanding. In this connection, the nature and meaning of an objectification of life or spirit (the "expression") may be determined. Since we can participate in the life of another, we are able to understand its manifestations through a psychological understanding that is directed toward internal motivations.[81]

Note the total absence of any Husserlian terminology here. Wach is a crucial summation of the prior work of the phenomenology of religion and transmitter of that work to subsequent generations of phenomenologists. It is clear that Hegel via Dilthey is his source of the phenomenological theory of consciousness, which lies at the heart of any kind of phenomenology. This theory of consciousness, while also being subjective (very subjective at times) is ultimately a theory of objective consciousness—both the subject and the object of study participate in it. So, the metaphysics, as well as the theory of *Geist* are an integral part of Wach's phenomenological program.

## The Foreign

Wach articulates the hermeneutical task with understanding the foreign so often that it would be impossible—and highly redundant—to cite all of its instances. Interestingly, one of the ways he taxonomizes religions is to differentiate the religion of Europe from all other religion: *Types of Religious Experience: Christian and Non-Christian* is a title of a book, as we have seen.

How, then, does Wach treat the Foreign? One would think that, given the emphasis on affinity as a part of understanding, the problem of understanding that which is "foreign" would not be a major issue. Recall that van der Leeuw did not find it problematic ("Nothing human is foreign to me"). Inner affinity allows one to overcome the distance between hermeneute and object of understanding, whether that distance is, as Seiwert noted, geographic or historical, or, we must add, a difference of culture, language, religion, of objective forms of spirit. However, Wach spends a great deal of time pondering the issue:

> But can you understand a religion other than your own? This question must be analyzed. There seems to be a sense in which the answer would have to be, "No," and yet there are indications that in some sense a positive reply is possible. Undoubtedly it is possible to "know the facts" in the sense of gathering and organizing all the available information. As we have seen, that was and is the task of our field according to the positivistically minded scholar. Yet, is that enough?[82]

The answer to the last question is clearly "No." Contra the positivists: "Modern epistemology, phenomenology, and psychology have analyzed both the prerequisites and the nature of the way we understand a foreign '*Thou*,' its nature, experience, and activity."[83] Affinity is one kind of answer he gives to this problem. However, he also argues that religion is a unique manifestation of spirit: "[I]n studying foreign religions the history of religions must proceed in a manner that is analogous to the other humanistic studies [*Geisteswissenschaft*]. The history of religions cannot simply be equated with these studies. In every realm of the spirit—law, art, morals—the process of objectification is unique; so, too, religious expression follows on its own laws."[84] Here again, we appear to have the traditional faculty psychology at work. The human self thinks, wills, and feels. It also is religious, for now he does argue, in effect that religion is an a priori essence. Finally, he pulls all of these threads together by arguing both ends: objective spirit is studied empirically, while the inner experience, the sui generis aspect, is grasped intuitively:

> After exploration, historians of religions must try to *understand* foreign religiosity and foreign religious forms. In understanding, the interpretive effort is intensified: the exegesis of sources is carried out from every angle; particular moments and views are related to others. Above all, the specific character of an object of religio-historical consideration is taken into account. A religious manifestation must be understood as a religious manifestation. Thus, whoever wishes deal with such data must possess a certain sensitivity for religious feelings and thought.[85]

The bridge between the foreign, by which he means the non-Christian, is, on the one hand the universal commonality shared by both hermeneute and subject of study, and on the other hand by the developed sensitivity to inner religious feelings, as Otto argued.

One would think that this view of the essential humanness would have as its corollary a radically egalitarian view of religions and persons. However, as we have seen before, that is not the case. What experience does Wach want us to call upon when understanding the "foreign"? This experience: "In this way the student of primitive religion will remember the experiences of his youth—the well-known Indian games of American boys and girls—and thus expand his understanding of the primitive mind."[86] The experience that it takes to understand exalted moments of religion are themselves exalted levels of high culture. However, to understand the primitive, the American Indian, it is childhood and play that help us understand this other—which amounts to the infantilization of "primitive" peoples (again, those mentioned are non-Europeans of color). We will see below that this is a very consistent pattern for Wach: every time American Indians are mentioned as examples, it is an example of a lower religion, a simpler state of culture, or a condition that is closer to nature than is the civilized as such.

## History of Religions, Society, and Culture

As with other chapters, we will now turn to some more localized treatments of concrete religious data so as to demonstrate how these notions work out in practice. This way we can see what Wach actually says about religions.

We have seen that Wach sets up the criterion for religion by differentiating between the authentic and the false. What is suppressed, I would argue, in this maneuver is a schema of the gradations of religion in light of the determination of essence, of true religion as distinguished from false. In order to get at these suppressed premises, it will be necessary to go through various regions of data (as defined by Wach himself) and demonstrate what these suppressed principles are and what they *do*, that is, how they shape his way of structuring representations of religion and specific religions. As noted before, representations are social facts. They will circulate and interact with other systems of representations, possibly systems the author never intended for them to interact with. This is how representations become socially objective and socially effective, that is to say, how they do something in the world.

The topics treated here will be Wach's comparative, cross-cultural treatment of reason or philosophy (closely connected to doctrine), his concept and treatment of the idea of salvation, of ethics, and of immortality. In each region will see recurrent patterns that closely resemble patterns in comparative religion we have seen in previous chapters.

### *Reason/Philosophy/Doctrine*

"Practically every positive religion, including every primitive religion, contains the beginnings of a philosophy of religion."[87] We start, then, with a micronarrative of the embryonic stage of the philosophy of religion: including "every primitive religion," that is, at "the beginnings" and by implication (and explicitly stated, as we shall soon see) not reaching to the consummation of an ethics in the primitive. The primitive is indeed "prima," the first, the origin, which contains the as of yet undeveloped embryo of reason. "What is expressed by the primitive mind as myth is conceived of in terms of doctrine at *a more advanced level of civilization*."[88]

Alongside this independent philosophy of religion, "there exists an explicitly formulated dogmatics—*the most intense refinement of doctrine*—as in Christianity, Judaism, Islam, and Buddhism."[89] We may define doctrine as the rational organization of beliefs, an organization by means of which the content of a religion, not in its totality but in its foundational structures, is clarified. In Hegelian terms, it is the mind or spirit becoming more conscious of itself *as* mind or spirit and recognizing its content via this progressive rationalization. This occurs in the "higher" religions, a term, as we can see, that is thoroughly logocentric: What makes higher religions higher? Is it not their increased "refinement," as opposed to primal beginnings? And is this refinement not coexistent with writing? All the religions cited as "higher" are religions that possess scripture; they are all "religions of the Book" (τα Βιβλια)? Has the research of the text been the dominant trend in studying religion until quite recently? And is not Wach's hermeneutics a hermeneutics, finally, of the text? The text, the logos, the word, differentiates the civilized from the noncivilized, to wit, the primitive. We must be attentive then to which religions and peoples are named as primitive and which are named as civilized. Therein lies the story of the suppressed element in the textual play at work here.

Having situated the primitive in a binary relation to the "refined" religions, which posses doctrine, we move to the next stage: "Even among the religions of higher cultures where for some reason or another a full-fledged philosophy of religion has never developed, sporadic reflections of a philosophic sort may nevertheless be observed, as in the religions of Egypt, Babylon, Iran, Japan, and Mexico."[90] Beyond the embryonic beginnings, we now have the adolescent stage; reason is there, but it is underdeveloped in these peoples. Although they are higher, they are not the consummation of the process of rationalization, and this despite their significant achievements as civilizations. Rather, they occupy a middle stage in what is clearly unfolding as a progressive narrative of greater and greater rationalization of religion.

Note how similar this is to Otto's criterion in his progressive narrative of the gradations of the history of religions. Whereas Otto clearly links the rational with *Geist*/mind and clearly opposes them to *Natur*/sensation, Wach is not so overt. This leaves room for doubt as to whether or not he is telling the same story. However, the order, grouping and characterization of the various peoples, especially vis-à-vis Europe, suggests that this narrative is quite similar, if not identical. Can we imagine that the logos is not *geistig*? Given the hermeneutics of Spirit and inner experience (free from all sensation, as both Dilthey and Otto asserted) does it not make the logos a dimension of Spirit?

"Where, however, the 'expansion' of dogma leads to a systematically developed worldview, albeit a worldview derived from a particular revelation, criticism, discussion, and opposition will arise. This stage has been reached by Christianity, Judaism, Islam, Zoroastrianism, Buddhism, and Hinduism, and also in China."[91] Reason is inherently self-reflective; it is in reason/philosophy proper that dialectics emerge. The dialectics of dogma in the various religions that posses writing is an advanced stage in the progressive development of the rational element in religion, a higher rung in its gradation in that, again, it is through dialectical reasoning ("criticism, discussion, and opposition") that Spirit advances to higher levels of self-realization.

From this list, it would seem that the sun does not rise in the East and set in the West. Wach's analysis includes the East, Judaism and Islam and other non-European religions in this stage. However, what the logos giveth, the logos taketh away:

> The emancipation of philosophical reflection from concrete religions and from worldviews based on them has taken place, strictly speaking, only in the Western world. Of course, in East Asia, thought is in general less constrained than anywhere else in the Orient, and there we do encounter "autonomous" thought. In India too, individual movements and persons have freed themselves from traditional speculations. But except for sporadic occurrences, such as mysticism, Greek influence on Judaism and Islam has led to no fundamental separation of philosophy from religion. In the West, by contrast, a *unique* "theoretical" and then a "scientific" attitude flourished first in Greece, and a radical separation of thought from the inherited faith was the result.[92]

Rather than a straight line from East to West (or South to North) as with Hegel, Wach zigzags, so to speak, from the "cradle of civilization," viz., Greece, to China back through the Middle East to *finally* end up in the West. Why this detour? Because: "In the East such independence has scarcely been achieved, even if we keep in mind that often in the East, especially in Islamic countries, the political situation necessitated dissimulation."[93] The state is a rational structure within which the spirit of a people may take definite form. As Hegel argued about the Hindus, Wach, in a less metaphysically aggressive manner (though not nonmetaphysical for that) seems to be claiming that "the political situation" hampered—rather than enhanced, as it did in the West, especially (eventually) in Germany—the full development of an independent philosophy of religion, that is, of an independent rationality, that, of independence in general. "The Orient only knows that one is free." So also in the philosophy of religion: the retarded condition of the state coincides with the retardation of independence, or, freedom, via the development of reason. The Orient remains stuck in—or, is *stuck* in, that is, placed in—the adolescence of Reason's history.

*Salvation*

Wach was especially interested in this topic. As noted in chapter 1, he wrote his dissertation on the phenomenology of salvation in the history of religions. His interest stems from the fact that he claims that salvation is the essence of religion: "The idea of salvation, which can be seen as constitutive of all religion, is of great significance to the philosophy of religion, too."[94] As constitutive of all religions, salvation is therefore a universal and essential notion: *homo religiosus* returns. As, so he argues, there are no humans without religion, there is no religion without salvation: it is the essence of the essence of man, so to speak. As essence, salvation is also the specific difference of the category "religion," as opposed to the sister category (as we saw above) "philosophy": "The presence of a savior is a mark that distinguishes religious from philosophical doctrines of salvation. Philosophical doctrines teach that human beings are saved by their own efforts; religious doctrines proclaim the principle of salvation by another."[95] Not only does salvation distinguish religion from philosophy, it is the "feeling of absolute dependence," *pace* Schleiermacher,[96] that is, divine, not human, that is, more the work of *Geist* or *das Heiligegeist* in a generic sense of the term, than it is of the limited, finite human.

In a move we have seen over and over again, despite the claim to the universality of salvation, it is not evenly developed (*Entwicklung* again) in all places, with all peoples in all times: "The degree to which the idea of salvation has been cultivated depends upon historical development, physical circumstances, and spiritual aptitude."[97] As Hegel argued in his *Philosophy of History*, geography (and other material factors) determines, to some degree, the capacity for the development of *Geist*. We saw above his statement that in the Orient, the political conditions did not allow for the development of independent, rational reflection on religion (i.e., philosophy of religion). What could Wach mean then by "spiritual aptitude"? This question can best be answered by tracing out the answers to the questions: Among *whom*, then, is this aptitude developed? *Where* and *when* is developed? The answers to these questions will hardly be surprising:

> As varied in details as the awareness of the depth and significance of the need for salvation may be, the earliest stirrings appear quite often—lead in a straight line to the deeper and universal conceptions found among the most highly developed cultures. The intensification of this awareness and the gradual development of the idea of salvation is one of the most important regions for the development of the spirit (*Geist*). Naturally, we must conceive of the development of this idea not as an even continuum but as proceeding by pushes and shoves.[98]

Like Tiele, Wach does not want to fall into speculative philosophy and see the development of history as a linear and dialectical *progressus*. In the attempt, as we saw in chapter 1, to hold a middle ground between positivism and Absolute Idealism, Wach tones down the story of *Geist's* development. It does not unfold according to an apodictic, a priori law of development. Rather, his concession, and rightfully so, it seems obvious, to the empirical dimension of history is to describe *Entwicklung* as occurring by "pushes and shoves."

It should also be noted that he describes the development of the concept of salvation as "one of the most important regions for the development of the spirit (*Geist*)." It will clearly, then, serve as a criterion for the spiritual aptitude and the stage of development of a religion, civilization, or people. And, indeed it does:

> We can already detect the beginnings of such notions in the religious beliefs of primitive peoples, for example, in the various sorts of culture heroes (*Kultur- und Heilbringer*) that we find among American Indians such as the Algonquins. Certainly, the saviors of the higher religions have traits that come from very different origins. It will never be possible to reconstruct an unbroken evolutionary sequence from these primitive *Heilbringer* to Gnostic, Buddhist, or Christian saviors."[99]

From like only like can come. Higher civilizations, which at this point I do not think it is unfair to equate with *Geist*, represent the "highest"—and we cannot take this term lightly; it is freighted with *enormous* meaning—if not the consummation, of the development of *Geist*. We again see that the American Indians, non-Europeans of color, are at the beginnings of the development of the religious notion of salvation. However, their savior figures are only "culture heroes," figures that reside somewhere between folklore, legend, and myth. The implication in the opposition between "these primitive *Heilbringer* to Gnostic, Buddhist, or Christian saviors" implies that the former are less developed: "prima," again, first, the embryonic (infantile?) not the fully developed equal of the religions of the Logos. This is so much the case that, again, a direct line of development must be denied, this time not because it seems to fit the empirically determined facts of the history of religion(s), but because of the *qualitative* difference between the two savior-types: "[T]he saviors of the higher religions have traits that come from very different origins."

*Ethics*

In his discussion of the ethical realm of religion, Wach claims that the criterion for the ethical, both as a first-order reality and as a category, is: "Generally speaking, in all religiously determined doctrines of man will be recognized according to which man is called upon to realize his highest possibilities."[100] The criterion of the ethical and its specific difference in the life of objective Spirit is "to realize his highest possibilities." We have in this phrase, taking it as a second-order concept, two components: the notion of the "higher" and the notion of the realization of possibility. This is, then, is it not, an enthymematic micronarrative of the history of religions? The gradual realization of possibility from lower to higher is the path, however nonlinear, moving by "pushes and shoves," Spirit takes to its fulfillment. Again, "higher" is a small philosopheme which does an enormous labor in this discursive structure.

That being said, again with whom, when, and where is this scenario played out?

> Religions differ in what may be regarded as the major hindrances in achieving this goal. "Among the American Indian peoples there is no conscious demarcation of classes of offense with respect to responsibility and object, such as is represented the civilized man's conception of crime as an offense against the law, vice as offense against society, and sin as an offense against the divine in nature or in human nature." Among the primitives, there is no clear distinction between the notions of spiritual and material,

psychical and physical. The history of religions shows us *gradations of recognition* of hindrances: from awareness of pollution to the ideas of vice ... crime ... and finally against the Deity.[101]

The American Indian is defined, again, by what he lacks vis-à-vis "the civilized man." As such, he is caught in a binary definition and suffers what Derrida called the "violent suppression" and hierarchical rendering that sustains an "economy of privilege," wherein the European always comes out on the higher end of any developmental or taxonomic scheme.

The American Indian is not conscious. Lacking self-consciousness, he does not and cannot make rational determinations of the spheres of objective Spirit, a point Hegel was at pains to make in his conjunction of history, morality, rationality, self-consciousness and the state. Being outside civilization, the primitive does not have the same intellectual/*geistig* "aptitude" that the civilized man does. Hegel's narrative once again.

Finally, those religions that stand before the deity, as opposed to an animistic principle or a totemic figure, are higher forms of ethics and religions. This is also the case, notice, between theistic religions and Buddhism, as was seen in the distinction between religious notions of salvation and philosophical-humanistic notions of salvation through self-effort. One cannot help but recognize the latter as Theravada Buddhism, that form of "religion" that complicates all delineations between religion and nonreligion. Insofar as that is true, Wach has performed a double movement: he relegates the primitives to the embryonic stage of *Geist* and subordinates the Buddhist to the theist. Which theist? We saw that he argued that there the political conditions did not favor the development of reason in Islam. Judaism develops to some degree a rational, ethical foundation. However, it is clear by a process of elimination, if no other, that it is the "consummate" theism of Christianity that realizes the fully ethical dimension of Spirit. In this double move, he has subordinated both the non-Europeans of color and the Orient, or the East to the West. The colonialist pattern of subjugation rendered in near perfect terms.

*Immortality*

Immortality can be seen as a subset of salvation. In this too, Wach's description follows the same pattern: there is an ideal of immortality followed by either an overt or an implicit hierarchical arrangement of gradations. On the topic of immortality the arrangement of the data is neither overtly progressive nor hierarchical. However, it is presented as a micronarrative that nearly exactly parallels Hegel's narrative of the stages of the development of history and religion. He lists in the following order—narrative succession?—the religion of: "primitive peoples of Australia," Egypt, Persian, India, including the Upanishads, Jainism, and Buddhism, Islam, and finally: "The highest good for the Christian is the *visio-beatifica*.... Far from regarding the past as gone and void, the Christian knows that it lives on in divine memory."[102] Regardless of what significance one attaches to the last statement (I would argue that it is significant but in no way decisive), the order in which these religions are presented follows in a near-perfect way the macronarrative of Hegel and Tiele and the micronarrative we saw in Otto. While Wach and/or his defenders may claim that he rejects evolutionary schemes of the progressive realization of spirit (in its various forms), or that classic phenomenologists of religion generally reject such schemas, this is far from the case. All protestations to the contrary, the text says what the text says. Wach's text is rife with gradations and rankings of religion. These gradations and rankings always start with "primitive religions" and move on to the "higher religions," most of the micronarratives of which end with Christianity—the religion that consummates the lists, if not the consummate religion.

It need not be added that Wach's hermeneutical-historical phenomenology of religion replicates the structure of the system of colonial representations. The "higher religions" are those with greater intellectual-rational development—logocentrism. The higher or highest religion is Christianity—Christocentrism, and, insofar as Christianity is the religion of Europe (or Euro-America), we have a Eurocentric perspective presented as an unbiased, *sympathetic*-intuitive, science of religion—again. Whatever imperfections in my general thesis there may be, or whatever defects in its application to other authors, Wach is as close to a perfect instantiation of the thesis as one could reasonably expect in such an overdetermined, historically complex body of data.

We may recall that it was Wach who gave the initial impetus for the development of the program of comparative religion at the University of Chicago, an institution, as noted before, which for some time dominated the field of Religious Studies. Ergo, what may have been seen as a distinctly European phenomenon, and it is by and large, had come to America in the person and work of Wach. This is precisely the case—in all senses dealt with here—with his successor at Chicago, Mircea Eliade. It is to his work we now turn.

## 10

# The Total Hermeneutics of the New Humanism

## Mircea Eliade's Agenda for *Religionswissenschaft*

It would be difficult to exaggerate the influence of Mircea Eliade on the project of Religious Studies. He is one of the most influential writers in the field. Douglas Allen says of Eliade that he was "one of the major interpreters of religion, symbol, and myth," and that he "was extremely influential."[1] Guilford Dudley quotes two sources with which he concurs: "Harvey Cox has said that Eliade is 'by nearly unanimous consent the most influential student of religion in the world today.' In the *Times Literary Supplement*, the reviewer of *The Quest* observed, 'Mircea Eliade is perhaps the best known living exponent of the history of religions.' " Finally, Gavin Flood rightly points out that Eliade is the c/site of the dissemination of the phenomenology of religion: "The teaching of religion, or rather about religion, largely follows from the work of the phenomenologists such as Eliade."[2] As noted before, the phenomenology of religion has very much influenced the introductory textbooks and world religion textbooks most often used in Religious Studies.

As such, it is important to see his work in its proper historical context. This is necessary if we are to understand fully the kinds of methodological and philosophical concept-practices he performs and recommends. One of the problems with both Eliade's critics and his disciples is that they have not critically evaluated the discursive tradition he is working within. This can now be accomplished and thereby conclude Part II of this study.

While this chapter will focus on his methodology, as with the other chapters, it will also go beyond that. Given Eliade's enormous role in disseminating the program of the phenomenology of religion, it will be necessary and highly useful for the thesis of this study to look at his statements about what he takes to be the cultural role of the phenomenology of religion. This role is summarized in his expression, a "New Humanism." The analysis of that concept will form a substantive part of this chapter. Finally, as with others, we will look at the way Eliade deals with actual historical materials, his history of religions in a strict sense of the term.

Eliade's book *Patterns of Comparative Religion* is his major work in what could properly be called a phenomenological approach to religion.[3] In the first chapter of that work he gives a compact statement of the principal motifs of his approach to religion. It begins with the problem of definition, of finding unity in the immense diversity of religious data, or manifestations, or hierophanies, as he calls them. He lists a wide range of such manifestations: Melanesian cosmogony myth, Brahmanic sacrifice, the writings of St. Teresa and those of Nichiren, Australian totems, initiation rites, the symbolism of a Borobudur temple, the ceremonies of a Siberian shaman, the rites of the Great Goddesses, and so forth. He then summarizes the approach that must taken if one is to find the *simile in multis*, the unity in this diversity: "Each must be considered as a hierophany in as much as it expresses in some way some modality of the sacred at some moment in its history; that is to say, some one of the many kinds of experience of the sacred man has had."[4] This statement will serve as the guiding thread of the explication of Eliade's phenomenology of religion.

## The Grounding of the Sacred as an "Irreducible Element"

Like Schleiermacher and Otto before him, Eliade sees religion as a sui generis something, a category independent of other categories: "[A] religious phenomenon will only be recognized as such if it is grasped at its own level, that is to say, if it is studied as something religious."[5] Religion has a unique status and independent being from society, psychology, etc. The antireductive polemic, which we have seen so often in this tradition, is clearly at work here, as is the same definitional strategy used by previous theorists.

Specifically, it is the sacred that is the irreducible element in religion: "To try to grasp the essence" of religion by other means "or any other study is false; it misses the one unique and irreducible element in it—the element of the sacred."[6] Like previous theorists, he uses the sui generis notion to make a stringent claim for the qualitative, even categorical difference of religion from other forms of human spiritual activity such as art, politics, or ethics. From this difference, the essential identity within it can be discerned, classified, and hierarchized.

This entails, further, that the sui generis character of religion is arrived at by delineating the specific difference of "religion" or "the sacred" (the two terms are interchangeable for Eliade) from other regions of Spirit, mind, or consciousness. The sacred "must be looked at first of all in itself, in that which belongs to it alone and can be explained in no other term. It is no easy task. It is a matter, if not of giving an exact definition of the religious phenomena, at least of seeing its limits and setting in its true relation to the other things of the mind."[7] Echoing Schleiermacher, Otto, and Kristensen, Eliade argues that religion is not morality, art, science, or any other of the categorical domains of human spirit. It is, or has, like Spirit, *Beisichselbstsein*, "self-contained being," and is not, as such, dependent, reliant upon, nor reducible to anything else.

The question is, then, on the basis of what is the sui generis, a priori, universal nature of the sacred explained? The answer, in short, is the same as that of Schleiermacher, Otto, Kristensen, and van der Leeuw, viz.: "[T]he 'sacred' is an element in the structure of consciousness," a statement I have often cited.[8] The sui generis nature of the sacred and of religion, the universality of religion, which allows one to see all historical manifestations as manifestations of the sacred, have their philosophical grounding in the notion of the transcendental structure of consciousness. Eliade, like the others in this tradition, subscribes to a philosophy of mind that holds that human consciousness is a unique phenomenon, not derivative from other realms of reality, for instance, biology or society. As a *category*, there is nothing further to which it can be reduced: it is the *Seelengrund*, the ground of the soul (consciousness), not merely one of its attributes. Gavin Flood rightly describes this as an "ahistorical philosophy of consciousness within the academic study of religion."[9]

"History" is unified and therefore only decipherable because it is an "expression" of this transhistorical consciousness: "But if we are to avoid sinking back into an obsolete 'reductionism,' this history of religious meanings must always be regarded as forming part of the history of the human spirit."[10] As we have seen before, the problem of "expressions" and their relation to human subjectivity form the core problematic of phenomenology of religion.

## Expression and Experience

"Preoccupied, and indeed often completely taken up, by their admittedly urgent and indispensable work of collecting, publishing, and analyzing religious data, scholars have sometimes neglected to study their meaning. Now, these data represent the expression of various religious experiences."[11] As a recurrent theme throughout his works, Eliade is constantly chastising the "timidity of scholars" for their refusal or inability to get beyond purely philological and historical-factual issues in the study of religion. The reason for this is that Eliade believes, much as van der Leeuw did, that religious texts, rites, symbols, and so forth, reveal something about *homo religiosus*. Consistent with his vehemently antireductive line, he holds that religious data are "expressions" of man's religious "experience."

For the most part, Eliade articulates the relationship between expression and experience negatively, by continually pointing out that neither is reducible to its historical context: "Every religious experience is expressed and transmitted in a particular historical context. But admitting the historicity of religious experience does not imply that they are reducible to non-religious forms of behavior."[12] One reason for this, as we have seen, is that Eliade subscribes to the view that religion is sui generis. As such, his claim about experience logically follows. However, his separation of history and experience is actually much more stringent than this. He claims that religion, and religious experience, is not merely nonhistorical, but actually nontemporal. In discussing the role of ecstasy in shamanism, he claims: "As an experience, ecstasy is a non-historical phenomenon; it is a primordial phenomenon in the sense that it is coextensive with human nature. Only the religious interpretation given to ecstasy and the techniques designed to prepare it or facilitate it are historical data."[13] Qua experience, "ecstasy itself" is a propensity, or capacity of the religious structure of human consciousness. As this consciousness is transcendental, it cannot properly be said to be in time. He argues the same point elsewhere: "[R]eligious forms are non-temporal; they are not necessarily bound to time."[14] As such, religious data must not be seen as merely historical documents but as "expressions" of the primal, sui generis experience of humanity: "He [the historian of religion] knows that he is condemned to work exclusively with historical documents, but at the same time he feels that these documents tell him something more than the simple fact that they reflect historical situations. He feels somehow that they reveal to him important truths about man and man's relation to the sacred."[15] *Homo religiousus* underlies all manifestations of religion in history, and, *homo religiousus* is *homo sapiens*.

Consequently, the historian of religion is not content with mere "facticity," but seeks the *meaning* of religious expressions: "The historian of religion does not act as a philologist, but as a hermeneutist. . . . He endeavors to understand the materials that philologists and historians make available to him in his own perspective, that of the history of religions."[16] Historical materials then are, again, the hyle from which the morphe is extracted. This morphe is grounded in the structure of consciousness as such. The extraction of meaning is accomplished by finding the structure of the religious reality in question.

## Structure, History, Intelligibility

The theme of the correlation of structure and meaning, and the relation of both to history, form the central problematic of Eliade's conception of phenomenological reconstruction, or method in comparative religion. In the quote from *Patterns* used at the very beginning of our discussion of Eliade, we saw that the methodological problematic for his phenomenology was the relation of unity to diversity, of finding the *simile in multis*. His question, like Seiwert's, Hegel's, and Otto's, is: How can things manifested in different times and places, that is, things manifested in history, be the same? His answer is that in the face of the enormous diversity of religious hierophanies

> [t]he safest method, is to make use of all these kinds of evidence, omitting no important type, and always asking ourselves what *meaning* is revealed by each of these hierophanies. In this way we shall get a *coherent* collection of common traits which . . . will make it possible to formulate a coherent system of the modalities [of the sacred].[17]

The key to the *simile in multis* is, again, meaning. What all the various manifestations of a religious type have in common, that is, what is of their essence, is their meaning. As we saw, Eliade sees the hermeneutical task as the specific difference of phenomenology/history of religion from other approaches to religion.

Meaning is, for Eliade as it was for van der Leeuw, an aspect of structure: "And, in the history of religions, as in other mental disciplines, it is knowledge of structure which makes it possible to understand meanings."[18] His method for delineating structure is virtually the same as was Kristensen's: "Suffice it to say that it is impossible to understand the meaning of [e.g.] the Cosmic Tree by considering only one or some of its variants. It is only by the analysis of a considerable number of examples that the structure of a symbol can be completely deciphered."[19] The method is *diaresis*: the collecting of many examples, of comparing them to one another, and finding the common element. Each of the examples collected will have differences, "historical accretions," as Eliade calls them;[20] but these differences are not essential. We have, again, the kernel/husk binary.

That the permanent elements always appear in various manifestations is the ontological ground for the eidetic, or structural approach to the study of religion: "History comes in as soon as man, according as his needs inspire, experiences the sacred. The handling and passing on of hierophanies also accentuates their 'historicization.' *Yet their structure remains the same* in spite of this and it is precisely the permanence of structure that makes it possible to know them."[21] Echoing an idea that harks back to Aristotle (i.e., hylemorphism), Eliade holds that it is a fact of the being of religious meanings that they are ahistorical, unchanging forms or structures, and, that it is by virtue of these structures that the otherwise chaotic mass of particulars is intelligible. Form is what is known, not particulars; and form is what gives meaning to the particulars. Like form, "meaning" is an abstraction, an object of the logos, not the hyle. Meaning is taken from these collections of hyle, of historical particulars. Among all the hierophanies the world over, the phenomenologist must extract from this global resource the goods latent therein. This extractive economy is in the service of the scholar and the scholarly enterprise; it is not in the service of those peoples from whom it is extracted. This is an example of what we will discuss in the last chapter of a colonial practice of forming "collections" (e.g., in museums) of "artifacts" from colonized countries. It is an academic form of an extractive economic practice. The "meaning" arrived at is for the hermeneute, not the instance of hyle, of the historical particular, for example, the person or people from whom it came—it cannot be, as they do not have the necessary (colonialist) comparative perspective.

*The Historical-Phenomenological Tension*

Eliade, and the literature on his work, struggle with what is called the "historical-phenomenological tension."[22] The problem is as follows: on the one hand, every religious phenomenon is *in* history, while on the other hand, every religious phenomenon manifests an *a*historical structure. How, then, can the two be related? If structure is the only issue, why use history at all? If the hierophanies are embedded within history, are we warranted in anything beyond merely historicist claims? Eliade's resolution to this problem is achieved by relying on the "essence and manifestation" paradigm, which, in Eliade scholarship is often referred to as the "dialectic of the sacred and the profane."[23] This is a crucial aspect of Eliade's methodology and must be examined carefully.

Eliade often states that he does not want to avoid or discredit history. He criticizes van der Leeuw, for instance, for not being attentive enough to history: "[H]e was not interested in the *history* of religious structures. Here lies the most serious inadequacy of his approach, for even the most elevated religious expression (a mystical ecstasy, for example) presents itself through specific structures and cultural expressions which are historically conditioned."[24] He argues, then, that "there is no such thing as a 'pure' religious datum that is not at the same time a historical datum."[25] We saw earlier in the discussion of Robert Segal's critique of Eliade that he does lay claim to taking an empirical approach to history, however qualified.

We have already seen how this tension is frequently described in the context of a polemic against reductionist or historicist theories of religion. The crucial point is to see how the notion is qualified. This qualification is effected by resort to the "dialectic of the sacred": "[F]or the sacred is always manifested through something. . . . The dialect of the sacred . . . expresses itself through something other than itself; it appears in things, myths or symbols, but never wholly or directly."[26] From what has already been said, it should be clear that Eliade means by "the sacred," the ahistorical, the universal, and the essential; and by the "historical" he means the temporal, the particular, and the accidental. Douglas Allen, a sympathetic commentator on Eliade, confirms just this correlation. In the dialectic of the sacred, Allen says, "something transcendent and transhistorical limits itself by manifesting itself in some relative, finite, historical thing."[27] Eliade also refers to this as the "paradox of incarnation" and argues that it is the basic structure of religion: "This paradox of incarnation which makes hierophanies possible at all—whether the most elementary or the supreme Incarnation of the Word in Christ—is to be found everywhere in religious history."[28] The paradox is, of course, that eternity can be present in and through time. It could be argued that the fact that Eliade makes this general, presumably universal statement about religion by means of appeal to a Christian doctrine is not incidental. While I would not make too much of it, it is there in the text. As we will see later, he indicates that Christianity is uniquely universal. What is clear, is that the power of his analytical operation literally stems from the Logos, the Word, that is, is logocentric, a pervasive fact of Eliade's method.

Allen points out that the dialectic of the sacred goes in two directions: from the sacred into the particular manifestation, and from each religious form back to its original archetype.[29] This latter point is Eliade's most serious qualification of any historicist approach to religion. It is part of the nature of a manifestation that it tends toward its ultimate realization: "[T]here is no religious form which does not try to get as close as possible to its true archetype,[30] in other words, to rid itself of 'historical' accretions and deposits."[31] Drawing loosely on Jung's notion of the archetype and connecting it with allusions to Plato's myth of the cave, he holds that the impetus within the manifestation is to "get back" to the primordial condition eternity: time, by nature, seeks its fulfillment in eternity. As with Otto, this view of the inner religious dynamic becomes a way of evaluating different hierophanies or manifestations of religion. Some can be more and some can be less full manifestations of *the* sacred. Thus, while we do not have an evolutionary criterion of religion, Eliade does have a synchronic criterion for assessing the "fullness," that is, World-Historical significance, of a hierophany.

A methodological problem that arises here is: If all manifestations of religion are essentially the same, how can Eliade explain the fact that they change? How is it that some religious manifestations appear and disappear in time? His explanation of this problem further qualifies his notion of essence and manifestation in an important way. He further argues that it is not only a fact of contingent history that manifestations change, but that it is of the nature of a manifestation to seek its most universal and complete expression:

> What we call syncretism can be seen at every point in the course of religious life. Every farming spirit of the countryside, every tribal god, is the culmination of a long process of being assimilated and identified with other divine forms adjacent to it. But it must be pointed out that these assimilations and fusions are not due solely to historical circumstances (the mingling of two neighboring tribes, the conquest of a given area and so on); the process takes place as a result of the very nature of hierophanies; whether or not a hierophany comes into contact with another religious form, like or unlike itself, it will tend, in the religious consciousness of those who perceive it as such, to be expressed as totally, as fully as possible.[32]

A list of a number of hierophanies from different times and places follows this statement, wherein Eliade tries to demonstrate how they exhibit, despite their differences, an essential continuity as the gradual, or episodic unfolding of ever more comprehensive aspects of their essence. He then summarizes the argument of *Patterns*:

> Here, at the conclusion of this, I should like simply to declare that almost all the religious attitudes man has, he has had from the most primitive times. From one point of view there has been no break in continuity from the 'primitives' to Christianity. The dialectic of the hierophany remains one, whether in an Australian churinga or in the Incarnation of the Logos.[33]

"What Spirit is, it has always essentially been," again. Again, on the basis of the Logos—literally and figuratively—he formulates the possibility, the reality, of an essential continuity to history. It is not in the immediate consciousness of the "locals," but put together in the workshop of the academician who, alone has access to Universal *history*, or the universal history of religions. Each only knows their own religion; the scholar, resident of the Metropole, knows them all.

At other places in *Patterns*, he indicates more specifically what the characteristic differences are between the various *levels* of manifestation. In an argument very similar to Kristensen's view of the nature of historical loss, Eliade says that some hierophanies have only a "local" meaning, while others are more universal in scope. Taking the cosmic tree as an example, he argues that "some hierophanies have a purely local purpose; others have, or attain, a world-wide significance."[34] The former, he describes as having "meaning only for them,"that is, the adherents of a specific group, locale or time period.[35] However, there are kinds of manifestations of the cosmic tree that are truly universal, which manifest the sacred structure of the Axis Mundi, "and this mythico-symbolic hierophany is universal, for we find Cosmic Trees everywhere among ancient civilizations."[36] He uses this exact language of local versus universal in several other examples, including the difference between priests and villagers, and the triumph of Yahweh over Baal. In each case, as the quote above indicated, what is essential to the process of one hierophany triumphing over another is neither political conquest nor historical activity as such, but the *entelechia* of religious consciousness, even of religious form, as it is being realized in and through history.

Methodologically, this means that we must take more universal manifestations as our norm in delineating the meaning of a manifestation: "[S]ome hierophanies are not clear at all, are indeed almost cryptic, as they reveal the sacred meaning embodied... in plant life in part... while others (more truly *manifestations*) display the sacred in all its modalities as a whole."[37] The relationship between structure, meaning, and history then, pivots on the distinction between universal essence and historical particular. Those hierophanies that appear virtually everywhere are taken as the norm for delineating the structure-meaning-essence of the phenomenon; the others are then hierarchically arranged in relation to them. The scholar knows what the locals do not know, cannot know. "He" is the witness to the Universal.

Some interesting differences between Eliade and earlier *Religionswissenschaft* are worth mentioning here, because they characterize the difference between the latter and classical phenomenology as a whole. Eliade rejects several other principles for establishing the universal form of a hierophany. For instance, he refuses the notion that the "elites" represent the higher religion and the masses represent the lower religion. He also rejects the idea, found in Hegel and others, that Occidental hierophanies are essentially more full revelations of the sacred than are Oriental ones. Finally, although he comes very close to favoring Christianity at times, and virtually always lists it at the "higher" end of any spectrum of manifestations he gives, he never *explicitly* uses the criteria "Christian/non-Christian" as the basis for a taxonomy of religious phenomena. He does not overtly assert the supremacy of Christianity, as did Hegel, Tiele, and Otto (Wach does so implicitly, while Kristensen uses Christianity as a major taxonomic division: "the West and all the rest").

In Eliade's attempt to resolve the "historical-phenomenological tension," then, we can only conclude, as does Allen, that he finally comes down on the side of nonhistorical essences: "What stands out is the primary methodological emphasis he places on, and the lofty status he grants to, nontemporal and nonhistorical universal structures."[38] And, as we have seen so often in this research tradition, this is articulated in terms of the "essence and manifestation of religion in history."

## *Religionswissenschaft*, a Total Hermeneutic and the New Humanism

Eliade, more than any other phenomenologist we have looked at, pursued an aggressive program for promoting and extending the scope of *Religionswissenschaft*, or the History of Religion. In doing so, he indicates some of the most important and comprehensive philosophical assumptions used in *Religionswissenschaft* about religion, history, metaphysics, and human nature. Here we can see very clearly what the ultimate entailments of this historic discursive formation are.

In a series of essays published together in a single volume entitled *The Quest: History and Meaning in Religion* (1969), Eliade makes a number of programmatic statements for what the true cultural function of *Religionswissenschaft* should be. To many in the field of religious studies, these statements have been seen simply as either subjective or theological bias. As such, they violate the objective and nondenominational norms to which any respectable scientific or academic enterprise should hold itself. Although I do not disagree with this completely, I simply feel that it misses a much larger point, viz., the themes Eliade announces have been an integral part of the science and the history and the philosophy of religion ever since its very inception. These themes, as we have seen ad nauseam by now, are continually reiterated throughout the history of this literature—it is a mistake, then, to locate their deficiencies in either dubious motivations or theological prejudice. Whatever deficiencies this discourse has, it goes to the very heart of its overall structure, not to some accidental (and fully indispensable, I would argue) feature of the persons who "activate" or deploy or engage it. Again, this is the difference between a holistic discourse analysis and an empirical-atomistic analysis that isolates individuals and therefore must psychologize/subjectify their production of discourse. That said, it remains to analyze Eliade's key pronouncements in these essays and see how they connect to the history of the discourse of the phenomenology of religion and what they tell us about that discourse.

Eliade complains that the history of religions has not fulfilled its proper role, not for lack of materials or effort, but because, unlike its "heroes" of the previous century, its contemporary practitioners "are more modest, more withdrawn, indeed more timid."[39] If the science of religion can overcome what may be called its "philological modesty," Eliade feels its promise is great, indeed: in preference of a "total hermeneutics" (using a distinction noted above), "[i]t is solely insofar as it will perform this task—particularly by making the meanings of religious documents intelligible to the mind of modern man—that the science of religion will fulfill its true cultural function. For whatever its role has been in the past, the comparative study of religions is destined to assume a cultural role of the first importance in the near future."[40]

The reason for this is that the science of religion does not deal with a merely "regional ontology," as do other humanistic disciplines (such as psychology or sociology), but with *homo religiosus*, and *"homo religiousus* represents the 'total man.' "[41] Religious meanings express the very structure of "Man's" mode of being-in-the-world, and are therefore all-encompassing in what they tell us about "him": "[B]y attempting to understand the existential situations expressed by the documents he is studying, the historian of religions will inevitably attain to a deeper knowledge of man. It is on the basis of such knowledge that a new humanism, on a world-wide scale, could develop."[42] In the context of what Pratt calls "planetary consciousness," which results from colonial exploration of the globe, a new kind of universality is possible, albeit located in the Metropole. As opposed to a regional ontology, the study of religion should aim at what Eliade calls a total hermeneutic: "The history of religions is not merely a historical discipline, as, for example, are archaeology or numismatics. It is equally a total hermeneutics, being called to decipher and explicate every kind of encounter of man with the sacred, from prehistory to our day."[43] The cultural aim of this hermeneutic is not merely to inform Western culture about religious history, but to renew it, to transform it:

> In the end, the creative hermeneutics changes man; it is more than instruction, it is also a spiritual technique susceptible of modifying the quality of existence itself. This is true above all for the historico-religious hermeneutics. A good history of religions book ought to produce in the reader an action of awakening—like that produced, for example, by *Das Heilege* or *Die Götter Griechlands*. But in principle every historico-religious hermeneutics ought to have similar results.[44]

His claim is that the science of religion should forego its "banal, excessive and narrow specialization"[45] and overcome "the inferiority complexes, timidity, and immobility of the last fifty years" to form an "integral science of the lived experiences" of real humanity, based upon "interpretive cultural syntheses" and a universal scope in its perspective on history.[46]

This last point is of special importance for our concerns. Against those who argue that classical phenomenology is concerned only with a synchronic taxonomy of religious data (and who, therefore, see the influence of Husserl writ large upon this school), I have been arguing that classical phenomenology is deeply and seriously concerned with history, even if in a rather "nonhistorical" way, that is, in a way that typical empirical approaches to history would treat the subject. Eliade is the best evidence for the survival—as late as 1969—of Hegel's influence on the brand of phenomenology practiced by this school. The philosophical foundation for the unity from diversity that Eliade believes the "total hermeneutic" can find in history is none other than "human spirit," human nature, consciousness, or "Man." In a long passage, he fully indicates the ground and aim of phenomenology of religion:

> The historian of religion recognizes a spiritual unity subjacent to the history of humanity; in other terms, in studying the Australians, Vedic Indians, or whatever other ethnic group or cultural system, the historian of religions does not have a sense of moving in a world radically "foreign" to him. Certainly, the unity of the human species is accepted *de facto* in other disciplines, for example linguistics, anthropology, sociology. But the historian of religions has the privilege of grasping this unity at the highest levels—or the deepest.... Today history is becoming truly universal for the first time.[47]

Spirit, here fully announced as such, but implicitly there ever since Hegel, is again the subject and *sub-stancia* of history, that which, by its "subjacency" gives unity, even identity to all of the various forms of difference which time, history, language, and politics might effect. In Spirit, all differences are subsumed and history becomes universal history: *allgemeine Geschichte*. The culmination of history of religions, then is philosophical anthropology, or a "New Humanism": "More than any other humanistic discipline, history of religions can open the way to a philosophical anthropology."[48] "Man" is the philosophical ground and center of all phenomenological structures, essences, and meanings. All meaning is, finally, "Man's" meaning; it points to him; it is his "expression." Consequently, historicism gives way to a new universalism, and now, "Western consciousness recognizes only one history, the Universal History," and the "ethnocentric history is surpassed as being provincial."[49] The phenomenology of religion forms the basis of a new Universalism: "From a certain point of view, one could say that a new *Phenomenology of the Mind* awaits elaboration by taking account of all that the history of religions is capable of revealing to us."[50]

In Eliade's view, this universality entails overcoming the narrow, ethnocentrism of Western history. "How to assimilate culturally the spiritual universes that Africa, Oceania, Southeast Asia open to us?"[51] The total hermeneute has no sense of moving in any area foreign to him; all cultures are now available to him for the enrichment of each. The use of materials from "Oriental and archaic societies," then, "will not only show us the point of view of the 'others,' the non-Europeans: for any confrontation with another person leads to enlightenment about one's own situation."[52] The goal of classical phenomenology of religion, then, is the same as that of Hegel's Science of Wisdom, viz., "the pure self-recognition in absolute otherness."

# Part III

# Poststructuralist, Postcolonialist Analyses

# 11

# "The Center Does Not Hold"

## Decentering the Centrisms" of the Discourse of the Phenomenology of Religion

> For we can say that deconstruction involves the decentralization and decolonization of European thought.
>
> —Robert Young[1]

The foregrounding of the pathologies inextricably woven into the history of the discourse of phenomenology of religion—and Religious Studies insofar as it is constituted by this discourse—is what a *poststructuralist* critique of the phenomenology of religion aims at accomplishing. Arguably, this could never be accomplished by an Anglo-American empiricist critique of phenomenology. This is what such a poststructuralist critique of phenomenology has shown to be at stake for the very project of Religious Studies: either it revises its entire foundation on radically different presuppositions or it silently perpetuates its collusion with a project both epistemologically and politically so profoundly pathological. This poststructuralist, discourse analysis and its elucidation of the metaphysical and ideological humanism of classical phenomenology of religion, have, it seems to me, several main serious pathologies inextricably embedded within the structures of the discourse of the phenomenology, both in its diachronic development and in the synchronic analysis of each author's "system." These have, or potentially have, serious implication for the enterprise of the Religious Studies.

Underlying these analyses is the argument that we cannot accept academic theories and methods as transparent media by which a universalized subjectivity "understands" its objects. Given the displacements discussed, it is more compelling to see theories as specific, historical discursive practices, which actively shape their objects.

Roland Barthes, in a discussion of the role of classification in rhetoric, indicates the ideological and prefigurative nature of systems of classification, including definitional statements: "[T]he taxonomic option implies an ideological one: there is always a *stake* in where things are placed: *tell me how you classify and I'll tell you who you are.*"[2] In a discussion of the divisions of the parts of speech in classical rhetorical theory, he reiterates this point in a way that further illuminates it: "[W]e must insist on the *active, transitive, programmatic, operational* nature of these divisions: it is not a question of the elements of a [given] structure, but of the actions of a gradual structuration."[3] If we transpose "these division" from rhetoric to Religious Studies, the same point holds.

From this perspective, the phenomenology of religion is just such a discursive, interpretive practice. Its central concept-operations, "experience," "expression," "essence," "manifestations/forms of," and "Man" all form an integrative schema within which "things" take on, *and can only take on, a determinate, selective identity*. This schema does not render phenomena "as such, clear and transparent" by means of "self-surrender to others." It is not a passive placeholder for the display of the true being of things, but an active, configurative structure that prefigures what can and cannot be placed in it. The resort to the notion of a "phenomenology" has been precisely the attempt to elide the fact of representation, the attempt to get back to "the things themselves," that is, to elide the mediated/mediating structures of representations—which are *their* constructions. Over and over again, phenomenologists of religion deny that phenomenology is a theory. The irony of this is that this elision has had precisely the opposite effect it intended. By its use of this schema, phenomenology does not represent the view of the believer, but imposes its own categorical structure onto those views. The humanism ("Man," "*Geist*," "[Cartesian] consciousness") upon which the notion of empathetic understanding is founded is wholly incompatible with the notion of self-effacement espoused by classical phenomenologists.

This imposition results in several characteristic pathologies embedded in the discourse of the phenomenology of religion. Each will be reviewed in turn.

## Logocentrism

"I have identified logocentrism and the metaphysics of presence as the exigent, powerful, systematic, and irrepressible desire for such a signified," that is, "the transcendental signified, which at one time or another, would place a reassuring end to the reference from sign to sign."[4] In the discourse of the phenomenology of religion, this transcendental signified is that "inner experience," either as posited in consciousness (Kristensen and Wach) or as the a priori condition for consciousness (Otto and Eliade). The gap between this "inner experience" and/or the a priori category and its "expressions" is precisely the hope for "a reassuring end to the reference from sign to sign." Expressions are signs, but they are grounded in a consciousness that is understood as unchanging and universal: "[R]eligious experience seeks to be expressed; this tendency is universal," as is the experience itself, so argued Wach. But this search for " 'origin' or 'ground,' those notions belonging essentially to the history of onto-theology, to the system function as the effacing of difference"[5] is itself logocentric. Effacing of difference: "[R]eligious experience is universal"; "[T]he holy is an a priori category"; "Spirit is what it has always essentially been." It is given to the very workings of this discourse, the limitations of the play of its elements, its philosophemes, that these must be determined—again, within a discourse; not ontologically—as a transcendental signified. The phenomenology of religion can do no other.

So also with the with the *Geist/Natur* dichotomy, again not simply in its contents but in its structural positioning of each term and their place with the system of ontotheology:

> Despite all its rejuvenations and disguises, this opposition is congenital to philosophy.[6] It is even older than Plato. It is at least as old as the Sophists. Since the statement of the opposition *physis/nomos*, *physis/techne*, it has been relayed to us by means of a whole historical chain which opposes "nature" to law, to education, to art, to technics—but also to liberty, to the arbitrary, to history, to society, to the mind and so on.[7]

This *opposition* to nature—in all senses of the word *opposition*, including *struggle against*—is the fundamental aim of the politics of *Geist*. It is the heart of the "violent hierarchy" and "economy of privilege" that comes into the discourse of the phenomenology of religion by way of this "whole historical chain," which has been relayed into the tissues of its fabric. The structures of our discipline, Religious Studies has been, I would argue, or at least I fear, infused with this opposition. It exists in the ideas of consciousness, experience, understanding, empathy, meaning, the sacred, the holy, the system of classification of "world religions"—those that are and those that are not—and the realities of the classification of our subject areas and the numbers of scholars at work in each. It also exists in the sheer ideality of our objects: "Buddhism," "Christianity," "Hinduism"; these are logocentric constructs in that they exist outside of the determinations of an individuality, that is, the ontological structures of human finitude. Their ideality sets them "above" (the violence and privilege of hierarchy again) the particulars, to wit, individual human beings and groups of human beings whose identities are subsumed into and by means of these idealities. The faulty structure of Religious Studies is not so obvious in what it includes but it is glaringly obvious in its systematic exclusions, exclusions that are constitutive of the structure of Religious Studies.

The emphasis on logocentrism is not simply a rejection or an attempt to disprove the validity of phenomenology. Rather: "Western metaphysics, as the limitation of the sense of being within the field of presence, is produced as the domination of a linguistic form. To question the origin of that domination does not amount to hypostatizing a transcendental signified, but to a question of what constitutes our history and what produced transcendentality itself."[8] *How* does phenomenology, the play of its elements, configure transcendentality? It is quite obvious that the phenomenology of religion is logocentric; that is not the issue. The question is: *how* is it logocentric? How does it stand within the history of ontotheology? The answers to these question lay bare the workings of this discourse, its "how," as opposed to its "what" (*quid est*; Quiditty), the question of essence, of definition, the initial and necessary gesture of philosophy in the broadest sense, including "theory").

Again, this is the difference between a poststructuralist critique and the kind of critiques aimed the phenomenology of religion from empiricist and those who claim that it is normative and subjective, and *therefore* invalid. In a sense, the phenomenology of religion is a perfectly valid discourse in that it conforms rather well to the ideational structure that would or could assess its validity. Ontotheology has no problem with the phenomenology of religion. However, a poststructuralist reading questions the nature of subjectivity as it arises within the discourse of the phenomenology of religion. It does not take the subject, neither the epistemological subject implicit in empiricist critiques of Eliade (et al.) nor the subject of the claim of "subjectivism." Nor does a poststructural analysis see the normative as necessarily problematic. Rather, it asks what is the *normativity* of norms? How is it configured in this discourse and what is its discursive function?

As Leela Gandhi points out, the difference between the attempt at an empirical invalidation of phenomenology and a poststructuralist and postmodernist critique "helps to undo the logic of the colonial civilizing mission ... *from inside* the Western philosophical tradition."[9]

The answers to the questions posed here reach well beyond the phenomenology of religion, or, they reach into that history in which phenomenology resides: "Metaphysics—the white mythology which reassembles and reflects the culture of the West: the white man takes his own mythology, Indo-European mythology, his *logos*, that is, the mythos of his idiom, for the universal form of that he must still wish to call Reason."[10] To which Derrida immediately adds in the very next sentence: "Which does not go uncontested." A poststructuralist, postcolonial genealogical analysis traces the discourse of the phenomenology of religion back to the deepest elements of the West, viz., rationality itself, and to the deepest pathologies of the West as it is governed by the logos which is a mythos: "The deconstruction of the Western theological [and ontotheological] network discloses the recurrent effort of human being to achieve a position of domination. This struggle appears to grow out of the conviction that mastery results from the ability to secure presence and establish identity by overcoming absence and repressing difference."[11] Whether by an evolutionary scheme that overtly subordinates the Other or by a static taxonomy that collects and subsumes the Other, otherness, difference, is negated while the subject/agent of these acts finds "the self-proximity of infinite subjectivity."

Derrida describes the basic categories of both ontotheology and the phenomenology of religion as logocentric in the following manner:

> The history of metaphysics, like the history of the West ... is the determination of Being as presence in all senses of this word. It could be shown that all the names related to fundamentals, to principles, or to the center have always designated an invariable presence—*eidos, arche, telos, energieia, ousia* (essence, existence, substance, subject) aletheia, transcendentality, consciousness, God, man ["Man," in my terms], and so forth.[12]

This genealogical analysis shows that the "phenomenology of religion" is a textual tradition, the dissemination and permutation of a discourse held together by the interconnection of a number of basic philosophemes, which, when woven together constitute a strategy for the formation of an historical identity, an object, "religion," is thus formulated. With the notions of "structure," "commonness," "morphology," "the sacred," "religious needs," "essence," "subject/object," "type," "the human essence," "consciousness," "understanding," and all their "others," especially *Natur* and its permutations, we have the appropriation and transmutation of Dilthey's appropriation and transmutation of Hegel (with some passing references to Husserl). For what all of these philosophemes speak to is the One and the Many: the One as found in determinate forms of the Many, found in and yet *founding* the very oneness of which they are many. In other words, this entire scheme is utterly unintelligible unless it is seen as a modified version of Hegel's founding paradigm of historical "forms" as revealing *Geist's* "essence and manifestations."

As such, the discourse of the phenomenology of religion reiterates the age-old relation of *eidos* and subject: "structure," "type," "morphé," "essences" are all variations on the theme of *eidos*. With *eidos* is articulated the correlative pair: *hylé/morphé*, form and matter, a correlative pair that is itself a permutation of the pair, *Geist/Natur*. The "History" (with its necessary capitalization) of "the History of Religion," is the *hylé* which, under the guiding agency of "Man," "expresses" itself in forms. As these forms are ideal, abstract objects, they participate more in their formality than in their *hylé*: thus, "[I]t does not matter in what religion we find them." The "permanence of structure" is unrelated to the content of the structure. The Logos is once again iterated; "phenomenology of religion" (and "Religious Studies"?) is yet another chapter in the history of ontotheology.

Why is this of concern to Religious Studies? Because: "War is congenital to phenomenality." "Hegel describes war [in] the dialectic of the *Master and the Slave*," and as such, war necessarily resides "within the realm of a science of consciousness, that is, of phenomenality itself, in the necessary structure of its movement: a science of experience and of consciousness." The "violence of metaphysics" lies in this: binaries are hierarchies. And, they are often vicious hierarchies: *Geist is itself* the denigration of *Natur*. *Natur* is nothing, *nil*, in its relation to *Geist*. In this binary, *Natur* and all things associated with it, for instance, Africans and Native Americans, Australian aborigines, etc., are reduced forever to an ontological subordination, in an ontology *of* subordination. There is no hope for an emancipation of *Natur* and her children. "War is another form of the appropriation of the other, and underpins all ontological thinking with its violence."[13]

It is noteworthy that the science of experience is included as a party to this war. We have seen that the science of consciousness is articulated via conflict. Hegel, Tiele, Otto, Wach, Eliade: all and always speak of the opponents of this science. This talk of conflict is not a derivative aspect of the discourse: it is the animating principle of the discourse itself. It is found it the endless chain of syntagmatic combinations: reductive/nonreduction; explain/interpret; explain/understand; consciousness/material conditions; and so forth. The discourse is literally constituted by the continuous opposition—and conjunction—of these binary philosophemes. Metaphysics, the White *Ideology*, including the science of consciousness, is the rationalization and legitimation for the hierarchies it established through this war. And, it is not just a war of words; it is also a war between continents as these hierarchies are also applied to religions *in toto*, to peoples *in toto*, to entire civilizations and epochs. Between the Logos, "us," "the West and all the rest," there can only be war.

The Logos-cum-Europe as *Geist* is entangled in several other braids that run throughout what we saw in our readings in the discourse of the phenomenology of religion: the "project Europe," to be discussed below, and, particularly, the state and history. Each of which will be treated in turn.

As Leela Gandhi argues, "[H]umanism has always functioned as an 'aesthetico-moral ideology' which is concerned with, and directed toward, the molding of ideal citizen-subjects."[14] This can be seen, again, in Hegel's theory of the state:

> A nation does not begin by being a state. The transition from a family, a horde, a clan, a multitude, &c., to political conditions is the realization of the Idea in the form of that nation. Without this form, a nation, as—an ethical substance—which is what it is implicitly, lacks the objectivity of possessing in its own eyes and in the eyes of others, a universal and universally valid embodiment in laws, i.e. in determinate thoughts, and as a result it fails to secure recognition from others. So long as it lacks objective law and an explicitly established rational constitution, its autonomy is formal only and is not sovereignty.[15]

There is a correlative set of interdependencies between phenomenological narratives of Spirit and Eurocentrism, logocentrism, and the humanities understood in the broadest sense: "[M]ost humanists were of the opinion that the State was the archetypal and representative form of *humanitas*."[16] The history of the humanities indicates this: "[A]s far back as Cicero and Petrarch, the *studia humanitatis* distinguished sharply between *Homo humanus* and *Homo barbarous*."[17]

As the quote from Hegel above indicates, using Spirit, "Man," and *the* human as an ideal inevitably leads to a ranking of humans vis-à-vis their "qualifications" to be members of a state or to form a state: "The story of political subjectivity has always been fraught by exclusions of gender, race, class, caste, and religion. Civil society has consistently refused admission and participation to those who . . . lack the attributes and capacities of the 'individual.'"[18] We saw that Hegel is not the only one who thinks this way about the state. Wach, for instance, consistently excluded Native Americans and other non-Europeans from those who possess a state and therefore possess the ethical, rational, *geistig* level of consciousness that both creates a state and a state makes possible. Tiele and Otto told similar stories. As a consequence, one could fairly say of this group of authors that they participate in a singular failing of Western thought: "The underside of Western humanism produces the dictum that since some human beings are more human than others, they are more substantially the measure of all things."[19] "Man" is the measure of all things in the discourse of the phenomenology of religion.

A survey of the history of the discourse of the phenomenology of religion also shows that, even when it is not explicitly marked as such—and let us not forget that it *is* marked as such at times—racial differentiation is at play. The play of race in this discursive formulation appears within theories of the state. As noted above, some humans are "more human," at least by implication, because they both form a state and exist within one: "Racial difference, much as sexual difference, becomes synonymous with political difference. Thus, unlike the colonizers who possess the privileges of citizenship and subjectivity, the colonized exist only as subjects, or as those suspended in a state of subjection."[20]

"History is always of great importance to a people; since by means of that it becomes conscious of the path of development taken by its Spirit."[21] Our survey of the structures embedded in the discourse of the phenomenology of religion showed a correlation between consciousness and history in that it is within history that consciousness is manifest, that is, once again *"Wesen und Erscheinung."* All narratives of consciousness end in Europe, or, Europe is *never* put in a subordinate stage to some other civilization. As such: "The postcolonial/poststructuralist intervention into this problem focuses accordingly on 'history' as the grand narrative through which Eurocentrism is 'totalized' as the proper account of all humanity."[22] Wach referred to his method as *Allgemeine Geschichte*: universal, totalizing history; it encompasses all of humanity: "Religious experience is universal." Its realization is not. The colonist has a universal gaze, which allows for, by the universal scope of his gaze, "the creation of a space for a 'subject peoples' through the production of knowledges."[23]

History, as knowledge, as *tellable* from the gaze of the colonist, functions, as does the theory of the state, as another assertion of Europe's unique and central place in "world history":

> [A] variety of postcolonial commentators have argued that "history" is the discourse through which the West has asserted its hegemony over the rest of the world. This idea becomes clearer when we consider that Western philosophy, at least since Hegel, has used the category of "history" more or less synonymously with "civilization"—only to claim both of these categories for the West, or more specifically, for Europe.[24]

Even in the "soft" colonialist theories of Kristensen and Wach, the world of religion is divided into "Christian" and "non-Christian." Europe remains the defining term around which the world's axis spins (including the "world" of "world religions"; that world is the world as colonized by Europeans). It goes without saying that the diachronic, developmental theorists see Europe as that civilization most closely associated with *Geist* and therefore as the true subject and substance of putatively Universal History. A more graphic version of the literal claim that Europe is the center of history is Hegel's description of the Mediterranean in his *Philosophy of History*: "the Old World—the scene of the World's History"; "For three-quarters of the globe the Mediterranean Sea is similarly the uniting element, and the center of World-History."[25]

This centering is accomplished by defining *Geist*, Europe in disguise, as both the subject/agent and substance (underlying, uniting force) of History: "It [the humanist view] supposes that there is a subject of history who, while also a subject in history, is the director of events in the theater in which he finds himself. This subject is always male: his name is Man. To enshrine this little man-god, the history of ideas fabricates its essential continuities: 'Continuous history is the indispensable correlative of the founding function of the subject.' "[26] By saying the subject is gendered, the claim is that it is particular, not universal. We have seen numerous examples of such "founding subjects" in the narratives of the history of religions. For Hegel, it was overtly named as Spirit. In Otto, it was the nonmaterial a priori category of the mind, the holy. For Wach, again, it was Spirit and for

Eliade it was the sacred as a category of consciousness. The latter was explicit in subordinating the local to the universal. Translated into geopolitical realities, we must ask: Who is local and who/what is universal? Individual peoples, less "developed" than those more perfect bearers of the logos are clearly the particulars while the logos bearers of the universal are the "higher religions," always Christianity included, often quite explicitly framed as the consummate religion, or the consummation of religion, that is, of Spirit or consciousness—and *not* just in Hegel.

"Like every effort to dominate, history and its narration represent a colonial enterprise. The logocentrism of history implies that narrativity functions to humanize time by giving it form."[27] This includes the discipline of history: "In Chakrabarty's words, 'Europe remains the sovereign, theoretical subject of all histories, including the ones we call "Indian," "Chinese," "Kenyan," and so on.' "[28] As I argued above, there is a politics, that is, a pattern of selection, of inclusion and exclusion with a metaphysical basis, that corresponds to the power to be included *in* history. "History" is a history of human beings forming the state, or an objective moral-rational structure, and moving toward the self-conscious realization of freedom. And it is no different with the History of Religion; it is a narrative of the realization of consciousness, the sacred, the holy, or Spirit. As such, there is an "inside" and an "outside" to history: some peoples are "in" history and some lack the sufficient development of *Geist* to contribute to the progressive realization of history and so are not "in" history—or have a deficient conception of themselves as moral beings or as beings having or being in a state. Phenomenology accepts a taxonomic distinction between "ethnographic" studies of peoples "who have no history."[29] The result of this power/knowledge formation is the connection between the discipline of history and the colonialist project: "It seeks authorization for its strategies by the production of knowledges of colonizer and colonized which are stereotypical but antithetically evaluated. The objective of colonial discourse is to construe the colonized as a population of degenerate types on the basis of racial origin, in order to justify conquest and to establish systems of administration and instruction."[30] A people, as Hegel argued about the Indians, who have no history have no state proper. Therefore, as we saw before, "it follows that there is no ethics to be found, no determinate form of rational freedom, no right, no duty. The Hindu people are utterly sunk in the depths of an unethical life"; "their humanity does not yet have within it the content of freedom."[31] In this, he says, "all Englishmen agree."[32]

A reflection: What if the state is crazy? What if the state of Hegel's history or as the subject of traditional historiography is *essentially*, necessarily violent, is mad, and thrives on chaos as its necessary other? Speaking of the idea of a rational state and rationally guided by "History," in Hegel but also in bourgeois optimistic theories of the state and history, Homi Bhabha notes that: "Forms of social and psychic alienation and aggression—madness, self-hate, treason, violence—can never be acknowledged as determinate and constitutive conditions of civil authority, or as the ambivalent effects of the social instinct itself. They are always explained away as alien presences, occlusions of historical progress, the ultimate misrecognition of Man."[33] This indicates why colonial discourse cannot admit the raw facts of colonialism and why it must displace the "blame" for colonialism onto the victims of colonialism. Not only is the legitimation of the West's position threatened by such facts, the deepest system of cultural values, even views of reality would be undermined by such admissions—or, at least, their claim to moral and other forms of superiority would be (and have been, are still being) seriously undermined. So, the lazy Negro, the obstinate Native American, the dreamy, chaotic Hindu, the rigid Mandarin *must* exist. Essentialism allows for the construction of ideal identities, which serve to organize "the Orient," or "the dark continent," that is, those domains defined as non-Europe. This essentialist system of identities is the basis for the assertion of Christian-Europe's superiority and supremacy, and hence its *right* to be master of all.

The failure to see this, to admit to it, or even its existence, is what Mary Louise Pratt calls "anti-conquest": "by which I refer to the strategies of representation whereby European bourgeois subjects seek to secure their innocence in the same moment they assert European hegemony."[34] Does this apply to Religious Studies? Wiebe, Segal, and others noted that Religious Studies was originally a kind of liberal Protestantism, which then transformed into a liberal, generic religiosity. Can such L/liberalism see how *it itself* is one of the sites of precisely this "anti-conquest"? *Insofar as* it cannot, the call for change must be a call to revolution, not a simple patching up of this deformed and dissimulating discursive structure. We must *start* with the will to power; we must *begin* with the facts of colonial domination to explain both "religion" and the history of our discipline. The idea, ideality, "Religion" takes the place in our narratives of the history of this, that, or another religion. What if religion is crazy? Can Religious Studies as currently constituted account for this? Can it even ask the question?

## Eurocentrism

"But why this emphasis on Hegel?"[35] Robert Young poses a question that would seem pertinent at this juncture. The answer, as Young explains, has to do with Hegel's relationship to Western imperialism: "Hegel articulates a philosophical structure of the appropriation of the other as a form of knowledge which uncannily simulates the project of nineteenth-century imperialism."[36] One of the central issues in the context of this "power/knowledge" correlation between Europe/non-Europe is the problem of the representation of the Other. Most often, this problem takes the form of "Eurocentrism," which is also a form of ethnocentrism. Robert Young explains how poststructuralism, representation, and Euro-, ethnocentrism entail one another:

> The politics of poststructuralism forces the recognition that all knowledge may be variously contaminated, implicated in its very formal or "objective" structures. This means that in particular colonial discourse analysis is not merely a marginal adjunct to more mainstream studies, a specialized activity only for minorities or for historians of imperialism and colonialism, but itself forms the point of questioning of Western knowledge's categories and assumptions.[37]

For the last several centuries Europe has approached its "others" with the dual interests of politico-economic exploitation and potential objects of knowledge. "Primitives" have been seen as a kind of laboratory in which "civilized" Europeans could learn about "Man." Hegelian philosophy was, in many ways, the culmination of this Eurocentric construction of self-and-other, or "the recognition of self in absolute otherness."

Heller and Feher have described the Eurocentrism of this transcendental philosophy, including, I would argue, the totalizing elements of the phenomenology of religion. They point out that

> the project termed "Europe," had always been more expansive and more expressly universalistic than other cultural projects. Europeans did not merely understand their culture as superior to others and these alien others as inferior to them. They also believed that the "truth" of European culture is in the same measure the as-yet-hidden truth (and *telos*) of other cultures, but that time had not yet come for the latter to realize it."[38]

We are what "they" should be. That is, Europe is what "the rest of the world" (in Mary Louise Pratt's phrase) *will* be, what they should be. The idea of universal structures or experiences or structures of consciousness predicated on the "white mythology" of European metaphysics elides the particularity, the specificity of those concepts. They are born in Europe and exported to the colonies. The history of the study of religion, including what Wiebe discussed as the transformation in Religious Studies from liberal Protestantism to a liberal generic religiosity, has been rife with the attempt to find the universal at the expense of the particular, the individual. In doing so, has it not been complicit in the extension of this project, "Europe"?[39]

This is also true of humanism. Humanism is a concept basic to both the phenomenology of religion and Religious Studies. Leela Gandhi notes that the Enlightenment concept of "mankind," as articulated by Kant, despite its pretensions to universality is, in reality, "a characteristically pedagogic and imperialist hierarchy between European adulthood and its childish, colonized Other."[40] She shows how "the Kantian conception of 'mankind' is prescriptive rather than descriptive. Instead of reflecting the radical heterogeneity of human nature, it restricts the ostensibly universal structures of human existence to the normative condition of adult rationality—itself a value arising from the specific historicity of European societies."[41] As we have seen so many times with the Logos, with one hand it offers equality and then takes it away with the other hand: "European rationality holds out the possibility of the improvement for all of humanity. Accordingly, those who are already in possession of the gospel of rationality are seen to have an ethical obligation or 'calling' to spread the word."[42] There is a categorical difference between those who possess reason and those who do not. The universalizing tendency of European categories is actually the tale of one society's ethnic "folk" concepts (metaphysics) used to dominate, subordinate, and infantilize other societies, which they have conquered.

Mary Louise Pratt has made a similar argument, focusing on certain European representations of non-Europe. She describes, for instance, the work of naturalists as they either were or as they accompanied explorers and colonizers. The naturalist, *qua naturalist*, produces a narrative "in which the naturalist naturalizes the bourgeois European's own global presence and authority."[43] This "narrative was to continue to hold enormous ideological force throughout the nineteenth century, and remains very much with us today."[44] She demonstrates this in two main areas: the circumnavigation of the globe and natural history. On the first, she argues that "circumnavigation and mapmaking had already given rise to what one might call a European global or planetary subject.... [T]his world-historical subject is European, male, secular, and lettered."[45] Recall what Hegel had said about this: "that urging of Spirit *outwards*—that desire on the part of man to become acquainted with *his* world. The chivalrous spirit of the maritime heroes of Portugal and Spain opened a new way to the East Indies and discovered America."[46] In the very next line, however, he says: "This progressive step also, involved no transgression limits of ecclesiastical principles or feeling." Pratt underestimates the role religion played in colonization. Now, we cannot "blame" phenomenologists of religion for that, but it does show that the use, definition, and meaning of religion were engaged in the colonial enterprise.

On "natural history," Pratt says:

> One by one the planet's life forms were to be drawn out of the tangled threads of the life surroundings and rewoven into European-based patterns of global unity and order. The (lettered, male, European) eye that held the system could be familiarized ("naturalized") to new sites/sights immediately upon contact, by incorporating them into the language of the system. The differences factored themselves out of the picture.[47]

Ergo, it was possible to create a series of metaphorical likenesses where Europe was the source domain onto which the target domain of "the rest of the world" was mapped. Plants, mountains, and so forth of "other countries" would be classified by the ways in which they resembled (*simile in multis*) European phenomena of the same kind. Europe is the norm for natural history, that is, science, that is, knowledge, thus demonstrating "the system's potential to subsume culture and history into nature,"[48] or the representation of nature.

Between the accounts of Enlightenment humanism and of natural history, we can see that the history of colonialism played a constitutive role in the very structures of that which is counted as "knowledge." Robert Young, points out: "Postmodernism can best be defined as European culture's awareness that it is no longer the unquestioned and dominant center of the world."[49] This is because, as noted before, postmodernism (which I take, for our purposes here to be synonymous with poststructuralism) *began* with a critique of "epistemology" as a Eurocentric form of domination, as a system that cannot approach otherness accept by subsuming it into itself, whether metaphysically or geopolitically. For phenomenology, "the fundamental problem concerns the way in which knowledge ... is constituted through the comprehension and incorporation of the other."⁵⁰ This other can never break through the system of European knowledge, a form of knowledge that strove to be Absolute Knowledge, not merely the knowledge of this or that region of being:

> In Western philosophy, when knowledge or theory comprehends the other, then the alterity of the latter vanishes as it become part of the same. This "ontological imperialism," Levinas argues, goes back at least to Socrates but can be found as recently as Heidegger. In all cases the other is neutralized as a means of encompassing it: ontology amounts to a philosophy of power, an egotism in which the relation with the other is accomplished through its assimilation into the self.⁵¹

Young cites Levinas's observation that "Hegel's philosophy represents the logical outcome of this underlying allergy of philosophy."⁵²

In conclusion: "Such is, I believe, the moment of [Eurocentric] colonial discourse. It is a form of discourse crucial to the binding of a range of differences and discriminations that inform the discursive and political practices of racial and cultural hierarchization."⁵³

## Christocentrism

A poststructuralist-postcolonialist reading slices open another vector in this discourse which is consistent with the previous vectors analyzed. With a notable exception here and there, phenomenology of religion and the braid of *Religionswissenschaft* of which it is a part, has been *programmatically* Christocentric. "Christocentric," is not a *theological* concept, that is, of a Christ-centered life, or making the Christian faith the center of one's life, or of society or of life in general. I mean it in a purely *descriptive* sense that almost all thinkers who either are phenomenologists of religion or who have made a significant contribution to its development, have argued, a fortiori—not ad hoc—that "Christianity is the supreme religion." The basis of this argument is on the one hand a simple extension of logocentrism:

> [M]ost of the Christian theological network rests on a dyadic foundation that sets seemingly exclusive opposites over against each other. Furthermore, these paired opposites

form a hierarchy in which one term governs, rules, dominates, or represses the other. For example, God governs the world, eternity and permanence are more valuable than time and change, presence is preferable to absence, spirit more worthy than body, etc.[54]

In the discourse of the phenomenology of religion, this logocentrism is directly tied to the claim that Christianity is not merely one religion among others, but the highest fulfillment of the innate, a priori, universal structure of *Geist*/consciousness/"Man." What is important to note here is that this position is the direct, logical outcome of their conception of an hermeneutical, empathetic approach to the science of religion.

Recall how, in the discussion of Eliade's view's, he argued that "the 'divine form' of Yahweh prevailed over the 'divine form' of Ba'al [because] it manifested a more perfect holiness.... This hierophany of Yahweh had the final victory because it represented a universal modality of the sacred," that is, as a manifestation of the sacred, Yahweh was "at once purer and more complete."[55] *Mutatis mutandis*, Eliade makes a similarly logocentric claim about Christianity: "that the image of the *Center* imposed itself *naturally*"[56] on that religion. "Universality," "more perfect," "purer," "more complete," "manifestation," "Center," "naturally," and "final victory": such are terms by which a Christocentricism is virtually synonymous with a logocentric methodology.

Recall also that a few pages later Eliade makes a similar argument concerning the greater universality, and hence truer manifestation, of the Christianity of the village priest over that of the peasants in the village. Again, this is not incidental to, but constitutive of, methodological principle:

> What we call syncretism can be seen at every point in the course of religious life. Every farming spirit of the countryside, every tribal god, is the culmination of a long process of being assimilated and identified with other divine forms adjacent to it. But it must be pointed out that these assimilations and fusions are not due solely to historical circumstances (the mingling of two neighboring tribes, the conquest of a given area and so on); the process takes place as a result of the very nature of hierophanies; whether or not a hierophany comes into contact with another religious form, like or unlike itself, it will tend, in the religious con-

sciousness of those who perceive it as such, to be expressed as totally, as fully as possible.[57]

Totality admits, as we can see, of degrees. Some religions are "more total" than others; it will never be a mystery in this discourse, again a fortiori—not ad hoc—that Christianity, if not the supreme religion, will always be ranked among them. The religions of Eskimos, Algonquians, Canaanites, Yorubans, Congolese, that is, the "losers" in the war between Europe and those that it would colonize, their religions are *theirs*: particular, ethnic, sensuous, lacking in all those things that make (apparently; victory is proof of superiority, is it not?) the Euro-imperialist not only greater than the colonized, but infinitely more fit to represent the universal.

Christ and Christianity are taken, most often, as the very model of the universal. The logocentric element in the Christ makes him/it interpretable as an exalted "structure," a manifestation marked by a higher degree of ideality than manifestations of religion whose being is a mixture of the ideal and the natural: "Universality," "more perfect," "purer," "more complete." For structure is a combination of an ordering of reality, a means of giving it shape, and an ideality, a nonmaterial, highly generic if not universal set of qualities. As such, there *is* a kind of natural affinity between the implicit universality, as ideal and generic, of structure and the Christ as the immortal, spiritual dimension, Logos/Word of the couplet "Jesus Christ." But this affinity must be read backward: it is not that Christ is more universal, it is that the model of/for universality is derived from the figure of the Christ—and that civilization that bears his name, "Christendom." All things are purer insofar as they resemble the ideality and genericity—not ethnic, not natural, not merely belonging to a given place and time, but *the* Logos—of the Christ of Christendom. As the rule and measure of ideal form itself, Christianity *is* the supreme religion. It is not simply derived from the fact that they are European Christians and so arbitrarily and willfully make their own religion "the supreme religion." This was the argument of Baird and the empiricist critics: the normative element of the phenomenology of religion was an individualized, subjective problem. However, a discourse analysis shows that such "norms" are the direct consequences of their methodology, not their private preferences.

On the other hand, the Christocentrism *is* a correlative of Eurocentrism/ethnocentrism. The criteria, or criteriology, by which Christianity comes to be the supreme religion are the projections of a "white mythology" a substitution of the false universality of a specific metaphysics for the limited history of a specific culture: "The deconstruction of the Western theological [and ontotheological] network discloses the recurrent effort of human beings to achieve a position of domination. This struggle appears to grow out of the conviction that mastery results from the ability to secure presence and establish identity by overcoming absence and repressing difference."[58] These metaphysical concepts are not limited to simple cultural prejudices (though they are likely that, too) but inform such basic, constitutive concepts as: structure, state, history, interpretation, as these are at work in the discourse of the *Geisteswissenschaften*, including—perhaps most especially?—*Religionswissenschaft*. It raises the question: Has our very concept of a human science, *as it has been historically articulated*,[59] been a Eurocentric projection? More specifically, is the very concept "religion" itself hopelessly ethnocentric? Does it do more to distort sociocultural historical processes than it does to aid in reaching a better understanding of those processes?

## Ethnocentrism

"Logocentrism is an ethnocentric metaphysics. It is related to the history of the West."[60] The discourse of the phenomenology of religion is Eurocentric and Christocentric in such a way as also to be *ethnocentric*. It takes a distinctly modern, European concept of consciousness and projects it upon the rest of "mankind" and the world as if it were a metaphysically certain universal—"nothing human is alien to me" (or, that which is alien is nothing? Nonhuman? As if Hegel's inability to understand the Eskimos makes them dogs?). "Man" turns out to be a European idea with a distinctly European history. Logocentrism is the means by which phenomenologists of religion essentialize and thereby universalize their conception of "Man." This projection entails any number of other, correlative universalizations of distinctly European concepts and categories, viz., the history of Cartesianism, a problematic of consciousness unique to Western thought. So, all the writers here will find "ethics," "politics," "aesthetics," and "religion" (etc.), to be natural, universal givens throughout the non-history of "Man." This is one result of the use of a faculty psychology, a maneuver that can be traced as far back as the first two chapters of Schleiermacher's *Speeches on Religion*. However, this configurative-configuring taxonomic operation uses domains of distinctively modern, European, even bourgeois culture which are taken to be the a priori categories and/or universal domains of the expression of the human spirit as such. This ontologization of the separation of spheres or domains allows them to make any number of otherwise totally spurious claims about the autonomy of spirit and its various manifestations in art, culture, the state, history, and most especially for our concerns, religion (itself a concept of European design as W. C. Smith demonstrated many years ago).

This also true of the category "Spirit." It is implicitly ethnocentric in that, again, it universalizes the Occident's own sense of self, gathering all the moments of history into itself. It is explicitly ethnocentric in that it is the means by which non-European, non-Christian religions are "ranked" as lower manifestations. The narrative of Spirit's full manifestation always ends up in the self-consciousness of the European self with itself. Or, conversely, a treatment of certain religions and certain kinds of religions, as ideal objects, which, in their very ideality, resemble the implicit criteria of Spirit's own fulfillment. These religions, almost all textual traditions, are "higher" religions insofar as they approach the true home of Spirit, the West. As with so many other cases in the discourse of the phenomenology of religion, the category Spirit would seem to be universal and yet, in its application by phenomenologists to "non-Christian" religions, it becomes an ethnocentric criterion for denying these religions equality.

"One can say with total security that there is nothing fortuitous about the fact that the critique of ethnocentrism ... should be systematically and historically contemporaneous with the destruction of the history of metaphysics."[61] That history begins at the apogee of colonialism-imperialism and continues through the breakdown of Europe's grip on the globe in such movements as, for example, existentialism, absurdism, feminism, and poststructuralism. One need not make a causal argument about the relationship between the two to see that, just as there are strong parallels between the discursive structure of phenomenology and colonial discourse, there is a parallel development of the fall of Egoic phenomenology and the fall of the empires. I cited Charles Long on this issue before (chapter 2), but it bears repeating, for it grasps the situation exactly as it is: "I do not mean to imply that the human sciences were simply and merely the ideological counterpart to this subjugation. *I should, however, make the case that these sciences came into being presupposing this situation.* A great deal of the practical and theoretical meaning of the 'others' is related to this colonial situation."[62] The data for the phenomenology/history of religions was drawn from those peoples colonists had conquered. Their sense of these peoples is inevitably filtered through that radically ethnocentric context.

Ethnocentrism itself raises many issues, including its potential circularity as a concept. "But there are several ways of being caught in a circle," as Derrida quipped. What is meant by the term *ethnocentrism*? More importantly, is ethnocentrism inevitable? Is the critique of ethnocentrism itself ethnocentric? David Hoy has described several different ways of being "caught in a circle" of ethnocentric reference. In a very useful discussion of the problem of ethnocentrism in hermeneutical theory, Hoy points out that the "specific features of ethnocentrism that are pernicious": "What is misguided is the further expectation that every other understanding of the world *converge* on one's own."[63] We have seen that the category of "unity" is one of the constitutive philosophemes in the discourse of the phenomenology of religion. It is a concept shared by Hegel and Otto, but also by Wach and Eliade. The category "unity," and its correlative terms, especially *Geist*, perform precisely the kind of convergence Hoy describes. This category is, as Derrida said, as old as the Pre-Socratics, that is, it is an integral part of ontotheology, a historical reality that is European. *Geist*, unity in action, one might say, underlies all individual manifestations of religious consciousness, of consciousness itself. As we saw: *Geist is Europe*. *Geist*, as both logocentric and Eurocentric is, finally: "the most original and powerful ethnocentrism, in the process of imposing itself upon the world."[64] Need it be added that this "convergence" has been a patterned, repeated form of violence? Of domination? Of exclusion? The scenes of this violence are *both* discursive and geopolitical. "The highest form of the will to power is interpretation."[65]

However, Hoy shows us how interpretation need not be based on such a pathological convergence. He draws a set of distinctions between two types of interpretive schemas: those which are Monistic versus those which are Pluralistic. These types are further qualified as being Critical versus those which are Metaphysical.[66] By Monism as a type of interpretive theory, he means: "Monism insists that all the possible question about all the features of an object of interpretation (paradigmatically, but not necessarily, a text) must be resolvable, at least at the ideal limit. More generally, monists have the intuition that there must be only one right interpretation of a text, problem, or subject matter."[67] By contrast, Pluralistic interpretive schemas "do not share the monists' intuition that there is a single right interpretation in the present are rationally adjudicatable. Pluralists believe that there can be rational disagreements that do not presuppose ideal convergence or consensus as the final arbiter of the dispute."[68]

The qualification "Metaphysical" primarily "posits that there is a unity of the object"[69] and is synonymous with the Kantian notion of "transcendent," or more simply, metaphysical realism, that is, that there are real, constant, objective phenomena in the world and that they can be known as such. By contrast: "The term 'critical' already means 'interpretive,' but it also suggests that interpretation can have a critical element in it. Kant sometimes spoke of his philosophy as critical philosophy, and the first *Critique* is a critique of metaphysics."[70] Critical, then, means an approach that questions its own basic categories, such as "unity" in the Monistic notion of the necessary unity of an object of interpretation. A critical-pluralist approach "resists this claimed necessity by holding that there can be more than one equally acceptable interpretation according to the best available standards."[71] By foregoing the insistence of the unity of the object and hence the singularity of correct interpretation, Critical-Pluralism is, at the very least, less prone to ethnocentrism. Or, put another way, Critical-Pluralism is self-conscious about the ways in which all interpretive schemas are ethnocentric, at least to some degree, and so can monitor that element in its own (and others') interpretations and underlying principles of interpretation.

From my reading of the phenomenology of religion, it is quite clear that its dominant tendency as a hermeneutic is toward a Metaphysical Monism. This is the most virulent type of convergence schema: it absorbs the Other into itself; "*self*-recognition in *absolute* otherness." The Other converges on *Geist*'s egoistic project of self-knowledge. In the history of the *Geisteswissenschaften*, in the history of *Religionswissenschaft*, in the history of the phenomenology of religion one of the keys to this Metaphysical Monism is the unrecognized features of the humanism (etc.) that is its foundation. As Mark Taylor has noted, "Though acutely sensitive to the problem of the other, transcendental philosophy is unable to provide an account of alterity that does not reduce difference to sameness."[72]

An example of this Metaphysical Monism at work is Eliade's treatment of "archaic man"—always in the singular. While Eliade valorizes archaic man, he also invents archaic man. The deployment of the trope, *simile in multis* (synecdoche), the One from the many, with its emphasis on sameness (another form of unity) is one of the oldest tropes of the Occident. Deployed as such, it is not really a valorization of archaic *man*, it is a self-valorization, a structural narcissism endemic to Eliade's quest for a final unity, a kind of methodological *parousia*, the "New Humanism," which, as it "transforms man," could arguably also be the "New Being." This project/projection does not allow the Other to be other, but subsumes all others into a network of concepts embedded, as we have seen, in Western, European ontotheology. Eliade's concept of "the sacred"—always in the singular—saturated with being and exalted as an *ultimate* reality, is another example of Metaphysical

Monism. As such, despite his protestations to the contrary, Eliade's *hermeneutic* is profoundly and uncritically ethnocentric.

When *Geist*, "Man," "consciousness," and/or "humanism" operates in such an unrecognized manner in the history of the study of religion it has always tended to substitute Nature for history, to render radically different social and cultural formations in such a way that their differences are negated by the impulse toward unity, which, as we have seen, is an integral, constitutive feature of phenomenology. Again, this Metaphysical Monism is ethnocentric in that these concepts are ahistorical, Platonic-like forms that "show up" in existence as sui generis phenomena. Rather, they are "related to the history of the West" as postcolonial critics had noted. They are, as we have seen, *located* and locatable. They exist in a complex historical-structural network of other concepts—without which, they would not exist.

Metaphysical Monism de-locates and therefore absolves. The phenomenologist is only working, after all, with the sui generis, a priori, given, universal structures of "consciousness as such." Who could doubt that we are conscious beings? Genealogy, the historicity of the category "consciousness," raises precisely that doubt. It is not a matter of being conscious; it is a matter of how "consciousness" is *theorized*. By lacking an awareness of this historicity, by refusing it in so many gestures of denial, the phenomenologist does not take into account the specificity, the locatedness, the genealogically ascertained play of structures and transformations—all of which are "housed" in the language of ontotheology. Thus, they impose categories foreign to the Others of Europe, resulting in *not* a "clear and transparent" grasp of "the things themselves." No, they form a virulent ethnocentrism dressed up as a science of experience. Insofar as it has followed the phenomenology of religion, Religious Studies is complicit in ethnocentrism.

## Phenomenology of Religion and/as Racism

We come, then, to a question that has been looming over this study since we encountered our first theorist, Hegel: Is the phenomenology of religion racist? It depends upon what the term means, or, more precisely, where to locate a phenomenon such as racism. If the issue is tantamount to asking after "personal" attitudes, etc., first off, that is irrelevant to a study like this, and secondly, no conclusions could be drawn about such an issue from *any or all* of the data presented here.

However, that is the wrong way to put the question, the wrong place to look. The question of racism, or of any methodological or political pathology—and racism is *both* a methodological and a political pathology—is never simply one of "personal attitudes." It is a question of the production, valorization, dissemination, and consumption of socially objective, publicly available, cultural representations. It is a structural, systemic problem, not an individual, subjective problem. This, again, is the difference that the use of discourse theory yields as opposed to the empiricists' approach. As they reduce knowledge to the individual, knowing subject, they must ask after "his" attitudes, etc. And, indeed they do: they are busy checking Eliade's papers for answers to this question. One need not read the letters and journals of any author to answer this question. Perhaps even more alarming: we need only read their *texts*. It is their *science* that is at issue, not their personalities.

Viewed in this way, this study has provided a *wealth* of material for assessing this crucial question. Unequivocally, the discursive structure known as "phenomenology of religion" is, was, and always has been racist—*pure and simple*. The metanarrative of *Geist*, whether articulated diachronically or synchronically, is a narrative of the ascendancy—their term, not mine—of white, Christian Europe out of black, "primitive" Africa and away from brown or yellow, "despotic" Asia. It moves *from* the South *to* the North; *away* from the East *to* the West. It moves out of Africa and into Germany; out of Asia, through Greece and into the heart of Europe. It moves away from "nature" *to* "spirit," out of bondage *to* freedom, it transcends "law" and culminates in "love," it goes beyond "sensualism" and so grasps "pure reason." And this narrative, this metaphysics of the subject, of *Geist*, or "Man" works thus whether its "articulator" is or is not "personally" racist or prejudiced, whether they are or are not "liberal" in any sense of the term, or conservative, whether they are or are not are believers or atheists, whether they do or do not consider themselves a theologian or a practitioner of *Religionswissenschaft*, whether they praise Hegel or damn him, whether they are known by the names Dilthey, Tiele, Otto, van der Leeuw, Wach, or Eliade. This is a racist discursive structure, more virulent at times, less at others admittedly, but racist nonetheless. It pretends toward a universalism but, in the end, time and time again, uses that very same universalism to marginalize the already marginal peoples of color and denigrate the already denigrated peoples of color, in the silent-so-all-the-more-insidious constant reiteration of its Logocentric, Eurocentric, Christocentric, and ethnocentric colonialist hegemony. When its core, constitutive, structural oppositions are analyzed, it is seen to be the vicious, self-aggrandizing, and monstrously narcissistic ideological formation that it is.

# 12

# The "End of Man" and the Phenomenology of Religion

"But it is easy to understand that the failure to search for the real center of a religion may be explained by the inadequate contributions made by the History of Religions to philosophical anthropology."[1] We saw this statement from Eliade before, but it is worth taking a moment to listen to its language more carefully. It is an acknowledgment of the failure of the discipline, first and foremost. That failure? A failure to find "the real center of a religion." Religions *have* a center, and there is a difference between a real center and an unreal center. In what does this center lie? It is framed within yet another failure or inadequacy: the lack of a contribution to philosophical anthropology on the part of the History of Religions. The solution to the failings of *Religionswissenschaft* is found in ανθροπος: "Man" is the center and this center is not only found in religion, it can be further revealed by the work of the phenomenologist of religion. A doctrine of "Man" is incomplete without the contributions of the History of Religions; "Man" cannot be fully understood, and therefore spiritually fulfilled, without this contribution. The History of Religions, then, performs a double function: it clarifies the science of "Man" by leading it to the center. This center is religion. Then, having brought man's self-awareness to the religious level, the History of Religions is the basis of a New Humanism, a new *Phenomenology of Spirit*, a new epoch in Spirit's awareness of itself as Spirit. It is the epoch of "Man."

Heidegger to Sartre: "This question proceeds from your intention to retain the word 'humanism.' I wonder whether that is necessary. Or is the damage caused by all such terms still not sufficiently obvious?"[2] Whence this damage? "Every humanism is either grounded in a metaphysics or is itself made to be the ground of one."[3] "Man," "humanism," are mythemes in the white mythology, which is also, as we have seen, a mythology of whiteness. "Man" is a white man. But *what*, after all, is "Man"? What, that is, is "Man" in the discourse of the phenomenology of religion? In the history of metaphysics? In the structure-structuration of ontotheology as it has existed in Modernity?

## "Man," Subject, Consciousness, *Geist*

### *"Man" as Subject*

What is "Man"? A subject. "Man" becomes a subject in a specific period of the history of the West: "The modern period in philosophy is generally acknowledged to have begun with Descartes' decisive turn to the subject."[4] Thus, the conditions for the possibility of any phenomenology of "Man" will lie in his/its historicity, not his/its transcendent qualities, because: "When fully developed, the Cartesian philosophy of the *cogito* leads to the 'theory of the subject,' which 'lies at the heart of humanism.' "[5] What, then, is (or was?) the subject?

> [T]he subject is a substance in which attributes inhere and a substantive to which predicates can be attached.... Common sense insists on the primacy of the subject and the secondariness of the predicates. The subject is viewed as ontologically *primal*. As such, it is the *antecedent* ground, base, and substance that underlies and unifies otherwise disparate predicates. From this perspective, the subject is supposed to be a discrete "thing-in-itself" that is extrinsically and accidentally associated with other subjects and entities.[6]

This is a solid answer to the *quid est?*, the question endemic to *philosophy*. There is, however, another way to put the point, viz., historically. In the transition from the European Middle Ages to European Modernity, "[w]hat is decisive is not that man frees himself to himself from previous obligations, but that the very essence of man itself changes, in that man becomes a subject ... when man becomes the primary and only real *subiectum*, that means: Man becomes that being upon which all that is, is grounded as regards the manner of its Being and its truth. Man becomes the relational center of that which is as such."[7] Again, this *historical* shift establishes the *Grundbegriffen* for phenomenology in general, that is, one could not have a phenomenology without the post-Cartesian notion of "Man" and consciousness. However, phenomenologists do not recognize this as a historical construct.

The damage, again? "The crux of this philosophy is, in other words, the all-knowing subject of consciousness—an entity that insists that our knowledge of the world is nothing other than the narcissism of self-consciousness."[8] Contained within itself, the subject of consciousness can only have itself as a reference, or, "Spirit is what it has always essentially been." The unity so important to the phenomenology of religion is this narcissism; the subject *can only* find itself in "absolute otherness."

As purely contained within itself, "[t]he Cartesian celebration of the human subject's epistemological possibilities is inevitably accompanied by an assertion of its power over, and freedom from, the external world of objects";[9] "mind is more certain than matter, and my mind is more certain than the minds of others."[10] We arrive back at Spirit/Matter, in a radical, qualitative separation of "mind" from non-mind. This separation is the cogito's, is Spirit's power: freedom. "I" am mind and as mind is "above" non-mind, "I" am free and have power over that sphere which is ultimately Other than "I," "the Cartesian philosophy of identity is premised upon an ethically unsustainable omission of the Other.... [T]he all-knowing and self-sufficient Cartesian subject violently negates material and historical alterity/Otherness in its narcissistic desire to always see the world in its own self-image."[11]

Why? Besides what has already been said, what is it about the cogito (which is but one link in the syntagmatic chain that is the history of metaphysics; one paradigmatic element in the *langue* of ontotheology) that gives it this purported power? In geopolitical terms, who or what is "Man"?

> The self in question is no ordinary self, no individual personality, nor even one of the many heroic or mock-heroic personalities of the early nineteenth century. The self that becomes the star performer in modern European philosophy is the transcendental self.... The transcendental self was *the* self—timeless, universal, and in each one of us around the globe and throughout history.[12]

The cogito, as a theory of the self, as a perspective on that "inner experience" of which Dilthey and Wach spoke, is the homogenous interiority of all of us. The problem is that it is not in "of us all." It has a location, a biography, a situatedness; it has an address: Europe. The self is, first and foremost "us," and only projected onto "the rest of the world." This is the damage done.

## "Man" and Consciousness

We must ask again: how is that the cogito-cum-"Man"-cum-*Geist* is endowed with this far-reaching power? Because "Man" is also synonymous with consciousness. He is the subject of the events of consciousness: "*I* think, *I* doubt, *I* feel," etc. More importantly, consciousness is the dividing line between "Man" and nonhuman. Consciousness makes man, "Man." As such: "Consciousness is the truth of man."[13] The science of consciousness, the science of experience, or phenomenology, would be a powerful instrument if a true science. And, as Eliade often proclaimed, "the sacred is a structure of *consciousness*," meaning that religion is an essential element of consciousness itself, Religious Studies is an integral—and therefore powerful—component in the science of man. In part, then, the battle over "Man" is a battle for the power over academic discourse or discourses. It is a battle over truth, academic, cultural, and religious. It is a battle over which discipline shall be the Queen of the sciences and which disciplines will serve her.

The unity of consciousness, "Man," and especially *Geist* is, as Derrida pointed out, in the centrality of consciousness, the privileging of consciousness as the unique site of the truth of man: "Consciousness is the truth of man, phenomenology is the truth of anthropology."[14] Consciousness is taken as the essence of "Man," and intentionality/meaning as the essence of consciousness. Speaking specifically of Husserl, Derrida makes a point that must be taken as an explication of one of the inner, core, driving assumptions of all the phenomenologies and theories of consciousness, all theories of meaning as products of inner, human consciousness we have reviewed. They are all qualified by, whether Platonic or Kantian, an insistence on "the autonomy of logical ideality as concerns all consciousness in general, or all concrete and non-formal consciousness. Husserl, for his part, seeks to *maintain* simultaneously the normative autonomy of logical or mathematical ideality as concerns all factual consciousness, and its original dependence in relation to a subjectivity in *general*; in *general* but *concretely*."[15] Finally, what qualifies consciousness is this "autonomy of logical ideality." We saw it as a series of binary philosophemes which played out through this history: in Hegel's qualitative distinction between Spirit/Matter; Dilthey's distinction between empirical experience and inner experience, Otto's locating the holy in the (autonomous) realm of the a priori, and, as cited many times, Eliade's locating the sacred in the (immutable) structures of consciousness. The very structure of these binaries aimed at this above all else: Spirit is Freedom.

The problematic, however, was to find a way for this transcendent structure to be the concrete acts of consciousness, to find in such acts, "subjectivity in general." And here we arrive at another set of philosophemes: "manifestation," "religious experience," "expression," and "history" as in the "History of Religion/s." All gestures of concretia, all movements encompassing the emperia, concretia, but also all movements *relating* such concretia to "subjectivity in general" as a logical or *geistig* ideality. As such, they both "aid" that subjectivity and threaten it. They aid it in that "without expressions we cannot access the inner experience of the Other"—Dilthey, Wach, van der Leeuw. Consciousness is consciousness *of*; without an object—an expression as object here—there is nothing for consciousness to be conscious of. Consciousness needs its other.

This is, obviously, the threat of the concrete to subjectivity in general. The concrete as such threatens the cherished "principle of principles," so to speak, viz., the autonomy of ideality as sheer otherness to non-ideality. In addition to this, and as a parallel concern, the concretia leaves subjectivity in general open to empirical reduction and therefore "explanation." The concretia, as the other of subjectivity in its autonomous ideality, can "drift away," as it were and attain an independence itself. Incipit the empiricists: their explanatory methods threatened to raise, a fortiori, methodologically, the concrete *above* the ideality of subjectivity in general. The empiricists claim that the concretia, qua concretia can be taken on their own term, and so need not be merely "understood," but can actually be explained. Insofar as this is the case, the concretia threaten to take away the ambrosia of Spirit/subjectivity in general, "Man," viz., "meaning." If they can be explained, and explanation does not lead to meaning, then the concrete leads to meaninglessness. "Man" is emptied out into his objectifications; subjectivity in general becomes, like God, an "unnecessary hypothesis."

*Incipit* Dilthey. Speaking of the common ground of Husserl and Dilthey, Derrida points out that:

> Dilthey has the merit of protesting against the positivist naturalization of the life of the mind. The act of "understanding" that he opposes to explanation and objectification must be the first and major route to be followed by the sciences of the mind. Husserl thus pays homage to Dilthey and shows himself quite hospitable . . . to the idea of a principle of "understanding" or of re-understanding, of "re-living" (*Nachleben*)—notions simultaneously to be

juxtaposed with the notion of *Einfühlung* ... and with the notion of *Reaktivierung*, which is the active re-living of the past intention of an *other* mind and the reawakening of a production of meaning—in question here is the very possibility of a science of the mind.[16]

The major method/ological philosophemes of the phenomenology of religion are then, rooted in a very specific theory, a theory of consciousness. We must bear in mind that it is a very specific kind of operation, it is a "theory" or "philosophy" of consciousness, it is not simply a factual, or phenomenal description of an obviously given item in the real, of the real. And, let us not forget, that "logical ideality" is a metaphysical notion, not simply syllogistic, obviously and necessarily not an empirical claim, and most certainly not simply, again, the product of a "raw" or "pure" phenomenalist examination of mind or consciousness or perception from within. It is, again, a "mathematical ideality as concerns all factual consciousness," an ideality that functions, as a norm, that is, an a priori commitment, of the *theory* of a phenomenological approach to consciousness. It belongs, part and parcel, to the system of metaphysical concept produced by the history of the West, to wit, it is a philosopheme at play within the structures, protean as they may be, of ontotheology.

Consciousness, once revealed as such, has "died," that is, no longer holds the pride of place in any theory of religion or of the human generally. David Hoy has given a comprehensive account of the role of consciousness in the history of philosophy:

> Although consciousness thus seems to some to be the pre-eminent topic of modern philosophy, others have suspected that the history of modern philosophy has disclosed not what consciousness really is, but that it is really not anything at all, or at least not much more than a matter of stipulative definition. On this view, a history of consciousness could only be a postmodern history of "consciousness," that is, a history not of some real thing but of a technical term.[17]

Contrary to the phenomenology of religion's claims of the universality and ahistorical nature of consciousness, "[t]he temporality of the subject, however, subverts the identity, propriety, presence, and property of selfhood. This subversion effectively dispossesses the subject."[18] Consciousness dies of its own history.

## "Man" and Geist

A point of clarification, for it is clear that "Man" and *Geist* are not identical, *in strictu sensu*, concepts. Their identity is complex; their relation is best described in the manner in which Derrida described the relation between Heidegger's *Dasein* and man: "We can see then that *Dasein*, though *not* man, is *nothing other* than man."[19] While "Man" is not *Geist*, it is nothing other than *Geist*.

The emergence into preeminence of this figure signals the reemergence of Hegel which was so apparently lost for *classical* phenomenology of religion (e.g., van der Leeuw) when the concept of "*Entwicklung*" was disregarded. For the figure "Man," the transcendental subject that unites classical phenomenology of religion's history, is none other than a reappearance of the founding figure of Spirit. Certainly Spirit is a very different figure than that of "Man," the "Man" of humanistic, philosophical anthropology. But the ability to see this difference is a product of *our* reading of the two, here at the beginning of the twenty-first century, after several decades of structuralism and poststructuralism.[20]

More importantly, the distance between the two figures is lessened by two factors. First, that Hegelianism comes to the phenomenology of religion via the neo-Hegelianism of Dilthey. What is most notable about Dilthey's appropriation of the figure Spirit is precisely the degree to which it is anthropologized. Karl Löwith tells us that, in Dilthey, "Hegel's world, dominated by spirit, becomes 'sociohistorical reality,' in itself neither rational nor irrational, but in an indefinite way, 'significant,'"[21] or, possess "meaning." The transmutation of World into "sociohistorical reality," signals the shift from a transcendent philosophy of the Absolute to an anthropological philosophy of history wherein the figure "Man" holds the place of the figure Spirit.

Secondly, as we have seen, the figure "Man" is explicitly articulated in religio-metaphysical terms. That is, in Otto, Wach, van der Leeuw, and Eliade, terms such as *consciousness, human nature, the spiritual unity of man, structure of consciousness* are all derived from the ontotheological tradition and fully retain their metaphysical content and function. "Man" has the equivalent function in the discourse of the phenomenology of religion that Spirit had in the inherited Hegelian discourse. So "Man" operates as a figure in the "diminished," if you will, metaphysical discourse of the phenomenology of religion by means of a double operation: the empirical reduction of Spirit and the metaphysical expansion of "man" into "Man."

## The Sickness unto Death of "Man"

"The individual's elaborate strategies of self-assertion are actually various efforts to secure self-presence by excluding the dangerous other."[22] As we have seen, this is true at the level of the discourse of the phenomenology of religion; the texts assert the supremacy of Christian Europe at the explicit expense of non-Christian non-Europeans. The Other is negated by and in the definition of the self. Hegel, Tiele, and Otto are particularly vicious about this, but the others are not much better. Van der Leeuw's imaginary of Islam is a case in point of a twentieth-century phenomenologist of religion who explicitly rejects the idea of "development," but yet finds a way to negate the Other in an act of the assertion of supremacy of the self.

Taken together, these are the specific "sicknesses" of "Man." While the discursive structures of the phenomenology of religion generate one set of pathologies, "Man," when put in the context of the colonial condition, carries with him a certain "sickness."[23] The inventory of these terminal illnesses, including the death scene, of "Man" shall conclude this study.

So, Derrida tells us: "To the extent that it describes the structures of human-reality, phenomenological ontology is a philosophical anthropology. Whatever the breaks marked by this Hegelian-Husserlian-Heideggerian anthropology as concerns the classical anthropologies, there is an uninterrupted metaphysical familiarity with that which, so naturally, links the 'we' of the philosopher to 'we men,' to the we in the horizon of humanity."[24] The problem here lies in a lack of specificity with regard to this "we men": "[T]he history of the concept man is never examined. Everything occurs as if the sign 'man' had no origin, no historical, cultural, or linguistic limit."[25]

In their obsession with a transcendental form of consciousness, "Spirit," "a priori categories," "consciousness" (in the singular, therefore as a totalizing category), "man as he exists now retroactively prolonged," as van der Leeuw said, left the phenomenologists at best insensitive, at worst blind, to the historicity of their own categories: "Lack of historical sense is the family failing of all philosophers; many, without being aware of it, even take the most recent manifestation of man, such as has arisen under the impress of certain religious, even certain political events, as the fixed form from which one has to start out. They will not learn that man has become . . ."[26]

The consequence of this critique of the metaphysics of subjectivity and the rejection of "Man" entails a shift in the paradigm for studying religion. A postmodern, poststructuralist, and posthumanist reformulation of the science of religion, of which this work is something of a prolegomena (only), entails the rejection of some of the most well established categories of the human sciences. The twentieth-century American anthropologist, Clifford Geertz, drew the obvious conclusion for the science of man/"Man" and the science of experience (anthropology and/or phenomenology) from Marx's and Nietzsche's analyses:

> [T]he image of a constant human nature independent of time, place, and circumstance, of studies and professions, transient fashions and temporary opinions, may be an illusion, that what man is may be so entangled with where he is, who he is, and what he believes that it is inseparable from them... that men unmodified by the customs of particular places do not in fact exist, have never existed, and most important, could not in the very nature of the case exist.[27]

Just as there is no lightning apart from the flash, there is no "Man" apart from his total contextually divergent components. Geertz also suggests that the category "mind" is not an obvious given either: "In fact, with some exceptions, the term 'mind' has not functioned as a scientific concept at all but as a rhetorical device.... More exactly, it has acted to communicate—and sometimes to exploit—a fear rather than to define a process, a fear of subjectivism on the one hand and mechanism on the other."[28] The fear that the self will lose its *esse*, its unique being, and therefore its freedom, is a motivating factor in the polemics and apologetics of the discourse of the phenomenology of religion. It is this fear, at least in part, that is the source of the pathologies of categories such as "subject," "consciousness," "Spirit," and "Man." Man's terminal illness turned out to be contagious. "Man" has "infected" academia directly and the colonized peoples of the world indirectly (how indirectly I honestly could not say; perhaps others can) in multiple ways. These sicknesses include: collecting the Other and "the transcendental pretense."

## The Sicknesses of "Man"

### Collecting the Other

"Man," as *Geist*, finds "self-knowledge in absolute otherness." How has this principle translated into a disciplinary practice? Perhaps in many ways but one concrete way is in the practice of collections.

Eliade's "validation" of primitive art, and therefore of the primitive as such, is arguably not as benign as it appears or as he intended it. James Clifford has shown how "modernist primitivism, with its claims to deeper humanist sympathies and a wider aesthetic sense, goes hand-in-hand with a developed market in tribal art and with definitions of artistic and cultural authenticity that are now widely contested."[29] Clifford offers us an ethnographic tour of the Museum of Modern Art's 1984 "Primitivism in Twentieth-Century Art: Affinity of the Tribal and the Modern." The express intent of the exhibition is very much in line with Eliade's remarks about the "creative contact" between early modern art and African and Oceanic art. What the exhibition does not do, Clifford says, is situate the tribal objects on display within the wider contexts of either their production or collection: "Cultural background is not essential to correct aesthetic appreciation and analysis: good art, the masterpiece, is universally recognizable. The pioneer modernists themselves knew little or nothing of these objects' ethnographic meaning. What was good enough for Picasso was good enough for the Museum of Modern Art."[30] This decontextualization via aestheticization is not merely a problem of correct interpretation of the meaning of the tribal objects in question, nor is it simply a matter of methodological neatness. What it does is elide "a more disquieting quality of modernism: its taste for appropriating or redeeming otherness, for constituting non-Western arts in its own image, for discovering universal, ahistorical 'human' capacities. The search for similarities requires justification."[31] In other words, "the scope and underlying logic of the 'discovery' of tribal art reproduces hegemonic Western assumptions rooted in the colonial and neocolonial epoch."[32] *Mutatis mutandis*, it would be fair to conclude that Eliade's valorization of the surrealist recovery of the primitive participates in a system defined by Edward Said (and others) as "colonial discourse." In support of this claim we must look at Eliade's own view of the study of non-Western cultures by Westerners, as well as his use of such terms as *primitive* and *archaic*.

Eliade displays an ambivalence about the study of non-European cultures. He is very self-conscious about the problem of intercultural translation and very critical of the tendency toward cultural imperialism demonstrated by the West toward the non-West. He says of anthropologists: "It is to be expected that some time in the future the political and cultural representatives of the new states of Africa or Oceania, that is, the descendants of what we still call 'primitives,' will strongly object to the anthropological expeditions and the other varieties of field work. They will rightly point out that their peoples have too long been the 'objects' of such investigations, with rather disappointing results."[33] In another place where he reiterates this same argument, he says such representatives will "regard many social scientists as camouflaged apologists of Western Culture." Why? "Because these scientists insist so persistently on the sociopolitical origin and character of the 'primitive' messianic movements, they may be suspected of a Western superiority complex, namely, the conviction that such religious movements cannot rise to the same level of 'freedom from sociopolitical conjuncture' as, for instance, a Gioachino da Fiore or St. Francis."[34]

What is "colonialist" about the social sciences is not that they extract cultural materials from foreign societies, but that they explain these extracted materials on reductive, nonspiritual, and nonreligious principles. It is to this that Eliade objects. As for the extraction of cultural materials, he is absolutely unambiguous in his avocation of this: "How to assimilate *culturally* the spiritual universes that Africa, Oceania, Southeast Asia open to us?"[35] It is, after all, Eliade's own claim that the social sciences compartmentalize religious and cultural data, and that the History of Religion demands a *"total hermeneutics*, being called to decipher and explicate *every kind* of encounter of man with the sacred, *from prehistory to our day.*"[36] Eliade's hermeneutics, then, is a totalizing discourse, that is, a discourse that subsumes all otherness into itself—the Family of *Homo Religiousus*, of man as essentially religious.

That Eliade's approach to non-Western cultures is aggressively assimilating in the name of the ethnocentric project of the modern, Western subject is further evidenced by his use of terms such as *primitive* and *archaic*. Again, prima facie, he seems to evince a critical self-consciousness on this issue. Thus, he will say of the term *primitive*, that it is "ambiguous and inconsistent"[37] and he often (though not always) puts it in scare quotes. However, his own descriptive, taxonomic practice belies this appearance of sensitivity.[38] In a number of places, he recites a concatenation of "peoples" such as "archaic and Asian," or "African and primitive," or "African, Oceanic, and archaic," and so forth. Our question is this: In what universe do these peoples belong together? In what universe do Africans—of all kinds, apparently—and Native North Americans, the peoples of Oceania—all of them—and the Aborigines of Australia belong together? Only in the universe of an essentialist consciousness, only in the universe of a universalist subjectivity that can assume as we saw that van der Leeuw does, that *"homo sum, humani nil a me alienum puto*: this is no key to the deepest comprehension of the remotest experience, but is nevertheless the triumphant assertion that the *essentially human always remains the essentially human, and is, as such, comprehensible,"* are these various cultures moments in a history of the same.[39] Eliade could say as easily as did Hegel: "Thus, what in religion was *content* or a form for presenting an *other,* is here the *Self's* own *act....* Our *own* act here has been simply to *gather together* the separate moments, each of which in principle exhibits the life of *Geist* in its entirety."[40] In short, Eliade's move to inclusiveness is bought by the elision of the difference of the other. These groups, completely distinct from each other and complexly plural in themselves, are all "the same" *only* vis-à-vis European "Man." *What they are is non-Europe* (and all peoples of color); they are images of the Other of Europe. Their sameness is nonexistent other than as a construct of the universalist ambitions of the modern European subject.

James Snead agrees with and extends Clifford's argument in a way that sheds much light on Eliade's invention of "archaic man" and valorization of the primitive. Referring to African literature, a type of indigenous-cum-primitive art, Snead notes that "few western readers seem unwilling to talk about its 'universality.' "[41] Eliade, again, arguing that the sacred is a structure of consciousness, ergo, is a universal feature of "Man," can certainly be counted among these readers. However, "universalism" means "even though the word 'universality' seems often merely to function as a code-word meaning 'comprehensibility for the European reader.' "[42]

Attributing "universality" to African writers—or expecting to find it in them—can merely be a question of (as in the case of political imperialism) a given observer projecting onto a neutral space a wish for power. That power, in turn, may be defined as *"the power to comprehend* and systematize within a European scheme, a wide and often perplexing range of non-European cultures and writings."[43] This power to comprehend, even to comprehend the innermost subjectivity, the place of the origin of religious experience, of the sacred or holy itself, is clearly something the phenomenology of religion claims for itself and claims in no uncertain terms. Its notion of universality allows it to enter into "foreign" (Wach) subjectivity. To clarify the nature of this act as an act of power, we may ask: When, in the discourse of the phenomenology of religion, does the "foreign" comprehend the "us"? Answer: never. This act is utterly unilateral—just as is the extractive, collecting economy of colonialism.

It is at this point where the Europeanness of phenomenology emerges: "When confronted with non-western cultures, European 'narcissism,' at first a mere 'repugnance' towards other peoples, develops into a myth of the past."[44]

On the logic of Eurocentric inclusion of the other, Europe,

> by a peculiar kind of magnanimity, needed to include the primitive within its imperial hoard. For eventually, the presumably flattering model of linear improvement tends to undermine itself. European artists and scholars began to suggest that if the non-western aesthetic is a potential, or primitive, or aboriginal manifestation of that which western man has brought to maturity, then it follows that potency, primacy, and originality themselves represent radically regenerative attributes that the mature post-Enlightenment west has already lost.[45]

This is, as is well known, Eliade's project of valorizing the primitive, at least in part, to regain the loss of the sacred in the modern, secular West. Eliade's "collection" (see *Patterns*) of the non-European is a project, or tied to a project, or possess the potentiality for the project of regeneration and recovery: "the New Humanism," that is, making *Religionswissenschaft* both the Queen of the Sciences, and a vehicle for cultural change. Eliade is a politician: he reaches out for power.

This pseudo-universality underlies the narcissistic European identity-formation:

> The European notion of "universality" often takes on the aspect of collection: it seems a drive to accumulate as many texts, artifacts, nations, peoples, as possible, all under one roof, one rubric, or one ruler.... [T]he European notion of "universality" is a mammoth power play... [driven by the] twin imperatives "exclude and accumulate" seem fitting under a kind of Hegelian linearism that wants to incorporate within one Spirit or mind ever greater areas of knowledge and material. "Realm" becomes "nation" becomes "empire" becomes "western" or "European" civilization, but stays *white*. Accumulation, then, is an almost metaphorical movement where things of differing values are lumped together under a single image or signifier for purposes of potential exchange.... Efforts both literary and political to include non-whites in this scheme have centered around white perspectives and maintained the dominance of the white narrative and white nations.[46]

While the hope of phenomenology was to render "the things themselves" "clear and transparent," from the analysis laid out in this study and others, it is clear that it is, in reality, precisely the transformative system of classification and analysis of which Barthes spoke at the beginning of the last chapter. It is a metaphysical "grid" through which the Others of Europe are screened, whereby some elements are valorized and appropriated, some are negated and ranked as lower, and some are outright demeaned and seen as worthless "dogs" vis-à-vis white, European "Man." In its claim to render "the things themselves" "clear and transparent," phenomenology is actually more susceptible to Euro-narcissism in that it cannot see its rather elaborate metaphysical filter *as* a filter. By dehistoricizing, it loses the ability to locate itself in history. By its emphasis on the abstract and universality, it loses the ability to see the specificity of its transformative operation, to wit, the way in which it actively constructs, rather than passively "perceives" its object.

*The Transcendental Pretense*

In the eighteenth century, vis-à-vis the feudal or semi-feudal states of Europe, "Man" appears on the scene as a heroic figure. However, vis-à-vis "the rest of the world," the whole idea has been what Robert Solomon describes as: "The transcendental pretense is the unwarranted assumption that there is universality and necessity in the fundamental modes of human experience."[47] As others cited in previous chapters have argued, the key to this notion was the convergence of all perspectives into one perspective, namely, one's own: "In its application the transcendental pretense becomes the a priori assertion that the structures of one's own mind, culture, and personality are in some sense necessary and universal for all humankind":[48] "Ultimately," Eliade argued, following Wach, van der Leeuw, following Otto, Dilthey, and Schleiermacher, "the historian of religion is forced by his hermeneutical endeavor to 'relive' a multitude of existential situations and to unravel a number of presystematic ontologies."[49] "Universality" as intelligibility to the European reader: universality as reducible to subjectivity, to *my* subjectivity, there being no such thing as "subjectivity as such." As I can relive, therefore the re: lives, lives, however, strictly within the confines of the discursive structure with both "founds" and is founded by "Man." In reliving the sacred, "Man's" transcendental pretense is extended even farther than Descartes and secularists imagined, just as Eliade et al. would want it: "The self is not just another entity in the world, but in an important sense it creates the world, and the reflecting self does not just know itself, but in knowing itself knows all selves, and the structure of any and every possible self."[50] "Man" is the center and the heuristic key to *all* things, past and present. This is the new world order of the subject of Modernity. Religious Study's use of the category "Man" makes it part of this order, including its neo- and postcolonial elements.

As such, the transcendental pretense denies variability and so becomes "an aggressive and sometimes arrogant effort to prove that there are no such (valid) possible alternatives."[51] When the religio-metaphysical concept of the self is put into the context of the extractive economies of European colonialism, it becomes clear that "[t]he transcendental pretense is no innocent philosophical thesis, but a political weapon of enormous power. Even as it signaled a radical egalitarianism, and suggested a long-awaited global sensitivity, it also justified unrestricted tolerance for paternalism and self-righteousness— 'the white philosopher's burden.' "[52]

We may understand the connection between the End of Man, the pathology of collecting, and the transcendental pretense by looking at Roland Barthes's famous analysis of the photographic exhibit "The Great Family of Man," held in Paris in the 1950s.[53] Here, the many facets of "man" are "moralized and sentimentalized"—the fear and the longing of which Geertz spoke—"which serves as an alibi to a large part of our humanism." According to Barthes:

> This myth functions in two stages: First the difference between human morphologies is asserted, exoticism is insistently stressed, the infinite variations of the species.... Then, from this pluralism, a type of unity is magically produced: man is born, works, laughs and dies everywhere in the same way; and if there still remains in these actions some ethnic peculiarity, at least one hints that there is underlying each one an identical "nature," that their diversity is only formal and does not belie the existence of a common mould.[54]

Ethnic peculiarity, that "context" of which, again, Geertz spoke, is the difference between man and man, is difference, but, ultimately difference is nothing: in the Family of Man, difference is nothing ("there is no difference").

There is a specific mechanism, if you will, that produces magically this unity and singularity out of a diversity and plurality: "This myth of the human 'condition' rests on a very old mystification, which always consists in placing Nature at the bottom of History. Any classic humanism postulates that in scratching the history of men a little, the relativity of their institutions or the superficial diversity of their skin . . . one very quickly reaches the solid rock of a universal human nature."[55] "Man's" nature and the "nature" conjoin, if by "nature" we mean, again, the universal of which Snead spoke. The Given as opposed to the made, is the distinction at work here: what is given in man is that man makes his world out of nature—and not in history.

However, this universality is a mistake: "Examples? Here they are: those of our Exhibition. Birth, death? Yes, these are facts of nature, universal facts. But if one removes History from them, there is nothing more to be said about them; any comment about them becomes *purely tautological.*"[56] This is a point that cannot be emphasized too strongly: our talk of "religion," of *homo religiosus*, of "world religions," all of it is tautological. "Man is religious by nature" is a tautology, not an analytical statement. "Man has a nature" is an abuse of grammar: man does not "have" what he is; he is what he is. Conceived as an a priori category or structure of consciousness, the statement: "Man is religious by nature" is also tautological in that a prior/structure of consciousness are the same things as "human nature" (at least conceptually if not rhetorically). We have again a case of metalipsis/metonymy: the lightning and the flash; the agent and the effect.

The problem then: "So that I rather fear that the final justification of all this Adamism is to give the immobility of the world the alibi of a 'wisdom' and a 'lyricism' which only make the gestures of man look eternal the better to defuse them."[57] The alleged *consensus gentium* weighs in: man has a nature. The aestheticization of man's achievements engenders the longing for a "human spirit," a universal creative drive in all of us, more so in the "geniuses" from all cultures, for all cultures have geniuses, and all genius is the same: the human spirit.

Uniting all of the threads of this critique is the figure, "Man." He is universal; the subject then can empathize with all subjects and so "understand" his collection of objects from the world of the Other, including sacred objects. However, he is also European and imperialistic. He comes from the North and West and has been a ready assistant in the imperative of "exclude and collect" for the sake of imperial domination so that he can achieve, again, self-recognition in absolute otherness. This emphasis on the project of the self is clearly, almost explicitly narcissistic as is the need for absolutizing the otherness of the Other. When the other is *absolutely* other, the self is left alone to gaze upon its own reflected image. Beautiful as that image can, in fact be, it is monstrous in its effects when we think of all the many, many horrors endemic to the conquering—which is, after all, the core reality of "colonizing," a sanitary term by contrast—these others. "Man" has blood on his hands. Insofar as the phenomenology of religion, which is clearly a kind of Euro-narcissistic method of collecting, has depended upon "Man" for its work, it has been complicit, however latently, in this domination via violent destruction of the colonized world. I emphasize the fact that this complicity is latent. At least for the twentieth-century phenomenologists, it is not an explicit feature of their program. It *is* explicit in nineteenth-century and early-twentieth-century phenomenology: Hegel, Tiele, Chantepie, and Otto are *not* innocent. They are, each in his own, semiotic way, ruthless. Later phenomenologists, for the reasons just given, however, in their desire to validate religion and defend "understanding" against "explanation," paid the price of taking on the basic structures of phenomenology as a *Geisteswissenschaft*, uncritically. Thus, they stumble into complicity with "Man" and *Geist, whom they never deny*. They are, as we have seen, quite aggressive in their appropriation of them both. As such, they are stricken with the sickness endemic to "Man." Or, perhaps more emphatically, the sickness that *is* "Man."

## Incipit: Post-"Man"

"Postcolonialism, then, derives from the anti-humanism of poststructuralism and the 'new humanities' a view of Western power as a symptom of Western epistemology and pedagogy . . . the postcolonial critique of colonial modernity is mapped out principally as an intervention into the realm of Western knowledge-production"[58]—including that "Western knowledge-production," Religious Studies. If the intervention is made, that is. If we do not simply patch "Man" up, fix his/its wounds, and return him to the battlefront once again as man. Can we think "religion" without "Man"? Without man? Without any of his proxies, Spirit, consciousness, subjectivity? Can we "think a way out of the epistemological violence of the colonial encounter?"[59] To do so, must we not first *unthink* "Man"? And must we not first unthink this couplet, "Man/Religion"? This study has attempted to take a small step in the direction of the unthinking of "Man/Religion." To reformulate positively, I would argue that Nietzschean genealogy and poststructuralism represent, among other voices, methodological paradigms which *might* (the subjunctive again) enable—*if not co-opted to the opposite project*—Religious Studies/the study of religion, to interrogate critically its representational practices and to abandon "the old theological and imperialistic impulses toward totalization, unification, and integration."[60] Religious Studies can accomplish this task, in part, at the level of theory and interpretation, by critically reinterpreting the activity of interpretation itself and the modes of representation-cum-identity-formation it has used in the past. We would, I believe, take a huge step in this direction by heeding Derrida's call for the Nietzschean *affirmation* of interpretation, a style of interpretation "which is no longer turned toward the origin," which affirms the play of the signifier without grounding it in the name of man, and which "does *not* seek ... the inspiration of 'a new humanism.' "[61]

# Notes

## Chapter 1. A Genealogy of the Phenomenology of Religion

1. Joachim Wach, *Introduction to the History of Religions*, ed. Joseph Kitagawa, trans. Gregory Alles and Karl Lucker (New York: Macmillan Publishing Co., 1988), 9. Cf. Charles R. Bambach, *Heidegger, Dilthey, and the Crisis of Historicism* (Ithaca and London: Cornell University Press, 1995), 81 on "the metaphysical tradition of speculative *Geschichtsphilosophie* common in the early nineteenth century" and the "radical split between *Natur* and *Geist*," later *Kultur* and *Natur*, upon which it was predicated.

2. Hubert Seiwert, "What Constitutes the Identity of a Religion?" in *Identity Issues and World Religions* (Netley, Australia: Wakefield Press, 1986), 3 and 4.

3. Ibid., 2.

4. When "Religious Studies" is put in capitals in this manner this is to indicate a *specific* institutional and academic reality, not a *general* phenomenon, "the study of religion." "Religious Studies" refers to that independent academic and intellectual enterprise embodied in academic departments at colleges and universities and in professional societies such as the International Association for the History of Religions or the American Academy of Religion.

5. I take the term *classical phenomenology of religion* from Jacques Waardenburg, *Classical Approaches to the Study of Religion* (The Hague: Mouton de Grouter, 1973), 51. Jeppe Sinding Jensen, in his masterful work, *The Study of Religion in a New Key: Theoretical and Philosophical Soundings in the Comparative and General Study of Religion* (Aarhus: Aarhus University Press, 2003) also uses the term (see pp. 28–34). As shall be discussed later, its main representatives include W. B. Kristensen, Gerardus van der Leeuw, and Mircea Eliade. Rudolph Otto and Joachim Wach are closely associated with, and according to some scholars, would be part of this movement. I treat the latter as important transmitters, so to speak, of the philosophemes and conceptual structures of the phenomenology of religion. Whether they are or are not, *in strictu sensu*, phenomenologists is, as such, not of any particular concern. They are both self-consciously part of this tradition and have been read into by the subsequent traditional narrative of the history of the study of religion. Ergo, they are part of my data and will be treated later in this study.

6. As shall be explained, throughout this study the term *Man* is put in quotes and capitalized because it is the argument of this work that it is *a historically specific, theoretical concept*, not simply a name for the human species.

7. Willard G. Oxtoby, "The Idea of the Holy," in *Encyclopedia of Religion*, ed. M. Eliade (New York: Macmillan), 436.

8. Walter Capps, *Religious Studies: the Making of a Discipline* (Minneapolis: Fortress Press, 1995), 117.

9. Ibid., 109.

10. Hans Penner, *Impasse and Resolution: A Critique of the Study of Religion* (New York: Peter Lang, 1989), 41. Cf. Clive Erricker who argues that a "philosophical influence upon which van der Leeuw drew was Edmund Husserl... his work provided valuable methodological starting-points for the phenomenological study of religion..." Clive Erricker, "Phenomenological Approaches" in *Approaches to the Study of Religion*, ed. Peter Connolly (London: Cassell, 1999), 77. It is important to note that some of the authors cited in support of the Husserlian origin go on in their texts to disclaim it. That does not change the fact that they concur with my thesis that there is a branch of the *Rezeptionsgeschichte* that places Husserl at its origin.

11. Penner, *Impasse and Resolution*, 41–42 citing Douglas Allen, "The Phenomenology of Religion," in *Encyclopedia of Religion*, ed. M. Eliade (New York: Macmillan, 1987). Elsewhere Allen gives a list of the generic concepts common to all he considers phenomenologists of religion and these are all Husserlian, not Hegelian concepts (see Erricker below). Douglas Allen, "Phenomenology of Religion," in *The Routledge Companion to the Study of Religion*, ed. John Hinnells (New York: Routledge, 2005), 196–99. Another more recent scholar also sees Husserl as influencing the phenomenology of religion, who wishes "to present a metatheoretical discussion, locating religious studies within the landscape I have outlined here, by showing how its predominant paradigm, the phenomenology of religion, assumes a Husserlian philosophy of consciousness." He continues in a way that foreshadows the conclusion of this work (and my next project): "this [philosophy of consciousness] can be criticized from the perspective of the philosophy of the sign." Gavin Flood, *Beyond Phenomenology: Rethinking the Study of Religion* (London: Cassell, 1999), 11. In the former point, he includes all of religious studies within the paradigm of a Husserlian theory of consciousness. I think, *mutatis mutandis*, this is likely correct but that we must *supplement* this with the Hegelian motifs outlined by Erricker below. See Murphy, *Representing Religion: Essays in History, Theory, and Crisis* (London: Equinox Press), 26–31 for a critique of the idea of consciousness in Religious Studies.

12. Clive Erricker, "Phenomenological Approaches," 76–77. ke Hultkrantz rightly points out that the use of the term *phenomenology*: "goes back to the philosophy of the outgoing 18th century and, for a long time, signified different doctrines concerning the essence of reality which lies behind the manifoldness of empirical existence. A classic work in this tradition is Hegel's philosophic dialectic treatise *Phänomenologie des Geistes* (1806)." ke

Hultkrantz, "The Phenomenology of Religion: Aims and Methods," *Temenos* 6 (1970): 69. Cf. Thomas Ryba, *The Essence of Phenomenology and Its Meaning for the Scientific Study of Religion* (New York: Peter Lang, 1991), 231: "The philosophical origins of phenomenology of religion are indubitable..." Cf. Tim Murphy, *Representing Religion: Essays in History, Theory, and Crisis* (London: Equinox, 2006), ch. 3, "The Concept of 'Essence-and-Manifestation' in the History of the Study of Religion" (first published in 1994). In the text, the term *essence-and-manifestation* is used in the German, i.e., *Wesen und Erscheinung*. Along with *Geist*, these are the exact themes I identified there as the Hegelian philosophemes (see chapter 2) that were basic to the structure of phenomenological discourse.

13. Erricker, "Phenomenological Approaches," 77. I will make this same argument in the chapter on van der Leeuw below.

14. Olof Pettersson, *Interpreting Religious Phenomena: Studies with Reference to the Phenomenology of Religion* (English edition: New Jersey: Humanities Press, 1981), 9. Scholars do not seem to agree when *The Phenomenology of Spirit* was published. I have always cited their dates with no attempt to correct them or make them uniform. The exact date of publication has no bearing on the argument of this study.

15. Ibid., 11.

16. Ibid., 17.

17. Walter Capps, *Religious Studies: The Making of a Discipline*, 109.

18. Ibid.,124.

19. This history of Hegelianism has been rather uncritically accepted as academic orthodoxy in the United States. By and large, most academics are unfamiliar with the history of the right wing of Hegelianism and this creates a very distorted view of its influence. In the Marxists or leftist history, it would appear that materialism had won the day, while in truth it was a highly marginalized point of view and few academics knew much, if anything, about Marx (yet were largely disdainful of him and simply assumed that he was wrong; they were of the middle class, by and large, after all). It is this right wing Hegelianism, obviously more conservative than the left wing, which influenced the history of the study of religion in that, as is discussed below, it became academic orthodoxy in the nineteenth century.

20. The former has been cited as influencing the phenomenology of religion, and indeed it did, but only as it had been thoroughly filtered by the latter work/reading. To put the point both literally and metaphorically: Eliade gives no evidence of ever having read Kojeve.

21. See below for the story of this establishment and appropriation of Hegel. As for the Marxist reading(s) of the narrative of the appropriation of Hegel, Karl Löwith explains this situation: "The German intelligentsia became aware of so-called Marxism [and therefore of the Hegelian Left] only through the political propaganda of National Socialism and its polemic staging." Karl Löwith, *From Hegel to Nietzsche: The Revolution in Nineteenth-Century Thought*, trans. D. Green (New York: Anchor Books, 1967), 134. In other words, again, it was Right Hegelianism which is totally disassociated from socialism, which

was academic orthodoxy, not Left Hegelianism. Most German scholars, being either Liberal nationalists or aristocratic Conservatives (Whigs and Tories in the English context) looked at Marxism with both suspicion and disdain. The materialism and embrace of Darwin was seen as a serious philosophical mistake (and threat, as is evident from Otto's work) and their leftist politics seemed both wrong and dangerous. Again, it is important for the understanding of the transmission of Hegel in this context not to assume the American narrative of Hegel-Feuerbach-Marx-Engels, etc. It is not that such a succession does not exist, but it is not the way Hegel was transmitted in the German academy of the nineteenth century.

22. Jacques Derrida, *Of Grammatology*, trans. Gayatri Spivak (Baltimore: Johns Hopkins University Press, 1974), 24.

23. Mircea Eliade, "Methodological Remarks on the Study of Religious Symbolism," in *The History of Religions: Essays in Methodology*, ed. M. Eliade and J. Kitagawa (Chicago: University of Chicago Press, 1959), 94.

24. Joachim Wach, *Types of Religious Experience Christian and Non-Christian* (Chicago: University of Chicago Press, 1951), 34. Cf. farther down where he says: "The phenomenology of the religious act show a great variety of ways of acting which we shall, for our purposes, arrange typologically" (41)—or synchronically.

25. Chantepie de la Saussye, *Manual of the Science of Religion* (London: Longmans, Green and Company, 1891), 4. See also 50–51, on the division of the religions: "On this subject again it is Hegel who has answered the question in a way which still influences scholars ... this division [of Hegel's] gives the analysis of the concept, and brings to light the nature of religion in its unity and in its many-sidedness [*des Begriffs giebt, das Wesen der Religion in ihrer Einheit und in ihrer Vielseitigkiet zur Anschauung bringt*]. At the same time the parts of this division form steps in the progress of development [*Entwickelungsgang*]; religion runs through this process from the lowest to the highest, for which the ages of man form a much used analogy."

26. See Derrida, *Margins of Philosophy*, trans. Alan Bass (Chicago: University of Chicago Press, 1982), 114ff, for his understanding of the history of metaphysics. See also the discussion of ontotheology in chapter 2.

27. Mark Taylor, "Introduction," in *Deconstruction in Context*, ed. Mark Taylor (Chicago: University of Chicago Press, 1986), 3; emphasis added. See that work for a discussion of the various readings of Hegel as well.

28. On the issue of history in Husserl's phenomenology see David Carr, *Phenomenology and the Problem of History: A Study of Husserl's Transcendental Phenomenology* (Evanston: Northwestern University Press, 1974).

29. Herbert Schnädelbach, *Philosophy in Germany 1831–1933*, trans. Eric Matthews (Cambridge: Cambridge University Press, 1984), 51. On the importance of *"des objectiv Geistigen"* in the study of religion, see J. Wach, *Introduction to the History of Religions*, (originally published 1924), 143ff. Wach also cites Droysen, Dilthey, and Rickert as of special significance in this respect.

30. See Schnädelbach, *Philosophy in Germany*, 81–85.

31. Ibid., 42ff.
32. Ibid., 45; emphasis added.
33. Ibid., 43.
34. Fredrick Gregory, *Nature Lost? Natural Science and the German Theological Traditions of the Nineteenth Century* (Cambridge: Harvard University Press, 1992), 43–44. Claude Welch completely concurs with this assessment, noting: "By the turn of the century the evolutionary principle was broadly accepted, even hailed, among Protestant liberal and moderate thinkers. . . . The general idea of evolution was also widely adopted as the key to the history of mankind and religion, both in the transition from primitive to higher forms of religion and the growth of the Judeo-Christian tradition." Claude Welch, *Protestant Thought in the Nineteenth Century* (New Haven: Yale University Press, Vol. I. 1972 and Vol. II, 1985), Vol. II, 209.
35. Wach, *Introduction to the History of Religions*, 150.
36. G. W. F. Hegel, *The Philosophy of History*, trans. J. Sibree (New York: Dover Publications, 1956), 17.
37. Rudolph Otto, *Naturalism and Religion*, trans. J. Arthur Thomson and Margaret R. Thomson (New York: G. P. Putnam's Sons, 1907), 295. Otto's somewhat convoluted argument is that spirit is independent of matter, has self-consciousness and therefore freedom, and cannot be negated by a concept or doctrine, i.e., materialism, which spirit itself has created. What is common to both statements is the idea that spirit is immaterial and that it is therefore free. Bondage to the "natural" is a common teleological principle in this tradition: spirit gradually frees itself from its natural consciousness to self-conscious, meaning spirit recognizes spirit as spirit. Otto shares this teleological scheme, as does C. P. Tiele, with Hegel.
38. Cf. Karl Löwith, *From Hegel to Nietzsche*, 61: "For Hegel, the spirit as substance and subject of history was the absolute and basic concept of his theory of being. Thus natural philosophy is just as much a spiritual discipline as are the philosophies of the state, art, religion, and history." Cf. also, Stanley Rosen, *G. W. F. Hegel: An Introduction to the Science of Wisdom* (New Haven: Yale University Press, 1974), 14: "This identity [of the divine and the human] is one of life in the deepest and most comprehensive sense: of Absolute Spirit as the activity which manifests itself in every finite mode of creation, without thereby limiting itself to any single mode or form." As noted above, this entails the notion that history, or historical moments, express Spirit, more or less partially, but always a manifestation (*Ersheinung*) of an essence (*Wesen*—also "being"); the "essence of essences," so to speak, is *Geist*. Eliade also describes some hierophanies, or manifestations, as more of less complete manifestations of "the sacred," which are understood *pace* Kant as an a priori structure of consciousness. See the chapter on Eliade for a full discussion of this point.
39. Hegel, *The Phenomenology of Spirit*, trans. A. V. Miller (Oxford: Oxford University Press, 1977), paragraph #26.
40. Charles Bambach, *Heidegger, Dilthey, and the Crisis of Historicism*, 21.

41. Ibid., 71. Windelband's dates are 1848 to 1915. He is a contemporary of Tiele and Chantepie de la Saussaye.

42. Ibid., 70. See Jane Samson, *Race and Empire* (London: Pearson Longman, 2005), 44–45 on the connection between German Humanism (as she calls it), colonialism, and academics: "The role of German theorists was crucial to [the] growing identification of culture with race.... German humanism had been extremely powerful in the early nineteenth century, giving rise to the liberal nationalism that (among other things) had enabled German unification. This humanism was most often expressed through literature, history-writing, and a study of the classics: the traditional humanities" or, *Geisteswissenschaften*. Given the sheer dominance of the names Kant and Hegel, we should hasten to add philosophy to the list of humanities; given the impact of Schleiermacher (even Feuerbach) one could, with some justice, add theology as well. The *Geisteswissenschaften* had a vast influence in the world of academics. As will be discussed in chapter 2, it was a world also deeply touched by colonialism.

43. Bambach, *Heidegger, Dilthey, and the Crisis of Historicism*, 128 n2, citing Dilthey.

44. Wilhelm Dilthey, *Selected Writings*, ed. H. P. Rickman (Cambridge: Cambridge University Press, 1976), 161, also cited in Bambach, 142, italics Dilthey's. See chapter 5 below for a full analysis of Dilthey's "science of experience" and its influence on the phenomenology of religion.

45. Hans-Georg Gadamer, *Truth and Method*, trans. Joel Weinsheimer and Donald G. Marshall (New York: Crossroad, Second, revised edition, 1990), 229.

46. Bambach, *Heidegger, Dilthey, and the Crisis of Historicism*, 136–37.

47. Ibid., 70 n22 on the translation and meaning of the term, "Geisteswissenschaften." He also notes (71) that "Hegel's *Enzyklopaedie der Wissenschaft* classified the sciences into a philosophy of nature and a philosophy of spirit (*Naturphilosophie, Philosophie des Geistes*)." Like Windelband, Hegel sees this both as a metaphysic and as an organizing principle of knowledge. As we will see throughout this study, this distinction is basic to the phenomenology of religion. Per our discussion above about the reception of Hegel, it is noteworthy that Windelband, a mainstream academic, even major institutional figure in creating a coherent structure for the general curriculum of "the University," draws upon the *Enzyklopaedie* and not the *Phänomenologie*.

48. Ibid.,128 n2.

49. J. Samuel Preus, in his book, *Explaining Religion: Criticism and Theory from Bodin to Freud* (New Haven: Yale University Press, 1987), has given us an excellent history of the explanatory approach to religion. On the preference for "naturalistic" over "reductive," see Preus, n2, ix–x. Two of the more ardent contemporary advocates of a strictly explanatory approach to the study of religion include Donald Wiebe *Religion and Truth: Towards an Alternative Paradigm for the Study of Religion* (The Hague: Mouton & Company, 1981) and Robert Segal, *Explaining and Interpreting Religion: Essays on the Issue* (New York: Peter Lang, 1992).

50. A new sensibility about how academic disciplines structure the objects of their investigations has produced a spate of interesting works on the history of the study of religion. See, e.g., Preus (cited above), Peter Harrison, *Religion and the "Religions" in the English Enlightenment* (Cambridge: Cambridge University Press, 1990), David Chidister, *Savage Systems: Colonialism and Comparative Religion in Southern Africa* (Charlottesville: University Press of Virginia, 1996), and Richard King, *Orientalism and Religion: Postcolonial Theory, India, and "The Mystic East"* (London: Routledge, 1999).

51. See Guilford Dudley, *Religion on Trial: Mircea Eliade and His Critics* (Philadelphia: Temple University Press, 1977), 142–43 for an excellent summary of the use of these philosophers of science.

52. In chapter 12 I will discuss Robert Solomon's concept of the "transcendental pretense," which is the view that the ideas of consciousness, "Man," *Geist*, etc., are seen as categories understood as a putatively universal subjectivity but which, in reality, turn out to be virulently Eurocentric and complicit in the maintenance of the system of colonial representations.

53. Penner, *Impasse and Resolution*, 32 and 56. Note how Penner collapses "the history of religion" and "the phenomenology of religion." This is in keeping with my assertion that the two are not separate schools or methods, but that the former is another way of naming the latter. See terminological section below.

54. Donald Wiebe, *The Politics of Religious Studies: the Continuing Conflict with Theology in the Academy* (New York: St. Martin's Press, 1999), 3. See chapter 10 of that work where he details how van der Leeuw's approach amounts to a religious quest.

55. Robert Segal, *Explaining and Interpreting Religion*, 29. See also p. 5 where he argues that "religionists wrongly laud contemporary social scientists for analyzing religion the way religionists profess to do: from the believer's point of view." This lauding is a strategy of absorption that leads to "defanging" the critical dimensions of Critical Theory, as well as more conventional social science approaches. I completely concur with Segal: there is a persistent misreading via very simple equivocations and often totally irrational "yes really means no" interpretive maneuvers. Most of this is simply bad scholarship and stands in our field with no intellectual warrant whatsoever. Robert Segal concurs: "Religionists, I contend, stand committed to the defense of religion" (op. cit., 1). As such, religionists are not playing by the rules of academic discourse—limited as they are and subject to critique, nevertheless the binding elements of a discursive community. Such a style of argumentation belongs in the Ecclesia, not the University.

56. This is very much the argumentative strategy of Schleiermacher in his *Speeches*, especially the second *Speech* where he painstakingly differentiates religion from ethics. That Bleeker cites Schleiermacher's *Speeches* on this issue (Bleeker, *The Sacred Bridge Researches into the Nature and Structure of Religion* [Leiden: E. J. Brill, 1963], 38–39) as late as 1963 indicates the persistence of this faculty psychology and its taxonomization of the sciences. Limits of space do not allow for a full treatment of Schleiermacher's work. He is, of course, a

seminal figure in this history. I hope to cover his views in a later companion volume on the theological treatment of the issues raised in this study.

57. Robert Baird, *Category Formation in the History of Religions* (The Hague: Mouton & Company, 1971), 131.

58. Penner, *Impasse and Resolution*, xv.

59. Dudley, *Religion on Trial*, 49; reference 169, n. 26 and 33. I argue that phenomenology's notion of the empirical in history is that of a manifestation of an essence, or a revelation of *Geist*'s meaning. Each concrete object is a member of an ideal class ("sacrifice as such") and as such, is an expression of the sacred/holy, which is in turn, an a priori structure/category of consciousness (or Consciousness as such). This is, of course, a nonempirical theory of the empirical.

60. See ibid., on Eliade and the empiricists, 19–21, for his view of this relationship and criticism.

61. Robert Segal, *Explaining and Interpreting Religion*, 19.

62. Ibid., 19, citing *Patterns*, xiii.

63. Segal, unlike Preus, seems to hold to more of a positivistic view of science. Preus explicitly uses the work of Thomas Kuhn in his definition of explanatory approaches to the study of religion. See Preus, *Explaining, Religion*, ix–xiv. Segal seems to be heavily influenced by Popper's and especially Lakota's use of the falsification concept. See Segal, op. cit., 38–40.

64. Roland Barthes's essay, "From Science to Literature" in his *The Rustle of Language* (Berkeley: University of California Press, 1989) expresses, along with my argument about the heuristic nature of the social sciences, my own views about the nature of the human sciences generally. Barthes argues (4–5) that "language is the *being* of literature [whether scientific literature or artistic literature], its very world: all literature is contained in the act of writing, and no longer in that of 'thinking,' of 'painting,' of 'recounting,' of 'feeling.' " As such, science and literature are a "certain ways of taking language" (5), albeit significantly different ways. For my own usage, "heuristic" could be replaced by "perspectivism," but for the fact that the latter retains the Cartesian epistemological model/problematic which is precisely what I am rejecting. Segal, Wiebe, et al. are very much still caught up within that epistemological problematic, hence their concern with subjectivity and objectivity.

65. W. Brede Kristensen, *The Meaning of Religion: Lectures in the Phenomenology of Religion* (The Hague: Martinus Nijhoff, 1960), 3. Cf. pp. 3–4 where he says: "Phenomenology is a systematic science, not just an historical discipline which considers the Greek, Roman, or Egyptian religion by itself. The problem is to determine what *sacrifice itself* is, not just what Greek, Roman, or Hebrew sacrifice is." Again, the identity of the subjects does not matter. It is, from a postcolonial perspective, elided and therefore denied. Peoples without an identity can be classified more easily by the power of the colonizer's system of "knowledge." It is also easier to justify imposing an identity and a system of governing such a people. They apparently do not have sufficient self-consciousness to do it themselves. Hegel will make precisely this argument. It is implicit in Tiele, but very much there nonetheless.

66. I am indebted to Bryan Rennie for the Kant-Plato correlation. See *Reconstructing Eliade: Making Sense of Religion* (Albany: State University of New York Press, 1996), 11–12.

67. Again, Rennie's astute comment above about how Eliade's—but it is just as true of Wach, van der Leeuw, and Kristensen—categories are a combination of Kant and Plato. Otto is explicit about using Kant; his definition of the holy as an a priori category is clear evidence of that (although he also has an explicit theory of history, to be discussed in detail later in this study). In his comparative work, Eliade uses purely formal categories that have a strong resemblance to Platonic forms. His oft-stated point that "the sacred is a structure of consciousness," with its echoes of Otto, is also very Kantian.

68. Cf. Juco Bleeker, *The Sacred Bridge*, 3, emphasis added: "Phenomenology of religion pays attention not so much to the historical surroundings of the phenomena, but rather to the ideological connections. That means that the facts are severed from their historical context and they are combined in such a way that the meaning of these phenomena as such becomes *clear and transparent*." Cf. Kristensen, the main author of the allusion about decontextualization, *The Meaning of Religion*, 3: phenomenology's goal is "to consider phenomena, not only in their historical context, but also in their ideal connection."

69. For an example of this kind of critique applied to Religious Studies, see Murphy, *Representing Religion*, ch. 5, "The 'Transcendental Pretense' and Eliade's Humanist Hermeneutics."

70. Penner, *Impasse and Resolution*, 60. He is citing Foucault, *Archaeology of Knowledge*, 203.

71. Capps, *Religious Studies*, 108.

72. While much of this information is public knowledge, I am largely reliant upon Eric Sharpe's *Comparative Religion: A History* (London: Duckworth, 1975), and Jacques Waardenburg's *Classical Approaches the Study of Religion* for the information in this section. As such, references will not be given except where direct quotations or other sources are used.

73. Sharpe, *Comparative Religion*, 121.

74. Space does not allow for a treatment of Söderbloom. He is not as *directly* influential as are those treated in this study.

75. Dudley, *Religion on Trial*, 9. Note how Dudley, like Penner collapses the "history" and the "phenomenology" of religions. As will be discussed later, this is common usage and reflects the "terminological field" in which and by which what I am calling *the* phenomenology of religion is known.

76. Sharpe, *Comparative Religion*, 167. See also Melissa Raphael, *Rudolf Otto and the Concept of Holiness* (Oxford: Clarendon Press, 1997), 47 on the inclusion, controversial as it may be, of Söderblom and Otto as phenomenologists: "The comparativism of both Söderblom and Otto qualified them as forerunners of the phenomenology of religion: they attempted to organize, observe, and empathize with all religious consciousness, and so isolate the essence of religion."

77. Sharpe, 238.

78. See Charles Long, *Significations: Signs, Symbols, and Images in the Interpretation of Religion* (Aurora, CO: The Davies Group, 1995), 27. His chapter, "The Study of Religion: Its Nature and Its Discourse," contains a wealth of interesting information on both the history of classical phenomenology of religion and the "Chicago School," the American institutional embodiment of the phenomenology of religion.

79. Wiebe, *The Politics of Religious Studies*, 100.

80. Ibid.

81. Bryan Rennie, *Reconstructing Eliade*, 208. He cites Alles's essay, "The Critique from Totality." It is clear from this otherwise unclear quote that Alles assumes the existence and prominence of the Chicago School.

82. Willard G. Oxtoby, "*Religionswissenschaft* Revisited," in *Religions in Antiquity*, ed. Jacob Neusner (Leiden: E. J. Brill, 1968), 594.

83. I must also express my regret for not being able to include two very fine works in this area, viz., Thomas Ryba's *The Essence of Phenomenology* and Jeppe Jensen's *The Study of Religion in a New Key*. It would an arduous task to bridge my work with theirs, a task that would be the subject of a study unto itself. The exclusion (in the main) of these works is by no means a criticism of them. Quite the contrary: to do justice to these excellent studies would require a considerable extension of this work. Though I have not analyzed them here, I have learned much about the phenomenology of religion from them.

84. On the idea of third wave, see Waardenberg cited in Penner, *Impasse and Resolution*, 56–57. Penner's assessment of this strand is not positive (57): "Unfortunately, the 'new style' of phenomenology of religion is a variation on the classical approach. All the classical problems are embedded in the reformulation." I completely concur with this argument. The new approaches simply appropriate the fundamental structures of classical phenomenology in a somewhat modified way. The situation is reminiscent of the way in which Hegel was appropriated via a rejection of his project. One should, however, acknowledge that these scholars were making a sincere attempt to overcome the pathologies and failures of their predecessors. Their critique, however, did not cut deep enough, and so they end up retaining more of that inherited structuring than they end up rejecting.

85. For the notion of a Scandinavian strand of phenomenology, see Jeppe Jensen, *The Study of Religion in a New Key*, 53ff. Also, the phenomenology of religion has been written about in Italy, but its reception there has been marked by ongoing criticism. Noteworthy in this respect are Raffaele Pettazoni's *Essays on the History of Religion* (Leiden: E. J. Brill, 1967) and Ugo Bianchi's *The History of Religions* (Leiden: E. J. Brill, 1975). See Mircea Eliade, *The Quest: History and Meaning in Religion* (Chicago: University of Chicago Press, 1969), 35-36 for a discussion of the Italian reception of the phenomenology of religion.

86. See Murphy, *Representing Religion*, 21–26 for an argument about the influence of classical phenomenology on the history of Religious Studies.

87. Dudley, *Religion on Trial*, 3.

88. Robert Segal misunderstands this distinction when he argues: "Eliade not only calls himself a historian of religions but even contrasts the historian

both to the theologian and to the phenomenologist." The phenomenologist, he argues, "deals with classes of religious phenomena, the historian is concerned with individual members of those classes." Segal, *Explaining and Interpreting Religion*, 141. What he fails to grasp is that the unity of both operations lies in the notion of objective *Geist*: both derive the meaning of religious phenomena from historical data because it is *Geist* manifested in each individual instance. His misunderstanding comes from applying a typical Anglophonic notion of "history" to Eliade (et al.), whereas Eliade is using a Hegelian expressionist view of history—which Hegel, of course, referred to as a *phenomenology* of the history of consciousness. I note this not to chide Dr. Segal, but because this is a typical misunderstanding of the phenomenology/history of religion by Anglophones who impose their own categories on these Continental thinkers. These two traditions of thought, as is well known in philosophy (a discipline that formally separates the two in job categories, at least in the United States), are quite separate and use quite different conceptual structures. The failure lies in not properly historicizing these thinkers. One of my aims in this study is to correct that failure by showing that these thinkers use an Hegelian theory of history, not an empiricist theory of history. As such, they cannot be criticized for failing to be good empirical historians; they never intended to approach religion that way. One could, of course, criticize the approach generally.

89. Douglas Allen, "The Phenomenology of Religion" in *Encyclopedia of Religion*, ed. Mircea Eliade (Chicago: University of Chicago Press, 1986), 273.

90. The terminal "s" in *Religions* indicates the genitive possessive, not the plural: "Religion's," not "religions."

91. W. C. Smith in particular advocated this term for a nonreductive, empathetic *approach* to the study of religion.

92. Dudley, *Religion on Trial*, 5. He goes on to note: "That scholars who were in roughly the same field called it by so many different names raised a question about the unity of the discipline." Indeed, there is a question about the *actual* unity of this diverse body of work. However, as I will argue, it is an important fact about Religious Studies, at least in the United States, but I believe also in Continental Europe, there has been the *perception* of such a unity. This unity is, as I will argue, the product of a *Rezeptionsgeschichte*, itself a fact even if the actual unity of the discipline is not. Having so thought it as a unity it has come to be, at least in some sense, a real unity.

93. On this term, see Preus, *Explaining Religion*, ix, n. 1: "Larry Laudin has a good definition of 'research tradition,' a term which he prefers to [the Kuhnian notion of] 'paradigm': 'a research tradition is a set of general assumptions about the entities and processes in a domain of study, and about the appropriate methods to be used for investigating the problems and constructing the theories in that domain.' " Both of these, with Foucault's "episteme" seem to me to be of interest. When speaking strictly, however, I will use the term, discussed (ad nauseam) in the next chapter, "discourse," for, in my sense, it has almost the precise meaning Laudin gives to "research

tradition"—except that the former is explicit about the linguistic nature of the phenomenon being named whereas the latter is, by comparison, vague (where is "tradition" if not embodied in symbolic memory, i.e., language, *langue*, or discourse?).

94. This overall school, as I will discuss in the next chapter, will be referred to as "the phenomenology of religion" (not *a* phenomenology of religion). It is not, I argue, a generic term. "Classic phenomenology of religion" refers to those core set of thinkers who formulated this approach into its most recognizable form, i.e., Kristensen, van der Leeuw, and Eliade in particular, Otto and Wach arguably. "Classic" therefore does not refer to the stature of these individuals (it varies considerably in degree and from locale to locale) or any specific features of their body of texts, e.g., that they are "greater" than others. It merely refers to a specific body of texts and thinkers whose influence was constitutive of *the* phenomenology of religion, the wider term in that it includes both the "classical" phenomenologists and other phenomenologists who do not fit that description. It is also clear that, to some degree, this a historical, periodic classification. "Classical phenomenology" refers exclusively to early to mid-twentieth-century scholarship whereas the broader term includes both earlier and later versions of phenomenology.

95. Gerardus van der Leeuw, *Religion in Essence in Manifestation*, trans. J. E. Turner (Princeton: Princeton University Press, 1986), xx.

96. I use the word here as an umbrella term only. Throughout this book the term *poststructuralism* is used as a stand-in for a complex and heterogeneous body of thought. I am not using it in a narrow or doctrinaire sense, if there be such a thing. It should be clear from the theorists and philosophers I cite what I mean by the term. It would be a fruitless discussion, in other words, to debate whether I "am" or am not a poststructuralist, or have gotten poststructuralism "right." I intend neither and make no claim to either. I merely use texts grouped under that heading as a heuristic, and use the term as shorthand for referring to those texts.

97. An autobiographical note: for a considerable amount of time, I *was* a phenomenologist. My encounter with poststructuralism persuaded me that it was the stronger argument and so I abandoned, with some travail, the position of a phenomenologist. On a broader theoretical level, the criterion, criteria, and criteriology involved in "disproving" a position leads to a labyrinthine search that has no obvious outcome. For my take on the complexity of this issue, see the section on metalanguages in *Nietzsche, Metaphor, Religion* (Albany: State University of New York Press, 2001), ch. 9, "Metaphor and the Death of God."

98. A recent and precise example of a plea to a "theory-less" reading comes from the historian of American politics (himself an American) James Patterson, who remarked on CSPAN (a U.S. cable network; he appeared on April 6, 2007), when asked about his methodology: "I am completely innocent of theory." Many exegetes, in Religious Studies and elsewhere, make a similar claim. W. B. Kristensen famously remarked: "The believer is always right," i.e., the exegete must not and cannot interpose anything between the pure statement and its rendering into a scholarly text. Many phenomenologists dismiss the

claim that phenomenology is itself a theory and, as historians and others often do, they lay claim to an act of mere "description," i.e., description "innocent of theory." To the contrary, however, Roland Barthes demonstrates, in *Writing Degree Zero* (New York: Hill and Wang, 1967), that there is no "zero" degree of writing, i.e., a writing free of some connotative stylistics or form. Advocates of a neutrality of writing have claimed a space in writing or "style" that is neither in the subjunctive nor in the imperative mood, but rather: "writing at the zero degree is basically in the indicative mood, or if you like amodal" (76). However, "amodal" is a *choice*, and *no* choice is free from bias, if in no other sense that it is a selection that precludes or foregoes other possible choices: "Form [must be] considered a human intention" (14). Thus: "Every Form is also a value," and all "writing is thus essentially the morality of writing" (15). *Mutatis mutandis*, there is no "zero" degree of exposition. All expository methods have consequences beyond their manifest intentions and claims. There is no "straightforward" reading; the term itself implies a teleology toward which reading moves ("accuracy," "canons of scholarship," "good philology," etc.) and that teleology determines the meaning produced by the "straightforward" reading. Such a teleology, however, is itself an extratextual entity; its life exists *outside* and beyond any individual text and so is not part of the text but is an added-on something. Ergo, it is not a "zero degree" of exegesis; it is utterly freighted with meanings that do not mimetically reflect the supposed inner core of an individual text. The political theorist William Connolly makes a similar point about claims to "neutrality" in the readings of major political theorists: "None of these exemplary thinkers was gentle with opposing thinkers of note. For that matter, few contemporary advocates of contextualization, appreciative interpretation or immanent critique are generous with those who do not accept the universality of their favorite mode." This suggests that "[a method of] interrogation is one of the ways thinking proceeds when it seeks to unsettle settled patterns of thought," William Connolly, *Political Theory and Modernity* (London: Basil Blackwell, 1988), 6. One could rather easily demonstrate that this has very much been the case with advocates of "nonreductive" readings, or readings that insist on taking a text "on its own terms." The obvious fallacy in the latter is that a hermeneutics *must select* which terms are a text's "own terms"—extratextual interpretation has already begun—this is what Barthes meant by his phrase "always already," of Foucault's phrase, "always already read." It is unavoidable; there is no "neutral" reading, not, nota bene, in the sense of a "for-and-against," but in the sense of a set of systematic selections and exclusions about what counts as the core elements of a text, about what counts as "context." In the next chapter I will discuss my own methodology in reference to this point.

## Chapter 2. Discourse, Text, Philosophemes

1. Jacques Derrida, "Structure, Sign, Play in the Discourse of the Human Sciences," in *Writing and Difference,* trans. Alan Bass (Chicago: University of Chicago Press, 1978), 278.

2. Which is not to say there is no order of logic. The order of logic is quite often an imminent fact of the mode of presentation of the philosophemes traced out. This order comes from within the text; it is not imposed upon the text as an extratextual demand as in conventional philosophical (often Analytical) expository methods. That is one theory of the text—*it is a theory of the text*, not the text *an sich*.

3. We must *ask* (and not presume), also, under what order of reading, under what theory of textual production and/or consumption, is the assertoric proposition or the "position" or the "argument" of a text is so privileged an object inside the text? While there no denying that such things exist and have their place and worth, it is the tendency of traditional philosophical exposition to deny, or at least elide (often derogate—A. J. Ayer's *Language, Truth, and Logic* comes to mind) any other linguistic entities that exist in the text, or for that matter, in language. This is a dogmatic failure of that method, as all contemporary linguistic *science* has clearly demonstrated (Analytic or Positivist philosophies of language most often have, ironically, failed to take *language itself* seriously). Texts and language do more than point at things or tie subject and predicate together (the assertoric function). Again, the argument is worthy of consideration—no disputing that—but so are other entities (tropes, metaphors, philosophemes, structural relations, intertextual allusion, etc.) in the text. The old method has confused, to some degree, the necessity to make arguments *about* the meaning of the text with the belief that the meaning of the text *must be* its argument. The latter claim is patently, even empirically, false.

4. Connolly, *Political Theory and Modernity*, 6. On the issue of neutrality, see Barthes and Connolly citations chapter 1 above.

5. Ibid., 4. My method has some interesting commonalities with that of Bryan Rennie. In his *Reconstructing Eliade*, 5, he says: "My initial task will be to clarify as much as possible Eliade's vocabulary, to settle on clear definitions of the terminology of his interpretative strategies: 'hierophany,' 'the sacred,' '*coincidentia oppositorum*,' '*illud tempus*,' and so forth." While I treat the issue of vocabulary in quite a different manner than he does, I also see it as the key element to interpreting these texts (I see them as philosophemes at play within the langue of the discourse). This common concern shares a common defect, or perceived defect: "If this has lead me to use overly long quotations, it is due to my desire for accuracy and my efforts to avoid the dangers of 'paraphraseology' " (5). Again, I share both of these concerns: accuracy comes from tracing out the play of the elements, not summarizing an argument. So, too, my analyses will, at times at least, apparently suffer from "overly long quotations" and chronic repetition of citations and problems. This is a necessary vice; we must read what has been written—not go on reputations or shorthand—and trace out the actual play, oppositions, narrations, and so forth, to lift off the vectors of text I am pursuing. Rennie does a fine job, but it is the job of the *exegete de texte*, not the job of the discourse analyst. So he will subjectify both ends of the process (his and the author's; 4–5), whereas I see the subject position as something *made possible* by the play of the text itself, not vice versa. See Murphy, *Representing Religion*, chapter 6, for my view of

the text-subject relationship. In short, I accept the "death of the author" and the transition from "work" to "text"—both in Roland Barthes's sense—and Rennie, in keeping with traditional modes of exegesis, does not. The benefit of Rennie's method is that it is easier for it to gain acceptance in the academic mainstream. The price paid for that acceptance is conformity: "Those who act within the confines of established concepts, actually have the perceptions and modes of conduct available to them limited in subtle and undetected ways." Connolly, *Terms of Political Discourse*, 1. So Rennie *reconstructs* Eliade et al., while I call for a *revolution* against Eliade et al.

6. E.g., on the model of Foucault's *The Order of Things* or Kuhn's *The Structure of Scientific Revolutions*. As Continental thought of the nineteenth century has been the object of unending fascination and quasi-obsessive scholarship, it could be argued that such "plowing of the field" has already been well accomplished.

7. Connolly, *Political Theory and Modernity*, 4 and 6, cited above.

8. Other texts and authors have said many similar things well before I have. This text is self-consciously set within that vein of critique.

9. Willard Oxtoby writes: "As late as 1959, the history-of-religions field in America seemed a sideline, even a dead end, peripheral to the main stream of scholarship in the study of religion. A scant eight years later, the field is prospering in American universities and colleges." "*Religionswissenschaft* Revisited," 590. Guildford Dudley concurs with Oxtoby's statement, if for different reasons: "The scholar Willard G. Oxtoby is probably correct in stating that 1959 was a watershed in the development of discipline, for the decade following saw a resurgence of interest and expansion unprecedented for such a brief period." Dudley, *Religion on Trial*, 13.

10. Oxtoby, "*Religionswissenschaft* Revisited," 590.

11. Dudley, *Religion on Trial*, 13. *Nota bene*: I am not arguing that this is the moment of origin of Religious Studies. Clearly, it had existed in some form before (although almost always as part of a theological faculty). I am only claiming that, as it is currently established, in the United States, it was in the process of *becoming* during this period. The major formative periods of the careers of all the authors analyzed in this study preceded this period by many years, even with Wach and Eliade, the last in the line of phenomenologists treated here.

12. Alexander Nehamas, *Life as Literature* (Cambridge: Harvard University Press, 1985), 82.

13. Friedrich Nietzsche, *The Will to Power*, trans. Walter Kaufman and R. J. Hollingdale (New York: Vintage Books, 1967), sections #551 and #557.

14. Nehamas, *Life as Literature*, 85.

15. It is obviously true that some authors reviewed here claimed the mantle of phenomenologist of religion. The German title of Van der Leeuw's famous text is *Der Phänomenology der Religion* (translated as "Religion in Essence and Manifestation"). However, the formulation of all of these texts into a specific group, coded with and by a specific set of concerns and forged into a "school," or unitary thing, is a retroactive work. While this may have

been the intent of people such as van der Leeuw, it is the *reader* that carries out that intention, not the author. The *Rezeptionsgeschichte* is a necessary condition for the continued existence of a body of texts as a school. Otherwise, the books do nothing but collect dust on the library shelves. I would also argue that "the phenomenology of religion," i.e., the product of this *Rezeptionsgeschichte*, is not the same thing as the work of the scholars who go by that name. By being structured together and institutionalized there are changes, many of them subtle, to their scholarly work. It is a different status to be doing new work in a field and being an institutionalized aspect of that field. The post hoc reading-together of these texts changes what they mean for Religious Studies and it changes the way they function in the field.

16. I.e., I am *not* interested in the "true history" of the phenomenology of religion, but rather, its history as *understood*, as appropriated by, as it lives within the present institutionalization of Religious Studies—including its *dissemination* via the publishing industry in World Religion textbooks, etc. While it clearly is not "all," to metaphorically quantify, of Religious Studies, it clearly is also not "none." To say "none" to the question of the influence of the phenomenology of religion on Religious Studies is flat out wrong. Further, I am not asserting that Religious Studies in its totality founded upon the phenomenology of religion. One only need contemplate the vast influence of Eliade to see how much it has, in fact, "invented" Religious Studies.

17. I am relatively certain that it is also an influence in European "History of Religion/s" as embodied in such organizations as the International Association for the History of Religions. However, I cannot substantiate that claim and so will leave it to others to decide whether or not it is true. I confine myself to a critique of the United States not out of a naïve American-centric view, all too often a national problem. I do so, rather, out of modesty: I simply do not claim to know whether or not what I say is true of other academic discourses and institutions in the rest of the Americas, Europe, Africa, or Asia. It seems rather clear that much of it is likely true of Western Continental Europe, as this is the origin of this discourse. Again, I leave it to others to confirm or disconfirm this. I need only be right about the situation in the United States for my argument to be valid.

18. See Murphy, *Representing Religion*, 25–26 where I cite Thomas Idinopulous on the use of Otto and Eliade to justify the existence of a separate department devoted to the study of religion in the 1960s at Miami, Ohio.

19. Recall the quote from William Connolly on the limitations created by the use of conventional methods. In short: they subtly reinforce the status quo, the regimes of truth and of power, insofar as they are connected.

20. See "Colonial Discourse" section below for a detailed analysis of this issue.

21. I recognize and fully embrace the paradoxical situation of a "subjunctive revolutionary."

22. See Jeppe Jensen, *The Study of Religion in a New Key*, 37, where he concurs that my reading and evaluation of the state of Religious Studies is "not timid, [is] radical, and acute." I am not interested simply claiming the

mantle of "a radical." I am interested in insisting that *my critique is radical*, in that it goes to the very root of our field. As such, it cannot merely be patched up. It has to be completely dismantled and completely replaced. As Segal noted above, there is a tendency of all institutions but also in Religious Studies to deny radical critiques, to claim that things merely need to be patched up and then we can continue with business as usual—i.e., radical critiques are elided by being absorbed in an intellectually false manner. The latter is usually achieved by a chain of equivocations, e.g., "scientists operate on faith, too"; "Marxism is a religion," i.e., antireligion is religion!

23. Stavrakakis, *Lacan and the Political* (London: Routledge, 1999), 89, quote from Lacan, XX: 32.

24. Michel Foucault, *The Archaeology of Knowledge and The Discourse On Language* (New York: Pantheon Books, 1972), 27.

25. Ibid., 117.

26. Sara Mills, *Discourse* (London and New York: Routledge, 1997), 17, citing Foucault; emphasis added.

27. Foucault, *Archaeology*, 47.

28. This may sound very much like the a priorism of Hegel and his view of the nature of science discussed in chapter 1. It should be clear, however that what is being offered here is a description of discourse as it actually functions in real world contexts, not a normative view about how discourse should be organized. It is not advocating this form of language use, but a description of how discourse *does what it does*—so that we may be able to see it for what it is and not just assume it in what *we* do.

29. Mills, *Discourse*, 70.

30. Diane Macdonell, *Theories of Discourse: An Introduction* (Oxford: Basil Blackwell, 1986), 11.

31. Ibid., 54.

32. Michel Foucault, "History of Systems of Thought," in *Language, Counter-Memory, Practice*, ed. Donald Bourchard (Ithaca: Cornell University Press, 1977), 200.

33. Mills, *Discourse*, 15.

34. Victor Burgin, *The End of Art Theory Criticism and Modernity* (Atlantic Highlands: Humanities Press International, 1986), 181.

35. Mills, *Discourse*, 18. See Nietzsche's in/famous essay, "On Truth and Lies in an Extra-Moral Sense" for a philosophical-linguistic argument about the construction of reality. See Luckmann and Berger's, *The Social Construction of Reality*, and especially, Berger's *The Sacred Canopy* for a social-scientific argument on how language shapes perception.

36. Leela Gandhi, *Postcolonial Theory: A Critical Introduction* (New York: Columbia University Press, 1998), 77.

37. Paul Rabinow, "Representations Are Social Facts," in *Writing Culture: The Poetics and Politics of Ethnography*, ed. James Clifford, and George Marcus (Berkeley: University of California Press, 1986), essay title.

38. Cf. Rabinow, 235–36 for a summary of the history of epistemology, including its end.

39. Macdonell, *Theories of Discourse*, 87, alluding to Foucault.
40. Ibid., 88, citing Foucault.
41. Foucault argues, in "History of Systems of Thought," 200, that "discourse" is not confined to language usage, but rather: "Discursive practices are not purely and simply ways of producing [verbal] discourse. They are embodied in technical processes, in institutions, in patterns for general behavior, in forms for transmission and diffusion, and in pedagogical forms which, at once, impose and maintain them." Colonial practices and the institutionally governed practice of scholarship (as opposed to the scholarship itself), then could both be analyzed as discursive practices. My argument is aimed directly at the textual/discursive practices that both constitute "the phenomenology of religion" and those by means of which the phenomenology of religion produces it objects of analysis. As discussed above, it is indirectly aimed as that object, Religious Studies, in precisely the way Foucault describes it above. It is more than a language practice per se, yet it is still a discursive practice.
42. Foucault, *Archaeology*, 27; emphasis added.
43. Mills, *Discourse*, 67.
44. Ibid., 54.
45. Alexandria Georgakopoulou and Dionysis Goutsos, *Discourse Analysis: An Introduction* (Edinburgh: Edinburgh University Press, 1997), 4.
46. Ibid., 5.
47. Nicola Wood, Describing Discourse: A Practical Guide to Discourse Analysis (London: Hodder Arnold, 2006), xi.
48. Ibid.
49. Ibid.
50. Some critics may harp on the use, for instance, of the name of an author as proof that I am *really* doing exposition. However, just as the text is diffused into discourse, the name of the author is diffused into the text—and the complex and nonoriginary history it presents to reading, if reading does not stop at the boundaries of the book/work. The authorial name is, again, a metonym by which the text, itself a metonym for the discourse, etc., is accessed. The use of the authorial name is an approach taken of necessity; "normal" research conditions do not allow for the exhaustive transversing of a field of texts in order to isolate these same tropes out of a broader swath of discourse (manuals, syllabi, job adds, curricula, "mission statements" of institutions and of journals and presses, etc.). However, again, such an exercise would finally be redundant in that, I would argue, we would find the same structures of discourse, only with infinitely more endnotes. It is not that the author said it; it is that it is part of *the said*, the "already said, the already written" of the archive.
51. Georgakopoulou and Goutsos, *Discourse Analysis*, 6.
52. Roland Barthes, "From Work to Text," in *Image-Music-Text* (New York: Hill and Wang,1977), 146.
53. Michel Foucault, *Archaeology*, 23. Cf. Roland Barthes "the metaphor of the text is that of the network," "From Work to Text," 161.

54. Barthes, "From Work to Text," 156–57. Cf. elsewhere where he elaborates, and radicalizes, this point. The text will come to be in and out of the various "alreadies," the systems of references, of codes, of discursive possibilities that preexist the text, and which the text can open up (in what Nietzsche called "discoveries" rather than "invention"). As such, "the Text is plural. Which is not simply to say that it has several meanings, but that it accomplishes the very plural of meaning: an *irreducible* (and not merely an acceptable) plural." Barthes, 159.

55. Ibid., 160.

56. I am not proposing any particular explanatory theory about why this discourse comes in this binary form. Neither do I assert that all discourses, thought, consciousness, etc., necessarily take the form of binary oppositions; this is a limited claim, not a universal claim—do not confuse me with Levi-Strauss! Clearly, many discourses are composed of binaries and the notion of "identity" seems to be necessarily structured by a self/other or is/is not, binary form. Be that at is may, my concern in *this* study is *only* with the discourse of the phenomenology of religion and secondarily with that discourse within which it is embedded, viz., ontotheology (as described by Nietzsche, Heidegger, Derrida, Taylor, and others), which clearly is also structured by binary oppositions.

57. Derrida, "Signature, Event, Context," 329.

58. Ibid., 329.

59. Mark C. Taylor, *Erring: A Postmodern A/theology* (Chicago: University of Chicago Press, 1984), 7.

60. Ibid., 9, emphasis added.

61. Charles Long, *Significations*, 86–87. Understanding colonial discourse as a hermeneutics is, to me, a fruitful concept. One could explore further the functioning, history, and structures of a colonial and/or imperial hermeneutics. "How does Euro-imperialism interpret the world?" A worthwhile question to ask.

62. Consider the meanings of the more current terms in international politics, "developed and undeveloped nations." Is this not an echo of earlier dichotomy, "civilized/savage," which is a variant of *"Geist/Natur"*? The *content* of each opposition is clearly different. The *structural relation* between each pair, and the geopolitical realities to which they refer, however, are virtually identical: it reflects "an economy of privilege," a hierarchy of value.

63. I take it as given that these distinctions also include distinctions of gender, distinctions within the natural sciences, of race, and other categories. I leave it to area specialists, many of whom have done excellent work, to cover these other issues. My focus is very specific and so very narrow. For instance, although *Geist* and *Natur* clearly have gender implications, they are rarely *actually* (i.e., overtly, empirically) gendered in the discourse of the phenomenology of religion. Race, however, *does* come up, as do fights over the meaning of science or *Wissenschaft*. Ergo, it will not be necessary to deal with gender here, while it will be necessary to touch on, mostly in passing, the other issues.

64. Jacques Derrida, *Of Grammatology*, trans. G. C. Spivak (Baltimore: The Johns Hopkins University Press), 3.

65. Jacques Derrida, *Positions*, trans. A. Bass (Chicago: University of Chicago Press, 1971), 28.

66. Mary Louise Pratt, *Imperial Eyes: Travel Writing and Transculturation* (London and New York: Routledge, 1992), 5.

67. Ibid., 213.

68. For a very detailed and vivid account of one of the most heinous episodes of Euro-imperialism, see Adam Hochschild, *King Leopold's Ghost: A Story of Greed, Terror, and Heroism in Colonia Africa* (Boston: Mariner Books, 1999). It was these atrocities in Belgian Congo that inspired Joseph Conrad's *Heart of Darkness*. I believe a fair and accurate description of this episode of colonialism is, indeed: "the horror, the horror."

69. Pratt, *Imperial Eyes*, 5. Though it is a separate issue, I would argue that the "world" of "world religions" is precisely the world as colonized by Euro-Americans. "World religions" is an imperialist concept.

70. Ibid., 5.

71. Charles Long, *Significations*, 86; emphasis added. I could not concur with this precise but limited statement of the relationship between the colonial situation and *Religionswissenschaft*/Religious Studies/phenomenology and history of religions more. However, Long does a *volte face* that is inexplicable to me, arguing that "Rudolf Otto's *The Idea of the Holy* speaks of the numinous and the irrational in terms that are neither pathological nor evolutionary." See chapter 7 on Otto below for an argument to the direct contrary. That someone such as Long, a member of the Chicago School, can have such acute and challenging insight into the colonial situation but such a disconnect when it comes to a phenomenological approach to religion is, to me, quite telling. It is likely that this disconnect is greatly facilitated by reading Husserl as its origin rather than the more blatantly "colonial/imperialist thinker," Hegel.

72. Jane Samson, *Race and Empire*, 45. Long, *Significations*, 86, makes a similar argument: "Whereas the history of the West is replete with historical events and heroes, the cultures of the world of 'others' is filled with static, eternally present social structures, and *mythological* events. The West is rational, the 'others' nonrational; the West is logical, the 'others' illogical or prelogical; the West is civilized, the 'others' primitive."

73. Leela Gandhi, *Postcolonial Theory*, 16.

74. Religious Study's inability to integrate "indigenous religions" into the category of "world religions" is the most suspect site where its structures are still informed by the colonial situation. Also, if one inventories the number of positions in subfields such as Native American religion, African religions, and the like, the disparity between those areas and those of Bible, theology, and (Christian) Ethics is astounding. The ratio is almost 100/1. For a contemporary and particularly egregious example of this structural exclusion of the indigenous other, see Stephen Prothro's book, *Religious Literacy: What Every American Needs to Know—And Doesn't* (New York: HarperOne, 2008). He argues that there are five world religions present in the America of the

twenty-first century and virtually pays no attention whatsoever to Native American religions nor to any of the religions of non-European immigrants who have become a significant element of the populations in certain places in the United States (e.g., Miami and New York), such as Haitian Vodou and (mostly) Cuban Santeria. This is a kind of "polite racism" that does not overtly derogate but denies by silence. As his goal is basically educational, he educates the American public to this form of racism.

75. Samson, *Race and Empire*, 45, citing Zimmerman.

76. Hegel, *Lectures on the Philosophy of Religion* trans. R. F. Brown, P. C. Hodgson, and J. M. Stewart (Berkeley: University of California Press, 1988), 229.

77. John Harvey, "Translator's Preface," in Rudolf Otto, *The Idea of the Holy: An Inquiry into the Non-Rational Factor in the Idea of the Divine and Its Relation to the Rational*, trans. J. W. Harvey (Oxford: Oxford University Press, 1958), ix–x.

78. Mills, *Discourse*, describes these differences about as well as anyone has so I will simply offer her distinctions:

> Colonialism is generally used to refer to a situation where the representatives of one country invade and settle in another country, and impose a legal system, a government and other institutional structures; imperialism is the more general term which is used to signify other exploitative relations, such as when there are enforced trading relations, the imposition of an alien religion, interference with the legal system or government by a foreign body ... but when there is no large-scale, planned settlement by civilians. However, since there is a great variety in imperial and colonial relations (over time and within a particular context), there is not a clear cut distinction to be made between imperialism and colonialism. (129)

On the other hand: "Post-colonialism is an equally problematic term, but is generally taken to refer to the socio-economic and cultural crises caused by colonialism" (129), or more precisely, in the wake of colonialism, i.e., the mess left after the colonialist leave, having been there for several centuries in many cases. Often, of course, they do not really leave; they set up corporations and put politicians in place that will ensure them favorable dealings with the former colony. Postcolonial subjects, then, are left with both a material-economic and political crisis as well as a crisis of identity, having been defined by colonial power for so long and with so much coercive force.

79. Ibid., 105–106.

80. Ibid., 128; emphasis added.

81. Ibid., 129.

82. Gandhi, *Postcolonial Theory*, 25.

83. Young, *White Mythologies: Writing History and the West* (London and New York: Routledge, 1990), 11.

84. Mills, *Discourse*, 106–107, citing Peter Hulme.
85. Ibid., 107.
86. Ibid. Cf. quote above from Foucault on the extensive sense of discursive practices.
87. Pratt, *Imperial Eyes*, 2 and 4.
88. Edward W. Said, *Orientalism* (New York: Vintage Books, 1978), 2.
89. Recall the discussion posited by Seiwert at the beginning of chapter 1. Essentialism creates a unified object by idealizing, i.e., rendering into a nonmaterial object, viz., a concept (so the argument goes). This logocentric maneuver allows for generalized characterizations of whole peoples, denying them difference, identity, and specificity. E.g., "the Asian mind," a term I have heard colleagues use, is only possible by such essentializing. It makes all Asians the same, thus giving the colonizer an easy means of reference and an easy way to insert this phenomenon into a taxonomy of similar phenomena. "The Asian mind," becomes "Eastern religion(s)," becomes non-European. As Europe is identified as white and Asian are not, it implicitly means "white" and "nonwhite." Again, our job categories also reflect this: we break down the West into careful and elaborate classifications. Asian religions jobs, by contrast, have only recently had their classification nuanced, but it is still crude: East Asia and South Asia. Most Asianists in a department are required to teach in both areas while we would not ask a scholar of Western religions to teach Judaism, Protestantism, Catholicism, and Islam. That would be the equivalent situation to what we ask—typically—Asianists to do.
90. Said, 45–46. Cf. the discussion of these passages in Ania Loomba, *Colonialism/Postcolonialism* (London and New York: Routledge, 1998), 44–47.
91. Loomba, *Colonialism/Postcolonialism*, 47; emphasis added.
92. Said, *Orientalism*, 3.
93. See Richard King's *Orientalism and the Making of the "Mysterious East"* for an excellent application of Said's and others' methods to the creation of "eastern religions" in mainstream academic scholarship.
94. Said, *Orientalism*, 206.
95 Ibid., 207.
96. Richard Beardsworth, *Derrida and the Political* (London: Routledge, 1996), 158.
97. Ibid., xiii.
98. The notion of better theories is a problem that cannot be dealt with here. From the critiques and methods outlined so far, it should be fairly clear what they could be.
99. Bhabha, 49.

## Chapter 3. *Geist*, History, Religion

1. Derrida, *Positions*, 77, cited in Taylor, *Erring*, 5.
2. Foucault, *Discourse on Language*, in *The Archaeology of Knowledge*, 235.
3. Derrida, *Margins of Philosophy*, 119.

4. Friedrich Nietzsche, *The Gay Science*, trans. Walter Kaufmann (New York: Vintage, 1974), #357.

5. Stanley Rosen, *G. W. F Hegel: an Introduction to the Science of Wisdom*, 10.

6. Philip M. Merklinger, *Philosophy, Theology, and Hegel's Berlin Philosophy of Religion, 1821–1827* (Albany: State University of New York Press, 1993), 4.

7. G. W. F. Hegel, *Hegel's Idea of Philosophy*, trans. and ed. Quentin Lauer (New York: Fordham University Press, 1971), 76.

8. See "*Entwicklung,*" in the *Oxford-Harrap Standard German-English Dictionary*. Cf. Also the *Oxford English Dictionary* on the verb, "evolve." The OED notes that the Latin means "to roll out," *e* (short for "ex")-*volvere*, and that the earliest English sense of the verb was "to unfold, unroll (something that is rolled up); to open out, expand." On the basis of this, it is easy to see why Germans might equate the two terms.

9. Ibid.

10. Hegel, *Hegel's Idea of Philosophy*, 77. Compare p. 76 where he claims: "This simple thing [the seed], however, is pregnant with all the qualities of the tree. In the seed is contained the whole tree, its trunk, branches, leaves, its color, odor, taste, etc. Nevertheless, this simple thing is the seed, not the tree itself; the fully articulated tree does not yet exist."

11. Quentin Lauer, in a footnote points out the way in which Hegel uses the term *Dasein*: "For Hegel, it [*Dasein*] signifies 'empirical being'—i.e., being as manifested in experience." *Hegel's Idea of Philosophy*, 77, translator's footnote.

12. Hegel, *Hegel's Idea of Philosophy*, 77.

13. Ibid.

14. Ibid., 78; emphasis added. Cf. p. 79 where he summarizes the process as follows: "If, in regard to realization, what came first was the in itself, the seed, etc., and second, existence, i.e., what emerges, then third comes the identity of both, more precisely the fruit of development, the result of the entire movement," or, being-for-itself.

15. Ibid., 79; emphasis added.

16. Ibid.

17. Ibid., 81.

18. Seiwert, "What Constitutes the Identity of a Religion?," 2.

19. Julian Roberts, *German Philosophy: An Introduction* (Atlantic Highlands: Humanities Press International, 1988), 70.

20. G. W. F. Hegel, *Philosophy of History*, trans. J. Sibree (New York: Dover Publications, 1956), 72–73.

21. Ibid., 78–79.

22. Hegel, *Introduction to the Lectures on the History of Philosophy*, trans. T. M. Knox and A. V. Miller (Oxford: Clarendon Press, 1985), 109.

23. Roberts, *German Philosophy*, 71.

24. Hegel, *Phenomenology of Spirit*, trans. A. V. Miller (Oxford: Oxford University Press, 1977), #35.

25. Ibid.
26. See Murphy, "The Concept of 'Essence and Manifestation' in the History of the Study of Religion," in *Representing Religion*, chapter 3.
27. Hegel, *Philosophy of History*, 78.
28. Ibid., 103–104.
29. Ibid., 105.
30. Ibid., 109.
31. Ibid., 1.
32. This list is concatenated in numerous places. One of its best summaries is in G. W. F. Hegel, *The Philosophy of Right*, trans. T. M. Knox (Oxford: The Clarendon Press, 1945), paragraphs 341–60.
33. For a very useful and quick overview of these substages, see the diagram provided in the *Philosophy of Religion*, 498–99.
34. Hegel, *The Philosophy of Right*, #355. The title of the book cited is "On the Decline of Natural States," which very much accords with Hegel's theme.
35. "But this unity is in the case of the family essentially one of feeling, remaining within the limits of the natural," *Philosophy of History*, 71.
36. Ibid.
37. Ibid.
38. Hegel, *The Philosophy of Right*, #355.
39. See *Philosophy of History*, 79–102 for a *very* telling geographical version of his historical narrative. In that section, Hegel makes his Eurocentrism quite explicit when he says, both of history and geography that "the Old Word [i.e., Europe]—the scene of the World's History" (87) and claims that: "For three-quarters of the globe the Mediterranean Sea is similarly the uniting element, and the center of World-History" (87).
40. Ibid., 354.
41. Ibid., 5–6, 19–29.
42. Ibid., 410; all italics Hegel's.
43. Ibid., 21.
44. Ibid., 25.
45. Hegel, *The Philosophy of Right*, #351.
46. Hegel, *Philosophy of History*, 39. Cf. *Philosophy of Right*, #349: "A nation does not begin by being a state. The transition from a family, a horde, a clan, a multitude, &c., to political conditions is the realization of the Idea in the form of that nation. Without this form, a nation, as—an ethical substance—which is what it is implicitly, lacks the objectivity of possessing in its own eyes and in the eyes of others, a universal and universally valid embodiment in laws, i.e. in determinate thoughts, and as a result it fails to secure recognition from others. So long as it lacks objective law and an explicitly established rational constitution, its autonomy is formal only and is not sovereignty."
47. See the discussion of Tiele in chapter 4.
48. Hegel, *Philosophy of History*, 39.
49. Ibid., 38.
50. Ibid.

51. Ibid., 39.
52. Ibid., 26–27, 50.
53. Ibid., 33–34, 35, 49.
54. See discussion of van der Leeuw below.
55. Hegel, *Lectures on the Philosophy of Religion*, 203.
56. Ibid., 76.
57. Ibid.
58. Ibid., 104. Hegel continues this thought in a way which is telling for his subsequent treatment of religious history: "Every realization, however, is a relationship in which two aspects must be considered: the elevation of the human being to God, the consciousness that itself is conscious of God, of spirit; and the spirit that realizes itself in consciousness" (104). As discussed below in the body, there is a correlation between the stage of consciousness that apprehends God as an object and the nature of the object which that consciousness can apprehend. Consequently, a "higher" stage of religion means a higher qualitative human being.
59. Ibid., 213–14.
60. Ibid., 214.
61. Ibid., 203; emphasis added.
62. Ibid., 207.
63. Ibid., 219.
64. Ibid., 215. Hegel see this at the level of thought as well: "What is primordial as a state, however, is savagery, while on the other hand what is primordial in thought is the concept, which realizes itself by releasing from the form of its naturalness" (215). The incapacity of the savage to release from the form of naturalness is the cognitive dimension of the savage's overall degeneracy.
65. Ibid., 208.
66. Which Hegel calls "magic"; see ibid., 221–22.
67. Ibid., 222.
68. Ibid., 251. Hegel here equates "Lamaism" with Indian Buddhism.
69. Ibid.
70. Ibid., 255–56.
71. Ibid., 252. Note how Hegel essentializes Buddhists as a group. They have a collective "character," nature, or *Wesen*. This move is possible by means of his idealization or Spiritualization of concrete reality. Again, in terms of the problem that we began with as articulated by Seiwert, Hegel opts for the notion that religions are finally not empirical matters; the "truth" of a religion or religion in general is an ideal object and/or Spirit. This idealization vis-à-vis both an antimaterialist idealism and the concept of Spirit runs through the whole of the discourse of the phenomenology of religion.
72. Ibid., 254–55.
73. Ibid., 256. Cf. p. 258, where he reiterates this point more forcefully: "This may appear to us as the most repugnant, shocking, and unbelievable tenet.... We must learn to understand this view, and in understanding it we shall see its justification. We shall show how it has its ground, its rational

aspect, a place in the evolution of reason.... It is easy to say that such a religion is just senseless and irrational. What is not easy is to recognize the necessity and truth of such religious forms, their connection with reason..."

74. Ibid., 267–69.
75. Ibid., 269.
76. Ibid., 270–71.
77. Ibid., 271.
78. Ibid., 275–82.
79. Ibid., 283. Again, note the essentialization of an entire people on the basis of the category of consciousness. Its ideality allows it to encompass a plethora of individual empirical instances. Were one to reverse the priority between the ideal and the empirical, it would not be possible to essentialize *in this way*.
80. Ibid., 290.
81. Hegel, *Philosophy of History*, 163.
82. Hegel, *Philosophy of Religion*, 291 and 289. Cf. *Philosophy of History*, 158: "Thus the moral condition of the Hindoos ... shows itself most abandoned. In this all Englishmen agree." Note the use of the European colonizer's perspective as a source for his information about Hindus.
83. Hegel, *Philosophy of History*, 161.
84. Ibid.
85. Ibid.
86. Ibid., 167. All of these arguments taken together form, of course, an apologia for colonization. That Indians would be "better off" under Euro-British-Christian rule is a rather obvious conclusion to be drawn.
87. Hegel, *Philosophy of Religion*, 328. The classification of some religions as "ethnic religions," and Judaism in particular as a "merely" ethnic religion, is a common feature of the metanarrative *and* the static taxonomy of the phenomenology of religion. While the particulars differ, the structural relationship in which this classification of Judaism and the category "ethnic religion" is embedded is consistent throughout this discourse.
88. Ibid., 357.
89. Ibid., 371–72.
90. Ibid., 393.
91. Ibid., 109.
92. Ibid., 391.
93. Ibid., 393. Cf. Richard Beardsworth, *Derrida and the Political*, 56: "For Hegel, the central experience of Christianity is, in philosophical form, the falling of the infinite into the finite and the subsumption of the finite into the infinite. Thus, grasped speculatively, the historic Good Friday is the mediation of the infinite and finite. No other religion apart from Christianity has 're-cognized' the limit between the infinite and the finite as mediation. This is why, for Hegel, Christianity is the true religion."
94. Hegel, *Philosophy of Religion*, 393.

95. Ibid., 391. Cf. Rosen, *G. W. F. Hegel*, 242: "Hegel unites ontology and logic"—theology and logic as well, and also theology and ontology.

96. Cf. Paul Tillich, *Systematic Theology* (Chicago: University of Chicago Press, 1951), 75: "Ontological reason can be defined as the structure of the mind which enables it to grasp and to shape reality. From the time of Parmenides it has been a common assumption of all philosophers that the logos, the word which grasps and shapes reality, can do so only because reality itself has a logos character [or structure]."

97. Hegel, *Philosophy of History*, 18–19.

98. Hegel, *Philosophy of Religion*, 110.

99. Hegel, *Phenomenology of Spirit*, #766. Cf. "Hegel's philosophy of history and his history of philosophy show how substance becomes subject." Beardsworth, *Derrida and the Political*, 56.

100. Recall how, in chapter 1, Hegel described matter as having its center out of itself.

101. Hegel, *Phenomenology of Spirit*, #25.

102. Hegel, *Philosophy of Religion*, 418.

103. Ibid., 415.

104. Ibid., 414.

105. Ibid.

106. Ibid., 415.

107. Ibid., 430.

108. Ibid., 431.

109. Ibid., 429.

110. Ibid.

111. Ibid., 431.

112. Ibid., 469.

113. Ibid., 528, from the glossary provided by the editors.

114. Ibid., 467.

115. Ibid., 464; emphasis added.

116. Ibid., 469.

117. Ibid., 462.

118. Ibid., 459.

119. Ibid., 76.

120. Ibid., 459–60.

121. Ibid., 413. Cf. "Thus Spirit is essentially Energy; and in regard to Spirit one cannot set aside its manifestation. The manifestation of Spirit is its actual self-determination, and this is the element of its concrete nature. Spirit which does not determine itself is an abstraction of the intellect. The manifestation of Spirit is its self-determination, and it is this manifestation that we have to investigate in the form of states and individuals." *Philosophy of History*, 26 html. Cf. p. 54 of same: "The very essence of spirit is *action*."

122. Hegel, *Philosophy of Religion*, 405.

123. Ibid., 443.

124. Hegel, *The Phenomenology of Spirit*, #767.

125. Hegel, *Philosophy of Religion*, 411.
126. Ibid., 411.
127. Ibid., 473.
128. Ibid., 434.
129. Hegel, *Philosophy of Right*, #346.
130. Hegel, *Philosophy of History*, 335.
131. Ibid., 335.
132. Ibid., 5, 19.
133. Ibid., 393.
134. Ibid., 4, 18.
135. Ibid., 349; Hegel's italics.
136. Ibid., 350.
137. Ibid., 351.
138. Ibid.
139. Ibid., 353.
140. Ibid., 417. Hegel is adamant that the Reformation is fundamentally a German event: "The Reformation originated in Germany, and struck firm roots only in the purely German nations." Hegel, *Philosophy of History*, 419.
141. Ibid., 416. Cf. "Thus subjective spirit gains emancipation in the Truth, abnegates [*aufheben*] its particularity and comes to itself in realizing the truth of its being" (416).
142. Ibid., 456.
143. Ibid., 416.

## Chapter 4. Religion in Essence and Development

1. Jonathan Z. Smith, "Classification," entry in *Guide to the Study of Religion*, ed. Willi Braun and Russell T. McCutcheon (London and New York: Cassell, 2000), 35. Cf. Eric Sharpe's statement in *Comparative Religion*, cited in chapter 1 in the discussion of the pedigree of the phenomenology of religion, that "Tiele was the Max Müller of the Continent."

2. Jonathan Z. Smith, *Relating Religion: Essays in the Study of Religion* (Chicago: University of Chicago Press, 2004), 167.

3. These lectures were both written and delivered in English so there are no issues of translation in the documents themselves. I have also used the English translation of *Outlines of the History of Religion* (full reference below) but again, I do not find any serious translation issues in that document.

4. Cornelius Petronius Tiele, *Elements of the Science of Religion* (London: William and Sons; New York: AMS Press, U.S.A. Distribution, Vol. I, 1896; Vol. II, 1898), Vol. I, 27. Subsequent references to Tiele's *Elements of the Science of Religion* will be given as *Elements*, volume number, and page number.

5. Ibid.

6. *Elements* I, 219. On the development of his concept of Development, Tiele notes that "In the '*Theologisch Tijdschrift*' of 1874 I wrote an article on 'The Laws of the Development of Religion.' " He goes on to say of that article:

"But I still adhere to the article as a whole, and have not altered my opinion in point of principle." *Elements* I, 213 and 214.

7. Ibid., 29–30 and 272.

8. Ibid., 30. Cf. p. 55: "Our proper task will thus be to show how one form not merely succeeds but grows out of another, and in such a way that the more developed form contains nothing essential that cannot be found, though in less perfect shape, or merely as a germ, in all the preceding forms from the very first."

9. Ibid., 32.

10. Ibid., 220.

11. *Elements* II, 187.

12. Ibid., 188.

13. *Elements* I, 226.

14. Ibid., 55.

15. See ibid., 51, where he concludes his discussion of Iranian religion: "All this proves, not that an existing lower religion was discarded in order to be replaced by a new and higher religion, but that the existing religion of Iran assimilated as much as it could from the Zarathustrian doctrine, and thus, although it mutilated the doctrine and applied it very imperfectly, was itself reformed and proceeded to develop itself in this direction."

16. Ibid., 243.

17. Ibid., 281.

18. Ibid., 295.

19. Ibid., 299–300. Cf. Chantepie de la Saussaye, *Manual of the Science of Religion*, 12: "Teleology seems so essential to the study of intellectual phenomena, that many who as a rule follow the theory of evolution (as Von Hartmann), cannot entirely renounce it."

20. *Elements* I, 233.

21. Ibid., 230. Cf. 33, 220, and 232.

22. Ibid., 214. See p. 216, where he makes this point in relation to the school of historians that deny the existence of historical laws: "But although we are grateful to" the historians for the results of their purely descriptive work, "and admit that they must be carefully reckoned with, we decline to rest satisfied with them, and we deem it our duty further to inquire what they teach us concerning the development of the human mind in different directions." Cf. also pp. 215 and 218.

23. Ibid., 232.

24. Cf. Schnädelbach, *Philosophy in Germany*, 85: "In the Germany of the nineteenth and twentieth centuries, empiricism has been a philosophy for natural scientists; in this form it has since Comte also been called positivism . . ." Throughout the *Elements*, Tiele has an ongoing polemic with positivistic conceptions of science. See, e.g., I, 51, 215ff., and II, 208ff. See also the discussion of this issue in chapter 1.

25. *Elements* I, 216 and 217.

26. *Elements* II, 186.

27. Ibid.

28. Ibid., 186–87.
29. Ibid., 187.
30. Ibid., 1.
31. Ibid., 3. Note the qualification "sound and normal." It opens the door to a normative evaluation of what counts as true religion as opposed to "degenerate religion," a move we will see more often than one would expect from a school that claims to be doing neutral description of the "contents of consciousness," as phenomenologists often describe themselves and their approach. This ranking of religions in relation to essence is a fortiori, I would argue, and not simply a "defect" of this approach. In the structurations of ontotheology, consciousness and Spirit are *necessarily* ranked higher than body and Nature.
32. Ibid., 187.
33. Ibid., 188.
34. Ibid.
35. Ibid., 187–88.
36. Ibid., 188.
37. Ibid., 14.
38. Ibid., 190–91. Cf. 78–79: "We must therefore, as I have already said, search for unity, for the abiding, for the essential, not in any conception, however general or enduring it may seem to be, but solely in the religious thoughts and aspirations to which the conceptions give expression. When we find such thoughts constantly reviving under new forms, we may reasonably assume that they are essentials of religion."
39. Ibid., 6–7.
40. Ibid., 75.
41. Ibid., 196.
42. Ibid., 197–98.
43. Ibid., 198.
44. Ibid., 233.
45. Ibid., 228.
46. Ibid., 231.
47. Ibid., 230.
48. Ibid., 235.
49. Ibid., 231.
50. Ibid.
51. *Elements* I, 60.
52. Ibid., 60–61.
53. C. P. Tiele, *Outlines of the History of Religion to the Spread of the Universal Religions*, trans. J. Estlin Carpenter (London: Kegan Paul, Trench, Trübner, 6th ed., 1896), 6; emphasis added. Henceforth cited as *Outlines* with page numbers following.
54. *Elements* I, 63; emphasis added.
55. Ibid. One of the things that an Idealist history does is depoliticize change. Tiele does not so much as entertain the notion that this change could be the result of a civil war within a society or the violent domination of

one society over another. Hegel, in some ways to his credit, does not fully depoliticize history: recall his remarks about the "slaughter bench" and the relative rights of developed peoples over their "barbarians."

56. *Outlines*, 3.
57. Ibid., 5.
58. Ibid., 9.
59. Ibid., 10.
60. Ibid., 11.
61. Ibid.
62. Ibid., 10.
63. Ibid., 15. For a contemporary version of this view, see Murphy, *Representing Religion*, 23–25, where there is a discussion of the treatment of "indigenous religions" in a contemporary world religions textbook. On one page of that section, I counted fifty different "indigenous" cultures referred to as examples of the idea being reviewed. We still do not treat "indigenous religions" the same way we treat "historical religions." The categorical scheme is a remnant of this tradition of classifying religions.
64. Ibid., 16. This denigration of the religion of Native Americans is a consistent theme in this history. Hegel, in his *Philosophy of History* and Wach in his *Types of Religious Experience: Christian and non-Christian*, both make similar arguments.
65. Ibid., 18. Cf. 19: "The character of the American with his somber earnestness, his sagacity and silence, his passionateness combined with a self-mastery which expresses itself outwardly in gravity and at least apparent indifference, and enables him to endure the most terrible torments with a smile, is reflected in his religion." Again, all Native Americans share essential, i.e., racial, characteristics, regardless of differences of material conditions, specific histories, languages, or other empirical markers of cultural identity. The kernel is ever unchanging even if the husk is variable.
66. Ibid., 20.
67. Ibid., 20–21. Cf. 22: "The names by which these nations designate the gods in general, *teotl* among the Mexicans, *guacas* among the Peruvians, signify nothing more than spirits." He includes the Inca on several occasions with the Aztecs and Mayans. By claiming that these groups worship "spirits" and not "gods" he is clearly claiming, *pace* Hegel, that they have a deficient conception of the divine.
68. Ibid., 21.
69. Ibid., 23.
70. Ibid.
71. Ibid., 24.
72. Ibid.
73. Ibid.
74. Ibid., 17. Cf. 15: "[I]t is necessary to point out the special causes which have led to its development among different races in such different forms and degrees. Of these the principal are (1) the different if characters of these races, (2) the nature of their home and occupations, and (3) the historic

relations in which some of them stood to their neighbors." To indicate that this is not simply an aberrant statement by Tiele, cf. also 16: "The great influence of national character on religion is specially apparent among peoples, which, though living in the same climate and engaged in the same occupations—like the Papuans, the Melanesians, and Polynesians—stand at such different stages of development: while the religion of the Americans, on the other hand, though they are spread over a whole quarter of the globe, and diverge so widely in civilization, exhibits everywhere the same character, and is everywhere accompanied by the same usages."

75. Ibid., 27.
76. Ibid., 28.
77. Ibid., 27.
78. On Confucianism as an ethical religion, as opposed to a nature religion, see *Elements* I, 121: "Let us first say a word about the religions which may be considered to have attained this pitch of development [i.e., ethical or nomic religions]. About some of them there can be no doubt. I need only mention Judaism, sprung from the Mosaic community, founded upon the sacred Torah, the law revealed to Moses by God himself, and upon the preaching of the inspired prophets; or the Brahmanic community with its Veda as a book of revelation, comprising the whole divine science of redemption, infinite and eternal, not imagined, but actually seen by the ancient bards; or Confucianism, which reveres Kong-tse, the great sage of China, as its founder, and possesses its sacred writ in the five Kings, or canonical books, and the four Shu, or classical books, of which the last-named emanated from the school of Kong." While ethical religions play an important part in *Weltgeschichte*, it is important to remember that Tiele sharply differentiates them from universal religions on the basis of their "particularism." However sophisticated, Confucius's ideas are still marked, *pace* Hegel, by εθνος, and have not emancipated themselves to full *Frieheit*, to full Λογος.

79. *Elements* I, 122.
80. This is a very consistent pattern of differentiation for Tiele. See *Elements* I, 200: "Among the Chinese, for example, the former is the case. There we find the somewhat sober Confucianism, the religion of the wise Kong, who in the sixth century before our era reformed the then existing imperial cult, a religion consisting mainly in the worship of spirits, especially of deceased ancestors, and in the observance of an elaborate morality, adapted to practice, and applied to private, social, and political life. And beside it we find Tao-ism, the religion whose adherents appeal to Lao-tse, Kong-tse's elder contemporary, with his bold, profound, and often gloomy speculations, his love of solitude and of escape from the duties of practical life, his unbounded belief in miracles—a religion which, among an undeveloped people, incapable of following the lofty flight of the Master, degenerated into dreary superstition, a combination of the ancient mythology with a poor-spirited morality and the silliest sorcerics."

81. *Outlines*, 37.
82. Ibid., 35.

83. Ibid.,37. He is quick to point out, however, that it would be a mistake to tie this morality to rationality: "It is altogether erroneous to regard Tao, with Rémusat, as the primeval Reason, λογος, and worse still to call the Tao-sse [sic] the Chinese rationalists. This character fits them least of all, and they do their utmost to be as unreasonable as possible."

84. That he thought thus is clear. See *Outlines*, 35: "The humane but prosaic Confucianism might satisfy the majority of cultivated Chinese, but it did not meet all wants." Speaking of the view that Tiele believes these Confucian Chinese have of Taoism, he says: "The cultivated Chinese now regard it with unmixed contempt." *Outlines*, 35. Need it be said that "cultivated" = "*Bildung*" = "*Kultur*" = *Geist*?

85. *Outlines*, 34. On this point regarding the "Orient," cf. Hegel (*Philosophy of Right*, #355): "The Oriental realm. The world-view of this first realm is substantial, without inward division, and it arises in natural communities patriarchically governed. According to this view, the mundane form of government is theocratic, the ruler is also a high priest or God himself; constitution and legislation are at the same time religion, while religious and moral commands, or usages rather, are at the same time natural and positive law."

86. Ibid., 30.
87. Ibid., 30–31.
88. Ibid., 31.
89. Ibid., 38.
90. Hegel, *Philosophy of History*, 16 html.
91. Hegel, Philosophy of Right, #347.
92. *Elements* I, 125.
93. Ibid., 61. The "modern world" is, of course, the world as colonized by Europeans.
94. Ibid., 233. The allusion to Hegel's *Philosophy of Religion* is clear. See Hegel, *Lectures on the Philosophy of Religion*, 391ff., where he describes Christianity as the "Consummate Religion," and discussion above.
95. *Elements* II, 254.
96. *Elements* I, 212.
97. He does, *in addition*, make this claim as one of "those who, like myself, are convinced that the Gospel, rightly understood, contains the eternal principles of true religion" (*Elements I*, 148). While I think it would be totally inaccurate to reduce Tiele's view to that of a Christian theologian, this statement (along with many others that could be marshaled) does lend weight to the fact that he held a starkly Christocentric—besides Eurocentric and logocentric—view of religion and of the world generally. His Christianity is, I would argue, a kind of Liberal *Kulturprotestantismus*, not an evangelical Christianity.
98. *Elements* II, 79–80.
99. Ibid., 80.
100. *Elements* I, 45.
101. Ibid., 126–27; emphasis added.

102. Ibid., 127–28.
103. *Elements* II, 254–55.
104. Ibid., 262–63; emphasis added.

## Chapter 5. "Experience, Expression, Understanding"

1. Richard E. Palmer, *Hermeneutics: Interpretation Theory in Schleiermacher, Dilthey, Heidegger, and Gadamer* (Evanston: Northwestern University Press, 1969), 106. Although he generally disagrees with Palmer's (and Gadamer's) rendition of Dilthey's philosophy, Andre Bowie agrees with Palmer about this tri-part structure in Dilthey: "A science like psychology belongs for Dilthey to the *Geisteswissenschaften* 'only if its object becomes accessible to us in behavior which is founded in the nexus of life [*Zusammenhang*], expression, and understanding': the trio of '*Erlebnis*, expression and understanding' therefore become the foundation of the *Geisteswissenschaften*." Andre Bowie, *From Romanticism to Critical Theory: The Philosophy of German Literary Theory*) London and New York: Routledge, 1997), 151, citing from Dilthey's *Der Aufbau der geschichtlichen Welt in den Geisteswissenschaft*, 99.

2. Palmer, *Hermeneutics*, 107.

3. Ibid.

4. Ibid. For an excellent history of the term *Erlebnis*, see Hans-Georg Gadamer, *Truth and Method*, 60–64.

5. Wilhelm Dilthey, *Introduction to the Human Sciences: An Attempt to Lay a Foundation for the Study of Society and History*, trans. with an Introductory Essay Ramon J. Betanzos (Detroit: Wayne State University Press, 1988), 72–73. Cf. Bambach, *Heidegger, Dilthey, and the Crisis of Historicism*, 132. Because of some differences of translation and availability at the time of writing, I have used two different translations of this work of Dilthey's: Betanzos's translation (cited here) and the more widely available translation edited by Makkreel and Rodi (Princeton: Princeton University Press, 1989). Wherever possible, I have given references to the latter. Where no indication is given, Makkreel's and Rodi's translation is being cited.

6. Dilthey, *Introduction to the Human Sciences* (Betanzos's trans.), 80 (60–61 in Makkreel and Rodi's translation).

7. Ibid., 248. Cf. 247: "We can call what has just been set forth the principle of phenomenality, since it involves insight into the phenomenality of what is real, that is, of all external facts. Everything is a fact of consciousness, and accordingly is subject to the conditions of consciousness. This principle cannot be derived from one more comprehensive. Only by bringing in intermediate terms can the principle be elucidated and exhibited as the general expression of what inner experience confirms in every case and at every moment."

8. Cf. Gadamer, *Truth and Method*, 65: "Following Descartes' formulation of the *res cogitans*, he defines the concept of experience by reflexivity, by interiority." Gadamer and others rightly argue, in my view, that for all his

attempts to do so, Dilthey never gets out of the Cartesian framework. He merely expands it to include the non-, or extrarational elements of subjectivity and then adds a Hegelian notion of culture as objective *Geist* (discussed below). This is largely true of the phenomenology of religion in general: they never get out of the "Cartesian theater of consciousness." When they attempt to do so, they resort to "objective spirit" and its corollaries.

9. Dilthey, *Introduction to the Human Sciences*, 248.
10. Ibid., 253–54.
11. Ibid., 247 n4, editor's note.
12. Ibid., 246.
13. Ibid., 245; emphasis added.
14. Ibid., 61. A brief side note: although I have not seen this mentioned by any Dilthey commentators, on the issue of the difference between *Erlebnis* as "lived experience" and *Erfahrung* as phenomenal experience (closely connected to the concept of *Vorstellung*, or representation), Dilthey seems to me to be very indebted to Schopenhauer's argument in his famous work, *The World as Will and as Representation* (*Vorstellung*). Dilthey frequently invokes experience of the will as typical and illustrative of the differences between the realms or modes of experience.
15. Ibid.
16. Bowie, *From Romanticism to Critical Theory*, 151. Bowie cites Derrida's *L'écriture et la différence*, 427 (the English version is listed in the bibliography of this work). He also refers the reader to Dilthey's *Die Geistig Welt: Einleitung in die Philosophie Lebens*, 151.
17. Dilthey, *Introduction to the Human Sciences* (Betanzos's trans.), 72–73 (50 in Makkreel and Rodi's translation). Cf. Bambach, *Heidegger, Dilthey, and the Crisis of Historicism*, 132.
18. Dilthey, *Gesammelte Schriften*, Vol. XIX, 446, cited in Frithjof Rodi, "Dilthey's Concept of 'Structure' Within the Context of Nineteenth-Century Science and Philosophy," in *Dilthey and Phenomenology*, ed. Rudolf A. Makkreel and John Scanlon (Washington, DC: Center for Advanced Research in Phenomenology and University Press of America, 1987), 107. This article has a short, but informative history of the concepts of structure and nexus in German thought.
19. On the use of the term *nexus*, or *der Zusammenhang*, Makreel and Rodi note: " 'nexus'—a favorite word of Dilthey's." Rudolf Makkreel and Frithjof Rodi, "Introduction," in Dilthey's *Introduction to the Human Sciences*, 9. Rodi ("Dilthey's Concept of 'Structure,' " 113) argues that the concept of the inner structure of lived-experience "does not belong merely to a 'psychologistic' phase which was overcome by the 'hermeneutical' approach of the later writings," i.e., it was a continuous idea held throughout his career.
20. Dilthey, Introduction to the Human Sciences, 263–64.
21. Ibid., 265.
22. Rodi, "Dilthey's Concept of 'Structure,' " 114.
23. Gadamer, *Truth and Method*, 225.
24. Dilthey, *Introduction to the Human Sciences*, 269.

25. Ibid., 270.
26. Ibid., 268.
27. Bowie, *From Romanticism to Critical Theory*, 151, citing from Dilthey's *Die Geistig Welt*, 151.
28. Gadamer, *Truth and Method*, 223. Gadamer is here quoting from Dilthey's *Gesammelte Schriften*, Vol. VII, 177.
29. Cf. Rodi, "Dilthey's Concept of 'Structure,'" 110, "By speaking of the articulation of the facts of consciousness, Dilthey points to the fact that the entirety of the facts of consciousness is not an inarticulate cluster of elementary relations a descriptive analysis would have to single out but, on the contrary, a complex whole for which, in his later terminology he would adopt the term 'structure' [*Struktur*]. In this sense 'structure,' along with 'nexus' [*Zusammenhang*], 'articulation' [*Gliederung*], 'differentiation,' etc., belongs to the basic categories of a holistic approach to the entirety of the facts of consciousness as lived experience." As an aside, it is probably a fair conjecture to say that is a point where Germanic-Continental philosophy and Anglophonic British-American philosophy differ in an important way. For Hume, the inner percepts are a mere "bundle" without, I believe it would be fair to say, any structure: Hume atomizes the contents of consciousness; separateness of percepts is the given, what must be explained is how they get unified. For Dilthey and Continental thought, structure is basic to the phenomena themselves, i.e., is the way they come packaged, so to speak. It is easy, therefore, for Continental thinkers to think of and with structured wholes, while Anglophones think of and with isolated, atomized elements. The differences between Adam Smith and Karl Marx are, arguably, a product of this more basic difference. The differences between Eliade and inductive empiricists may be due, in part, to this difference as well.
30. Dilthey, *Introduction to the Human Sciences*, 263–64.
31. Ibid., 265.
32. Gadamer, *Truth and Method*, 223.
33. Dilthey, *Pattern and Meaning in History*, ed. H. P. Rickman (New York: Harper and Row, 1961), 99–100, 74–77. This is a translation of the selections from Dilthey's *Gesammelte Schriften*, Vol. VII, and references to that work are given in the translation by the editor.
34. Ibid., 74; italics added.
35. Gadamer, *Truth and Method*, 67.
36. Dilthey, *Pattern and Meaning in History*, 99–100 and 74–77.
37. Ramon Betanzos, "Wilhelm Dilthey: An Introduction," in *Introduction to the Human Sciences: An Attempt to Lay a Foundation for the Study of Society and History*, 34. The slogan in Hegel was, readers will recall, "*das Wahre ist das Ganze*."
38. Dilthey, *Pattern and Meaning in History*, 105.
39. Ibid., 103. Gadamer, (*Truth and Method*, 61) notes that, for Dilthey, "something becomes an 'experience' not only insofar as it is experienced, but insofar as its being experienced makes a special impression that gives it lasting importance." That is to say, the definition of something as *Erlebnis* is, in part,

the fact that it stands out as "significant" in relation to the whole. This is, Gadamer wants to argue, part of the etymology of the term *Erlebnis*: "For we have seen that the coinage *Erlebnis* has a condensing, intensifying meaning. If something is called or considered an *Erlebnis*, that means it is rounded into the unity of a significant whole" (Gadamer, 66). By connecting the concepts of experience and meaning so closely, Dilthey is, in essence, saying that human life is inherently meaningful. This is a point of which later phenomenologists would make a great deal. It is part of the story of how "religion" became defined as a sphere of meaning, or "ultimate meaning." By elevating the category of meaning to the level of scientific method, Dilthey opened the door to a science of religion that could use hermeneutics as its foundation—rather than the reductive (and often dismissive) explanatory approaches.

40. Those seeking to rehabilitate Dilthey from what they argue is a misinterpretation (particularly by Gadamer), viz., Bowie and Bambach, will certainly take issue with any exposition of Dilthey that is reliant upon this work. Were our concern here to "get Dilthey right," there would be every reason to argue this way. However, the aim here is to read Dilthey as he was read by phenomenologists of religion, and, rightly or wrongly, in the *Rezeptionsgeschichte* of Dilthey, this work figures quite prominently.

41. Wilhelm Dilthey, *Poetry and Experience*, ed. Rudolf Makkreel and Frithjof Rodi (Princeton: Princeton University Press, 1985), 34. Cf. the statement from a document (drafts of the "Althoff Letter") included by the editors of *Introduction to the Human Sciences* (495): "Thus the foundation is created for dealing with the following question: How can the sciences of mankind, society, and history come into being from the experiences of human-cultural life? The claim that reality—the only complete reality that we possess—is given in inner experience, with its corresponding understanding of other people, forms the first part of the epistemology of the human sciences."

42. Dilthey, *Poetry and Experience*, 35.

43. Ibid., 35. Andre Bowie (*From Romanticism to Critical Theory*, 149), makes an interesting and astute point on this issue: Compared with "Derrida's assertion that the subject is merely an 'effect of the general text' ... The key problem is the relationship between the 'general' aspect of the text and what Schleiermacher and Dilthey see as the inherently individual aspect of 'literature.' " Clearly, the tradition of hermeneutics that stems from Schleiermacher and Dilthey is centered on the subject. As will be discussed below, the only issue here is whether the subject is better understood as more of an individual phenomenon or more of a collective phenomenon. Schleiermacher seems to have rather clearly kept his emphasis on the former, while Hegel emphasized the latter. Dilthey's career is marked by the move from an early emphasis on the individualistic paradigm of the subject (as seen in his famous work, *Poetry and Experience*) and a later emphasis on a more collective notion of the subject (discussed below). In either case, my argument is that he never broke out of the "metaphysics of the subject," and it was this dimension of his thought that was appropriated by the phenomenology of religion.

44. Dilthey, *Pattern and Meaning in History*, 67. In fact, Dilthey makes this connection between inner experience and literary object almost the definition of literature: "[O]nly to the extent that a psychic element, or a combination of them, stands in relation to a lived experience and its presentation can it be a constituent of literature." Dilthey, *Poetry and Experience*, 56.

45. Dilthey, *Poetry and Experience*, 56.

46. Dilthey, *Pattern and Meaning in History*, 117.

47. Ibid., 75.

48. Dilthey, *Poetry and Experience*, 104; italics Dilthey's.

49. Dilthey, *Selected Writings*, 249; emphasis added.

50. Bowie, *From Romanticism to Critical Theory*, 148.

51. Dilthey, *Pattern and Meaning in History*, 76.

52. Ibid., 123; italics Dilthey's. In his "General Introduction" to this work (22), Rickman, who is also its translator, explains the choices he made in translating the various meanings of the terms "*Geist*" and "*objektiver Geist*": "One set of problems which faces the translator is concerned with the terms '*Geist*,' '*geistige Welt*,' '*objektiver Geist*,' and '*Geisteswissenschaften*.' These terms convey quite clearly certain connections which underpin Dilthey's central arguments. The '*objektive Geist*' is the creation of '*Geist*' and constitutes the '*geistige Welt*.' The latter is the subject matter of the '*Geisteswissenschaften*' and in them '*Geist*' grasps what '*Geist*' has created. This connection cannot, as far as I can see, be fully conveyed in an English translation. '*Geist*' I have translated as 'mind' and '*objektiver Geist*' by which Dilthey refers to such things as language, poetry, religion, science, art, social organizations, as 'objective mind.'" I find the choice of "mind" in both cases somewhat unfortunate and would prefer "spirit," although the reasoning is clear enough. In the German tradition, and I see no difference in Dilthey (quite to the contrary, in fact), the difference between "mind" and "spirit" is that the former is the passive receptacle of that which is, as it were, "non-spirit," i.e., sensory experience, while the latter connotes the self-originating action of that which is spirit upon itself. This distinction is absolutely crucial for both Dilthey and the entire tradition being reviewed here.

53. Gadamer, *Truth and Method*, 224; italics Gadamer's.

54. Ibid.

55. Ibid., 228; italics Gadamer's.

56. Dilthey, *Pattern and Meaning in History*, 120.

57. Ibid., 121.

58. Ibid., 127.

59. Gadamer, *Truth and Method*, 228.

60. Dilthey, *Selected Writings*, 261–62.

61. Note how similar this is to Hegel's narrative of *Geist's* coming to self-knowledge. "Knowing" is, ultimately, knowledge of self. Again, Dilthey tries to ground this in a Cartesian phenomenalism of inner experience, and so, *in his sense*, in a kind of empirical manner. As such, he hoped to have avoided the a priorism of Absolute Idealism.

62. Dilthey, *Pattern and Meaning in History*, 67–68. Cf. elsewhere (*Selected Writings*, 261–62) where he argues that historical reconstruction and/or the interpretation of texts "is possible only on the conditions that the other person's expression contains nothing which is not also part of the observer. The same functions and elements are present in all individuals and their degree of strength accounts for the variety in the make-up of different people. The same external world is mirrored in everyone's ideas..."

63. Dilthey, *Pattern and Meaning in History*, 67.

64. Dilthey, *Gesammelte Schriften*, Vol. VII, 148, cited in, and translated by, Bambach, *Heidegger, Dilthey, and the Crisis of Historicism*, 150.

65. Bambach, *Heidegger, Dilthey, and the Crisis of Historicism*, 150, citing paragraph 331 of Vico's *Scienza Nuova* (reference to English translation given below).

66. Giambattista Vico, *The New Science*, trans. Thomas G. Bergin and Max H. Fisch (Ithaca and London: Cornell University Press, 1968), 96, paragraph 331. Vico's full statement on this is worth noting, as it very much resembles Dilthey's argument here. Vico argues that, despite the lack of information about ancient civilizations, it is nevertheless possible to reconstruct them by analogy, because, "the world of civil society has certainly been made by men, and that its principles are therefore to be found within the modifications of our own human mind" (Vico, 96, paragraph 331).

67. Gadamer, *Truth and Method*, 222.

68. Dilthey, *Gesammelte Schriften*, Vol. XIX, 347, cited in Rodi, "Dilthey's Concept of 'Structure,' " 115.

69. Dilthey, *Pattern and Meaning in History*, 66.

70. Gadamer, *Truth and Method*, 222.

71. Dilthey, *Pattern and Meaning in History*, 107; italics Dilthey's.

72. Ibid., 106.

73. Ibid.

74. Ibid., 108.

75. Ibid.,77.

76. Ibid.,112.

77. Derrida, *Of Grammatology*, 24 and 26.

78. Dilthey, *Selected Writings*, 248.

79. Bowie, *From Romanticism to Critical Theory*, 149.

80. Dilthey, *Selected Writings*, 248. He touches here on the issue of *Nachleben*, which van der Leeuw and Wach elevate to a doctrine and to which Eliade makes frequent reference.

81. Ibid.

82. Ibid.

83. Ibid.

84. Ibid.,249.

85. Ibid.

86. Ibid., 248. Cf. 249: "Understanding takes its place beside the analysis of inner experience and both together demonstrate the possibilities and limits

of general knowledge in the human studies [*Geisteswissenschaften*] in so far as it is determined by the way in which we are originally presented with mental facts."

87. Ibid., 258. Cf. farther down on the same page: "In the process of interpretation itself we can only distinguish two aspects to grasping an intellectual creation through linguistic signs. Grammatical interpretation proceeds from link to link to the highest combinations in the world of the work. The psychological interpretation starts with penetrating the inner creative process and proceeds to the outer and inner from of the work and from there to a further grasp of the unity of all his works in the mentality and development of their author." Again, on the same page, the play of inner and outer is key to both thinkers: "Here we have reached the point from which Schleiermacher developed the rules of interpretation in a masterly fashion. His theory of inner and outer form is fundamental..."

88. Dilthey does not, by any means, abandon the concept of *Entwicklung*. See Dilthey, *Pattern and Meaning in History*, 105. "Thus the present is filled with the past and carries the future within itself. This is the meaning of the word 'development' [*Entwicklung*] in the human studies." This is very much in line with Hegel's theme of the cumulative nature of Spirit, which grows but remains constant at the same time. This process is for Dilthey, too, a rational one wherein the idea of structure plays a vital role: "With this concept of development goes that of formation [*Gestaltung*]. Formation is a general characteristic of life." *Pattern and Meaning in History*, 105. That is, life itself is structured; conversely, structure is a feature of life, not an a priori category imposed upon objects of interpretation. He is implicitly arguing that he has found an "object" feature of the world which grounds his theory. Phenomenologists of religion will make similar claims; their hermeneutics are, they will argue, not arbitrary but reflect the very structures of consciousness itself. This is in keeping with the phenomenological pursuit of an apodictic foundation. Phenomenology, in virtually all its forms, is a foundational project. The search for such immutable, indubitable foundations is very much part of the legacy of ontotheology—itself a term naming such foundations.

89. Bowie, *From Romanticism to Critical Theory*, 149.
90. Bambach, *Heidegger, Dilthey, and the Crisis of Historicism*, 164.
91. Ibid., 136.
92. Ibid., 136–37.
93. Rudolf Makkreel and Frithjof Rodi, "Introduction" to Wilhelm Dilthey, *Poetry and Experience*, 18.
94. Gadamer, *Truth and Method*, 227.
95. Dilthey, *Gesammelte Schriften*, Vol. VII, 136, cited in Gadamer, *Truth and Method*, 229.
96. Gadamer, *Truth and Method*, 229.
97. Dilthey, *Introduction to the Human Sciences* (Betanzos's trans.), 81.
98. Ibid., 79.

## Chapter 6. *Geist*, Nature, and History

1. Clive Erricker, "Phenomenological Approaches," 80. The English translation of Otto's book appeared in 1923 while the original German edition appeared in 1917.

2. Eliade, *The Sacred and the Profane: The Nature of Religion* (New York: Harcourt, Brace, and World, 1959), 8 and 10.

3. Thomas Ryba, "Manifestation," *Guide to the Study of Religion*, 177–78.

4. While the major exegetical work will be on *Das Heilige*, other of his works will be used to support and expand key themes in it.

5. See discussion of Eliade in chapter 10.

6. See Ryba, "Manifestation," 177–79, on this issue.

7. Hegel, *Philosophy of History*, 17.

8. Rudolf Otto, *Naturalism and Religion*, trans. J. Arthur Thomson and Margaret R. Thomson (New York: G. P. Putnam's Sons, 1907), 295. Cf. the argument of Adina Davidovich: "My analysis showed that Otto accepted the Kantian dualism of nature and freedom." Adina Davidovich, *Religion as a Province of Meaning* (Minneapolis: Fortress Press, 1993), 216. Despite their very real differences, in broad terms Kant and Hegel were more alike than different on the issue of nature versus mind or Spirit (both are squarely within the tradition of, and the structures of, ontotheology). Davidovich's point adds weight to mine: for Otto the difference between nature and Spirit was extremely important.

9. Rudolf Otto, *The Idea of the Holy: An Inquiry into the Non-Rational Factor in the Idea of the Divine and Its Relation to the Rational*, trans. J. W. Harvey (Oxford: Oxford University Press, 1958), 112.

10. Otto, *Naturalism and Religion*, 306.

11. Ibid., 332.

12. Ibid., 300.

13. Ibid., 335.

14. Ibid., 221.

15. Otto, *The Idea of the Holy*, 112. See discussion above where this quote was introduced.

16. Ibid., 113.

17. Ibid.

18. Ibid.

19. Ibid., 162.

20. Ibid., 135.

21. Ibid., 8. Cf. Davidovich, *Religion as Province of Meaning*, 165: "Otto is by no means the only proponent of 'sympathy' as a method in the study of religion. In fact 'sympathy' is one of the key terms used by various scholars of religion in their attempt to convince us that, somehow, we all can acquire the ability to 'walk in the shoes' of other people and to see the world through their eyes. It is often assumed that a certain common denominator, the nature

of which is not always explicitly defined, makes it possible for members of one tradition to understand the meaning of foreign religious phenomena." I would take issue only with the claims that this common denominator is "not always explicitly defined." The idea of a transcendental subjectivity, as we have seen repeatedly, is that common denominator.

22. Davidovich, *Religion as Province of Meaning*, 167.
23. Otto, *The Idea of the Holy*, 1.
24. Otto, *Naturalism and Religion*, 318.
25. Ibid., 351. Cf. Phillip Almond, *Rudolf Otto: An Introduction to his Philosophical Theology* (Chapel Hill: The University of North Carolina Press, 1984), 94: "The rational elements of deity are consequently a priori because they can be generated in Friesian manner by the completion of the analogous aspects of human personality. They are derived not from any sensuous experience but from reason alone." Otto himself says: "Just as Kant's 'intelligible character' was not added to the empiric character, but is its eternal basis, so the ground of the soul is not added to the parts or the powers of the soul. It is *homo sub specie aeterni* (man in his eternal aspect) in distinction from *homo sub specie temporis* (man in his temporal aspect)." *Mysticism East and West*, trans. Bertha L. Bracey and Richenda C. Payne (New York: The Macmillan Company, 1932), 220.
26. Otto, *Naturalism and Religion*, 336.
27. Ibid., 337.
28. Ibid., 324.
29. Otto, *The Idea of the Holy*, 4.
30. Ibid., 5.
31. Ibid., 7.
32. Ibid., 175–76.
33. Ibid., 176.
34. Ibid., 112.
35. Otto, *Naturalism and Religion*, 301.
36. Almond, *Rudolf Otto*, 113.
37. Otto, *The Idea of the Holy*, 133.
38. Ibid., 91.
39. Ibid., 132.
40. Ibid., 133.
41. Ibid., 134.
42. Ibid.
43. Otto, *Mysticism East and West*, 179.
44. Ibid., 185.
45. Ibid., 191.
46. Ibid., 194.
47. Ibid., 229.
48. Ibid.
49. Ibid., 186.
50. See Hegel, *The Philosophy of History*, 161–67.
51. Otto, *Mysticism East and West*, 187.

52. The etymology of the word *Entwicklung* shows that it means to wind (*wickeln*) out from within as with a scroll. To develop, then, is the process of unfolding from within: "that which Spirit is, it has always essentially been."

53. Otto, *Mysticism East and West*, 188.

54. Ibid., 187.

55. Ibid.

56. Ibid., 188.

57. Ibid., 231.

58. Ibid.

59. Otto, *The Idea of the Holy*, 72.

60. Ibid., 72.

61. Ibid., 83.

62. Ibid.

63. Ibid.

64. Ibid., 75.

65. Ibid., 90–91.

66. Hegel, *Philosophy of Religion*, 203.

67. Otto, *The Idea of the Holy*, 163; emphasis added.

68. Ibid., 56.

69. Ibid., 1; emphasis added.

70. Otto, 56. Cf. Wach's argument that the idea of salvation is the core of religion generally. His dissertation was on this subject and it will be treated below in chapter 9.

71. Otto, *The Idea of the Holy*, 6.

72. Rudolf Otto, *The Philosophy of Religion*, trans. E. B. Dicker (London: Williams and Norgate, 1931), 202–203.

73. Otto, *The Philosophy of Religion*, 203, emphasis added. There is a clear echo here in his notion of "absolute unlikeness" or difference and Hegel's definition of knowledge as "pure self-recognition in absolute *otherness*." The self and its other are seen, in both cases, albeit for somewhat different reasons, as not merely different, not even a different gradation along a continuum, but as different as the concept of difference itself can posit. Obviously, when we shift from metaphysics to a taxonomy of human beings (and their religions), this is what Said described as one of the "less than admirable ends" colonists seek in making such distinctions.

74. Melissa Raphael, *Rudolf Otto and the Concept of Holiness* (Oxford: Clarendon Press, 1997), 7.

75. Ibid., 8.

76. Ibid., 7.

77. Ibid. For a discussion of a similar valorization of Otto by Charles Long, see note 71, 391.

## Chapter 7. Phenomenology as Empathetic Taxonomy

1. Erricker, "Phenomenological Approaches," 78.

2. van der Leeuw, *Religion in Essence and Manifestation*, xx.

3. Capps, *Religious Studies*, 109–10.

4. Recall that this was noted in chapter 1 in the section on the pedigree of the phenomenology of religion.

5. Capps, *Religious Studies*, 124. While I agree in the main with what Capps is claiming, as will be seen, in Kristensen's conception of *Religionswissenschaft* as a whole (a tripart science as with others) he is concerned with, and considers it necessary to define, the essence of religion.

6. P. D. Chantepie de la Saussaye, *Manual of the Science of Religion*, 3.

7. Ibid., 4. A segment of this could be better translated as "the Concept and the manifestation of religion." The difference between Idee and Begriff is an important distinction in Hegel's view.

8. Ibid., 7 and 9. Cf. Ryba, *The Essence of Phenomenology*, 234ff.

9. Chantepie, *Manual of the Science of Religion*, 8; emphasis added.

10. Ibid.
11. Ibid., 67.
12. Ibid., 71.
13. Ibid., 72.
14. Ibid.
15. Ibid., 76.
16. Ibid.
17. Ibid.
18. Ibid., 80.
19. Ibid., 81.
20. Ibid., 124.
21. Ibid.
22. Ibid., 127.
23. Ibid.
24. Ibid., 127–28.
25. Ibid., 244.
26. Ibid., 245.
27. Ibid., 245–46.
28. Ibid., 246.
29. Ibid., 249.
30. Ibid.
31. Ibid., 248–50.

32. He mentions Mayans, Hindus, African nations, as well as some others. This category allows him to subordinated urbanized peoples of color to the "high cultures," of which Europe is the supreme example, while accounting for their differences from "savages" in a reasonable way.

33. Chantepie, *Manual*, 250.
34. Ibid.
35. Ibid.
36. Ibid., 251.

37. I should here remind readers that it is not my goal to point out the fact *that* phenomenology is, in this case, racist but rather *how* it is racist via its logocentrism, Eurocentrism, etc. This instance, which is a quite obvious case,

is also clearly an instance of the construction of race via the metaphysics of *Geist*. The construction of race is therefore a structural feature of this discourse, not an incidental feature that could be dismissed as a product of the times, a moral lapse, and so forth.

38. Chantepie, *Manual*, 251.
39. Ibid.
40. Ibid., 250.
41. Ibid., 336–37.
42. Ibid., 499.
43. Ibid.
44. Ibid., 517.
45. Ibid., 538.
46. Ibid., 521.
47. Ibid.
48. Ibid., 507.
49. Ibid., 537.
50. Ibid., 499.
51. Ibid., 499–500.
52. Ibid., 499.
53. Ibid.
54. Ibid., 500.
55. Olaf Pettersson and Hans Åkerberg, *Interpreting Religious Phenomena*, 17. Virtually all commentators on Kristensen draw from this work. For other commentaries on Kristensen and *The Meaning of Religion*, see Eric Sharpe, *Comparative Religion*, 228, and Douglas Allen, *Structure and Creativity in Religion: Hermeneutics in Mircea Eliade's Phenomenology and New Directions* (The Hague: Mouton, 1978), 64. I am unaware of the existence of a German translation of this work.
56. Wilhelm Brede Kristensen, *The Meaning of Religion: Lectures in the Phenomenology of Religion* (The Hague: Martinus Nijhoff, 1960), 11.
57. Ibid., 2. We saw how this *was* the case with Hegel, Tiele, and Chantepie: finding the essence of a given religion, they could compare it with the essences of other religions—each taken as a whole.
58. Ibid., 3; emphasis added. This statement echoes, perhaps only faintly, Chantepie's statement about savage nations, viz., "They have no history." Does this kind of dehistoricizing deny the cultural identity of the subject of phenomenological analysis?
59. Ibid.
60. Ibid., 2.
61. Ibid., 3.
62. Ibid., 3 and 4; emphasis added.
63. Åke Hultkrantz, "The Phenomenology of Religion: Aims and Methods," 71, specifically connects Kristensen and phenomenology of religion to Dilthey. Pettersson and Åkerberg, 10, also connect both to Schleiermacher and Hegel.
64. Kristensen, 7.

65. Ibid., 10.
66. Ibid., 13.
67. Ibid. Again, we find the notion (and we will see it in other theorists) that understanding of "our own" religion is not problematic; it seems to be fully accomplished and therefore further analysis is unnecessary. We know who "we" are; we want to know who "they" are. We have then, at the very foundations of the phenomenological method, the "us/them," "self/other" dichotomies. While Kristensen's treatment of the Other is far less negative than that of other theorists we have seen (and will see), he does classify religions as "our European type" and what he calls "Ancient" religions. This issue will be discussed farther on in the text.
68. Ibid., 2.
69. Ibid., 7.
70. Ibid., 3; emphasis added.
71. Ibid., 2–3.
72. Ibid., 3.
73. Ibid., 8; emphasis added.
74. Ibid., 14.
75. Ibid., 3–4.
76. Ibid., 3.
77. Ibid., 8.
78. Ibid.
79. Ibid., 9 and 12.
80. Cf. Pettersson and Åkerberg, *Interpreting Religious Phenomena*, 20 on this point as well as Kees Bolle, "Myths and Other Religious Texts," in *Contemporary Approaches to the Study of Religion in 2 Volumes*, Volume I: *The Humanities*, ed. Frank Whaling (Berlin: Mouton, 1983), 323, who says that "for all his pupils and admirers, Kristensen was the supreme practitioner of empathy."
81. Kristensen, 10.
82. Ibid., 9.
83. Ibid., 1.
84. Ibid., 8.
85. Ibid., 9.
86. Ibid., 6.
87. Ibid., 7.
88. Ibid., 7–8.
89. Ibid., 7.
90. See Eliade, *The Quest*, on this issue, discussed below in chapter 10.
91. Kristensen, 14.
92. Ibid., 15.
93. Ibid., 13.
94. Ibid., 16.
95. Ibid.
96. Ibid., 17.

97. Ibid., 18.
98. Ibid., 19.
99. Ibid.
100. Ibid., 20.
101. Ibid.
102. Ibid.
103. Recall the very strong emphasis that Hegel, Tiele, and Chantepie put on the difference between those peoples who have a history and those who do not. Whatever it is, myth is *not* history.
104. Kristensen, 21.
105. Ibid.
106. Ibid.
107. Ibid.
108. Ibid., 23.
109. Ibid., 19.
110. Ibid.
111. That would necessarily be Catholicism, would it not? Hegel clearly identified Protestantism with European Modernity; does Kristensen imply this here?
112. Note that he uses the term *won* here. It implies a struggle of some kind which further implies the existence of an opposition of some kind. From whom or what did this rationalism win something? It would *appear* that it was the Ancients.
113. Kristensen, 20. The translator of Kristensen's text affixes a footnote (20) to the term *enlightened-classical*. The footnote reads, in part, as follows: "Prof. Kristensen makes a sharp distinction between the terms 'Ancient' and 'Classical' with reference to the ancient civilizations, identifying 'Classical' with 'rationalistic' and 'enlightened.' . . . The meaning of 'enlightened' as the author uses the term is: similar to the rationalism of the Eighteenth Century *Enlightenment* (Dutch *verlichting*; German, *Aufklärung*)."
114. Kristensen, 20.
115. See 186 for original citation. The quote continues: "And because for him only data of his own consciousness exist, a result is that every value and every goal in life has its locus in this independently functioning intellectual world within him, and every goal of his activities consists in producing intellectual results. And so he distinguishes nature from history, in which, surrounded though it is by that structure of objective necessity which nature consists of, freedom flashes forth at innumerable points in the whole."
116. It is Logocentric in that it relies on the abstraction of purely formal features which are completely dehistoricized.

## Chapter 8. Experience, Expression, Empathy

1. Gerardus van der Leeuw, *Religion in Essence and Manifestation*, trans. J. E. Turner (Princeton: Princeton University Press, 1964; paperback

edition, 1986), 671. All English quotes of van der Leeuw are taken from 1964 translation, which is based on the second German edition and was republished in 1986 (the 1986 page numbers being the same as the 1964 edition). All German references are from *Phänomenologie der Religion* (Tübingen: J. C. B. Mohr (Paul Siebeck), 1933), page numbers for which will appear in parentheses after the English citation where relevant.

2. Van der Leeuw, *Religion in Essence and Manifestation*, 671. Interestingly enough, although this is clearly a Husserlian theme, *nowhere* in this section—this section in which van der Leeuw is giving his philosophical exposition of the basis of phenomenology—does he cite Husserl. He cites Spranger, Binswanger, Heidegger, and, most of all, Dilthey. Given that van der Leeuw is not in the least shy about citing his sources this is strong evidence that he does not understand himself to be following Husserl's program for phenomenology. At best, one could say that he does not distinguish Husserl from those just noted. George A. James, *Interpreting Religion: The Phenomenological Approaches of Pierre Daniël Chantepie de la Saussaye, W. Brede Kristensen, and Gerardus van der Leeuw* (Washington, DC: The Catholic University of America Press, 1995), 231–32, concurs that Husserl is *not* van der Leeuw's primary source on phenomenology: "He [van der Leeuw] refers to Husserl in only two places in his phenomenology of religion, one of which is in a quotation from a work of Scheler." In a footnote (232, n37), James continues: "He refers repeatedly, however, to Jaspers, Binswanger, Heidegger, and others; some of whom acknowledge the influence of Husserl."

3. Van der Leeuw, *Religion in Essence and Manifestation*, 671. On van der Leeuw's view of "the phenomenon," cf. George James, *Interpreting Religion*, 203. Cf. also Thomas Ryba, *The Essence of Phenomenology*, 232.

4. Van der Leeuw, *Religion in Essence and Manifestation*, xxi.

5. He directly correlates (674, n1) "phenomenology of religion" with *Religionswissenschaft*: "What I myself understand by the phenomenology of religion is called by Hackmann 'The General Science of Religion' [*Allgemeine Religionswissenschaft*]."

6. van der Leeuw, *Religion in Essence and Manifestation*, 671, n2 (634).

7. Ibid., 462.

8. Ibid., 461.

9. Ibid., 451, n5.

10. Ibid., 673.

11. Ibid., 671, quoting Dilthey. This quote from the body of the Epilogomena is the text to which the note (cited in German above) about *Erlebnis* is attached. There, the cross-reference to the section on religious experience is given. In the footnote to that section (cited above), van der Leeuw continues: "Understanding is not a supplementary activity on the part of the investigator, but pertains essentially to life itself; cf. Heidegger, *op. cit.* [*Sein und Zeit*], 164; similarly, 'what the disciple of Sais unveils is not life, but form' " (461, n5). Thus, the circle of references is closed. Not to belabor the point, but it is clear that Husserl is "not in the loop."

12. van der Leeuw, *Religion in Essence and Manifestation*, 459, quoting Goethe's *Epirrhema*. George James, *Interpreting Religion*, 247ff., notes how van der Leeuw makes frequent reference to poets at highly strategic points in his analyses.

13. van der Leeuw, *Religion in Essence and Manifestation*, 460. Cf. the discussions throughout this study concerning the metaphors of "inner/outer." This metaphor set is, I would argue, constitutive of the phenomenology of religion as understood.

14. Ibid., 459.

15. Ibid., 445. Cf. Wach on this issue in the next chapter.

16. Ibid., 672.

17. Ibid. Cf. Thomas Ryba, *The Essence of Phenomenology*, 233. Cf. also George James, *Interpreting Religion*, 206–207.

18. van der Leeuw, *Religion in Essence and Manifestation*, 672.

19. Ibid., 673.

20. Ibid.

21. Ibid.

22. Ibid.

23. Ibid.

24. Ibid., 674.

25. Ibid.

26. Ibid.

27. Ibid., 638.

28. Ibid., 674.

29. Ibid.

30. Ibid., 675 (639). Cf. George James, *Interpreting Religion*, 245–55: "While Kristensen emphasizes the specific nature of the religious intuition, van der Leeuw places emphasis upon the common nature of humankind that enables him to achieve understanding of what appears. With van der Leeuw the irreducible in religion pertains to the nature of humanity as a fundamentally religious species."

31. van der Leeuw, Religion in Essence and Manifestation, 677.

32. Ibid., quoting Jaspers.

33. Ibid., 676, quoting Dilthey.

34. Ibid., 676.

35. Ibid., xx. In relation to the historical thesis being argued here, it is interesting that he connects this work, as noted in chapter 1, to that of Chantepie: "As regards Phenomenology itself, Chantepie's volume should be consulted" (xx).

36. Ibid.

37. Ibid., 591.

38. Ibid., 594.

39. Ibid., 688 (652–53). Cf. George James, *Interpreting Religion*, 213.

40. van der Leeuw, *Religion in Essence and Manifestation*, 593, quoting Dilthey.

41. Ibid., 593.

42. Ibid. For a discussion of van der Leeuw's theory of historical types, see George James, *Interpreting Religion*, 244–46.

43. van der Leeuw, *Religion in Essence and* Manifestation, 594.

44. Ibid., 596. The higher religions are not included because they "are also found in other religions, and thus possess no specific form of their own."

45. Ibid., 594.

46. Ibid., 597.

47. Ibid., 641.

48. Ibíd.; all elipses van der Leeuw's. The author of the letter is Hendrik Kraemer, a theologian and phenomenologist of religion discussed briefly in chapter 1.

49. Ibid., 642.

50. Ibid., 643.

51. Ibid., 644.

52. This would present a serious challenge to the overall "payoff" of George James's exposition of the history of the phenomenology of religion, as he structures, in part, it around its purported ahistorical, nondevelopmental approach. Given the concurrence of judgments about religions made by both evolutionists (including those who argue for spiritual evolution only) and anti-evolutionists, it is clear that there is something more afoot here. It is the argument of this study that that something is, first of all, the spirit/nature (*Geist/Natur*) dichotomy, and, more centrally, a metaphysical conception of human consciousness, or the subject.

53. van der Leeuw, *Religion in Essence and Manifestation*, 645; italics van der Leeuw's.

54. Ibid., 646.

55. Ibid.

56. As discussed in chapter 2, this is an important difference between the kind of structural critique I am making against phenomenological discourse and the more individualistic critique made by Donald Wiebe in his "Phenomenology of Religion as Religio-Cultural Quest: Gerardus van der Leeuw and the Subversion of the Scientific Study of Religion," in *Religionswissenschaft und Kulturkritik: Beiträge zur Konferenz: The History of Religions and Critique of Culture in the Days of Gerardus van der Leeuw (1890–1950)* (Marburg: diagonal-Verlag, 1991). Wiebe argues that "Van der Leeuw, I shall attempt to show, was concerned to transcend such a scientific mandate; he was also concerned to show, I think, that transcending that mandate constitutes not the abrogation of science but rather its ultimate fulfillment" (68). No disagreement there; that is built in to the logic *Geist*. However, Wiebe (quoting Herbert Hahn) goes on to argue that for members of the *Verstehen Schule*, of which van der Leeuw must certainly be counted, " 'no merely intellectual understanding was adequate; there must be the kind of 'spiritual' appreciation that comes from personal commitment as well' " (Ibid.). It is that last phrase, "personal commitment" with which I take some

(qualified) exception. Throughout the history of this discursive structure, atheist and theist, Christian and agnostic, alike have subscribed to the kind of valuational-cum-ontological-cum-historical scheme just presented in the body of the text. This is not best understood, as Wiebe's critique implies, as the contingent and/or aggregate choices of individuals; that scheme is built into a discursive structure.

57. van der Leeuw, *Religion in Essence and Manifestation*, 646; italics van der Leeuw's.
58. Ibid., quoting Galatians, 4:19.
59. Ibid., 647.
60. Ibid., 692. Recall what Chantepie (*Manual of the Science of Religion*, 4, quoted above in chapter one) had said about Hegel's importance for *Religionswissenschaft*, who "made us see the harmony between the idea and the realization of religion [*zwischem dem Begriff und der Erscheinung der Religion zur Anschauung zu bringen*]." Cf. George James's discussion of the relationship between Hegel and van der Leeuw in *Interpreting Religion*, 211.
61. van der Leeuw, *Religion in Essence and Manifestation*, 595.
62. Ibid., 595–96.
63. Ibid., 596.
64. Ibid., 435.
65. Ibid., 37–38.
66. Ibid., 441. Cf. 445, where, speaking of law, he says: "But it also receives a fixed mould and becomes a formula that is spoken, and subsequently written, which as such pertains to the category of sacred words."
67. Ibid., 445.
68. Ibid., 645–46. Cf. George James's discussion of the relationship between Husserl and van der Leeuw in *Interpreting Religion*, 231–33.
69. van der Leeuw, *Religion in Essence and Manifestation*, 646.
70. Edmund Husserl, *Ideas: General Introduction to Pure Phenomenology* (New York: Collier Books, 1962), 100.
71. van der Leeuw, *Religion in Essence and Manifestation*, 675.
72. Ibid.
73. See Husserl, *Ideas*, ch. 2.
74. Ibid., 38; italics Husserl's.
75. van der Leeuw, *Religion in Essence and Manifestation*, 677.
76. Ibid.
77. Ibid., 686.

## Chapter 9. Overcoming the Foreign through Experience, Expression, Understanding

1. Joseph Kitagawa, "Life and Thought of Joachim Wach," in Joachim Wach, *The Comparative Study of Religion* (New York: Columbia University Press, 1958), xxiii.

2. Joseph Kitagawa, "Introduction," in Joachim Wach, *Essays in the History of Religions*, ed. Joseph M. Kitagawa and Gregory D. Alles (New York: Macmillan, 1988), xx.

3. Joachim Wach, *Types of Religious Experiences: Christian and Non-Christian* (Chicago: University of Chicago Press, 1951), 32.

4. Joachim Wach, *Introduction to the History of Religions*, ed. Joseph M. Kitagawa and Gregory D. Alles (New York: Macmillan, 1988), 60–61. Please note: all of the German terms in parentheses are the editors' of Wach's work and not mine.

5. Ibid.

6. Wach, *Types of Religious Experiences*, 33.

7. Ibid., 32–33.

8. Ibid., 33.

9. Wach, *Introduction to the History of Religions*, 115. Cf. 29: "the conviction that religion is not dead but alive, that more or less innately, more or less purely actualized, it lives in all of us; that the soul's final attitudes, experiences, and decisions are 'eternally human,' and that this 'eternally human' includes not only the general attitudes toward life that are expressed in particular religions but also the modalities in which they express themselves."

10. Ibid., 106–107.

11. Wach, *The Comparative Study of Religion*, 39. See there where he cites Marett: "Our common human nature, I believe, embraces a permanent possibility of religion." On p. 38, he peppers his texts with citations from Malinowski, Otto, Bergson, and others, all arguing for the universality of religion.

12. Wach, *Types of Religious Experience*, 33. For the thesis being expounded here it is worthy of note that he cites colonialists in relation to the primitive, "*even* the primitive." Unlike Eliade, Wach is closer to Hegel more inclined to see "true religion" as part of high culture, i.e., part of developed *Geist*.

13. Ibid., 64.

14. Joachim Wach, *Understanding and Believing*, ed. Joseph M. Kitagawa (New York: Harper and Row, 1968), 133. Again, the *editors* of Wach's work insert the German terminology, thus the parentheses and not brackets.

15. Wach, *The Comparative Study of Religions*, 27.

16. Wach, *Introduction to the History of Religions*, 22.

17. Ibid., 120.

18. Ibid., 21.

19. Wach, *Sociology of Religions*, 21–22.

20. Eliade's treatment of the archaic is, of course, a notable exception to this tendency. We will see, however, some surprising similarities in both his theory of development and in his actual narratives. Eliade's approach, however, does in the main require different strategies of critique.

21. Wach, *Understanding and Believing*, 151. Cf. Kitagawa, "The Life of Joachim Wach," xliv: "Wach as a phenomenologist distinguishes between a genuine and a non-genuine revelatory experience." As we have seen

elsewhere, this normative position is offered as the result of a non-normative science. To put my argument another way: the phenomenologists of religion are *right*, i.e., this is the logical outcome of the *structures* of this discourse, not an ad hoc, subjectivist preference. Again, arguing this way is indicative of the difference between a discourse analyasis and either Wiebe's or James's exegesis, good as they are, of individual works written by individual authors (who have *personal* beliefs, etc.).

22. Wach, *Understanding and Believing*, 139. Cf. *The Comparative Study of Religion*, 37, where he discusses pseudo-religion. He includes Marxism and Communism in that category.

23. Wach, *Essays in the History of Religions*, 177.
24. Wach, *Types of Religious Experiences*, 33–34.
25. Wach, *Sociology of Religions*, 15.
26. Wach, *Introduction to the History of Religions*, 29.
27. Ibid., 112.
28. Ibid.
29. Wach, *Types of Religious Experiences*, 34; emphasis added.
30. Ibid., 47.
31. Ibid., 34.
32. Ibid., xxi.
33. Ibid., 38.
34. Wach, *Understanding and Believing*, 135.
35. Wach, *Introduction to the History of Religions*, 114. Recall that Dilthey argued that humans can only understand what they have made. Or, humans can only *understand* the human.

36. Wach, *Essays in the History of Religions*, 179.
37. Ibid., 184.
38. Wach, *Introduction to the History of Religions*, 112.
39. Ibid., 25–26.
40. Ibid., 114.
41. Ibid.
42. Wach, *Essays in the History of Religions*, 171.
43. Wach, *Introduction to the History of Religions*, 113.
44. Wach, *The Comparative Study of Religions*, 18.
45. Wach, *Introduction to the History of Religions*, 26.
46. Ibid., 112.
47. Ibid.
48. Ibid., 112–13.
49. Ibid., 112.
50. Ibid.; emphasis added.
51. Ibid., 114.
52. Ibid.
53. Ibid., 140.
54. Ibid., 120.
55. Ibid., 138.
56. Ibid., 123.

57. Wach, *Essays in the History of Religions*, 95.

58. Ibid., 94–95. Again, whatever just criticisms they have, this indicates one of the several ways in which Weibe and Segal, but especially the latter, misread the "history" in the "History of Religions" and/or the "history and phenomenology of religion."

59. Ibid., 131.
60. Ibid., 124.
61. Ibid., 133.
62. Ibid., 137.
63. Ibid., 29.
64. Ibid., 132.
65. Ibid., 133–34.
66. Ibid., 135.
67. Ibid., 137.
68. Ibid.
69. Ibid.
70. Ibid., 37–38.
71. Ibid., 165; italics Wach's.
72. Wach, *Introduction to the History of Religions*, 117.
73. Ibid., 114. Cf. 157: "Beyond the factual prerequisites, we must have an affinity with the subject matter, an affinity that in general hermeneutics is expressed in terms of kinship of spirit (*Geisterverwandtschaft*) or congeniality, and that in theology is conceived of as an 'attunement' of spirit (*Geistesbestimmetheit*)."

74. Ibid., 29.
75. Ibid., 94.
76. Ibid., 144.
77. Ibid., 167,
78. Ibid., 144.
79. Ibid.
80. Ibid., 160.
81. Ibid., 155.
82. Wach, *The Comparative Study of Religions*, 10.
83. Wach, *Introduction to the History of Religions*, 155.
84. Ibid., 160.
85. Ibid., 162.
86. Wach, *Essays in the History of Religions*, 179.
87. Wach, *Introduction to the History of Religions*, 169.

88. Wach, *Sociology of Religions*, 20; emphasis added. Again, I am not arguing that this is necessarily false; I do not know whether nonliterate societies use myth instead of doctrine. Even if what Wach asserts is true, that is of no interest to my argument here. What is of interest is the way in which this claim operates in the overall structure of Wach's narrative(s) of the history of religion/s. *Just to be clear*: I do not subscribe to the idea of the "primitive," nor do I see one society as more "advanced" than any others.

89. Wach, *Introduction to the History of Religions*, 169; emphasis added.

90. Ibid., 169.
91. Ibid., 172.
92. Ibid.; emphasis added. Wach seems to be asserting the common notion that Europe has a unique place among the nations of the world. Clearly, a non-Eurocentric comparative view would argue that every specific civilization is unique. However, like Hegel and Otto, Wach seems to single out in a very consistent manner "things European" as more advanced and always on the list of anything ranked as "higher." Note that the all mentions of "lower" or primitive religions are people of color: Africans, aboriginal Australians, and Native Americans. While Asians are not so ranked, they often occupy a middle ground between the most advanced and the least advanced. The religions of Asia, again, that he singles out are all religions with significant literary traditions. One could argue that the reason they are ranked higher is that, as religions of the book, they resemble Christianity, whereas the nonliterate religions do not. Insofar as this is the case, it is obviously an example of a Christocentric criterion in terms of which all religions are ranked. Note how similar this is to Otto's method of ranking religions.
93. Ibid., 172.
94. Ibid., 189.
95. Ibid., 179.
96. "What Schleiermacher recognized in his *Speeches* must never be forgotten." Ibid., 161.
97. Ibid., 187.
98. Ibid., 189. The editors inserted the word *Geist* in the text (as are, again, all German terms in Wach's text). This idea of "pushes and shoves," as noted, recalls Tiele's language, but, more importantly it is a casual way of describing the dialectics of Reason/Spirit.
99. Ibid., 179.
100. Wach, *The Comparative Study of Religions*, 92–93.
101. Ibid., 93, citing H. B. Alexander; emphasis added.
102. Ibid., 95–96.

## Chapter 10. The Total Hermeneutics of the New Humanism

1. Douglas Allen, "Phenomenology of Religion," 194 and 195.
2. Gavin Flood, *Beyond Phenomenology*, 6.
3. Bear in mind the terminological confusion noted in chapter 1. Eliade uses the term *History of Religions* to refer to his project. It is, however, not distinguishable from phenomenology nor from *Religionswissenschaft*. See Douglas Allen, *Structure and Creativity in Religion*, 107ff on Eliade as a phenomenologist.
4. Mircea Eliade, *Patterns of Comparative Religion* (New York: The New American Library, 1958), 2.
5. Ibid., xiii.
6. Ibid.

7. Ibid.; emphasis added.
8. Mircea Eliade, *The Quest: History and Meaning in Religion*, i.
9. Flood, *Beyond Phenomenology*, 11.
10. Eliade, *The Quest*, 9; emphasis added.
11. Ibid., 2.
12. Ibid., 7.
13. Eliade, *Myths, Dreams, and Mysteries: The Encounter between Contemporary Faiths and Archaic Realities*, trans. Philip Mairet (New York: Harper and Row, 1960), 154.
14. Ibid., 178.
15. Eliade, *The Quest*, 53.
16. Mircea Eliade, *The Sacred and the Profane: The Nature of Religion* (New York: Harcourt, Brace, and World, 1959), 91.
17. Eliade, *Patterns*, 8; italics Eliade's.
18. Eliade, *Myths, Dreams, and Mysteries*, 110. Cf. 178: "The history of religions is concerned not only with the historical becoming of a religious form, but also with its *structure*. For religious forms are non-temporal; they are not necessarily bound to time." Eliade continually associates essence, structure and meaning. See, e.g., *Patterns*, 35: "The different historical and historicist schools have reacted strongly against the phenomenologists' claim that they can grasp the *essence* and the *structure* of religious phenomena."
19. Eliade, *Sacred and the Profane*, 94. Cf. *Patterns*, 3–4.
20. Eliade, *Patterns*, 462.
21. Ibid.; emphasis added. Cf. Allen, *Structure and Creativity*, 176: "It is true that all hierophanies are historical manifestations, but what is most crucial for Eliade's methodology is that their structures remain the same. Only because there is a permanence and continuity of structure can we participate in the life-world of the other and interpret religious data with some sense of objectivity."
22. See Eliade *The Quest*, 35ff., Allen *Structure and Creativity*, 173ff., and Pettazoni, *Essays on the History of Religion* (cited in chapter 1) on this issue.
23. The phrase recurs in Eliade a number of times, but it was popularized by Thomas Altizer's book by that name. Allen gives, perhaps, the best discussion of it. See *Structure and Creativity*, 123ff., and "Eliade and History," *The Journal of Religion* 68, no. 4 (1988): 560ff.
24. Eliade, *The Quest*, 35.
25. Eliade, 7. Cf. *Patterns*, xiii: "Obviously there are no *purely* religious phenomena; no phenomenon can be solely and exclusively religious."
26. Eliade, *Patterns*, 26.
27. Allen, "Eliade and History," 560.
28. Eliade, *Patterns*, 26.
29. Allen, *Structure and Creativity*, 127, and "Eliade and History," 560.
30. For Eliade, and I would argue for Jung also, "archetype" is not meaningfully different than "essence." Both stem from the Platonic, rationalist heritage and, as far as I can tell, perform the same function in their respective places. See Joseph Campbell's description of the Jungian archetype in his "Editor's Introduction," in *The Portable Jung* (New York: Penguin Books,

1971), xxii: "[T]he archetypes or norms of myth are common to the human species, they are inherently expressive neither of local social circumstance nor of any individual's singular experience, but of common human needs, instincts, and potentials."

31. Eliade, *Patterns*, 462.
32. Ibid., 463.
33. Ibid.
34. Ibid., 3.
35. For Kristensen, the temporal dimension is predominant; he sees truer manifestations as those which endure through time. Eliade's taxonomy is synchronic, because of his view that religious consciousness is essentially atemporal, and so he emphasizes a horizontal, geographic metaphor for the fullness of a manifestation.
36. Eliade, *Patterns*, 3.
37. Ibid., 8; italics Eliade's.
38. Allen, "Eliade and History," 552.
39. Eliade, *The Quest*, 55.
40. Ibid., 2.
41. Ibid., 8.
42. Ibid., 3.
43. Ibid., 58.
44. Ibid., 62.
45. Ibid.
46. Ibid., 68–70 and 66.
47. Ibid., 69.
48. Ibid., 9.
49. Ibid., 52. The fact that it is Western consciousness that recognizes only one history, *the* Universal History, is a clear indication of the way in which the discourse of the phenomenology of religion is "nestled" within colonial discourse. The Western domination of the globe, the empire upon which the sun never sets, is the material precondition for the universalism Eliade announces. He both draws this material from the colonized and denies knowledge of its universal nature to "them."
50. Ibid., 9.
51. Ibid., 70.
52. Mircea Eliade, *Myth, Dreams, and Mysteries: The Encounter between Contemporary Faiths and Archaic Realities*, trans. Philip Mairet (New York: Harper and Row, 1960), 233; emphasis added.

## Chapter 11. "The Center Does Not Hold"

1. Robert Young, *White Mythologies: Writing History and the West* (London and New York: Routledge, 1990), 18.
2. Roland Barthes, "The Old Rhetoric: An Aid-Memoire," in *The Semiotic Challenge* (New York: Hill and Wang, 1977), 47.
3. Ibid., 50.

4. Derrida, *Of Grammatology*, 49.
5. Ibid., 23.
6. One may add Whitehead's adage, "All philosophy and science is but a footnote to Plato." The *Geisteswissenschaft*, as noted above, seen as predicated upon a metaphysical distinction between *Geist* and *Natur*, are clearly part of this "whole historical chain." As such, so is the phenomenology of religion.
7. Derrida, *Writing and Difference*, trans. Alan Bass (Chicago: University of Chicago Press, 1982), 283.
8. Derrida, *Of Grammatology*, 23.
9. Leela Gandhi, *Postcolonial Theory: a Critical Introduction* (New York: Columbia University Press, 1998), 34.
10. Derrida, Margins of Philosophy, 213.
11. Taylor, *Erring*, 15.
12. Derrida, *Writing and Difference*, 279–80.
13. Young, *White Mythologies*, 13.
14. Gandhi, *Postcolonial Theory*, 49. In this section, while allowing for their differences, the terms *humanism*, *Man*, and *Spirit* will be used interchangeably. This is for the sake of convenience only; a careful reader will see both the overlap of these terms and their differences.
15. Hegel, *Philosophy of Right*, #349, cited in note 44 in chapter 3.
16. Gandhi, *Postcolonial Theory*, 49.
17. See ibid., 47–48.
18. Ibid., 169.
19. Ibid., 30.
20. Ibid., 169.
21. Hegel, *Philosophy of History*, 163. Cf. ???: "Reason governs the world and has consequently governed its history. In relation to this Reason, which is universal and substantial, in and for itself, all else is subordinate, subservient, and the means for its actualization."
22. Gandhi, *Postcolonial Theory*, 171.
23. Homi K. Bhabha, *The Location of Culture*, 70.
24. Gandhi, *Postcolonial Theory*, 170–71.
25. Hegel, *Philosophy of History*, 87. Cited in note 37 of chapter 3.
26. Macdonell, 86–87, citing Foucault.
27. Taylor, *Erring*, 70.
28. Gandhi, *Postcolonial Theory*, 171.
29. See discussion of Tiele in chapter 4.
30. Bhabha, *Location of Culture*, 70.
31. Hegel, *Lectures on the Philosophy of Religion*, 291 and 289.
32. Hegel, *Philosophy of History*, 158.
33. Bhabha, *Location of Culture*, 43.
34. Mary Louise Pratt, *Imperial Eyes: Travel Writing and Transculturation* (New York: Routledge, 1992), 7.
35. Young, *White Mythologies*, 3.
36. Ibid.

37. Ibid., 11.

38. Agnes Heller and Ferenc Feher, *The Postmodern Political Condition* (New York: Columbia University Press, 1988), 2.

39. Young, *White Mythologies*, 19, points out: "Postmodernism can best be defined as European culture's awareness that it is no longer the unquestioned and dominant center of the world."

40. Gandhi, *Postcolonial Theory*, 32. Cf. 52, where she shows how cultural elitism is also a Eurocentric colonialist idea by citing, among others, "[Matthew] Arnold's humanism, in particular, asserts the need to maintain the integrity and sovereignty of Europe in the face of its multitudinous and barbaric Others"

41. Ibid., 31–32.

42. Ibid., 33.

43. Pratt, *Imperial Eyes*, 28.

44. Ibid.

45. Ibid., 30.

46. Hegel, *Philosophy of History*, 410; all italics Hegel's.

47. Pratt, *Imperial Eyes*, 31.

48. Ibid.

49. Young, *White Mythologies*, 19.

50. Ibid., 12.

51. Ibid., 13.

52. Ibid., 12.

53. Bhabha, *Location of Culture*, 67.

54. Taylor, *Erring*, 108–109.

55. Eliade, *Patterns*, 4.

56. Eliade, *A History of Religious Ideas*, Vol. 2, 402; emphasis added.

57. Eliade, *Patterns*, 493.

58. Taylor, *Erring*, 15.

59. Which is a very different argument than claiming that they are *necessarily* or by nature ethnocentric. I doubt that argument can be cogently sustained, but I leave it to others to work out that issue. My claim is much more limited: I am only saying, *as it actually exists in* these *texts*, in *these* discourses, there is little doubt that the *Geisteswissenschaften*, aka., "the Humanities," have been rather profoundly Eurocentric and therefore ethnocentric in the way in which the modalities, subjects, and objects of knowledge have been configured. It is worth noting, however, that this discovery has *also* been part of the work of those very same sciences.

60. Derrida, *Of Grammatology*, 79.

61. Derrida, *Writing and Difference*, 282.

62. Charles Long, *Significations*, 86; emphasis added.

63. David Hoy, "Is Hermeneutics Ethno-centric?" in *The Interpretive Turn: Philosophy, Science, Culture*, ed. D. Hiley and J. Bohman (Ithaca: Cornell University Press, 1991), 156. Note the strong similarity between the hermeneutical notion of convergence and the "project called 'Europe'" described by Heller and Fehr above.

64. Derrida, cited in Young, *White Mythologies*, 18.
65. Friedrich Nietzsche, *The Will to Power*, ????
66. Hoy, "Is Hermeneutics Ethno-centric?," 157–59.
67. Ibid., 157.
68. Ibid., 157–58.
69. Ibid., 158.
70. Ibid., note 1.
71. Ibid., 158.
72. Mark C. Taylor, "The Stranglehold of Transcendentalism," *Journal of the American Academy of Religion* 53, no. 2 (1985): 280.

## Chapter 12. The "End of Man" and the Phenomenology of Religion

1. Eliade, *The Quest*, 11.
2. Martin Heidegger, "Letter on Humanism," in *Basic Writings*, ed. David Farrell Krell (New York: Harper and Row, 1977), 195.
3. Ibid., 202.
4. Taylor, *Erring*, 21.
5. Ibid., 22, citing Foucault.
6. Ibid., 132.
7. Martin Heidegger, *The Question Concerning Technology and Other Essays*, trans. William Lovitt (New York: Harper Torchbooks, 1977), 128.
8. Gandhi, *Postcolonial Theory*, 35.
9. Ibid.
10. Ibid., citing Bertrand Russell.
11. Ibid., 39.
12. Robert Solomon, *Continental Philosophy Since 1750: The Rise and Fall of the Self* (New York: Oxford University Press, 1988), 4.
13. Derrida, *Margins of Philosophy*, 120.
14. Ibid.
15. Derrida, *Writing and Difference*, 158; all italics Derrida's.
16. Ibid., 160.
17. David Hoy, "A History of Consciousness: From Kant and Hegel to Derrida and Foucault," *History of the Human Science* 4, no. 2 (1991): 262.
18. Taylor, *Erring*, 14.
19. Derrida, *Margins of Philosophy*, 116.
20. See ibid., 116ff., on the anthropologistic reading of Hegel, Marx, Husserl, and Heidegger.
21. Löwith, *From Hegel to Nietzsche*, 122.
22. Taylor, *Erring*, 140.
23. Which is to say that, apart from that context, if "Man" can or could be separated from the colonial situation, a different set of arguments would likely arise.
24. Derrida, *Margins of Philosophy*, 115–16.

25. Ibid., 116.
26. Friedrich Nietzsche, *Human All-Too Human*, #3.
27. Clifford Geertz, *The Interpretation of Cultures* (New York: Basic Books, 1975), 35.
28. Ibid., 56.
29. James Clifford, *The Predicament of Culture: Twentieth-Century Ethnography, Literature, and Art* (Cambridge: Harvard University Press, 1988), 198.
30. Ibid., 200.
31. Ibid., 193.
32. Ibid., 197.
33. Eliade, *The Quest*, 7.
34. Ibid. His argument here is based on a distinction that most anthropologists would *not* share. That is, religious essentialists such as Schleiermacher, Hegel, and Otto would argue for such a difference, whereas a reductive anthropologist such as Weston LeBarre, who compared Plato to the Cargo Cults and the Ghost Dance, would not grant such a difference.
35. Ibid., 70.
36. Ibid., 58.
37. Eliade 1973, xii n. 2.
38. Eliade does not, as did Otto, van der Leeuw, and earlier practitioners of *Religionswissenschaft*, argue for the outright supremacy of Christianity. He does often see Christianity as one of the purest hierophanies in history, but never overtly ranks it above other "higher" hierophanies such as Vedantic Hinduism or Buddhism. He also does not disparage Islam as a deviant form of monotheism, as do virtually all of these other thinkers. All of this gives him the appearance of a much more inclusive, "ecumenical" approach, but I am arguing that his form of exclusion is of a different kind than that. It is not Eliade's Christocentrism that makes him ethnocentric; it is his logocentrism, his insistence on ideal, universal, structures, which are, in fact, products of his own history, and so *imposed* upon the histories of other social groups.
39. van der Leeuw, *Religion in Essence and Manifestation*, 675.
40. Hegel, *The Phenomenology of Spirit*, #485.
41. James Snead, "European Pedigrees/African Contagions: Nationality, Narrative, and Communality," in *Nation and Narration*, ed. Homi K. Bhabha (London: Routledge, 1990), 237.
42. Ibid.
43. Ibid., 238; emphasis added.
44. Ibid., 235.
45. Ibid.
46. Ibid., 244.
47. Solomon, *Continental Philosophy Since 1750*, 7.
48. Ibid.
49. Eliade, *The Quest*, 10.
50. Solomon, *Continental Philosophy Since 1750*, 6.
51. Ibid., 7.

52. Ibid., 6.
53. Roland Barthes, *Mythologies* (New York: Hill and Wang, 1972), 110.
54. Ibid., 111.
55. Ibid., 112.
56. Ibid.
57. Ibid.
58. Gandhi, *Postcolonial Theory*, 54.
59. Ibid., 63.
60. J. Z. Smith, *Imagining Religion: From Babylon to Jonestown* (Chicago: University of Chicago Press, 1982), 18.
61. Derrida, Writing and Difference, 292.

# Bibliography

Allen, Douglas. *Structure and Creativity in Religion: Hermeneutics in Mircea Eliade's Phenomenology and New Directions*. The Hague: Mouton, 1978.
———. "Eliade and History." *The Journal of Religion* 68, no. 4 (1988).
———. "Phenomenology of Religion." In *Encyclopedia of Religion*, ed. Mircea Eliade. New York: MacMillan, 1995.
———. "Phenomenology of Religion." In *The Routledge Companion to the Study of Religion*, ed. John Hinnells. New York: Routledge, 2005.
Almond, Phillip C. *Rudolf Otto: An Introduction to his Philosophical Theology*. Chapel Hill: The University of North Carolina Press, 1984.
Baird, Robert D. *Category Formation and the History of Religion*. The Hague: Mouton, 1971.
Barthes, Roland. *Writing Degree Zero*. New York: Hill and Wang, 1967.
———. *Mythologies*. New York: Hill and Wang, 1972.
———. "From Work to Text." In *Image-Music-Text*. New York: Hill and Wang, 1977.
———. "The Old Rhetoric: An Aid-Memoire." In *The Semiotic Challenge*. New York: Hill and Wang, 1977.
———. "From Science to Literature." In *The Rustle of Language*. Berkeley: University of California Press, 1989.
Bambach, Charles R. *Heidegger, Dilthey, and the Crisis of Historicism*. Ithaca and London: Cornell University Press, 1995.
Beardsworth, Richard. *Derrida and the Political*. London: Routledge, 1996.
Betanzos, Ramon J. "Introductory Essay." In *Introduction to the Human Sciences: An Attempt to Lay a Foundation for the Study of Society and History*, trans. with an introductory essay, Ramon J. Betanzos. Detroit: Wayne State University Press, 1988.
Bhabha, Homi K. *The Location of Culture*. London: Routledge, 1994.
Bianchi, Ugo. *The History of Religions*. Leiden: E. J. Brill, 1975.
Bleeker, C. J. *The Sacred Bridge: Researches into the Nature and Structure of Religion*. Leiden: E.J. Brill, 1963.
Bolle, Kees. "Myths and Other Religious Texts." In *Contemporary Approaches to the Study of Religion in 2 Volumes*. Volume I: The Humanities, ed. Frank Whaling. Berlin: Mouton, 1983.
Bowie, Andre. *From Romanticism to Critical Theory: The Philosophy of German Literary Theory*. London and New York: Routledge, 1997.

Burgin, Victor. *The End of Art Theory: Criticism and Modernity*. Atlantic Highlands: Humanities Press International, 1986

Campbell, Joseph. "Editor's Introduction." In *The Portable Jung*. New York: Penguin Books, 1971.

Capps, Walter. *Religious Studies: The Making of a Discipline*. Minneapolis: Fortress Press, 1995.

Carr, David. *Phenomenology and the Problem of History: A Study of Husserl's Transcendental Phenomenology*. Evanston: Northwestern University Press, 1974.

Chantepie de la Saussaye, P. D. *Manual of the Science of Religion*. London: Longmans, Green, 1891.

———. *Lehrbuch der Religionsgeschichte*. Freiburg: J. C. B. Mohr (Paul Siebeck), 1897.

Chidister, David. *Savage Systems: Colonialism and Comparative Religion in Southern Africa*. Charlottesville: University Press of Virginia, 1996.

Connolly, William. *Political Theory and Modernity*. London: Basil Blackwell, 1988.

Clifford, James. *The Predicament of Culture: Twentieth-Century Ethnography, Literature, and Art*. Cambridge: Harvard University Press, 1988.

Davidovich, Adina. *Religion as a Province of Meaning*. Minneapolis: Fortress Press, 1993.

Derrida, Jacques. *Positions*, trans. A. Bass. Chicago: University of Chicago Press, 1971.

———. *Of Grammatology*. Trans. Gayatri Spivak. Baltimore: Johns Hopkins University Press, 1974.

———. *Writing and Difference*. Trans. Alan Bass. Chicago: University of Chicago Press, 1978.

———. *Margins of Philosophy*. Trans Alan Bass. Chicago: University of Chicago Press, 1982.

Dilthey, Wilhelm. *Pattern and Meaning in History: Thoughts on History and Society*. Ed. H. P. Rickman. New York: Harper and Row, 1961.

———. *Selected Writings*. Ed., trans., and Introduction, H. P. Rickman. Cambridge: Cambridge University Press, 1976.

———. *Poetry and Experience*. Ed. Rudolf Makkreel and Frithjof Rodi. Princeton: Princeton University Press, 1985. Selected Works, Vol. V.

———. *Introduction to the Human Sciences: An Attempt to Lay a Foundation for the Study of Society and History*. Trans. with an Introductory Essay by Ramon J. Betanzos. Detroit: Wayne State University Press, 1988.

———. *Introduction to the Human Sciences*. Ed. Rudolf Makkreel and Frithjof Rodi. Princeton: Princeton University Press, 1989.

Dudley, Guilford. *Religion on Trial: Mircea Eliade and His Critics*. Philadelphia: Temple University Press, 1977.

Eliade, Mircea. *Patterns of Comparative Religion*. New York: The New American Library, 1958.

———. *The Sacred and the Profane: The Nature of Religion*. New York: Harcourt, Brace, and World, 1959.

———. "Methodological Remarks on the Study of Religious Symbolism." In *The History of Religions: Essays in Methodology*, ed. M. Eliade and J. Kitagawa. Chicago: the University of Chicago Press, 1959.

———. *Myths, Dreams, and Mysteries: The Encounter between Contemporary Faiths and Archaic Realities*. Trans. Philip Mairet. New York: Harper and Row, 1960.

———. *The Quest: History and Meaning in Religion*. Chicago: University of Chicago Press, 1969.

———. *A History of Religious Ideas, Vols 1–3*. Trans. William R. Trask. Chicago: The University of Chicago Press, 1982.

Erricker, Clive. "Phenomenological Approaches." In *Approaches to the Study of Religion*, ed. Peter Connolly. London: Cassell, 1999.

Flood, Gavin. *Beyond Phenomenology: Rethinking the Study of Religion*. London: Cassell, 1999.

Foucault, Michel. *The Order of Things: An Archaeology of the Human Sciences*. New York: Vintage Books, 1970.

———. *The Archaeology of Knowledge and The Discourse On Language*. Trans. A. M. Sheridan Smith. New York: Pantheon Books, 1972.

———. "History of Systems of Thought." In *Language, Counter-Memory, Practice*, ed. Donald Bourchard. Ithaca: Cornell University Press, 1977.

Gadamer, Hans-Georg. *Truth and Method*. Trans. Joel Weinsheimer and Donald G. Marshall. Second, revised edition. New York: Crossroad, 1990.

Gandhi, Leela. *Postcolonial Theory: A Critical Introduction*. New York: Columbia University Press, 1998.

Geertz, Clifford. *The Interpretation of Cultures*. New York: Basic Books, 1975.

Georgakopoulou, Alexandria, and Dionysis Goutsos. *Discourse Analysis: An Introduction*. Edinburgh: Edinburgh University Press, 1997.

Gregory, Fredrick. *Nature Lost? Natural Science and the German Theological Traditions of the Nineteenth Century*. Cambridge: Harvard University Press, 1992.

Harrison, Peter. *Religion and the "Religions" in the English Enlightenment*. Cambridge: Cambridge University Press, 1990.

Harvey, John. "Translator's Preface." In Rudolf Otto, *The Idea of the Holy: An Inquiry into the Non-Rational Factor in the Idea of the Divine and Its Relation to the Rational*, trans. J. W. Harvey. Oxford: Oxford University Press, 1958.

Hegel, G. W. F. *Hegel's Philosophy of Right*. Trans. T. M. Knox. Oxford: The Clarendon Press, 1945.

———. *The Philosophy of History*. Trans. J. Sibree. New York: Dover Publications, 1956.

———. *Phänomenolgie des Geistes*. Frankfurt am Main: Suhrkamp, 1969.

———. *Vorlesung über die Philosophie der Religion*. Frankfurt am Main: Suhrkamp, 1969.

———. Vorlesung über die Philosophie der Geschichte. Frankfurt am Main: Suhrkamp, 1970.

———. *Hegel's Idea of Philosophy*. Trans. and ed., Quentin Lauer. New York: Fordham University Press, 1971.
———. *Phenomenology of Spirit*. Trans. A. V. Miller. Oxford: Oxford University Press, 1977.
———. *Introduction to the Lectures on the History of Philosophy*. Trans. T. M. Knox and A. V. Miller. Oxford: Clarendon Press, 1985.
———. *Lectures on the Philosophy of Religion*. Trans. R. F. Brown, P. C. Hodgson, and J. M. Stewart. Berkeley: University of California Press, 1988.
Heidegger, Martin. *The Question Concerning Technology and Other Essays*, trans. William Lovitt. New York: Harper Torchbooks, 1977.
———. "Letter on Humanism." In *Basic Writings*, ed. David Farrell Krell. New York: Harper and Row, 1977.
Heller, Agnes, and Ferenc Feher. *The Postmodern Political Condition*. New York: Columbia University Press, 1988.
Hochschild, Adam. *King Leopold's Ghost: A Story of Greed, Terror, and Heroism in Colonial Africa*. Boston: Mariner Books, 1999.
Hoy, David Couzens. "A History of Consciousness: From Kant and Hegel to Derrida and Foucault." *History of the Human Sciences* 4, no. 2 (1991).
———. "Is Hermeneutics Ethno-centric?" In *The Interpretive Turn: Philosophy, Science, Culture*, ed. D. Hiley and J. Bohman. Ithaca: Cornell University Press, 1991.
Hultkrantz, Åke. "The Phenomenology of Religion: Aims and Methods." *Temenos* 6 (1970).
Husserl, Edmund. *Ideas: General Introduction to Pure Phenomenology*. New York: Collier Books, 1962.
Idinopulous, Thomas A. "Understanding and Teaching Rudolph Otto's *The Idea of the Holy*." In *The Sacred and Its Scholars: Comparative Methodologies for the Study of Primary Religious Data*, ed. Thomas A. Idinopulous and Edward A. Yonan. Leiden: E. J. Brill, 1996.
James, George A. *Interpreting Religion: The Phenomenological Approaches of Pierre Daniël Chantepie de la Saussaye, W. Brede Kristensen, and Gerardus van der Leeuw*. Washington, DC: The Catholic University of America Press, 1995.
Jensen, Jeppe Sinding. *The Study of Religion in a New Key: Theoretical and Philosophical Soundings in the Comparative and General Study of Religion*. Aarhus: Aarhus University Press, 2003.
King, Richard. *Orientalism and Religion: Postcolonial Theory, India, and "The Mystic East."* London: Routledge, 1999.
Kitagawa, Joseph. "Life and Thought of Joachim Wach." In *The Comparative Study of Religion*. New York: Columbia University Press, 1958.
———. "Introduction." In Joachim Wach, *Essays in the History of Religions*, ed. Joseph M. Kitagawa and Gregory D. Alles. New York: Macmillan, 1988.
Kristensen, Wilhelm Brede. *The Meaning of Religion: Lectures in the Phenomenology of Religion*. The Hague: Martinus Nijhoff, 1960.
Lauer, Quentin. "Preface." In *Hegel's Idea of Philosophy*, trans. and ed. Quentin Lauer. New York: Fordham University Press, 1971.

Long, Charles H. *Significations: Signs, Symbols, and Images in the Interpretation of Religion*. Aurora, CO: The Davies Group, 1995.
Loomba, Ania. *Colonialism/Postcolonialism*. London and New York: Routledge, 1998.
Löwith, Karl. *From Hegel to Nietzsche: The Revolution in Nineteenth-Century Thought*. Trans. D. Green. New York: Anchor Books, 1967.
Makkreel, Rudolf, and Frithjof Rodi. "Introduction." In Wilhelm Dilthey, *Poetry and Experience*, ed. Rudolf Makkreel and Frithjof Rodi. Princeton: Princeton University Press, 1985.
———. "Introduction." In *Introduction to the Human Sciences*, ed. R. A. Makkreel and F. Rodi. Princeton: Princeton University Press, 1989.
Macdonell, Diane. *Theories of Discourse: An Introduction*. Oxford: Basil Blackwell, 1986.
Merklinger, Philip M. *Philosophy, Theology, and Hegel's Berlin Philosophy of Religion, 1821–1827*. Albany: State University of New York Press, 1993.
Mills, Sara. *Discourse*. London: Routledge, 1997.
Murphy, Tim. *Nietzsche, Metaphor, Religion*. Albany: State University of New York Press, 2001.
———. *Representing Religion: Essays in History, Theory, and Crisis*. London: Equinox Press, 2007.
Nehamas, Alexander. *Nietzsche: Life as Literature*. Cambridge: Harvard University Press, 1985.
Nietzsche, Friedrich. *On the Genealogy of Morals: A Polemic*. Trans. Walter Kaufmann and R. J. Hollingdale. New York: Vintage Books, 1967.
———. *The Will to Power*. Trans. Walter Kaufman and R. J.Hollingdale. New York: Vintage Books, 1967.
———. *The Gay Science*. Trans. Walter Kaufmann. New York: Vintage Books, 1974.
———. *Human, All-too-Human*. Trans. R. J. Hollingdale. Cambridge: Cambridge University Press, 1986.
Otto, Rudolf. *Naturalism and Religion*. Trans. J. Arthur Thomson and Margaret R. Thomson. New York: G. P. Putnam's Sons, 1907.
———. *Das Heilige: Über das Irrationale in der Idee des Göttlichen und Sein Verhältnis zum Rationalen*. Gotha: Leopold Klotz, 1929.
———. *The Philosophy of Religion*. Trans. E. B. Dicker. London: Williams and Norgate, 1931.
———. *Mysticism East and West*. Trans. Bertha L. Bracey and Richenda C. Payne. New York: Macmillan, 1932.
———. *The Idea of the Holy: An Inquiry into the Non-Rational Factor in the Idea of the Divine and Its Relation to the Rational*. Trans. J. W. Harvey. Oxford: Oxford University Press, 1958.
Oxtoby, W. G. "*Religionswissenschaft* Revisited." In *Religions in Antiquity*, ed. Jacob Neusner. Leiden: E. J. Brill, 1968.
———. "The Idea of the Holy." In *Encyclopedia of Religion*, ed. Mircea Eliade. New York: Macmillan, 1987.
Palmer, Richard E. *Hermeneutics: Interpretation Theory in Schleiermacher, Dilthey, Heidegger, and Gadamer*. Evanston: Northwestern University Press, 1969.

Penner, Hans. *Impasse and Resolution: A Critique of the Study of Religion*. New York: Peter Lang, 1989.
Pettazoni, Raffaele. *Essays on the History of Religion*. Leiden: E. J. Brill, 1967.
Petterson, Olaf, and Hans Åkerburg. *Interpreting Religious Phenomena: Studies with Reference to the Phenomenology of Religion*. New Jersey: Humanities Press, 1981.
Pratt, Mary Louise. *Imperial Eyes: Travel Writing and Transculturation*. London: Routledge, 1992.
Preus, J. Sammuel. *Explaining Religion: Criticism and Theory from Bodin to Freud*. New Haven: Yale University Press, 1987.
Rabinow, Paul. "Representations Are Social Facts." In *Writing Culture: The Poetics and Politics of Ethnography*, ed. James Clifford and George Marcus. Berkeley: University of California Press, 1986.
Raphael, Melissa. *Rudolf Otto and the Concept of Holiness*. Oxford: Clarendon Press, 1997.
Rennie, Bryan S. *Reconstructing Eliade: Making Sense of Religion*. Albany: State University of New York Press, 1996.
Rickman, H. P. "General Introduction." In Wilhelm Dilthey, *Pattern and Meaning in History: Thoughts on History and Society*. Ed. H. P. Rickman. New York: Harper and Row, 1961.
Roberts, Julian. *German Philosophy: An Introduction*. Atlantic Highlands: Humanities Press International, 1988.
Rodi, Frithjof. "Dilthey's Concept of 'Structure' Within the Context of Nineteenth-Century Science and Philosophy." In *Dilthey and Phenomenology*, ed. Rudolf A. Makkreel and John Scanlon. Washington, DC: Center for Advanced Research in Phenomenology and University Press of America, 1987.
Rosen, Stanley. *G. W. F. Hegel: An Introduction to the Science of Wisdom*. New Haven: Yale University Press, 1974.
Ryba, Thomas. *The Essence of Phenomenology and Its Meaning for the Scientific Study of Religion*. New York: Peter Lang, 1991.
Said, Edward W. *Orientalism*. New York: Vintage Books, 1978.
Samson, Jane. *Race and Empire*. London: Pearson Longman, 2005.
Schleiermacher, Friedrich. *On Religion: Speeches to its Cultured Despisers*. Trans. John Oman with an introduction by Rudolf Otto. New York: Harper and Row, 1958.
Schnädelbach, Herbert. *Philosophy in Germany 1831–1933*. Trans. Eric Matthews. Cambridge: Cambridge University Press, 1984.
Segal, Robert. *Explaining and Interpreting Religion: Essays on the Issue*. New York: Peter Lang, 1992.
Seiwert, Hubert. "What Constitutes the Identity of a Religion?" In *Identity Issues and World Religions*. Netley, Australia: Wakefield Press, 1986.
Sharpe, Eric. *Comparative Religion: A History*. London: Duckworth, 1975.
Smith, Jonathan Z. *Imagining Religion: From Babylon to Jonestown*. Chicago: University of Chicago Press, 1982.
———. "Classification," entry. In *Guide to the Study of Religion*, ed. Willi Braun and Russell T. McCutcheon. London and New York: Cassell, 2000.

———. *Relating Religion: Essays in the Study of Religion*. Chicago: University of Chicago Press, 2004.

Snead, James. "European Pedigrees/African Contagions: Nationality, Narrative, and Communality." In *Nation and Narration*, ed. Homi K. Bhabha. London: Routledge, 1990.

Stavrakakis, Yannis. *Lacan and the Political*. London: Routledge, 1999.

Taylor, Mark C. *Erring: A Postmodern A/theology*. Chicago: The University of Chicago Press, 1984.

———. "The Stranglehold of Transcendentalism." *Journal of the American Academy of Religion* 53, no. 2 (1985).

———. "Introduction." In *Deconstruction in Context*, ed. Mark Taylor. Chicago: University of Chicago Press, 1986.

Teile, C. P. *Outlines of the History of Religion to the Spread of the Universal Religions*. Trans. J. Estlin Carpenter. London: Kegan Paul, Trench, Trübner, 6th ed., 1896.

———. *Elements of a Science of Religion*. Part I: Morphological. London: William Blackwood and Sons, New York: AMS, 1896.

———. *Elements of a Science of Religion*. Part II: Ontological. London: William Blackwood and Sons, New York: AMS, 1898.

Tillich, Paul. *Systematic Theology*, Volume I. Chicago: The University of Chicago Press, 1951.

van der Leeuw, Gerardus. *Religion in Essence and Manifestation*. Trans. J. E. Turner. Princeton: Princeton University Press, 1964.

———. *Phänomenologie der Religion*. Tübingen: J. C. B. Mohr (Paul Siebeck), 1933.

Vico, Giambattista. *The New Science*. Trans. Thomas G. Bergin and Max H. Fisch. Ithaca and London: Cornell University Press, 1968.

Waardenburg, Jacques. *Classical Approaches to the Study of Religion*. The Hague: Mouton de Grouter, 1973.

Wach, Joachim. *Sociology of Religions*. Chicago: The University of Chicago Press, 1944.

———. *Types of Religious Experience: Christian and Non-Christian*. Chicago: The University of Chicago Press, 1951.

———. *The Comparative Study of Religions*. Ed. Joseph M. Kitagawa. New York: Columbia University Press, 1958.

———. *Understanding and Believing*. Ed. Joseph M. Kitagawa. New York: Harper and Row, 1968.

———. *Essays in the History of Religions*. Ed. Joseph M. Kitagawa and Gregory D. Alles. New York: Macmillan, 1988.

———. *Introduction to the History of Religions*. Ed. Joseph M. Kitagawa and Gregory D. Alles. New York: Macmillan, 1988.

Welch, Claude. *Protestant Thought in the Nineteenth Century*. New Haven: Yale University Press, Vol. I., 1972 and Vol. II, 1985.

Wiebe, Donald. *Religion and Truth: Towards an Alternative Paradigm for the Study of Religion*. The Hague: Mouton, 1981.

———. "Phenomenology of Religion as Religio-Cultural Quest: Gerardus van der Leeuw and the Subversion of the Scientific Study of Religion."

*Religionswissenschaft und Kulturkritik: Beiträge zur Konferenz: The History of Religions and Critique of Culture in the Days of Gerardus van der Leeuw (1890–1950)*. Marburg: diagonal-Verlag, 1991.

———. *The Politics of Religious Studies: the Continuing Conflict with Theology in the Academy*. New York: St. Martin's, 1999.

Wood, Nicola. *Describing Discourse: A Practical Guide to Discourse Analysis*. London: Hodder Arnold, 2006.

Young, Robert. *White Mythologies: Writing History and the West*. London and New York: Routledge, 1990.

# Index

Absolute Knowledge, 10–11
Allen, Douglas, 5, 28, 259, 265, 318, 361
*allgemeinen Geistes*, 73, 75
Almond, Phillip C., 167, 358
animism, 115, 117–19, 121, 124
*Ausdruck*, 133, 144–5, 209, 213, 229

Baird, Robert D., 18, 291
Bambach, Charles R., 25, 27, 149, 153, 317, 350–51, 353
Barthes, Roland, 37, 51, 276, 312–13, 324, 329, 331, 335
Beardsworth, Richard, 64, 342, 343
*Beisichselbstsein*, 74, 261
Betanzos, Ramon J., 143, 350
Bhabha, Homi K., 285
Bianchi, Ugo, 326
binary: Dilthey's treatment of, 235; of *Geist/Natur*, 32, 37, 49, 53, 84, 235–36, 280; of kernel/husk, 37, 52, 101, 106–8, 264; paired philosophemes, 32, 36–37, 42, 49, 51–53, 281, 302; of primitive/civilized, 252, 257; Said's treatment of, 62–63; Taylor's treatment of, 52–53; Tiele's treatment of, 106
Bleeker, C. J., 38, 180, 235, 323, 325
Bolle, Kees, 362
Bowie, Andre, 138, 140, 146, 151, 153, 350, 351, 353
Buddhism: as compared to Christianity by Tiele, 128–30; as compared to Christianity by von Hartmann, 126; as compared to religions with notions of salvation, 257; Hegel's treatment of, 86–87; on immortality, 258; as Indian philosophy, 170, 220; as logocentric construct, 278; as a non-empirical category, 3–4, 73, 81; Otto's treatment of, 253; van der Leeuw's treatment of, 222; Wach's treatment of, 257
Burgin, Victor, 45

Campbell, Joseph, 372
Capps, Walter, 5, 7, 180
Carr, David, 320
*causa sui*, 171, 185
Chantepie de la Saussaye, P. D., 6–9, 24, 179–80, 191, 322, 345, 364
Chidister, David, 323
China: in analysis of historical religion, 219; Buddhism in, 3; as "the childhood of History," 75; as Europe's "Other," 188–89; Otto's treatment of Chinese religion, 253; Tiele's treatment of Chinese religion, 122–25
Christianity: as the "consummate religion," 126–30; Eliade's treatment of, 239, 265, 267–68; Hegel's treatment of, 77–78, 80–81, 89–93, 95, 98–100; as "higher religion," 284, 289–91; India as contrast for, 189; Kristensen's treatment of, 193, 201, 203, 205; as logocentric construct, 278;

Christianity *(continued)*
 Otto's treatment of, 168, 173–77; the systematic study of religion and, 4; as treated by the evolving *Religionswissenschaft*, 158–59; van der Leeuw's treatment of, 221–23, 227; Wach's treatment of, 229, 235, 242–43, 251, 253, 257–58
Christocentrism, 289, 291, 100, 258, 127
class domination, 56
Clifford, James, 308, 209
colonialism: anti-humanism and postcolonialism, 315; "blame" for, 285; colonialism-imperialism, 293; defined, 57; knowledge and, 288; Modernity and, 70; phenomenology and, 20, 33, 53, 55, 310; the relations between postcolonial theory and poststructuralism, 60; the self and, 313; the shift from, 56; Young's treatment of, 286
comparative religion: the ambiguities of, 28; colonialism and, 53, 57; Eliade and, 263–64, 269; "the Orient" and, 172; phenomenology and, 7, 192, 237–38; van der Leeuw and, 226; Wach and, 8, 25, 251, 258
Connolly, William, 36–37, 318, 329, 331, 332

consummate religion, the, 82, 89–92, 126, 176, 223, 257–58, 284
*cultus*, 88, 120, 246

*Dasein*, 227, 305
Davidovich, Adina, 163, 357
Derrida, Jacques, 8–9, 14, 18, 23, 35–36, 52, 54, 62, 64, 71, 138, 148, 151, 234, 257, 279, 294, 302–6 passim, 316, 335, 351, 353
Dilthey, Wilhelm, 9–15 passim, 29, 36, 65,

Dudley, Guilford, 20, 27, 28, 38, 259, 323, 324, 325, 327, 331

Eliade, Mircea, 4–5, 7–9, 12, 15, 17, 20–22, 25–31, 36, 38–39, 41, 47–48, 54, 59, 65, 70, 75, 80, 83, 131, 138, 143, 144, 157–58, 180, 192, 200, 213, 217, 228, 234, 235, 239, 258, 259–71, 277–78, 280, 284, 290, 294–97, 299, 302, 305, 308, 309–12, 317, 319, 321, 327, 328, 330, 332, 352, 355, 368, 371
*Entwicklung*: Chantepie and, 185–87; *Contra*, 201–2; Dilthey and, 153; Hegel and, 10, 71–74, 79, 85–87, 93, 115, 305; the stages of, 168; Tiele and, 102, 104, 116–17, 124, 126–27; Otto and, 173; van der Leeuw and, 12, 31, 218, 224; Wach and, 231, 235, 255
*Erlebnis*, 133–34, 136, 138, 144–45, 147, 150, 208–12, 214, 229
Erricker, Clive, 6–7, 318
*Erscheinung*, 6, 9–10, 25, 74–75, 81, 106, 145, 181, 217, 234, 237, 282
Eskimos, 57, 291–92
essence, *see* ontology
ethnocentrism, 100, 271, 286, 291–96
Euro-expansionism, 56
Euro-imperialism, 20, 56, 335
Eurocentrism, 62, 281–82, 286
*explication de texte*, 36, 42, 50

Feher, Ferenc, 286
Flood, Gavin, 259, 261, 318
Foucault, Michel, 23, 43–44, 46, 48, 50–51, 69, 201, 325, 327, 329, 331
Frithjof, Rodi, 351

Gadamer, Hans-Georg, 41, 47, 140–42, 147–48, 150, 154, 353
Gandhi, Leela, 57, 60, 279, 281, 375
Geertz, Clifford, 307, 313, 377
*Geist*: as basis for similarities between Hegelianism and the

INDEX 389

phenomenology of religion, 32;
Buddhism and, 86; Chantepie's
treatment of, 185; Christocentrism,
290, 297; Dilthey's treatment
of, 15, 138, 146–48, 153–54;
Eliade's treatment of, 7–8,
234, 310; expression and, 247;
*Geisteswissenschaften*: 10–11,
14–15, 20–21, 31, 55–56, 62, 69,
81, 110, 138, 141, 145, 172, 207,
292, 295; Hegel's treatment of,
6, 31, 74–75, 84, 100; and the
history of the study of religion,
96, 220; as informant of the
taxonomic structure of classical
phenomenology, 10; Kristensen's
treatment of, 197, 205;
logocentrism and, 281, 283–84,
294–95; and "Man," 216, 276, 302,
305, 307, 310, 315; matter/nature
as underlying the metanarrative
of, 12; Metaphysical Monism and,
296; and *Natur*, the relationship
of: 13–15, 22, 28, 32–33, 37, 47, 49,
52–54, 58–59, 72, 78, 80, 84, 86,
94, 120, 154–55, 158–63, 167–69,
178, 185, 187, 211, 231, 277, 280;
as ontotheological, 54; Otto and,
158–61, 168, 178, 252; the politics
of, 56, 63–65, 70, 100; stages of
history and, 75, 78, 80, 82; sui
generis as reformulation of, 4; van
der Leeuw's treatment of, 209,
223; Wach's treatment of, 235–36,
249, 255
*Gemüt*, 98–99, 240–41
geneology, 7, 37, 39, 42, 52, 58, 157,
180, 229, 296, 315
Georgakopoulou, Alexandria, 49
gothic personality, 169–72
Goutsos, Dionysis, 49
Gregory, Fredrick, 321

Harrison, Peter, 323
Harvey, John, 160

Hegel, G. W. F., 4–12, 14–16, 28–30,
32, 36, 38, 44, 47–48, 54–55, 57,
60, 63, 65, 69–100, 101–5, 108–11,
113–16, 118–20, 122, 124–25, 127,
138, 140, 143, 146–48, 150, 153–55,
158–59, 164–66, 168–71, 173,
175–77, 180–82, 184, 186, 188–90,
198–99, 201–2, 206, 209–10,
214–20, 222–25, 229–31, 236, 243,
247–48, 252–54, 257–58, 263, 268,
271–72, 280–86, 288–89, 292, 294,
296–97, 302, 305, 306, 310–11, 315,
318–22, 324, 326–27, 333, 336, 339,
340, 341, 342, 343, 344, 347, 348,
349, 351, 352, 353, 354, 356, 357,
359, 360, 361, 363, 367, 368, 371,
374, 377
Heidegger, Martin, 9, 18, 54, 64, 162,
289, 299, 305–6, 317, 364
Heller, Agnes, 286
hermeneutics, 26, 53, 151–52, 178,
216, 234, 240, 248, 252, 259,
269–70, 309
heterosexism, 56
hierophany, 83, 217, 260, 266–68, 290
Hinduism: Chantepie's treatment
of, 189; Hegel's treatment of,
86–89; as Indian philosophy, 170,
220; as logocentric construct, 278;
Otto's treatment of, 177, 253;
taxonomic treatments of, 32, 81;
Tiel's treatment of, 123; "white
mythology" and, 62
"Historical School," the, 10–11, 146
History of Religions (the field),
24–30, 38, 40, 107, 115, 179, 188,
237, 247, 299
Hochschild, Adam, 336
"holy, the": defining religion as,
40; Otto and, 65, 157–68 passim,
176–78, 202, 277, 283, 302
Hoy, David Couzens, 294, 304, 375
Hultkrantz, Ake, 27, 318–19, 361
humanism: anti-humanism, 315;
Derrida and, 316; empathetic

humanism *(continued)*
understanding and, 275; in the enlightenment, 288; Heidegger and, 299; human nature and, 313; ideological humanism, 16; as integral to the phenomenology of religion and Religious Studies, 287; Metaphysical Monism and, 295; "New Humanism," 235, 259–60, 270–71, 311; structurally compared, 54, 275; the subject and, 300; Western humanism, 282
Husserl, Edmund, 4–10, 23, 40, 44, 135, 136, 138, 158, 180, 187, 194, 199, 208, 209, 210, 212, 225, 227, 228, 229, 235, 248, 270, 280, 302, 303, 306, 318, 320, 336, 364, 367, 376

Idinopulous, Thomas A., 332
inner experience: consciousness and, 14; Dilthey's treatment of, 133–44 passim, 154, 241–42, 301–3; as the essence of religion, 241, 250; Hegel's treatment of, 70; the subject and, 65; van der Leeuw's treatment of, 212, 303; verses outer expression, 37, 237–39, 242, 277; Wach's treatment of, 235, 241, 250, 303
Islam: as monotheistic, 173; Otto's treatment of, 174–76; as Orient, 223; taxonomic treatments of, 32; Tiel's treatment of, 128–20; van der Leeuw's treatment of, 220–21, 306; Wach's treatment of, 251–53, 257–58

James, George A., 364, 365, 367, 369
Jensen, Jeppe Sinding, 317, 326, 332

King, Richard, 323, 338
Kitagawa, Joseph, 25, 28
Kristensen, Wilhelm Brede, 4, 5, 9, 22, 24, 29, 41, 58, 59, 75, 179–81, 191–206, 213, 235, 237, 244, 245, 261, 263, 267–68, 277, 283, 317, 324, 325, 328, 360, 361, 362, 364, 365, 373

Lauer, Quentin, 339
lived-experience, *see Erlebnis*
logocentrism: and Christocentrism, 289–90; Derrida's treatment of, 148; and ethnocentrism, 292; Euro- and ethnocentrism and, 100; of history, 284; and phenomenology, 276–81 passim; and Tiele, 127; and Wach, 258
*logos*: the course of history as, 98; Derrida's treatment of, 54; Dilthey's treatment of, 93, 241–42; Eliade's treatment of, 265, 267; Hegel's philosophy of, 8, 77, 79, 91, 100, 190; Kristensen's treatment of, 198; "meaning" and 264; mythology as, 279; as the third stage of civilization, 186; van der Leeuw's treatment of, 216; Wach's treatment of, 253, 256
Long, Charles H., 25, 28, 53, 56, 293, 326, 335, 336
Loomba, Ania, 62
Löwith, Karl, 305, 319

Macdonell, Diane, 44–45, 48
Makkreel, Rudolf, 153, 350, 351
Man, the construct of, 4, 32, 65, 76, 78, 232, 237–39, 270–71, 276, 279–97 passim, 299–316
materialism, 13, 54, 105, 187, 235
mediation, 35, 72, 98, 208
Merklinger, Philip M., 70
*methexis*, 240–41, 243
Mills, Sara, 43, 48, 59, 337
morphology, 50, 127
Murphy, Tim, 318, 319, 325, 326, 330, 332, 347

*Natur*: Confucianism and, 125; and *Geist*, the relationship of, 13–15, 22, 28, 32–33, 37, 47, 49,

52–54, 58–59, 72, 78, 80, 84, 86, 94, 120, 154–55, 158–63, 167–69, 178, 185, 187, 211, 231, 277, 280; Hegel's treatment of, 83–86, 89, 100, 164–67; and "Nature," 107, 138; *Naturvölker*, 13, 57, 64, 100, 122–23, 182; *Naturwissenschaften*, 14
natural history, 288
Nature, see *Natur*
nature religions, 32, 47, 84–86, 92, 96, 100, 114–18, 121, 125, 173, 236
Nehamas, Alexander, 39
New Humanism, 235, 259–60, 270–71, 295, 299, 311, 316
Nietzsche, Friedrich, 18, 39, 65, 69, 307, 315, 316, 333, 335

objective spirit: as anthropological fact and hermeneutical necessity, 237; Dilthey's treatment of, 15, 147–48, 153–54, 247–48; ethics and, 256–57; *Grundhaltung* and, 246; Hegel's bias of *Wissenchaft* and, 28; history as manifestation of, 9, 11; as metaphysical category, 32; reason as, 98; religion as manifestation of, 12; "state" and 81; structure and, 243; as studied empirically, 250; the study of religion as the study of, 96; van der Leeuw's treatment of, 218, 224
ontology: Hegel's treatment of, 8; ontological subordination, 280; phenomenological ontology, 306; as philosophy of power, 289; "regional ontology," 269, 270
ontotheology: axiological categories as part of, 20; Derrida's "metaphysics of presence" and, 23, 52; *Geist* and, 53–55, 277, 294; Hegel and Husserl as located in the discourse of, 9; as historical construct, 36; historical retention and, 201; insignificance of the finite and, 238; logocentrism and, 278–80; phenomenological texts as situated in, 50; as phenomenology's problem, 18; the shift from theology towards, 19
Orientalism, 61–63, 169, 176
Otto, Rudolf: 4, 5, 9, 13, 15, 24, 25, 27, 29, 38, 41, 47, 55, 58, 65, 70, 75, 90, 110, 113, 131, 138, 140, 155, 157, 158 159, 160, 161, 162, 163, 164, 165, 166, 167, 168, 169, 170, 171, 172, 173, 174, 175, 176, 177, 178, 181, 189, 194, 198, 201, 202, 209, 214, 218, 219, 222, 229, 232, 234, 241, 252, 258, 260, 261, 263, 266, 268, 277, 280, 282, 283, 294, 297, 302, 305, 206, 312, 315, 317, 320, 321, 325, 328, 332, 336, 357, 358, 359, 368, 371, 377
Oxtoby, W.G., 5, 26, 38, 331

Palmer, Richard E., 133, 350
*parole*, 32, 36, 44, 49–50, 54
patriarchy, 76
Penner, Hans, 5, 17, 19, 20, 23, 323, 325, 326
Pettazoni, Raffaele, 326
philosophemes: as binary pairs, 51–53; the category of "unity" and, 294; Chantepie and, 187; as the constitutive structuring principle of history, 82, 279–81, 302–3; as implying rationalization, 117; the necessity of genealogy and, 42, 230, 277; the representation of non-European religions and, 33; as rooted in a theory of consciousness, 304; as situated in ontotheology, 35–39; subordination and, 64; van der Leeuw and, 217
*piety*, 111–12
"planetary consciousness," 56, 233
postcolonial theory: in the analysis of classical phenomenology, 16, 31, 33, 35, 43, 50, 58–60, 63, 315;

postcolonial theory *(continued)*
  Christocentrism and, 289; of Kristensen and Wach, 283
poststructuralism: in the analysis of classical phenomenology, 16–17, 20, 31–32, 35, 50, 60, 315; as "de-Hegelianization," 69; as derived from ontotheology, 54; on the distinctions between "Man" and *Geist*, 305; Euro-, ethnocentrism and, 286
Pratt, Mary Louise, 56, 61, 233, 270, 285, 287, 288, 336
Preus, J. Sammuel, 322, 323, 324, 327
Protestantism, 26, 99, 285, 287
psychology: Dilthey's concept of, 141, 248, 249–50; faculty psychology, 108, 111, 232, 292; Otto and, 162; phenomenology and, 17–18, 21, 182, 208, 210, 228, 260

Rabinow, Paul, 45
racism, 296–97, 337
Raphael, Melissa, 325
reflexive awareness, 135–36
relational center, the, 136, 300
*Religionswissenschaft:* Chantepie and, 181, 190–91; Eliade and, 268–69, 311; Hegel and, 6–10, 73–74, 181; the Hegelian paradigm as informative to, 69–70; the impact of anthropological collections on, 57–58; "objective spirit" as fundamental premise of, 81; Otto and, 158, 167, 172, 174, 176; phenomenological discourse and, 53; as programmatically Christocentric, 289, 292; the reformulation of, 4; separation from "classical phenomenology of religion," 202; as synonymous with "history of religions," 28–29, 40; as synonymous with phenomenology of religion, 27; 29; Tiele and, 100–1, 121, 127; van der Leeuw and, 207, 217, 225; Wach and, 3, 230, 248; "world religions" and, 56
Religious Studies: binaries as informative to, 53; colonial representations and, 33, 57–59, 63, 81; the development of, 4–5, 15–16, 38–42, 179, 158, 259; Eliade and, 259, 269; Müller and, 23; Otto and, 157, 159, 178; poststructuralist critique of, 275–315 passim; Protestantism and, 26; theology and, 17–18; *see also* "third wave," the
Rennie, Bryan S., 26, 325, 326, 330, 331
*Rezeptionsgeschichte*, 29, 38–40, 50
Rickman, H. P., 322, 325, 354
Roberts, Julian, 73
Rodi, Frithjof, 139, 140, 153, 350, 351, 352, 353
Rosen, Stanley, 69, 73, 321, 343
Ryba, Thomas, 157, 179, 319, 326

Said, Edward W., 61, 62, 63, 172, 176, 308, 338, 359
Samson, Jane, 322, 336
Scandinavian school, the, 27
Schleiermacher, Friedrich, 9, 29, 30, 110, 111, 113, 148, 152, 153, 158, 176, 181, 193, 197, 209, 217, 222, 226, 228, 232, 254, 260, 261, 292, 312, 322, 323, 350, 353, 356, 361, 371, 377
Schnädelbach, Herbert, 11, 320, 384
Segal, Robert, 17, 21, 22, 265, 285, 322, 323, 324, 326, 327, 333, 370
Seiwert, Hubert, 3, 4, 7, 10, 71, 72, 73, 166, 231, 238, 249, 263, 338, 341
self-differentiation, 71, 88, 92
self-estrangement, 72
sensation, 64, 135, 160–65, 168, 241, 252
Sharpe, Eric, 23, 24, 25, 325, 344, 361

*simile in multis*, 22, 180, 192, 260, 263, 288, 295
Smith, Jonathan Z., 40, 101, 293, 344
Snead, James, 310, 314
sociology, 21, 28, 270
Spirit, *see Geist*
state, the, 70, 76, 79–82, 89, 98–100, 122, 124–25, 147, 253–54, 257, 281, 282–85, 292–93, 308, 312
subjective turn, the, 9, 46
sui generis: Dilthey and, 242; Eliade and, 160–62; experience and, 138–40, 150; *Geist* and, 122, 154; and the holy, 167; Metaphysical Monism and, 296; the phenomenology of religion as, 83; reductivism and, 163; the reformulation of *Religionswissenschaft* and, 4; as retroactive creation, 40; Wach and, 234, 239

Taylor, Mark C., 52, 53, 62, 295, 320, 335
Teile, C. P., 179
text (*versus* discourse), 35–55 passim
theology, *see* Protestantism
"third wave," the, 27
Tillich, Paul, 136, 230, 343
*Totalität*, 73–74, 240

van der Leeuw, Gerardus, 4–6, 9, 12, 15, 24, 26, 29, 30, 31, 38, 41, 48, 59, 75, 82, 90, 143–44, 157–58, 179–80, 194, 199, 200, 207–13, 215–29, 237, 240–41, 245, 249, 261–63, 265, 297, 303, 305–6, 309, 312, 317–19, 323, 325, 328, 331–32, 341, 355, 363–67, 377

Vico, Giambattista, 149, 355
*Volk*, 98

Waardenburg, Jacques, 26, 27, 317, 325
Wach, Joachim, 3–4, 8, 9–12, 15, 23, 25–29, 41, 107, 157, 213, 228–45, 247–58, 268, 277, 280, 282–83, 294, 297, 301, 303, 305, 310, 312, 317, 320, 325, 328, 331, 347, 355, 359, 369, 371
Welch, Claude, 321
*Weltgeschichte*, 75–76, 91, 95, 99, 125
West, the: Eliade and, 271; ethnocentrism and, 292–93, 295–97; Hegel and, 283, 285–86, 289; History of Religion and, 188, 190, 204; Kristensen and, 268; "Man" and, 300, 304, 308–11, 314–15; Otto and, 169–73, 176, 178; van der Leeuw and, 219–20; Wach and, 253–54, 257; "Western critique of Western civilization," 60–63; Western history, 19, 36, 54, 56–57, 60, 69, 75, 86, 99, 118, 279, 281, 292, 300; Western metaphysics, 9, 18–19, 37, 278, 282–83
white supremacy, 56, 178
Wiebe, Donald, 17, 21–22, 25, 26, 285, 287, 322–24, 366–67, 369
Wood, Nicola, 49–50
world religions, 53, 56, 63, 86, 96, 278, 283, 314

Young, Robert, 60, 275, 286, 288–89, 375

*Zusammenhang*, 139, 140, 214